WHITE BUT NOT QUITE

Central Europe's Illiberal Revolt

Ivan Kalmar

First published in Great Britain in 2022 by

Bristol University Press
University of Bristol
1-9 Old Park Hill
Bristol
BS2 8BB
UK
t: +44 (0)117 374 6645
e: bup-info@bristol.ac.uk

Details of international sales and distribution partners are available at
bristoluniversitypress.co.uk

© Bristol University Press 2022

British Library Cataloguing in Publication Data
A catalogue record for this book is available from the British Library

ISBN 978-1-5292-1359-1 hardcover
ISBN 978-1-5292-1360-7 paperback
ISBN 978-1-5292-1361-4 ePub
ISBN 978-1-5292-1362-1 ePdf

The right of Ivan Kalmar to be identified as author of this work has been asserted by him in accordance with the Copyright, Designs and Patents Act 1988.

All rights reserved: no part of this publication may be reproduced, stored in a retrieval system, or transmitted in any form or by any means, electronic, mechanical, photocopying, recording, or otherwise without the prior permission of Bristol University Press.

Every reasonable effort has been made to obtain permission to reproduce copyrighted material. If, however, anyone knows of an oversight, please contact the publisher.

The statements and opinions contained within this publication are solely those of the author and not of the University of Bristol or Bristol University Press. The University of Bristol and Bristol University Press disclaim responsibility for any injury to persons or property resulting from any material published in this publication.

Bristol University Press works to counter discrimination on grounds of gender, race, disability, age and sexuality.

Cover design: blu inc
Bristol University Press use environmentally responsible print partners.
Printed and bound in Great Britain by CMP, Poole

Contents

List of Figures, Tables, and Maps	iv
Acknowledgements	vi
Introduction: Race, Illiberalism, Central Europe	1
1 How Eastern Europeans Became Less White	33
2 How Central Europeans Became Eastern European	46
3 How Central Europeans Became Central European (Time and Time Again)	74
4 Central Europe: Half-Truths and Facts	105
5 The Last of the White Men: Central Europe's White Innocence	146
6 'Have Eastern Europeans No Shame?' Anti-Semitism, Racism, and Homophobia in Central Europe	160
7 Imitators Spurned: Why the West Needs Central Europe to Stay in its Eastern European Place	182
8 'We Will Not Be a Colony!'	199
9 Slavia Prague v. Glasgow Rangers: Lessons from a Football Match	227
Conclusion: When the Migrants Come	241
Postscript: Confessions of a Canadian Central European	249
Notes	251
References	275
Index	312

List of Figures, Tables, and Maps

Figures

1.1	Alleged Irish Iberian, 'Anglo-Teutonic', and 'Negro' facial features	43
2.1	The Western image of Central Europe's location in Europe, before the end of the Second World War	53
4.1	Global Freedom scores, 2021	114
4.2	Liberal Democracy Index, 2020	115
4.3	Press Freedom Index for selected countries	116
4.4	Corruption Perception Index (CPI) scores of selected countries	118
4.5	Global Peace Index for selected countries	124
4.6	Number of sex workers per 10,000 population in selected countries in 2018	125
4.7	Human Development Index for selected countries	126
4.8	Happiness Index for selected countries	127
4.9	World Happiness Index for selected cities, 2017–19	128
4.10	Gross domestic product in selected countries, purchasing power parity dollars, per capita, 2019	130
4.11	Gross domestic product in selected countries, regions, and cities, purchasing power parity dollars, per capita, 2019	131
4.12	Gini Index of inequality for selected countries	137
4.13	Human flight and brain drain in selected countries, 2020	142
6.1	Percentage per country of people willing to accept a Muslim or a Jew into their family	171

| 6.2 | Percentage of people who said they 'favoured' or 'strongly favoured' legalizing same-sex marriage | 180 |

Tables

4.1	Degree of democracy in selected states	112
4.2	Capital flows in selected countries	134
4.3	Net annual wage in selected countries and regions in Europe, for a single person without children working full time and earning the medium wage, in euro, 2018	138
6.1	Selected countries ranked by the percentage of respondents who are willing to accept a Jew or a Muslim into their family	172

Maps

I.1	The location of 'Central Europe', as discussed in this book	9
4.1	Which Europeans consider their culture superior to others	107
4.2	The state of democracy in European countries	113

Acknowledgements

The work of a writer is thought to be a lonely one, but bringing this book to the light of day has allowed me to be in touch with some of the most interesting and supportive people I know. There are too many to include all of them here, and I apologize to those whom I may have missed.

Among the scholars who have enriched, through personal contact, my understanding of issues connected to this book, I would like to mention Veronika Ambros, Robert Austin, Huub van Baar, Pavel Barša, Monika Bobako, Omri Grinberg, Farid Hafez, Anikó Imre, Yolande Jansen, Deepa Kumar, Petr Kupka, Michael Lambek, James Mark, Nasar Meer, Kasia Narkowicz, Bronislav Ostřanský, Norbert Pap, Alejandro Paz, Konrad Pędziwiatr, Jiří Pehe, Derek Penslar, James Renton, Salman Sayyid, Victoria Shmidt, Nitzan Shoshan, Ondřej Slačálek, Zdeněk Tarant, Anya Topolski, Nicholas Worby, Alexander Yendell, and Reza Zia-Ebrahimy.

The research associates and assistants whose skills and knowledge I came to depend on were Adrien Beauduin, Miguel Gonzalez, Rhiain Lefton, Robin Martin, Chiara Olivieri, Teresa Pian, Nara Salis and Christopher Stevens.

Aleksandra Lewicki, my valued collaborator on several projects related to this work, made a decisive contribution not only through insights that she has shared, but also by suggesting, when considering several offers that I was honoured to receive, that I choose to publish with Bristol University Press. My editor, Stephen Wenham, has provided invaluable comments, encouragement, and assistance, ensuring that I would never regret that choice.

My sons Ethan de Jonge-Kalmar and Daniel Davidson-Kalmar have made many greatly insightful comments and engaged in many conversations with me, which found their imperceptible way into this book.

ACKNOWLEDGEMENTS

Last, but not least, I must thank my wife Diane Davidson for patiently enduring the times when I tuned out of everything in order to turn out this book. It is the priceless comfort of her companionship that makes anything and everything seem possible.

The work that went into researching this book has been generously supported by a grant from the Social Sciences and Humanities Research Council of Canada.

While all these parties share in whatever may be the merits of this book, its errors and eccentricities should be viewed as entirely mine.

Introduction: Race, Illiberalism, Central Europe

Who would have thought? A village boy noted for his soccer prowess. Football is his life, but he's not good enough to become a pro. Makes it to a good university, but never breaks into the circle of chic students from better-connected families. Maybe he doesn't even want to. Starts to dabble in politics. Speaks at the reburial of a communist leader who rebelled against the communists. He has no patience for reform communism; to him it's an illness that must be expounded. The cure is the party, Fidesz, that he founds mainly with other friends with similar, relatively unprivileged, backgrounds. Wins a scholarship to Oxford. Feels out of place, quits, returns to Budapest where the communist regime is busy dismantling itself. After it does, Fidesz wins one election, then loses, then comes back reborn as a movement of 'illiberal democrats'. 'Liberal' and 'globalist' become the names of the enemy, a vast conspiracy of money men pulling the strings behind the scenes, ruling the world, Washington, Brussels, and Budapest. Some hear anti-Semitic dog-whistles, but he denies that he means 'the Jews'. Dines with Silvio Berlusconi in Italy, sits around the Oval Office fireplace with Donald Trump. When Trump falls, the two stay in touch.

In his village, Felcsút, folks are proud of Viktor Orbán. They love the world-class football stadium he built there. The Puskás Arena seats 3,500, almost double the population of the community. Amenities include a fine hotel reported to have cost nearly $35 million of taxpayers' money.[1]

Lőrinc Mészáros, one of Orbán's childhood buddies, became the mayor of the village as soon as Orbán was re-elected prime minister in 2010. With Orbán's protection, this humble gas installer's wealth rose spectacularly, until *Forbes* named him Hungary's richest man, with a finger in every pie, from construction and hotels to agriculture. In 2017 Lőrinc confessed, 'My fortune is due to three factors: God, luck, and Viktor Orbán'.[2] Many people think he *is* Viktor Orbán, the real owner of the assets.

Not since the fiery nineteenth-century revolutionary, Lajos Kossuth (half Slovak, half German by descent, now largely forgotten outside of Hungary), or the composer Franz Liszt (who grew up and lived outside the country), has a Hungarian been as much the talk of the world as Viktor Orbán.[3] As prime minister of an East European mini-country of some 10 million people, whose Gross Domestic Product is only about 1½ times the reported net worth of Jeff Bezos,[4] Orbán succeeded at positioning himself at the forefront of the global assault on liberal democracy,[5] in the company of Vladimir Putin, Recep Erdogan, Jair Bolsonaro, and Donald Trump.

When, during the 2015–16 'European migration crisis', Orbán had a wire fence erected to keep out the mostly Muslim refugees, the usually reserved German chancellor, Angela Merkel, passionately decried his action as contrary to 'humanity'. But such lecturing by representatives of the Western establishment only gained Orbán admirers within the ranks of right-wing nationalists across Europe and America. The criticism certainly energized leaders among Hungary's neighbours to turn their long-standing frustrations with the West into political capital. Soon, the countries of the Visegrád Alliance or 'V4' – Hungary, Poland, Czech Republic, and Slovakia – turned into an rebel bloc within the European Union (EU). Poland's Prime Minister, Tadeusz Mazowiecki, promised that 'the day will come when we will succeed and we will have a Budapest in Warsaw'.[6] The Czech president, Miloš Zeman, described Orbán as a 'genuine leader', of the sort that is rare in contemporary politics.[7]

The revolt of the ex-communist periphery shocked the West. The reunification of Europe, like the reunification of Germany, had taken place entirely on Western terms. Westerners expected Easterners to continue thankfully accepting Western political domination, along with the handouts provided by the EU. Some in the West spoke of 'backsliding' towards authoritarian Russia. And many saw awakened, in the ungrateful East, a backward cultural inclination that had lain dormant during the years of communist rule. These critics suggested that there was a connection between illiberalism of the Orbán variety and a long history in Central Europe of authoritarianism and anti-Semitism.

Orbán-style illiberalism has been a continuing influence on Central Europe's relationship with the West, in spite of strong local opposition and regardless of electoral reversals; it is all but guaranteed to survive Orbán's personal hold on power. Yet illiberalism is not unique to Central Europe or to the character of its peoples. Orbán built a network of political fans reaching well beyond the post-communist parts of Europe. The Italian leader of the ultra-right Lega, Matteo Salvini, declared Orbán a 'good friend' and supported his anti-democratic endeavours, from the unlimited emergency powers Orbán declared at the height of the coronavirus crisis, to his infamous law against 'presenting homosexuality' in schools.[8] When Salvini's frenemy Giorgia Meloni, the head of the Fratelli d'Italia, a party of neo-fascist heritage, had herself photographed with Orbán, Orbán captioned the photo on his Facebook page, *due fratelli* (two brothers).[9] Marine Le Pen, of the French illiberal party, Rassemblement National, said the Hungarian leader was the only one willing to protect the EU's borders.[10] That did not prevent him from feting her rival, Eric Zemmour, who was then preparing to run for president of France, at a Budapest anti-liberal fest also featuring former US Vice President Mike Pence.[11] Tucker Carlson, America's most popular right-wing talk show host, spent a week in Budapest sending back praise after praise of the Hungarian leader. Donald Trump, retired from his stint at the White House, sent a note from Florida affirming that Orbán and he shared the same 'values'.[12] Whoever thought that Orbán's rule was a local, 'Eastern European' affair with few consequences for the West, should think again.

The rise of the Hungarian villager to global prominence was undoubtedly due to his personal qualities, but also, luck. He was at the right place at the right time. Neoliberal capitalism and globalization, which had seemed omnipotent in 1989 when communism fell in Europe, was experiencing a crisis, leading among other things to illiberalism. The illiberal revolt was, as we will see, both an ill-conceived response against, and in other ways a continuation of, the neoliberal policies that had decades ago come to the fore with Reagan and Thatcher. The revolt did not begin in Hungary or Central Europe, but engulfed much of the world; in America it would greatly contribute to the election of Donald

Trump as president. Everywhere, it was far more than a personal affair. It will remain a serious threat to liberal democracy, whether it holds the reins of government or challenges it from outside. And for a long time, Central Europe is certain to endure as one of the hotbeds of illiberalism in the world – not by far the only one, but one with its own characteristics, which this book aims to address.

These characteristics include the special appeal of Central Europe to the white racists who, as we will see, make up a significant part of the public who support illiberal leaders. One of the things that appeals to racists in the West most about Central Europe is that the population there is still almost entirely white (apart from the long-oppressed and still largely silenced Roma residents). They so wish that were still the case in their own lands! Whiteness is something that forms a bond between them and illiberals in Central Europe, though more polite 'conservatives' like to use 'Christianity' and 'European values' as euphemisms. Illiberal Central Europeans wish to protect their whiteness from the migrants of colour who have 'invaded' the West (while they welcome white refugees from Ukraine).

Racism, as always, is a tool wielded by people to advance their interests. The Central European landscape is dotted by assembly factories, largely belonging to foreign manufacturers. Here workers toil at wages that are much lower than in the West, but still higher than those of their competitors, workers of colour in the Global South. The competition has been transferred to the West, too, where Central European migrants work alongside people from the former colonies. On the basis of a rational analysis, Central Europeans should see the need for solidarity with the Global South. That would, however, not sit well with the crony capitalists who have gained the most from illiberal movements. As I will show, they have their problems with the multinational corporations of the West, but they do need Western investment for their own projects, and so have been happy to encourage 'competitive' low wages. Against that reality they offer as a balm the emotional or (to use the technically more correct term) *affective* politics of imagined kinship felt among people of the same nation and race.[13] Illiberal Central Europeans (which is by far not all of them!) are insulted by the notion that they should be at the level of people of colour, or even anywhere near there. They are white and want to be treated as quite. The dream of the 'transition' from communism was that they would fully access white privilege – live at the same standard as the West and be accepted as equals by it.

It is a central contention of this book that such was never meant to be the case. It is in the nature of capitalism to create groups and regions destined to provide cheap labour and to become a captive market for goods.[14] This was also the logic that applied to the 'Eastern enlargement' of the EU. The East has had to compete with a much richer and more powerful West. When it became apparent that, as a result, the East was not 'catching up', its 'failure' was attributed, by many in the West, to its being congenitally, inherently, culturally backward. But Central Europe's failure to become as prosperous and as liberal as the West must be viewed as largely wrought by the invisible hand of intervention by Western-dominated, global market neoliberalism (the *neo-* stands for the return of the idea of 'freeing' markets aimed at dismantling the postwar welfare state).[15] To be blind to this, and instead to blame 'Eastern European' backwardness for what is very much the West's doing, is racist.

I suggest that post-Cold War conditions have created, or at least greatly strengthened, a new racism that I call 'Eastern Europeanism'. It is, to be sure, not comparable in severity to the racisms that originated in colonial oppression. Yet it does treat Central Europeans and others in or from post-communist Europe as a different and inferior breed.

What is different here from the colonial situation is that Eastern Europeans are white, even if treated as not quite so. Being white gives at least potential access to white privilege, which gives every white person, other things equal, a head start over a person of colour.

Yet to white racists that is not enough. They expect their whiteness to guarantee the kind of security that people of all races have seen slip away from them. This sentiment appears to have taken hold of some among the groups most affected by the ravages of unbridled global capitalism in the 1990s and in the first decade of the twenty-first century. Worldwide, they include what may be called the white periphery: some white middle-class and working-class people of the depopulating countryside and rust belts; some in the cities seeing secure jobs replaced by precarious positions without benefits, and many in Central Europe, having seen not only the political repression but also the extensive social security of the communist period severely savaged during a fast and chaotic changeover to a 'market economy'. Their white privilege is the last privilege they have and want to defend.

Race, illiberalism, Central Europe

Three of the crucial terms here are: race, illiberalism, Central Europe. None has strict boundaries. Race spills over into nationality and class. Illiberalism is almost impossible to separate from its near-synonyms: populism,[16] authoritarianism,[17] right-wing nationalism, reactionary[18] or majoritarian[19] democracy, national conservativism,[20] authoritarian[21] or authoritarian-ethnicist[22] neoliberalism, electoral authoritarianism[23] and the like; some speak simply of 'fascism'.[24] More, illiberalism shares some elements (not least a tendency toward racism) even with its seeming opposite: liberalism. Central Europe has been said by some to range from Finland to Turkey and from Switzerland to Belarus, although in this book I focus, with deliberate simplification, on the Visegrád Four: Poland, the Czech Republic, Slovakia, and Hungary.

That race, illiberalism, and Central Europe are hard to define is not a deficiency. Pliability is part of their very nature. Each refers to a fluid process and not a static fact. All three (even Central Europe, I will argue) are concepts under constant construction. My aim is to show that they are constructed together, and to discuss how.

First, race. Specifically, I am concerned here with whiteness. The illiberal racism *of* Central Europeans is that of white people against people of colour; the racism *against* Central Europeans is a racism (largely) of whites against whites. 'White' is one of those words that illustrate well the idea of 'prototype semantics' introduced by the philosopher Ludwig Wittgenstein.[25] Each word has a central, prototypical meaning, from which more peripheral meanings radiate. A robin may be the prototypical bird for many English speakers; a chicken is still a bird, but somehow less so. When it comes to whiteness, Northwest Europeans and their overseas descendants are the prototype, but other people considered white are less so. It should be clear that what I mean by 'white' here is 'possessing white privilege'. 'White but not quite' means white, but not possessed of full white privilege.

Clearly, the racial othering and the attendant racial discrimination against people who are white, even if not quite, is only partial compared to the much more obvious and far more nefarious discrimination against non-white groups including Black and Indigenous people. To interpret this book as relativizing anti-Black racism and equating it with Central or Eastern European victimhood would be a severe misunderstanding. Rather, my point is that the same system that produces such radical racial oppositions as White and Black or colonizer and colonized, also produces ambiguous positions of partial privilege coexisting with oppression, such as 'Eastern European' (which subsumes Central Europeans). Other such ambiguous categories that have been identified in the academic literature include Southern European,[26] Southeast European,[27] and Asian American.[28] (And then there are, of course, the many millions of mixed-race people in the world, a group that is rapidly increasing in the West.) Recognizing that race penetrates insidiously the fabric of social distinctions even where it is somewhat less visible, should serve to highlight, not obscure, the singular importance of cases, like anti-Black racism, where racism is too overwhelming to be missed.

Thomas C. Holt, a leading scholar of race and African-American history, believes that in the twenty-first, unlike in the early twentieth century, 'race no longer follows a color line. The racialized other may well be white and hail from the Caucasus'.[29] It is still rather unusual to refer to race in Europe, however. Some even consider it inappropriate to speak of racism in Europe in a way that at all compares it to racism in America.[30] When it comes to white-on-white racism, they may recognize intolerance within Europe, but hold on to an old-fashioned distinction between race and ethnicity and the ethnically defined nation. That is, they insist that white-on-white discrimination in Europe is national, not racial; that it is 'chauvinism' not racism. (In Holt's words, 'Race is something blacks have; ethnicity belongs to whites.'[31]) But rejecting the relevance of race for this reason would be just another way to miss the opportunity to understand it in its full complexity and geographic reach. We are dealing here with much more than terminology; the substance of race and race-making is explored in Chapter 1.

Second, illiberalism. We are dealing with the kind of political arrangements that have characterized governments such as Donald Trump's in America, Vladimir Putin's in Russia, Jair Bolsonaro's in Brazil, and, to cite the most famous (or infamous) Central European example, Viktor Orbán's in Hungary. 'Illiberalism' is only one of the many terms that, as mentioned above, can be used to describe this type of political arrangement. There is no shortage of academic literature discussing the nature of what may be covered by all these terms, which, to refer to Wittgenstein again, clearly hold a certain 'family resemblance' by which we recognize, in spite of differences, that they cover the same kind of political style. I prefer 'illiberalism' over such terms as 'populism', for one thing because as an anthropologist I respect the terms the groups I study use themselves. 'Illiberal democracy', although a phrase invented with a disapproving connotation by the political commentator Fareed Zakaria,[32] has been popularized by Orbán himself, who has proudly used it to describe his ideal social arrangement. But also, I believe that illiberalism more than the other terms refers, in addition to politics, to a mood. The supporters of illiberalism (whom I call 'illiberals') typically stress conservative, patriarchal 'European' or 'Christian' values. They hold these 'values' with an intense and combative emotional conviction. So 'illiberalism' functions well to support an approach that I follow here, to combine a study of relatively objective geopolitical facts with an examination of moods and emotions, or what has been called affective politics.[33]

In terms of its objective characteristics, illiberalism is, as I have already mentioned, not the opposite of liberalism. Unlike neoliberalism it may favour strong state control including arbitrary intervention both in the market and in politics, and national over global scales of action. However, like market liberalism it has little taste for providing social welfare for the poor (as opposed to measures to increase the birth rate in order to prevent the need for migrants). It tends to favour low and regressive tax rates. For this and other reasons, as we will see, many observers have considered illiberalism to be a new phase of neoliberalism.[34] They point out that its features were already observable in Margaret Thatcher's Britain.[35] The Scottish sociologist Neil Davidson in fact suggested, though using different terminology, that illiberalism has always been an option inherent in liberal capitalism, to which it resorts at times of crisis.³⁶

Third, Central Europe. I use the term here mostly in its narrowest geographic sense, to include Poland, the Czech Republic, Slovakia, and Hungary (Map I.1). Sometimes, the term is used also to include Germany (a fact that, we will see, is crucial to understanding the history of Central Europe) and often Austria and other parts of the erstwhile Austro-Hungarian Monarchy: Croatia, Slovenia, and Romania. Ukrainians and Belarusians who want closer ties with the West would include themselves, too. There was even a time, as we will see, when Finland and Turkey were envisioned within Central Europe by some. But Poland, the Czech Republic, Slovakia, and Hungary are the core of what is meant by 'Central Europe'; no one would dispute that *they* belong there.³⁷ Certainly, these are the countries that Orbán means when he says 'we Central Europeans' – 'the spirited Poles, the ever-thoughtful Czechs, the sober Slovaks, and the romantic Hungarians'.³⁸ The only other group he regularly refers to as 'we' is Hungarians themselves.

Map I.1: The location of 'Central Europe', as discussed in this book

Again, I am an anthropologist by training, and in anthropology we insist on respecting the insider perspective of the people we study. So the fact that 'Central Europe' is a major point of self-reference for residents of the four countries – and it is, whether they otherwise agree with Orbán or not – is, for me, significant. A considerable part of this book is devoted to the distinctive history and current geopolitical relations of Central Europe, which I believe to be indispensable to understanding its part in the worldwide illiberal revolt. One of my objectives is to introduce the unfamiliar reader to the specific politics – and emotions – of Central Europe and Central Europeans today, especially as they relate to their relationship to the West.

In the West, 'Central Europe' is not much known or discussed as a separate area. It appears perhaps most often as part of the phrase, 'Central and Eastern Europe'. The *and* in this expression is rarely taken seriously. In fact, it is not required; most of the time, it is acceptable to say 'Eastern Europe' without the 'Central and', and to mean the same thing. There are good reasons for such a conflation in some contexts. It makes good sense when our focus is on the common communist past, or its common effects today. But one of the major points of this book is that illiberalism in Central Europe is not only or mainly the result of its communist experience. Illiberalism is global and has global causes. These are, obviously, inflected by local conditions. Yet those conditions are very different in the part of the post-communist world that is now within the Western alliances, NATO and the EU, on one hand, from Russia, which since the invasion of Ukraine has unequivocally positioned itself as the West's enemy.

Yet the prototypical country of 'Eastern Europe' is Russia, so the term 'Eastern Europe', when applied to Central Europe, gives it a Russian tint. This serves to cover up, not to reveal, the specificities of East–West relations in Central Europe. Conflating Central *and* Eastern Europe raises unjustified suspicions that Central Europe, and especially its illiberals, are a Russian fifth column. I will argue, instead, that illiberalism in this region is primarily a matter of relations between Central Europe and the West – not between Russia and the West.

This flattening of difference, this insistence that Central Europe *still* resembles Russia, *still* is separate from the West, *still* remains incapable of being fully European (I say: fully white), this othering of Central Europe is not an innocent one. It is a distancing fundamental to the structure of East–West relations in Europe since the end of communism. It is meant to justify the refusal to allow Central Europe, construed as forever different, forever other, forever 'Eastern', full access to the Western structures of privilege, and so to keep it in the quasi-colonial condition to which many Central Europeans so firmly object – though sadly not by attacking coloniality as such, but rather by joining the misguided revolt of illiberalism.

In Western Europe, and in particular in Brexit Britain, this effort to distance, to send back, to keep in their Eastern European place, people from Central Europe whom EU membership entitled to come, manifested itself in ways that have become ever more recognizably racist. Here, capital's interests in creating racially defined pools of cheap labour competing in the race to the bottom of the wage scale, that is, the same interests that make some Central European workers resent those of the postcolonial Global South, now induce some Western European workers to oppose Central European migrants. They, too, are oblivious to recognizing their *Schicksalgenossen*, to use the German expression, their partners in fate.

Partial privilege and the semi-periphery

There is a fourth term, in addition to race, illiberalism, and Central Europe, that is essential to the argument of this book: *partial privilege*. In geopolitical terms, Central Europe is more privileged than the Global South (and, by virtue of its membership in the EU, arguably also more privileged than Russia or the rest of 'Eastern Europe' outside the EU). To repeat, discrimination against Central European migrants cannot be compared to racism against people of colour (including discrimination *by* Central Europeans). But the privileges of whiteness are not fully granted to Central Europeans.

Central Europe's place in the system of white privilege can be captured by the phrase, *semi-periphery*. The notion of 'periphery' is crucial to my position. The scholar who has made the most of the term is the Yale sociologist, Immanuel Wallerstein. His 'world systems theory' is an approach to geopolitics developed in his monumental *The Modern World System*.[39] This work eventually appeared in four volumes, between 1974 and 2001, and remains influential today. Wallerstein's 'world systems' consist of relations between a 'core' and a 'periphery'. The countries of the core benefited the most from the rise of capitalism and continue to do so. They included Northwestern Europe and the United States. The periphery most unambiguously included the former colonies, for example, in Africa. But Wallerstein also posited the existence of an intermediate category, the *semi-periphery*:

> The core-periphery distinction, widely observed in recent writings, differentiates those zones in which are concentrated high-profit, high-technology, high-wage diversified production (the core countries) from those in which are concentrated low-profit, low technology, low-wage, less diversified production (the peripheral countries). But there has always been a series of countries which fall in between in a very concrete way, and play a different role.[40]

These semi-peripheral countries vary widely in character. Wallerstein saw among them even such rich countries of the 'old white Commonwealth' as Canada and Australia, along with Latin America, Southern Europe, and definitely 'most of Eastern Europe'. 'In part they act as a peripheral zone for core countries,' he wrote, 'and in part they act as a core country for some peripheral areas.'[41] The four Central European countries discussed here function as a periphery for the core areas of the EU. For example, they provide a network of assembly plants employing relatively cheap labour for Western and Asian multinationals, such as automobile makers. At the same time, the area continues to benefit collectively, as part of the EU and due to its intensive integration with the Western economy, from the economic and political privileges enjoyed by the West vis-à-vis the peripheral regions of the former colonies. These include but are not limited to transfers of technology, managerial know-how, and practices of democratic governance.

Partial privilege is the condition experienced by semi-peripheral groups. I will be using, and even extending, Wallerstein's term 'semi-peripheral', but with a reservation. In fact, a semi-peripheral group, engaged as it is in a constant struggle for its contested privilege, is not necessarily or usually located half-way between the core and the periphery, as the term *semi-* may suggest. At some times, and in some contexts, it is closer to one or the other. Clearly there are degrees of 'coreness' and peripherality, related to local as well as global hierarchies of power and prestige. London is more core than Manchester, and Warsaw more than Poznań. But also, England is more core than Austria, which is more core than Hungary. Eastern Europe *as a whole* is peripheral vis-à-vis Western Europe. Yet Central Europe is still more core than Bulgaria or Ukraine.

In an insightful analysis of what I call partial privilege, Anca Parvulescu suggests that 'Eastern European' is one of the conditions produced by a 'racial triangulation' that locates populations in-between such ultimate contrasts as black and white, or colonizer and colonized. Rather than producing a 'neat hierarchy of oppressor and oppressed', writes Parvulescu, 'the three terms of the triangle *co-produce* each other ... in multidirectional ways, with multiple, often contradictory and unstable effects'.[42] However, this always mobile, unstable process cuts a more complex figure than a triangle. It produces a hierarchy of racialization also *within* 'Eastern Europe'. To use one important example, discrimination against Ukrainian migrants in Poland has a remarkable resemblance to that practised against Poles and other 'Eastern Europeans' in Western Europe.[43]

As we progress in this book, I will stay focused on the partially privileged position of Central Europe between the core and the periphery, though we need not be committed to the detail of Wallerstein's work. I will use the term 'peripheral' when focusing on Central Europe's position outside the Western core, and the more specific 'semi-peripheral' when concentrating on its position between the West and the rest of the world.

Semi-peripherality and partial privilege mark distinctions among people not only horizontally, in geographic space, but also vertically, in the social hierarchy. Wallerstein's geopolitical analysis can be extended to recognize core and periphery within a society. Groups engaged in 'high-profit, high-technology, high-wage diversified production' and high-paying professions are the core within each society, including in Central Europe. These 'elites', as illiberals like to call them, tend to live in the more globally connected cities. Within those cities, they live in the more prosperous and/or more glamorous areas. They also tend to be most resistant to illiberal rhetoric and politics. So, going beyond Wallerstein's use, I would like to generalize the notion of peripherality to the vertical stratification of a society, that is its class system. The most powerful segments of a capitalist class society are the upper and upper middle classes, and the least powerful are the ever growing underclass of the chronically unemployed. (In Central Europe, many are members of the Roma minority.) If we transfer the notion of peripherality to this situation, then the upper and upper middle class are the core, and the chronically unemployed and the lower working class are the ultimate periphery of the class system. The lower middle class and the upper working class (skilled blue-collar workers, mostly) are also not part of the core. They are peripheral, but less so. Compared to the poorest and the least privileged, they are a semi-periphery.

There is a related, gendered dimension to this, captured by the phrase, 'men without postsecondary education' – a peripheral position relative to other men. And there is an urban–rural dimension, with rural residents peripheralized compared to the urban core. By extension of Wallerstein's terminology, these can be called semi-peripheral groups; they have, and struggle to defend, their partial privilege. The point that I am anticipating here is that these socially semi-peripheral groups show tendencies to support illiberalism that are quite comparable to those shown by the geographically defined semi-periphery, including rural areas everywhere, and also including Central Europe as a whole.

A number of cautionary points need to be made to qualify such generalizations. To say that white lower-middle-class and upper-working-class people as a whole are, as a group, responsible for the illiberal revolt would be an unjustified insult, and it is not what I am saying. Auriel Mondon and Aaron Winter detail many of the necessary reservations, focusing on the case of the Brexit referendum and on the 2016 American presidential election that brought Donald Trump to power.[44] The authors demonstrate as a misconception the idea that the victory of what was largely an illiberal cause depended on a generalized 'working class', an especially misleading conclusion if this class is misrepresented as entirely white. But even if only the white working class is taken into account, Mondon and Winter show that their vote was not the only one ensuring that Trump and Brexit prevailed; voters from classes above the working class played a major role.

Similarly, in the 2019 parliamentary elections in Poland, the illiberal PiS party got 40.2 per cent of its votes from people with a secondary education and 26.8 per cent from university graduates, and only 34 per cent from those without either of these educational qualifications.[45]

Nevertheless, even if less socially privileged voters do not make up the majority of illiberal voters, the support for illiberal and related causes among white, working- *and* lower-middle-class, rural, and male voters throughout Europe and North America is typically more pronounced than among other groups. In Poland, the reason the majority of PiS's vote did not come from people with less than a secondary education is that they are a minority in a country where most people have graduated from at least secondary school. But among people without a secondary education, PiS won over 60 per cent, considerably more than among those with higher educational status.[46]

If we go beyond education, and especially if we are careful to focus on the upper working class and lower middle class, rather than just 'working class', then the generalization, that *illiberalism appeals strongly to white groups with precarious, partial privilege*, appears to stand. In this respect, Central Europe when taken as a whole is part of the partially privileged white periphery, which also includes groups and regions in the West. And just like in the West, the relative success of illiberal ideas and politics in Central Europe is not the result of cultural baggage, but largely a misdirected reaction to the region's position in the global hierarchy of power.

That reaction is complex and to understand it we may approach it from many directions. My contribution is to investigate it in terms of the conjunction of race, illiberalism, and the notion of Central Europe. These are factors that interact dynamically in a way that changes from time to time and from place to place. I am not suggesting a total, deterministic explanation that predicts when and where illiberalism will necessarily appear and to what extent. Rather, I am discussing the conditions of possibility where illiberalism has found fertile ground in Central Europe.

How this books fits in

This book complements other approaches to its topic and related issues; often it expands them, occasionally it contradicts them. Timothy Snyder's *The Road to Unfreedom: Russia, Europe, America* has given me much food for thought, especially in its emphasis on how undemocratic regimes present themselves as representing the eternal, unchanging essence of the nation (and also, how they therefore have trouble surviving change, especially the succession from one leader to the next).[47] Anne Applebaum is, as always, a source of endless insight into the nuances of how dangers to democracy develop. Her work is especially revealing about the human context of interaction, among both leaders and ordinary people. She is astute in tracing the descent of the political right, with which she may initially evidence more sympathy than most observers, into anti-democratic illiberalism (though that is not her favourite term). And she, a long-time observer (and resident) of Poland, makes it clear in *The Twilight of Democracy: The Seductive Lure of Authoritarianism* that illiberalism is not an Eastern European specialty, that '[g]iven the right conditions, any society can turn against democracy'. Worse, 'if history is anything to go by, all of our societies eventually will'.[48] This in particular makes studying authoritarianism in Central Europe important for the lessons it holds as a case study of a global threat.

The Austrian historian Philipp Ther's *Europe Since 1989: A History* is particularly powerful in its recognition of the effects of global neoliberal capitalism on Central Europe, in connection to other places, including the West.[49]

Ivan Krastev and Stephen Holmes, in *The Light That Failed: A Reckoning*, speak of the 'failed light' of liberal democracy in Central and Eastern Europe and in Trump's America, attributing this alleged fiasco, in the case of Russia and of the East of the EU, to a so-called 'Imitation Imperative'.[50] They claim that Russia imitated the West for a while after the fall of communism, but that their imitation was insincere. Eastern Europe within the EU (including what I call here Central Europe), on the other hand, really meant it. However, Krastev and Holmes argue, it was bound to fail because Western liberal democracy was not a model that could, in their region, be successfully imitated, at least in the conditions that have historically obtained after 1989. I am less inspired by Krastev and Holmes' approach, for reasons that I will set out later in this book.

There are many other major and widely read books about illiberalism and/or related threats to democracy (populism, authoritarianism, ethnonationalism). Among these, one might rather randomly pick Benjamin Moffit's *Populism*,[51] Jan-Werner Müller's *What Is Populism?*, or Steven Levitsky and Daniel Ziblatt's *How Democracies Die*. Without a doubt more will appear at the same time as, and following, the appearance of this book.

Academic work on illiberalism/populism/ethnonationalism and so on is expanding by leaps and bounds, and is impossible to cover from a totalizing scope. Much of it will be referred to in the various chapters of this book. It may be worth singling out a few of the research initiatives undertaken with a partial or complete focus on Central Europe, often with significant participation by scholars in the area.

The EU's Horizon 2020 research grant programme has made a major contribution. The DEMOS research project is a large cooperative effort located at 15 European institutions, whose main aim is to study populism in terms of the 'democratic efficacy', that is, the conditions under which different publics will engage in different ways with populism.[52] The *FATIGUE* and *POPREBEL* projects, led respectively by Richard Mole and Jan Kubik, investigate the recent rise of 'neo-traditionalism' as part of a 'rebellion against modernity'. Neo-traditionalism is characterized, according to the researchers,

> by the emphasis placed on outcomes rather than procedures of the political processes; protection of a (national) collective rather than an individual; safeguarding of the 'traditional' social, particularly gender, roles; and an overriding concern with protecting the purity of the (national) collective against the perceived threats of cosmopolitanism and multiculturalism.[53]

A certain 'neo-feudalism' is detected from this perspective in illiberal society; that is an approach that has found some response among others in the area and beyond.[54]

One of the most enlightening contributions from Central Europe is a collection of essays entitled *Central European Culture*

Wars: Beyond Post-Communism and Populism. The introduction by the editors, the Czech researchers Pavel Barša, Zora Hesová, and Ondřej Slačálek, insists, as do I in this book, that the 'culture wars' in Central Europe are not the result primarily of the communist heritage, but rather 'part and parcel of the anti-globalist moment of the 2010s and its pan-European and global reach'.[55] This 'moment' happened as the liberal consensus that governed the post-communist 'transition' unravelled because the market economy that had been its goal had been established. When it led to various crises both in the area and globally, it stimulated the defection from liberal democracy of an important part of the political elite and their supporters. Barša and his colleagues make a connection here to the French political scientist Jacques Rupnik's notion that, once the consensus to establish a market economy was accomplished, liberals 'no longer had any collective project to put forward'.[56] The political economy scholar, Adam Fabry, too, sees a liberal (or neoliberal, in his terms) consensus existing after 1989, and he relates in detail its unravelling as the neoliberal system, and the prosperity it began to produce, crashed during the 2008 financial crisis.[57]

To return to concerns of race and comparisons with the postcolonial condition, these are particularly important in some of the research literature that focuses on people who move from Central Europe (and the rest of the post-communist space), to work temporarily or to settle in the United Kingdom and Western Europe. This relatively new area of research is expanding so swiftly that to address all of it would be impossible, given the energy with which new work is produced by an ever increasing number of scholars. A special issue of the *Journal of Ethnic and Migration Studies* brings together research focusing on race and illiberalism on location in the east of the EU, with that concerned mainly with the migration context.[58] As one of the guest editors of the issue (the other is Aleksandra Lewicki of the University of Sussex), I see the migration context as closely related to my concerns here.

These and other works have helped me to develop this book's discussion of whiteness as an object of struggle in Central Europe, in the context of the illiberal tendency on the rise there and in the world.

Awful East, awesome West?

As all the literature just mentioned agrees, there was once a near-complete consensus around the need to integrate post-communist economies and political systems in the West as the West appeared in the years after 1989, when it was beholden to the alleged magic of the market and global deregulation.

Neoliberal globalization once saw the fall of communism in 1989 as perhaps its greatest triumph – but no more. Long gone is the euphoria of the early November day in 1989, when East German guards stepped back, weapons still unsheathed, and throngs of cheering Berliners, from the East and from the West of the cursed wall dividing them, climbed atop and embraced as brothers and sisters. It was the last of the great victory celebrations in Europe: the return home of the East. Germans revelled at the reunification of their country, but also the whole continent rejoiced that East and West had survived the forced separation of the Cold War, long imposed by the Russian outsider.

In the next months and years, disappointment began to appear on both sides of the former wall. In the East, the peace and prosperity that many expected was far from arriving; on the contrary, what ensued was chaos, corruption, criminality, and economic recession. Although many of these were later at least partially reversed, even now the East of the EU lags behind the West on measures of wealth and social security. In the West, where neoliberal dogma dictated that freeing up markets would lead to affluence, many were disappointed in the East's performance. They charged its inability to catch up to its cultural backwardness. The patient, not the bad medicine, was blamed for the apparent lack of cure, as well as the side effects.

Perhaps, many in the West thought, Russian influence was not just a temporary, 40-year interlude; maybe these Eastern Europeans resembled the Russians by nature. Perhaps they always had. Leading historians now claimed to discover that 'Eastern Europe' had been imagined as the West's contrasting Other, as far back as the Enlightenment of the eighteenth century, if not before.[59]

If the free-market medicine didn't seem to take in Central Europe, it seemed that neither did liberal democracy. Freedom of thought and speech seemed to disappointed observers to have done little more than release disturbing expressions of hate that, as they saw it, surfaced from deep reserves of intolerance that had survived decades of communist repression. Even if there were a potential in Eastern Europe for shaking the legacy of anti-Semitism, anti-Roma racism, and belligerent, authoritarian nationalism, as many observers saw it that potential was not realized during the years when the area was cut off from the West. It would be pointed out by self-satisfied Westerners, that the dark past of intolerance had been 'mastered' (*bewältigt*, as the Germans say) in the West through decades of discussion and education directed by the liberal state. They would add that this self-cleansing exercise had not taken place in the Soviet-led Eastern Bloc, and still wasn't taking place after it dissolved.

When the impact of the American Black Lives Matter movement made itself felt in Europe, at least some Western Europeans began to see, however, how false that feeling of having mastered racism – including anti-Semitism – in the West really was. Racism was alive and well, and ingrained in the invisible fabric of daily life, both in the West and in Central – and Eastern – Europe.

Nevertheless, critics were right to point to shocking manifestations of racism in the post-communist East. My goal is to put Central European racism and other, related forms of hate and intolerance, in a perspective that does not locate it all in 'Eastern Europe' and I may point to cases where the origins and/or the persistence of racism there is actually due to practices that come from the West. But that emphatically does not mean that I would like to justify racism in Central Europe. If I explain (not defend) the awfulness of Central European illiberalism with reference to a not-so-awesome West, it is in the hope that this broader understanding may help us to combat hate in both.

The first manifestation of hate after communism that was widely noticed was anti-Semitism, openly propagated on the political fringe by groups nostalgic after prewar fascist movements, and coopted in more subtle form by mainstream politicians. Less than a year after the Fall of the Wall, in October 1990, a scholarly conference in Jerusalem examined the 'old-new scourge of anti-Semitism' in Central and Eastern Europe. István Deák, an influential Hungarian-American historian and essayist, who has some Jewish roots, noted that in his country of origin a writer from the ranks of the anti-communist dissidents now came out openly and loudly with the idea that Hungarian Jews could not empathize with the suffering of Hungarians. This was because of the different experiences Jews and gentiles in Hungary had after the First World War, when Jews played a prominent role in an ill-fated communist revolution and, of course, during the Holocaust. Sándor Csoóri concluded that 'we are experiencing a reverse assimilationist trend'. It is now not Hungarians wanting to assimilate Jews, but 'liberal Jewry that wants to assimilate the Hungarian nation. For that purpose it possesses a more powerful weapon than it has ever possessed, namely, the parliamentary system'.[60] Here, Csoóri meant to bring down with one fell swoop his country's 'liberal' Jews and the entire liberal democratic system, which he saw, as the fascists and Nazis did before him, as the work of Jews.

In Slovakia, tens of thousands of Jews had been deported to German death camps and hundreds were slaughtered, including by Slovak paramilitaries (as were my own grandparents), under the wartime president, Jozef Tiso. Tiso was a convicted war criminal, yet in 1990 some nationalists wanted to honour him with a controversial commemorative tablet. Though this particular attempt was not successful, efforts to commemorate Tiso have occurred repeatedly since then. Slovak state TV shocked critics in 2017 by allowing a nomination of Tiso for the title of 'Greatest Slovak', which they then withdrew.[61]

In Poland, as in Hungary and Slovakia, extreme nationalist groups and groupuscules have openly celebrated prewar and wartime anti-Semites and occasionally even Nazis. But even in the political mainstream, anti-Semitically tinted pronouncements have proliferated in Hungary and Poland, though usually with some plausible deniability added. Viktor Orbán takes care to protest that he and Hungary are friends of the Jews,[62] but it does not take too much interpretive acumen to understand whom he at least partially means when he speaks of an enemy, '[n]ot open, but hiding; not straightforward but crafty; not honest but base; not national but international; does not believe in working but speculates with money; does not have its own homeland but feels it owns the whole world'.[63]

Orbán chose as the focus of his anti-liberal attacks the figure of the Hungarian-born American-Jewish financier, George Soros, whom Orbán like other authoritarians accused of financing anything from Hungarian oppositional leaders to the migrant 'invasion' of Europe in 2015–16. (Orbán was biting the hand that, at least briefly, fed him; it was Soros' philanthropic foundation that had sent him to Oxford.) But if accused of anti-Semitism, Orbán took advantage of the fact that his obsessive hatred of Soros has been supported also by Israeli leaders, such as Benjamin Netanyahu.

During his tenancy as prime minister in the second decade of the century, Netanyahu also had very good relations with Mateusz Morawiecki, his Polish counterpart, at a time when the latter presided over a law prohibiting the criticism of the 'Polish nation' for collaborating in the Holocaust and persecuting Jews even after (although it is generally agreed by historians that many Poles did just that). It became a little more difficult for the next Israeli leadership to support the Polish government, when the latter decreed in 2021 that it would no longer be possible for family members to claim Jewish property confiscated by the Nazis and later nationalized by the communist government.

Anti-Semitism in Central Europe has been said to be related to the other forms of hate that surfaced more powerfully later. When more than a million migrants entered Europe in 2015 and 2016, Central European governments surprised and shocked the West by pulling together to block them from entering their countries. This effectively meant hindering their progress to the more prosperous Western countries of the EU, which is where they really wanted to go. Orbán had his infamous wire fence erected on his country's border with Serbia. Serbia was outside the EU and the 'Schengen Zone' of essentially border-free travel. But Hungary was inside, meaning that, in principle, those who managed to enter its territory could move on unhindered toward Austria and their favoured destination, Germany. The Czechs, Slovaks, and Romanians joined the Hungarians in refusing an EU-decreed quota of refugees. The issue played a large part in Poland in an election that deposed the liberals and brought to power the illiberal PiS (Rights and Justice Party) of Jarosław Kaczyński. Orbán's energetic anti-migrant agenda went a long way to achieve his goal of creating a common Central European front consisting of the four countries that are the focus of this book: Hungary, Poland, the Czech Republic, and Slovakia.[64]

Most of the migrants were from outside of Europe and were people of colour, many of them Muslim. The rhetoric against them was full of Islamophobic references, ranging from the alleged incompatibility of Muslim culture with Christian Europe, to fears of Muslims as terrorists and sexual assaulters. The President of the Czech Republic, Miloš Zeman, for example, suggested that even when Muslim terrorists are born in Western Europe, they continue to belong instead to Muslim countries like Algeria or Mali, attributing this to 'a kind of genetic determination'.

> A Czech remains a Czech, however, even if he lives in France. With Czechs there is no cultural difference problem. Whereas a Czech in France manages to adapt wonderfully, *viz* Milan Kundera [the author discussed in this book in Chapter 3], people from these countries don't have an ability to adapt. That's not an opinion, it's a fact.[65]

The president added that if Muslims cannot adapt to their host country then they should be deported. Given his view of Muslim adaptability as non-existent, that meant all of them.

Many observers attributed the virulent and open Islamophobia of such public pronouncements in Central Europe to the very same heritage that allegedly made the area predisposed to anti-Semitism. 'Have Eastern Europeans no shame?', asked one of the major historians of the Holocaust in Poland. Jan Gross played such a prominent role in uncovering Polish complicity in murdering and robbing Jews that the above-mentioned law against blaming the Polish nation as a whole was informally called in the country *lex Gross* (the Gross Law). To Gross, the antimigrant stance of the 'Eastern Europeans' was caused by the same revival of local traditions of intolerance that one of the participants of the 1990 Jerusalem conference just mentioned, Otto Dov Kulka, saw as the reason for revived anti-Semitism: 'What we are witnessing today in Central and Eastern Europe, is a return to the area's point of departure – its pre-totalitarian historical complexities – and not the adoption of a more or less uniform pattern of Western European political culture.'[66] In other words, there was a Western and an Eastern European political culture; the Western being liberal and tolerant, and the Eastern racist and intolerant. I will dispute this simplistic opposition throughout the book, but especially in Chapter 6.

The next round of hate speech, as anti-Semitism and Islamophobia lingered on but provided fewer active targets, was based mostly on sexual orientation. LGBTQ+ was declared an 'ideology' alien to Christian Europe, which among other things aimed to change innocent children's sexual orientation – something that reputable scholars today believe to be impossible. The campaign began with particular virulence in Poland. Dozens of Polish jurisdictions declared themselves an LGBT-propaganda-free zone, banning depictions of homosexuality. When the EU took funding away from such locations, the Polish government doubled it. In the 2020 presidential campaign, the successful candidate, Andrzej Duda, declared that 'LGBT ideology' was a worse enemy than communism.[67] He was only repeating the point made by Krakow Archbishop Marek Jedraszewski, who opined during a mass that the 'red pestilence no longer marches across our land, but a new, neo-Marxist one has appeared, which seeks to conquer spirits, hearts and minds – not red, but rainbow'.[68]

The Peace and Justice Party's anti-gay campaign, which (ironically given Kaczyński's anti-Russian emotions) mimicked that of Putin's Russia, began in Catholic Poland,[69] reached new heights in Orbán's Hungary, which is both less religious and less Catholic (Orbán is a Protestant). Here Orbán borrowed a page from Putin's book and, in spite of the impotent protests of the opposition, had his obedient Fidesz Party put through parliament a law that bans 'representing' homosexuality to children under the age of 18. The supposed motivation, to protect children from paedophiles, raised even more outrage through its equation of paedophilia and homosexuality. It tried the patience of the EU leadership, with Ursula von der Leyen, the President of the European Commission, calling the bill 'a shame' because it 'clearly discriminates against people on the basis of their sexual orientation and it goes against all the fundamental values of the European Union'. She asked the Commission to write a letter expressing 'legal concerns',[70] which was the most she could do. Hungary under Orbán had already stacked the courts and the universities with his minions, and manipulated the country's media so that the only independent voices heard by the public were constrained to speaking from relatively small platforms. To be sure, they were not speaking from jail. Nor were any journalists murdered by the Fidesz government as they are accused to have been in Russia.

While this might make the repression of the media in Orbán's Hungary slightly less repellent, it is in a sense more frightening than the Russian case to the EU and the rest of the West, because it represents a clever subversion, rather than a muscular destruction, of the structures of liberal democracy.

Liz Fekete, one of the keenest observers of the area, has been one of the scholars who have commented on the gendered nature of illiberalism in Central Europe, including its homophobic tendencies. She believes that illiberals prefer, to democracy, 'order and responsibility as the foundational values of a patriarchal Christianity, one that starts from the protection of kith and kin and proceeds to love of country and culture'.[71] One might have gone on beyond 'country and culture' to race. The ultimate privilege that Central European, like Western, illiberals mean to protect is that of the White Man. Much more on that later, but suffice it to say that illiberals, especially those inspired by conservative Christianity, also favour traditional gender roles for women and men. Gender fluidity and transgender identities frighten and threaten this type of illiberal (less commonly seen in the largely atheist Czech Republic than in the other three countries). The word 'gender', imported from English, is used by some illiberals to refer to what they think is an 'ideology': the idea of the social construction of gendered behaviour. The Hungarian scholar Andrea Pető saw the attacks on gender critique in Hungary as 'a fundamentally new phenomenon that was launched to establish a new world order',[72] an illiberal one that opposes the authority of scientific research, including in the social sciences and humanities, and rejects the considerable advances that have been made by scholars reconfiguring our understanding of gender.

This anti-gender rhetoric does resemble classic patriarchal discourse by advocating that the main task of the nation's women is to raise nationally conscious Poles or Hungarians. This is in part to prevent having to use migrants of colour to solve the demographic problem caused by the fact that too many people are leaving and that those who remain are getting old. In both countries, illiberal governments have implemented highly popular bonuses for large families, though as Fekete and others point out, these were carefully calibrated to avoid supporting the poorest families and the Roma.[73] For the very poor, who are disproportionately Roma, the Orbán government instituted workfare: you work at a job we say you will, and you get little or no welfare.

Such discriminatory welfare support functions in the context of an authoritarian state that drains resources in favour of the nouveau-riche cliques close to the government. This 'reverse distribution of wealth toward the wealthy', as Fekete calls it, became most advanced in Orbán's Hungary. The Hungarian analyst, Péter Magyari, noted that Orbán promoted friendly individuals to many important posts in government, the courts, the media, academia, and the cultural institutions, ensuring that his and his cronies' power would survive any regime change.[74] He did all of this more or less legally. The Central European illiberals' 'respect' for the law is the reason why their success is a more direct warning to Western liberal democracies than the Russian, Chinese, or Turkish models that rely on physical coercion and worse.

Even though democracy has been under siege in Central Europe, even where it is most threatened there is still enough democracy to demand significant support for the rulers by the ruled. An alliance of the very rich and the not-so-poor is the key to illiberal success today everywhere, including Central Europe. How that is formed is examined in Chapter 8. Essentially, it relies on the affect of identity, the feeling of being 'kith and kin' with others of the same race and nationality. Nationalism and racism operate here in the classic mode of 'false consciousness'. Instead of acting on feelings of exploitation, the exploited are swayed by the family-like solidarity of nationhood. On this half-articulated emotion, the real nation are those who are white, Christian, patriarchal, and allegedly 'hard-working'. These are the individuals that people in Central Europe as in many other parts of the world are thinking of when they say 'among us' – *u nas, u nás, nálunk, bei uns, chez nous*. The 'among' here is meant in the sense of a location as well as group membership. *U nás na Slovensku* means roughly 'in our country, Slovakia', but in English the domestic echo of *u nás*, which also means 'in our home' and 'in our family', is missing. The notion of family is both inclusive and exclusive. Extended to the nation, it includes those of the same 'background' (white, Polish, Catholic conforming to patriarchal gender role expectations), and excludes others (Jews, Roma, Muslim migrants). But also, it includes emotionally those who appreciate this feeling of identity and excludes those, of one's own background, who allegedly betray it. These are the 'liberals', the 'leftists', and other careerists and bleeding hearts who, so the illiberals say, advance their careers through obeying 'politically correct' dogma and prefer sympathy for the outsider to solidarity with their own kind. In other words, they prefer career or false pangs of conscience to the dictates of protecting what the illiberals see (wrongly of course) as the endangered species of white privilege.

This chimera of danger (a fearful fantasy that I, in this book, present as absolutely crucial to understanding illiberalism in Central Europe), finds political expression in what some have called 'majoritarian democracy', the right of a majority defined by a sense of common, family-like identity, to disregard the wishes and the rights of everyone else, whom they consider as outsiders or renegades.[75] In practical political policy terms, that means undermining the institutions that protect those with minority backgrounds or opinions; above all, the courts. Efforts in Central Europe to limit the checks and balances provided by the courts were spearheaded by the Polish leader, Jarosław Kaczyński, though Orbán did not trail far behind.

Kaczyński is the one other person, in addition to Orbán, whom history books will most remember as responsible for initiating Central Europe's illiberal revolt. The Polish leader is considerably more discreet than Orbán. True, he, too, has a sports passion. Like Orbán, he likes boxing, but among his serious sports passions is the rodeo; he dreams of having a bull ranch if ever he retires. (It is a safe bet, however, that he plans to watch others handle the wild bulls, not to be thrown off their backs himself.)

Kaczyński's twin brother, Lech, served as President of Poland from July 2006 to November 2007, with Jarosław running the government as prime minister. Together they had founded the Law and Justice Party in 2001, known even in English by its Polish acronym, PiS. Lech Kaczyński was among the almost 100 passengers who died in a plane crash near Smolensk in Russia, as they were on their way to commemorate a wartime massacre of Polish officers by Soviet forces near Smolensk. Although declared an accident by all official investigators, Polish and Russian, Jarosław Kaczyński has continued to support a conspiracy theory according to which the plane was shot down by the Russians.

Kaczyński ran for president and lost in 2010, but when his party won the 2015 parliamentary election riding the illiberal wave in response to the migrant crisis, he chose not to hold any office other than party leader. He decided to rule from the shadows as a grey eminence, or an official 'chief of state', as some called him, alluding to the prewar autocratic leader, General Piłsudski. In 2020, he did take on the official post of deputy prime minister, with his portfolio including responsibility for the justice system. Attempts to weaken the justice system in Poland and Hungary received not only informal, but even formal, legal condemnation from the EU. The EU officially invoked a process based on Article 7 of the Treaty on European Union, which provides sanctions, but short of expulsion, against states that are suspected of a 'serious breach' of EU values.

It was reported that in June 2021, alone, the European Commission launched 16 different probes into Poland and Hungary's behaviour, most of them related to justice issues, including regulations against 'LGBT ideology'. In both countries, illiberal governments used various types of legal subterfuge to stack the courts with judges obedient to the regime. In September 2018, the EU added Hungary to Poland as targets of the Article 7 process. But punishment has to be voted on unanimously by all EU members, and Hungary and Poland vowed to protect each other by vetoing any serious censure.

Poland and Hungary could also count on the support of the Czech Republic and Slovakia, but not unconditionally. The common front presented to 'Brussels' during the migration crisis was felt as emotionally satisfying throughout Central Europe, long disappointed with the deal it was getting from the West. The experience taught the leaders in the two countries sandwiched between Poland and Hungary that there was strength in Central European unity. However, at times support from the Czechs and Slovaks has been lukewarm at best. Mikuláš Dzurinda, a liberal Slovak politician, rejected Orbán's demand that the EU's power structure should change from a French-German axis to a French-German-V4 triangle. Dzurinda thought this would unnecessarily fragment the EU. Orbán's angry repartee was: 'Dear Mikuláš, should we not finally start behaving as equal partners to the western member states? Has the time not come for us to get organized and stand up for our interests? Why should we remain the EU's dupes?'

As the criticism from Brussels of Warsaw and Budapest's attacks on the rule of law intensified, and Orbán's resistance continued to harden, the Slovak minister of justice, Mária Kolíková, protested that Hungarian attempts to differentiate a Visegrád policy on law separate and different from that of the EU were a 'misuse of the V4 brand'.[76] The nature of such disagreements evidently reached even the Vatican. In his 2021 visit, Pope Francis only spent seven hours in Hungary, before moving on to a three-day visit of Slovakia. It was widely believed that he was trying to send a message.

The Czech Republic or Slovakia have, on the whole, shown a greater resistance to illiberal trends than their northern and southern neighbours. Certainly, the former Czechoslovakia has also produced notable illiberal personalities. Of these, the most mediatic is Miloš Zeman, who has repeatedly held the largely ceremonial role of President. One of the most stubborn Islamophobes of the continent, Zeman had declared, in support of the Islamophobic organization, 'We Do Not Want Islam in the Czech Republic' (Islám v České Republice Nechceme): 'I also don't want Islam in the Czech Republic'.

It was partly due to Zeman's public support that Andrej Babiš was elected prime minister of the Czech Republic in 2017. Babiš, proudly wore a red baseball hat, encouraging comparisons with Trump. Born in Slovakia, where he appears to have once been a minor agent of the communist secret police, Babiš became a powerful businessman, focusing on agriculture. Wealth eventually brought the trappings of class: Babiš purchased a Michelin-star restaurant on the French Côte d'Azur as well as a small chateau. He came to own extensive property, among other places, in Wittenberg, the eastern German city of Luther. He established a party, ANO (an acronym that is the Czech equivalent of 'YES'), one of whose aims was to fight corruption. But Babiš himself became the target of corruption investigations by the EU. Suspicions about Babiš's character increased when Monika Hohlmeier, chair of the EU Parliament's Committee on Budgetary Control, declared that she had received death threats.[77] Babiš's popularity continued to decline until, in a fall, 2021, election that included an appearance by Orbán in his support, he was defeated by a coalition of opposition parties. The new prime minister, Petr Fiala, warned against 'populism' as a danger to Czech society.

That illiberalism would no longer reign without significant challenge had been demonstrated even earlier in Slovakia. Here, a kind of proto-Orbán had taken power after the dissolution of Czechoslovakia. Vladimír Mečiar had himself been very much responsible for the breakup, having negotiated it with his Czech counterpart, Václav Klaus. The 'Velvet Divorce' left Mečiar in charge of a new country, where he proceeded through corruption and cronyism to establish his influence in Slovak institutions and the economy. Criminal gangs thrived under the protection of corrupt police, a modern Slovak tradition that the country appears to be seriously trying to free itself of, at last (see Chapter 4). Voters were able to remove Mečiar definitively from power in 1998, but subsequent governments have regularly fallen short of expectations. Prime Minister Robert Fico, who headed the Slovak government during the 2015–16 'migration crisis', was revealed to have suspicious links to the underworld, perhaps reaching as far as Italy. Massive demonstrations by citizens marching under the banner 'For a Decent Slovakia', led to the fall of Fico and his social democrats, and the victory in presidential elections of an environmentalist lawyer and activist, Zuzanna Čaputová, in 2019. Greeting the public not only in Slovak but also in the languages of the country's minorities, including Hungarian and Roma, Čaputová gave notice that the illiberal and racist style which had certainly penetrated Slovak politics was not to her taste. What ensued was a series of striking police actions, including the arrest of high-ranking judges, and a sequence of governments, none of whom was, however, able to gain the confidence of the majority of Slovaks.

These reversals of fortune for illiberals in Slovakia and the Czech Republic may be seen as marking the end of the triumphant, initial phase of the illiberal revolt in Central Europe, which had begun during the 'European migrant crisis' of 2015-16. By the winter of 2022, the illiberal leaders of Hungary and Poland, too, had more to fear than the wildfire spread of the Omicron variant of the Covid-19 coronavirus. In both countries, the opposition was making great strides to unite in challenge to the increasing authoritarianism of Orbán, Kaczyński, and their coterie.

Illiberalism was not, however, nearly defeated, even where illiberal politicians were unseated. The conditions that gave rise to it did not disappear. And indeed, some of the opposition included elements with quite an extreme anti-liberal heritage, as in the case of Hungary's nationalist Jobbik party.

Cronyism, racism (including anti-Semitism and Islamophobia), and homophobia continue to exist to an alarming extent in Central Europe. Opposition to racism and homophobia is comparatively timid, even if pursued by significant groups of courageous activists, and leaves the potential that hate toward the other may be exploited by authoritarian leaders in the future.

That said, much of the stimulus for hate actually comes from the West. Not only Islamophobia but anti-Semitism also should not be discussed without examining connections to the West, as had become obvious to me on a visit early after the fall of communism to the Slovak city of Komárno, where I spent most of my childhood. I discovered that the surviving little synagogue, built long ago in a church-like, neo-Gothic style by a community anxious to adapt to the Christian majority, had been vandalized. All of its windows were shattered, awaiting repair. On the walls and the doors I found stickers in Hungarian, the language of many in this border town. One said, 'We are back!' Another commanded, 'Foreigners out!' I recognized that the last slogan at least was a direct translation of a favourite rallying cry of the German far right. This, along with the red-white-and black graphic design recalling the Nazi flag, made me think that the stickers originated in Germany. I had a closer look, however, and the small print at the bottom made the provenance of the hate propaganda clear: Portland, Oregon, USA.

Practically every manifestation of hate in Central Europe has been seen in the West as well. In general, illiberalism has certainly been more visible in Central Europe, which is one of the issues that needs to be explained in this book, and is addressed in particular in its Conclusion. However, Donald Trump's rise to the presidency in the US should have put to rest the wishful thought that illiberalism will never conquer the West because of the West's superior, liberal democratic culture. Trump encouraged racism, anti-Semitism, and Islamophobia, and he, too, attempted to subvert American institutions by installing personal friends and/or obedient lackeys in positions of power.[78] No wonder when the American illiberal lost the 2020 election, the Hungarian illiberal missed him so much. The next summer he sent Trump a letter of support, for which Trump thanked him profusely. 'I am grateful for your enduring friendship and enduring commitment', replied Trump, 'to the ideals you and I cherish – freedom, patriotic pride, and liberty.'[79] Trump certainly did not feel that the 'ideals' he was sharing had anything singularly 'Eastern European' about them; they were global. On that, at least, he was right.

The evidence is just not there, when it comes to illiberalism, for the simplistic contrast between the awful East and the awesome West. Hate and illiberal encroachments on democracy and human rights also exist in the West. This alone is not, however, the only or the main reason to object to considering them as a specifically 'Eastern European' defect. A much bigger problem with leaving the West out of sight is that it is precisely in the West and its handling of the post-communist space that we should be seeking some of the major reasons for the very real problems for which, as I will show, Central European illiberalism proposes a false, deeply misguided, and self-defeating solution.

1

How Eastern Europeans Became Less White

Jozef Chovanec, a Slovak traveller, boarded a plane at the Charleroi airport in Belgium on 23 February 2018. The 39-year-old, who suffered from episodes of mental illness, reportedly became violent before take-off. At 7:30 pm, the captain called the police, and a doctor approved placing Chovanec in a cell, where he was at first allowed to sleep. A video shows officers entering at about 4:30 am. They proceed to bind the man's hands and feet. Soon, as many as seven officers are seen in the cell. One applies pressure to his neck; another kneels on his chest for about 16 minutes. A policewoman presents a mock Nazi salute. Smiles on the other officers' faces show they are quite amused. Initial reports said that Chovanec died in hospital a little later, but his lawyer and family maintain that he was dead on arrival. At the time of writing, a court investigation is still going on.[1] Chovanec's wife Henrieta saw a parallel to the well-known death of an African American who choked to death under the knee of a white policeman in the summer of 2020. 'After the videos of the arrest of the American George Floyd,' Henrieta recalled, 'I immediately thought, "my husband died the same way". Except that police also laughed out loud at my husband and a policewoman next to him did a Hitler salute'.[2]

How right was Chovanec's widow, to compare the police brutality toward her husband to one of the most notorious cases of police killing a Black man in America? Would Chovanec still be alive today if he was not a Slovak, like, we must surmise, Floyd would be alive had he not been an African American? Would he be alive if he wasn't an Eastern European?

I call racism against people seen as Eastern European (including Central Europeans), 'Eastern Europeanism'. Eastern Europeanist racism reared its head quite visibly during the 'Brexit' debate in the United Kingdom. Decades after the end of Soviet hegemony, the Eastern Bloc certainly lived on – or was it revived? – as an enemy in the minds of the owners of a little fishing lake in Oxfordshire. 'No Polish or Eastern Bloc fishermen allowed', a warning they posted at the pond said. 'No children or dogs.'[3] The British sociologist Alina Rzepnikowska-Philipps, who herself has Polish roots, notes that 'shared whiteness between East European migrants and majority has not exempted the former from racialization'.[4] Many Polish residents of Great Britain whom she interviewed felt a great increase in hostility during and following the 'Brexit' campaign for the UK to leave the EU (although there was some before as well). 'A neighbour who has been living here for several years', says one female immigrant, 'always used to talk to me, you know, she asked "how are you, how is it going, is everything OK?", and everything was fine. Now, when I see her, she turns her head away and pretends she doesn't see me'.[5] The experience of another Polish resident of Manchester was more frightening:

> I was attacked in a public place most likely because I was speaking Polish or my foreign accent. I asked him to leave me alone. He was English. He said 'I don't understand what you are saying' in a very negative way ... and he attacked me. It was terrible. I was in a hospital. I couldn't walk. It was a serious and brutal attack.[6]

The sociologist Aleksandra Lewicki has shown how migrants, including from Eastern Europe, are said to siphon off what remains of austerity-strapped social support. They are criminalized as 'tricksters and traffickers'. During the coronavirus crisis, they were blamed for spreading disease. All of which is used to justify arguments against their admission as migrant workers or permanent immigrants.[7]

Resentment of Central European workers has crystallized, for example, in France in the image of the *plombier polonais*, the 'Polish plumber', who allegedly destroys the livelihoods of local tradespeople by offering cheap labour without demanding the social benefits French workers have acquired through decades of labour activism.[8] The wave of negative sentiment against Polish workers (seen as 'Eastern European' and akin to other immigrants from post-communist Europe) may appear surprising, given France's record of absorbing white immigrants into the French majority. In fact, in 2005 when the *plombier polonais* first appeared as a stock phrase in the country, the minister responsible for immigration was Nicolas Sarkozy, the future president of France, who was the son of a Hungarian immigrant of aristocratic roots but modest social standing. Discrimination against people of colour has a long history in France, as elsewhere in Europe. Now the Eastern European joins their ranks, making up what Rzepnikowska has called the 'New Other'.

One of her Polish migrant interviewees recognized this, though one can perhaps hear in her voice a racially motivated tinge of resentment as well:

> I said that it would have been better if I was black, I mean, if I was from Africa, because people would stop treating me as an intruder from Europe, because that's how they treat me sometimes, and they feel guilty about those from Africa because of the history, because they have to make it up to them. And now 'them' from Europe? What do they want here?[9]

Still, compared to racism against Black people and people of colour, prejudice against Eastern Europeans is, to be fair, tame. Any discrimination, including *by* Central Europeans against the few migrants of colour in their lands, and especially against the many Roma who live there,[10] far outweighs Eastern Europeanism in frequency and intensity. The violent incidents recounted to Rzepnikowska-Phillips by Polish migrant women are relatively rare.

Most Western Europeans probably do not *hate* Poles or Romanians. Yet in the general discussion of Eastern Europeans one does detect, if not hatred, then contempt. (Ironically, this contempt can be expressed even by 'progressive' anti-racists who accuse Eastern Europeans of an inherent predisposition toward intolerance.) But then, let us remember that, as Zadie Smith put it, 'hate is not ... the right word' that best describes the 'virus' of racism, 'contempt is'. Contempt 'is truly not believing at a fundamental level that this person in front of you is a person as you are. That to me is far more dangerous,' Smith adds, than in-your-face hatred, because, rather than an evil personality trait, it is something that deeply and invisibly permeates much of society.[11]

Nevertheless, surely when hate is added to contempt then racism is more likely to erupt in violence. All racism potentially produces violence; but racism against Eastern Europeans, unlike that against people of colour, has not, so far, morphed into systemic, as opposed to personal and sporadic, violence.

One of the possible objections to calling the undeniable contempt, discrimination, and occasional violence toward Eastern Europeans 'racism' is that Eastern Europeans are overwhelmingly white. Regarding them as targets of white racism clashes with the popular perception that race is a matter of phenotype – of physical appearance, that is, and especially skin colour. Can one speak of racism by whites against whites? The answer is yes, but to understand why, we need to take a short detour from the specific 'Eastern European' situation, and examine the history of whiteness and race in general.

My argument is that racism is part of capitalism and is in all of its many varieties, spurred on by the same processes of capital's need for cheap labour and compliant markets.[12] This is so also in the case of Eastern Europeanism. 'Race' was not always necessarily associated with phenotype. In the nineteenth century, racialization followed the lines of linguistic classification, sometimes even overriding those of colour. Iranians and Northern Indians were often thought of as white, because they spoke 'Indo-European' languages, also known as 'Indo-Aryan' and, especially in Germany, as 'Indo-Germanic' (*indogermanisch*). Infamously, the Nazis used the term 'Aryan' and the swastika, a symbol of auspiciousness and spirituality known to them from India, as signs of their Germanic racial pride. But 'Semites', speaking a group of languages different from 'Indo-Germanic', where also generally considered a branch of the white race, if often an inferior one.¹³ Semitic languages include Arabic and Hebrew. 'Semites' include Arabs and Jews.

In America, Lebanese immigrants (included with 'Syrians') and their descendants were counted in the census among the white population, although with hesitation, so that their 'whiteness' required several court cases to be established.[14] With increasing immigration of people who were neither of European nor Sub-Saharan origin to the United States and other parts of the West, the identity of 'brown' people, especially Hispanics but also South Asians and people from the Middle East and North Africa, became problematic. No longer wishing to be counted as white in the 2020 census, some Lebanese-Americans and others of Middle Eastern and North African (MENA) origin lobbied, supported by a 2015 suggestion by the Census Bureau, for the recognition of MENA origin as identifying a separate race. Their request was unsuccessful; the census forms continued to suggest that Lebanese or Egyptians were 'white'.[15]

Today some white supremacists such as the Ku Klux Klan leader David Duke state emphatically, 'No – JEWS ARE NOT WHITE!'.[16] The Nazis, however, considered Jews to be white; their hatred for the Jewish 'race' – and they certainly did call Jews a *Rasse* – was not based on colour.

These examples demonstrate that you can become white and you can stop being white, or at least you can try. In the academic literature, this is taken a little further than in ordinary language. 'Became white' figures as a phrase in a number of books and articles, referring especially to the Irish, to Jews, and even to white people themselves. The classic is *How the Irish Became White* by Noel Ignatiev, which originally appeared in 1995.[17] Karen Brodkin's *How Jewish Folk Became White* followed in 1998.[18] Since then, others discussed as 'becoming white' have included, other than Syrians or Lebanese, a number of different groups, including French Canadians and even Mennonites.[19]

The tradition of discussing how groups became white is part of a broader scholarly agenda to show that the white race itself is an invention. The foundational work is Theodore Allen's two-volume *The Invention of the White Race*, published in 1994 and 1997, which was the direct inspiration for Ignatiev's ground-breaking book about whiteness and the Irish.[20] Allen argued that, essentially, even white people have only become white in relatively recent history. He suggested that the 'white race' first appeared as an idea, as an imagined categorization of people, at the same time as, and in contrast with, the 'Black race'. This happened on the plantations of seventeenth-century North America. Following Oscar and Mary Handlin's work in the 1950s, Allen believed that Africans forcibly imported to the colonies in the early seventeenth century were not slaves. In principle, they would be freed after a period of time. Crucially, the Black plantation workers shared this status with white workers brought from the British Isles.[21] By the eighteenth century, however, a differential treatment set in, based on continental origin and skin colour. Africans were enslaved in perpetuity, including their offspring. To Allen, this was a matter of divide and rule. Regardless of skin pigment, the plantation workers had been capable of uniting, as in the Bacon's Rebellion of 1676, when they together demanded the end of unfree labour. The owners therefore set about to divide and rule their workers by inventing, and eventually setting into law, race as we know it and racial oppression. They equated, or just about, blackness with slavery and whiteness with freedom.

According to Allen, the American example of racial oppression had antecedents within Europe, in the oppression of the Irish by the English. Noel Ignatiev detailed how in America the Irish, who had already been racially oppressed in Ireland without reference to skin colour, entered a society where colour had become indelibly a defining feature of race. 'The Catholic Irish, an oppressed race in Ireland', says Ignatiev, 'became part of an oppressing race in America'.[22] In America, this meant 'becoming white', a privilege the Irish had to struggle to acquire.

The historian Geraldine Heng defines race as 'attached' to a

> repeating tendency ... to demarcate human beings through differences among humans that are selectively essentialized as absolute and fundamental, in order to distribute positions and powers differentially to human groups. Race-making thus operates as specific historical occasions in which strategic essentialisms are posited and assigned through a variety of practices and pressures, so as to construct a hierarchy of peoples for differential treatment.[23]

This definition of race, which I adapt in this book to 'Eastern Europeanism', does not insist that skin colour or any other bodily feature must be the basis on which racial hierarchies are constructed as 'strategic essentialisms' – ways to imagine a group as essentially different and alien, so as to justify asserting power over it.

Heng suggests that race and racism, thus defined, predate modernity and have defined what it means to be European since at least the thirteenth century. Other scholars consider modern racism to have originated in late fifteenth-century Spain.[24] There, the fateful year 1492, when Columbus sailed to America, began with the surrender of the last Muslim ruler in Spain. Muhammad, nicknamed 'King Boabdil', the ruler of Granada, handed the spectacular Alhambra fortress to the 'Catholic Monarchs' Isabelle and Ferdinand, on 2 January. On 31 March, the pair proclaimed, from the same citadel, the expulsion of all Jews who would not convert to Christianity. But the *Reconquista* and the forced absorption of many Jews and Muslims into the Christian fold did not end, and may even have increased, their persecution. 'New Christians' of Jewish and Muslim extraction were accused, often falsely, of practising their old family religion in secret. This opened them up to investigation by the Inquisition, and to imprisonment or execution. In the fifteenth and increasingly from the sixteenth century on, the rights of people of Jewish or Muslim descent were curtailed regardless of how sincere they were in their Christian faith. It was believed that even conversion did not gain them the precious qualities of Christian blood. This judgement was accompanied by official rules for keeping 'New Christians' out of important state, church, and military appointments. The Spanish church authorities infamously issued certificates of *limpieza de sangre*, 'purity of blood', to protect those free of a Jewish or Muslim background from discrimination. This racism did not stress differences in colour or other features of physical appearance. In fact, certificates would not have been needed if one could reliably detect a Jew or Muslim by just looking at them. But like all racism, it created an exploitable group defined by imagined common descent.[25]

The persecution of alleged crypto-Jews or *marranos* and alleged crypto-Muslims or *moriscos* became particularly severe in the seventeenth century, contemporaneously with the beginning of the widespread use of African slave labour in the Americas. With race now a familiar concept underlying social control at home, Spanish *conquistadores* implemented new versions of racism in the Americas, just as English settlers brought with them racial practices aimed at the Irish.

The Spanish and the English colonial adventure both began with absolutist rulers attempting to assert their sway over an expanding territory. Their greed was amplified by the mercantilist philosophy that equated prosperity at home with importing more wealth than was exported. In other words, absolutist states sought to accumulate a surplus of capital. Because capitalism is an economic and geopolitical system driven by the impulse to accumulate surplus capital, absolutism can be considered to be the first stage of capitalism.

'Capital' in the wider technical sense is not just money but any material means for raising wealth. Land is the most traditional example. Surplus capital can be accumulated by outright theft or by acquiring part of the value produced by the labour of someone else, such as an employee. Both processes happened in colonial expansion when, for example, Indigenous lands were stolen to create plantations where slave labour was exploited. But over the same period, they also occurred 'back home' with such developments as the enclosure by landlords of lands previously used by poor farmers, and the related move of much of the rural population to cities where they were put to work for wages.

In an article entitled 'Racial Capitalism', the British sociologist Satnam Virdee reviews the literature that considers racialization to be a process essential to the economic and geopolitical organization of the world under capitalism. Racial discrimination has been used, Virdee suggests, from 'the 17th century colonization of Virginia to Victorian Britain and beyond' as a means to deny rights to subordinate classes 'with a view to making the system safe for capital accumulation'.[26] Capitalism is widely but falsely believed to encourage a free market with each individual participating as an abstract entity, a rational being essentially the same as and equivalent to all other rational beings. Virdee cites Stuart Hall to the effect that in fact, capitalist modernity 'has always advanced as much by way of the production and negotiation of difference as it has through enforcing sameness, standardization, and homogenization'.[27] The difference produced is that between the owners and accumulators of capital and those who labour to produce wealth. The logic is to racialize the latter as inherently incapable of exercising the same rights accorded to their 'betters'. In the words of Lisa Lowe, writing on racial politics concerning Asian-Americans,

> Capitalist states and classes come to understand that the maximization of profits is most effectively secured not by 'rendering labour abstract' but by willfully entangling the objective of profit maximization with 'the social production of difference, of restrictive particularity and illegitimacy marked by race, nation, geographical origins, and gender'.[28]

We have moved from the popular consideration of race as a matter of looks or phenotype, to the today more commonly accepted scholarly understanding of it as the result of socioeconomic factors, particularly under capitalism. It has to be recognized, however, that the race-as-colour approach is so deeply ingrained in the public's perceptions that discussing race without reference to phenotype constitutes an obstacle for reaching the broad public, on a topic of public interest and significance.

Perhaps for that reason, some writers have argued that Irish and Jews, to use the two main examples of who 'became white', actually became white also visually. They claim that Irish and Jews actually did not, before they moved up on the whiteness ladder, even *look* white to people who were.

The influential cultural historian Sander Gilman, in particular, suggested in 1994 (so during the same year that the first volume on Irish of Allen's *Invention of the White Race* appeared), that '[t]he Jews were quite literally seen as black'.[29] Ran HaCohen, however, has detailed how this and other references to Jews as 'Black' have been misinterpreted and mistranslated. Essentially, what was meant was 'swarthy', not Black. Darkish skin colour was attributed to only some Jews: those who lived among equally swarthy Europeans. In the eighteenth century, Count de Buffon was among other writers, mentioned by HaCohen, who knew that Jews came in different colours:

> It has been pretended that the Jews, who came originally from Syria and Palestine, have the same

> brown complexion they had formerly. As Misson, however, justly observes, the Jews of Portugal alone are tawny. As they always marry with their own tribe, the complexion of the parents is transmitted to the child, and thus with little diminution preserved, even in the northern countries. The German Jews, those of Prague, for example, are not more swarthy than the other Germans.[30]

The reader is invited to make a mental note here that Prague was described as inhabited by 'German' Jews and 'other Germans', not Czechs – this will become important later. For now, what matters is that, to Buffon, Prague Jews appeared to be no less white than non-Jews.

As for the Irish, Ignatiev notes, though without his usual carefully selected citations, that 'in the early years ... Irish were frequently referred to as "n-----s turned inside out"; the Negroes, for their part, were sometimes called "smoked Irish"'.[31] But surely the point of such turns of phrase, as of the illustrations in the book that liken yet clearly distinguish Black and Irish people, was not to say that the Irish were *not* white, but that they were whites who could in some ways be compared to non-whites. They were white, though the message was that they weren't quite.

What racists held against groups who had to 'become white' was not that their whiteness was absent, but that it was of questionable quality. A much reproduced (today) pseudo-scientific drawing published in 1888 by the racist and anti-vaccination activist, Henry S. Constable, showed an Irish profile with some allegedly African features (Figure 1.1). The point was not that the Irishman was Black, but that he was mixed with an 'African race' called 'Iberians',

> who thousands of years ago spread themselves through Spain over Western Europe. [...] They came to Ireland and mixed with the natives of the South and West, who themselves are supposed to have been of low type and descendants of savages of the Stone Age, who, in consequence of isolation from the rest of the world, had never been out-competed in the healthy struggle

of life, and thus made way, according to the laws of nature, for superior races.³²

Jews were also sometimes 'accused' of admixture with Africans. Karl Marx, himself a baptized Jew, wrote to his friend Friedrich Engels that the Jewish-German socialist LaSalle, descended, judging by the 'shape of his head and the way his hair grows', from the Negroes who accompanied Moses' flight from Egypt (unless his mother or paternal grandmother interbred with a n-----)'.³³ Some racists, such as Houston Chamberlain, author of the best-selling *Foundations of the Nineteenth Century*, understood Jews to be a mixed race who stopped mixing with others.³⁴

Such musings about racial impurity do not suggest that Irish or Jews are not white. They do suggest that their whiteness is incomplete, of a lesser worth than that of a person of 'Anglo-Teutonic' extraction. The subtext is, of course, that only the fully white person is entitled to full white privilege.

Now we can see how this discussion of race and whiteness applies to Central Europeans – who are racialized in the West together with others as 'Eastern Europeans.' Like the Irish and Jews, Eastern Europeans, at least the Slavs among them, have been said to be racially impure. (As we will see, this is because of their alleged admixture of 'Asiatic' blood.) And similarly to the other groups, in Western countries Eastern European migrants of the

Figure 1.1: Alleged Irish Iberian, 'Anglo-Teutonic', and 'Negro' facial features

IRISH IBERIAN   ANGLO-TEUTONIC   NEGRO

Source: Henry Stickland Constable, *Ireland from One or Two Points of View*, 1888 (Wikimedia Commons)

previous generations could easily be said to have 'become white'. Polish, Czech, Slovak, and Hungarian Americans are just as well assimilated, just as fully 'white', as are the Irish or the Jews; that is, very nearly white, if still not quite. The Hungarian extraction of Nicolas Sarkozy made him no less fully French and white than the Italian extraction of his wife, Carla Bruni, made her.

Why then is there no comparable discussion in the academic literature about how Eastern (or Central) Europeans became white? Possibly, the answer is that recently things have become different. The British sociologist Nasar Meer has given a memorable informal definition of white privilege. He noted that life was not necessarily easy for white people, but 'being white doesn't make life harder'.[35] But we have seen examples that being Eastern European today makes life harder. Unlike the Irish and the Jews, Eastern Europeans have been becoming not more, but less white.

Perhaps, during the heyday of the 'became white' literature in the 1990s, it may have been felt subconsciously that Eastern Europeans did not fit the bill. Eastern Europeans, who were widely seen as faltering in their assimilation to Western standards, including the standards of liberal democracy, appeared to fail to become properly white. This was just the time when communism had fallen and the 'transition' to capitalist democracy was beginning. The chief expectation on both sides of the Berlin Wall was that the cousins from East and West were to be reunited after the nightmare of Soviet domination. The expectations of a joyous coming back together were almost as strong across the expanse of Central and Western Europe as they were within Germany. But the eastern relatives who were emerging onto the global scene appeared, as viewed from the West, not quite presentable. Much like the Irish and Jewish immigrants to London or New York a hundred years earlier, they seemed oddly dressed and uncultured. They were used mostly for low-paid service and factory work, no matter if they joined the Western economy from home, as their countries were being transformed to giant assembly plants and 'emerging markets' for Western companies, or by physically picking up and going to work in the West. In their destination countries as on the world economic marketplace, the 'Eastern Europeans' of Central Europe were now a nearshore alternative for cheap labour in Asia and Africa.

Eastern Europeanism was needed to racialize Central Europeans in order to attribute their continuing 'immaturity' as Western-style liberal democracies and as capitalist market economies, not to the conditions of a wild wave of privatization and the colonial-style domination of their economies by 'globalized' capital, but rather to some obscure and obscurantist Eastern essence, to an ingrained character that forever tied them to the backwardness of ostensibly less than fully European Russia. The Soviet domination of the Cold War era needed to be rethought as a form of cultural and racial kinship, going back not to the Yalta Conference of 1945, when Churchill and Roosevelt gifted Central Europe to Stalin, but to the deep centuries before. This would make the 'Eastern European' character of Central Europe appear to be eternal, explaining why Central Europe not only didn't, but couldn't quite become part of the democratic West. If, to use the terms of the 'becoming white' literature, they were *not* becoming white, then that would only be the fault of their own 'Eastern European' character. It would not be the fault of the West.

2

How Central Europeans Became Eastern European

In the previous chapter, I examined a tendency to blame Central European inability to catch up with the West, not on the way Western-dominated economic and political structures were introduced in the area, but on an alleged cultural difference between West and East in Europe. The West is said to be culturally predisposed to freedom and democracy, and the East not.

This mechanism for racializing Eastern Europe's alleged failure includes work by academics who argue that an unbridgeable East–West gap has existed in Europe centuries before the fall of communism. In the 1990s, some of them came to entertain a thought that had never occurred to Churchill, namely, that the Iron Curtain he saw in his famous 1946 speech descending across the continent only replaced an imagined divide of a much longer date, possibly going back to the eighteenth century and the Enlightenment. These scholars were quick to give the academic imprimatur to the litany of complaints about the eternal and intractable backwardness of Eastern European culture. While economists discussed the post-communist region as one of the world's 'emerging markets', what these historians and social scientists saw emerge was an iceberg of obscurantism re-emerging, having been partly kept underwater by communist oppression.

But 'Eastern Europe', as a uniform, culturally distinctive, and socially and politically inferior area, was not invented in the eighteenth century. Nor in the nineteenth. If it was, it was not known to a British traveller like the soldier and priest George

Robert Gleig, who in the 1830s described the average labourer in early nineteenth-century Bohemia (now Czech Republic) as better off than an Englishman of comparable social station, and considered the political heritage of Bohemia to be superior to that of Germany (though no match for the superior state of liberty in England). Prague provided him with 'the pomp and splendour of a great capital', except for the unparalleled squalor of its Jewish Town.[1] No, the invention of 'Eastern Europe' in the form that we know it did not yet happen, either in the Enlightenment, as some scholars claim, or in the 19th century, as do others. It is of much more recent vintage, essentially produced in the Cold War, and only getting more intense after it. But to demonstrate that, we need to examine both of these proposed dates of origin carefully.

The Enlightenment is the period when the imagined East–West distinction appeared according to one of the most influential proponents of its deep historical pedigree, the New York University historian Larry Wolff. In *The Invention of Eastern Europe* (1996), Wolff's declared inspiration was Edward Said's *Orientalism*, and he frequently and insightfully likens orientalist representations of predominantly Muslim areas of Asia and North Africa (which was Said's principal subject)[2] to representations by Western Europeans of the East of the continent. An additional, probably subconscious motivation may have been to redefine 'Russian and East European Studies' (or 'Russian and Slavic Studies', as Wolff's New York University department is called), giving the unified study of Central *and* Eastern Europe a new meaning. For just like 'Oriental Studies' was invested in 'producing' the Orient as an object of investigation, so was 'Russian and East European Studies' in perpetuating its own area of study, which similarly needed, as a result of a new turn of events, to be rescued from irrelevance.

In one of his many entertaining anecdotes, Wolff discusses a time when Wolfgang Amadeus Mozart was riding in a coach on one his trips to Prague. Later the composer recalled to his good friend, the botanist Gottfried von Jacquin, how he and his companions spent their time making up funny names for each other and people they knew.

> Now farewell dearest friend, dearest Hikkiti Horky! That is your name, so you will know it; we have all of

us on our trip invented names ('*auf unserer Reise Namen erfunden*'); they follow here. I am Punkititi. – My wife is Schabla Pumfa. Gofer is Rozka Pumpa. Stadler is Notschibikitschibi. Joseph my servant is Sagadarata. Goukerl my dog is Schomanntzky – Madame Quallenberg is Runzifunzi. – Mademoiselle Crux Ps: Ramlo is Schurimuri. Freistädtler is Goulimauli. Have the Kindness to communicate to the last-mentioned his name.

As Wolff saw it,

> It was just the sort of silliness that contributed to the Mozart legend, but it was also the comical expression of alienation that attended the imaginative eighteenth-century traveler to Eastern Europe. Mozart, born in Salzburg, resident in Vienna, a German by native tongue, was not at home in Slavic Bohemia where the language he heard around him sounded like nonsense. In fact, Mozart was a cosmopolitan European who could understand the language almost anywhere his musical career might take him: to Italy, to France, all over Germany. He did not understand Czech. Ignorance of the language was an inconvenience for travelers, but it also offered a sort of imaginative liberation, and Mozart seized the opportunity to create new identities for everyone in his party and even for his friends at home. He freely employed the elements of pseudo-Slavic and pseudo-Oriental sounds ... [3]

How extraordinary an interpretation of Mozart's word play! One might agree that 'Rozka' and especially Schomantzzky sound Slavic (though many Austrians had such Slavic sounding names even then). But Sagadarata? Punkititi? Schurimuri? It is difficult to see what makes such delightfully nonsensical monikers either Slavic or Oriental, if not the desire to prove Wolff's point that a civilizational border existed at the unmarked transition from what is now Austria to what is now Czech Republic, both of which were at the time considered equally parts of Habsburg Austria. Nothing in the rest of Mozart's correspondence gives the slightest reason to believe that he felt alienated in Bohemia. He probably heard some Czech in Vienna, and certainly heard a lot of German in Prague, where it was the native tongue of perhaps most of the residents at the time, a fact that we'll return to later. But in his letters there is hardly a comment on any linguistic or cultural difference between Vienna and Prague. In the letter itself quoted by Wolff, Mozart simply writes about how Prague was 'a beautiful and pleasant place', where his friend would have enjoyed the society ball featuring all the local beauties.[4]

Wolff's work was one of a crop of books with 'invention' in the title, starting with Eric Hobsbawm and Terrence Ranger's collection of highly instructive and often very amusing essays in 1986, called *The Invention of Tradition*.[5] (Theodore W. Allen's *The Invention of the White Race* appeared in the same year, 1994, as Wolff's volume.) Like the Hobsbawm and Ranger anthology, *Inventing Eastern Europe* dazzles with a sweep of scintillating or salacious anecdotes. For example, Wolff titillates the reader with a lengthy discussion of Casanova purchasing a 13-year-old Russian peasant girl, a virgin, from her father. He dresses her in the French style, and teaches her some Venetian. Casanova calls the girl Zaire, after Voltaire's tragic character, a slave girl in the Ottoman sultan's harem. The harem was a well-known cliché of orientalist fantasies linking Western and male domination. Wolff observes that Casanova is orientalizing Russia in his mind, comparing serfdom in Russia to slavery in the Ottoman Empire.

One wonders how Russian serfdom might have come across to the Venetian as a sign of civilizational backwardness, while he himself was committing an unspeakable crime using an under-aged Russian girl as a sex slave, and of course while slavery was still practised unimpeded in the United States and the British Empire, as well as by 'enlightened' western France in Haiti. But since Wolff mentions it in his influential book, it may be useful to examine the issue of serfdom in some more depth.

It is in fact true that serfdom is one of the features of European history that does distinguish between East and West. But it does not do so in the Eastern Europeanist sense of placing an imaginary iron curtain between two civilizations, with forced labour practised on the eastern side and not on the western one. As Allen pointed out in his study of race in America, unfree labour existed in Ireland and was forcibly exported overseas along with Africans. But serfdom in Casanova's time did increase in frequency and severity in a roughly West-to-East direction in Europe. By the end of the eighteenth century, unfree agricultural work was indeed far less prevalent and far less brutally supervised on the British Isles than in Russia. It was abolished in the latter under Tsar Alexander II only in 1861. Austria and Prussia occupied an intermediate position, with serfdom officially abolished in 1781 and 1810, respectively, although some feudal obligations did remain for decades longer.[6] In other words, eastern Germany and Austria need to be included in the area of Eastern Europe characterized by late serfdom. That is not the prevailing definition of 'Eastern Europe', however, which does not usually include places that were, during the Cold War, included in the West.

Nevertheless, serfdom in Central and Eastern Europe did resemble slavery. The sociological historian Manuela Boatcă has argued that both developed in response to Western Europe's increasing demand for agricultural products.[7] With the Industrial Revolution advancing more rapidly and population growing faster in the West than in the East, and with the East of Europe possessed of large tracts of land suitable for cereal production, Eastern land owners had incentives similar to overseas plantation owners to integrate forced labour into the emerging global agricultural industry. Boatcă's work nuances the classic narrative reproduced by Wolff, that '[f]rom the sixteenth to the eighteenth century, in Eastern Europe in contrast to what happened in the West, the peasant mass increasingly lost its freedom'.[8] On that view, serfdom simply moved from the West, where it had been more prevalent earlier, to the East, where it was less so (with peasant farmers sometimes holding land communally). In fact, Boatcă shows, what was developing in the East was not a revived or a transferred serfdom, but a new form of labour organization – the 'coloniality of labour'[9] – that, unlike mediaeval serfdom, was not a local relationship between landlord and serf, but rather a part of a global network of production, trade, and exploitation that also included slavery.

Boatcă also details that after the serfs were emancipated in Russia, their lot only worsened, because the landlords were able in various ways to assert even more control over agricultural production. The peasants, having few opportunities to become industrial workers because the Industrial Revolution was slow in the tsar's empire, were struck by increasing, not decreasing, poverty and unemployment. Similar developments of 'neo-serfdom' may be observed in Romania and in eastern Poland, Slovakia, and Hungary.[10] However, in Germany and today's Austria and Czech Republic, as well as the western regions of Poland, Slovakia, and Hungary, where nineteenth-century industry made increasing inroads, nothing of the mass misery witnessed in Russia was seen. Poverty did, unfortunately, afflict poor farmers as it did industrial workers across Europe. But the village folk celebrated in the operas of Smetana or Dvořák barely resemble the suffering characters languishing on the estates described by Tolstoy and Gogol.

The sexual exploitation of poor women perhaps also did not reach the same extent in Central Europe as it did in Russia. Casanova does not appear to have purchased a sex 'slave' in Prussia or (German) Austria. But neither did he in Poland or in Bohemia. Casanova does make it clear that Russia is, to him, the home to unbridled patriarchal authoritarianism, both in the council chambers and in the bedrooms of its rulers. In this, his view conforms very clearly to the contemporary Western Christian view of the Muslim Orient, including that of Europe's greatest rival, the Ottoman Empire.[11] Wolff is, therefore, making a convincing argument that the famous adventurer gave an example of how a Westerner (if an Italian could fully be considered as one) regarded Russia as Orientalized and, in general, as a backward civilization. The problem, however, still remains with Wolff's claim that Casanova generalized his view of Russian difference and backwardness to all of 'Eastern Europe', contrasting it in a binary fashion to the West.

My aim is not to dispute the validity of Wolff's presentation of the Enlightenment image of Russia and of some other parts of the eastern periphery of Europe, which, like some parts of the South (Andalusia, Sicily)[12] were viewed as exotic and mysterious, and eroticized and Orientalized partly through imaginative fiction and artistic representation. But, as the case of Mozart's glossolalia demonstrates, Wolff was wrong to incorporate so uncritically Central with Eastern Europe. In fact, neither in the Enlightenment nor later, even in the first half of the twentieth century, was there in the Western consciousness a sharp imagined distinction between

East and West. What did unquestionably exist is a scale of prestige that decreased from its pinnacle in Northwestern Europe in both the North-to-South and the West-to-East direction.

Slavoj Žižek, the celebrated and controversial Slovenian scholar, identified the process in the context of 'Balkanism',[13] which combines these two directions: the Balkans is the part of Europe that is the most Eastern part of its South.

> For the Serbs, [the Balkans] begin *down there*, in Kosovo or in Bosnia, and they defend the Christian civilization against this Europe's Other; for the Croats, they begin in orthodox, despotic and Byzantine Serbia, against which Croatia safeguards Western democratic values; for Slovenes they begin in Croatia, and we are the last bulwark of the peaceful *Mitteleuropa*; for many Italians and Austrians they begin in Slovenia, the Western outpost of the Slavic hordes; for many Germans, Austria itself, because of its historical links, is already tainted with Balkan corruption and inefficiency; for many North Germans, Bavaria, with its Catholic provincial *flair*, is not free of a Balkan contamination; many arrogant Frenchmen associate Germany itself with an Eastern Balkan brutality entirely foreign to French *finesse*; and this brings us to the last link in this chain: to some conservative British opponents of the European Union, for whom – implicitly, at least – the whole of continental Europe functions today as a new version of the Balkan Turkish Empire, with Brussels as the new Istanbul, a voracious despotic centre which threatens British freedom and sovereignty ... . Is not this identification of continental Europe itself with the Balkans, its barbarian Other, the secret truth of the entire movement of the displaced delimitation between the two?[14]

We may call this scale of prestige, in our terms, whiteness. In the West-to-East direction, full whiteness decreased (before the post-communist binarization of the scale) gradually from England to Russia. But there were areas in-between. Germany was grouped with England on account of its 'Teutonic' race but, as we will soon see, in the East it blended with 'Slavdom'. The Slavs and Hungarians of Central Europe appeared, both in the imagination and in fact, associated with German culture and the millions of ethnic Germans who lived among them until they were brutally expelled in the ethnic cleansing following the Second World War. On the eastern side, Central Europeans were linked, through their Slavic race and/or physical proximity, to Russia.

If the reader will excuse me for what is clearly a simplification, I suggest that, historically, the Western view of the continent may be pictured as in the Venn diagram of Figure 2.1. The Western end constitutes the most clearly 'civilized' and, since the Industrial Revolution, 'advanced' area, and the Eastern end the least so. 'Anglo-Saxons' is a term still commonly used outside the English-speaking world, and was once a popular self-referential, racialized term used also by white English, Americans, Canadians, and so on.

Everyone on the left of the map looks down on everyone on the right. Everyone has an inferiority complex about everyone on the left. Those far to the left are barely sensitive, however, to the differences felt by those on the right, and vice versa. The French do not differentiate clearly between Czechs and Russians. Russians have little awareness of differences between the French and the English, though perhaps slightly more; power relations mean that the West knows much less about the East than the East knows about the West. The circle representing Central Europeans is smaller, to indicate that this area is less familiar and less important to outsiders than the other four.[15]

To collapse, in the Western imagination, this gradual differentiation into a single contrast between East and West was, on my view,

Figure 2.1: The Western image of Central Europe's location in Europe, before the end of the Second World War

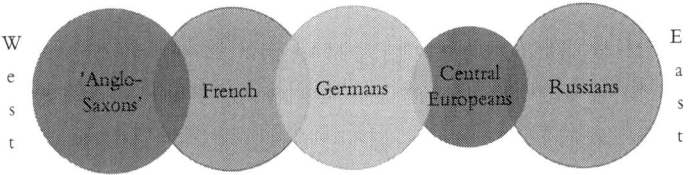

the work of the Cold War. After 1989, the lumping together of Central and Eastern Europe continued. Scholarship has reinforced such binarism, in tandem with public discourse, together serving the interests of Western capital, while also providing fodder for both Eastern Europeanist racism in the West, and resentment in Central Europe.

Anti-Slavism and German-Slavic rivalry

There is much more to this gradual 'Easternization' of parts of Europe than just some mildly amusing display of snobbery. In the case of the Balkans, Žižek's gradation of prejudice reflects what other scholars have shown to be part of a broader discourse of East–West difference resulting from conditions of exploitation that privileged Northwest Europe during the heyday of nineteenth- and twentieth-century imperialism. What we see in Figure 2.1 is that the large circles represent a hierarchy of colonial powers, with Britain (and in more subtle ways the US) the most important, followed by France, with Germany struggling to catch up and Russia confined to expanding to nearby regions overland. But also, the West-to-East dimension in the figure represents the degree to which the Industrial Revolution penetrated each region.

As mentioned earlier, it is in the nature of capitalism to create divisions of not only class but also of race or ethnicity (recall Thomas C. Holt's dictum that '[r]ace is something blacks have; ethnicity belongs to whites').[16] The divisions into which it categorizes people, and how those categories are spatialized (that is, the geographic borders between them), are, however, flexible and they evolve through history. It is true that, as Wolff showed, the Enlightenment, when capitalism and colonialism were in their youth, privileged Western Europe over Eastern Europe. But Western and Eastern Europeans were not explicitly named as different groups. The borders of the East, moreover, were undefined and did not coincide with those established later, during the Cold War. Basically, what he (and not the citizens of the Enlightenment) describes as 'Eastern Europe' roughly applied only to the Russian Empire and perhaps parts of Poland.

The error committed by Eastern Europeanist history is to assume a pre-existing division into peoples and their spatialization within borders, and then to project it onto history, as opposed to recognizing that it is in history that those divisions and spatializations are formed, and that they change with the historical context.

There is little evidence that Eastern Europeanism (as opposed to a disdain for *some* parts of what we but not Enlightenment Europeans call 'Eastern Europe') existed in the eighteenth century at all. On my view, it did not come into existence in the nineteenth either. We do, however, see the formation then of an attitude and a rhetoric that would later prove to be amenable to transforming into the binary, Eastern Europeanist, opposition between Western and Eastern Europe. I have in mind the bitter rivalry in Central Europe between self-identified Germans and Slavs.

German-Slavic rivalry increased in the course of the nineteenth century, as Germans developed their national consciousness and established a new German state. Anti-Slavism did not include the non-Slavic populations of 'Eastern Europe' such as the Hungarians and Romanians, although arguably it did influence German views of such peoples. Eastern Europeanism not only targets a broader population than anti-Slavism did, but also its rhetoric is quite different and its causes, which are to be sought in the post-communist relationship between East and West in Europe, are, as I will continue to argue, completely dissimilar.

Yet some of the forms of anti-Slavic prejudice have resurfaced in post-communist Eastern Europeanism. One of these is the idea that 'Eastern Europeans' have physical characteristics due to mixing with Asians, often described in the past as Tatars or Mongols. A casual internet search will show how this is still the case. A Quora contributor from Norway answers the question, 'What are Eastern European facial features?':

> Eastern European men at least (since they tend to have shorter hair than their women of course) are most easily identified by their skulls than their facial features compared to Western European men. Their back head is much flatter whereas the Western skulls (including North, Central and Southern European) are more rounded. Some Eastern European populations also have broader faces in general (e.g. Poles), others not.

> It's hard to generalize in this matter because there is so much variation within both Western and Eastern + Southern Europe, but still, in general I would say I can walk into a shop and immediately pick out Eastern Europeans if they are present.[17]

There are social media users who have the East–West European physiognomy down to the colour of the skin: not quite white. 'The physical characteristics of Eastern Europeans (Slavs) are that they tend to have a darker tint of skin when compared to North Western Europeans', says one. Eastern Europeans 'are usually able to tan unlike say northwestern europeans [*sic*], when they are exposed to the sun they almost never get burned but they get red and then they tan', says another. At least one believes falsely that Eastern European bodily features have been confirmed by science, and relates it to invasions of Europe from the East. Commenting on what others have said about high cheeks and other features of 'Eastern European' physiognomy, this commentator writes,

> When understanding the reason, one can realize why. With the Mongol invasion of the lands of now Eastern Europe led by Genghis Khan's descendants in the 13th century, there was a significant introduction of Mongolian DNA into the population.
> This has been confirmed by the accelerating inroads in various genetic testings since the start of the Human Genome Project.[18]

True, the same Quora thread includes contributors who completely disagree that there is a unified Eastern European look. (These are mostly but not exclusively people from Central or Eastern Europe.) But the posts like the ones just quoted are a clear verbalization of the mixed-race thesis about the white-but-not-quite populations of Europe. In the previous chapter, we have seen the example of the suspected African genetic admixture of the Irish.

The Asian-influenced look of the 'Slavs' is an extension of a long tradition of understanding Russia as profoundly affected by the oriental character of the Mongols. Stalin's Soviet autocracy has been explained as an oriental despotism.[19] Chauvinistic

Germans, including Nazis, used the term 'semi-Asiatic' (*halb-Asiatisch*) frequently to deride Russians. But the term was first made popular in the German-speaking world through the relatively benign, romanticizing prose of the Austrian author, Emil Franzos. Many of Franzos' books consisted of slice-of-life episodes from the eastern regions of the Habsburg Empire, an area he referred to as *Halb-Asien* (Half-Asia). *Aus Halb-Asien* ('From Half-Asia') appeared in 1876. Franzos' works were extremely popular, and a collection of his vignettes was published posthumously as late as 1912, bearing the title *Vom Don zur Donau* ('From the Don to the Danube').[20] The peasant population in the area was mostly Ukrainian-speaking, Slavic but not Russian, though it is worth remembering that Ukrainians were then sometimes called 'Little Russians'. Even if the exoticism of Franzos' portrayal was often charming, the 'half-Asiatics' came across as living in a state of premodern backwardness that could only be relieved, the author seemed to be saying, by becoming Germanized. Franzos himself, after all, was born in 'half-Asiatic' Galicia. He did grow up, however, in the largely German-speaking and German-cultured city of Czernowitz (Chernivtsi, now Ukraine), a member of its large Germanized Jewish population.

Any understanding of Central Europe that writes out the presence of self-identified Germans (including people of non-German, 'Slavic' or Jewish, origin) and of German culture legitimizes the expulsion of millions and the subsequent rewriting of history. The German presence was strongest along Poland's, Czechoslovakia's, and Hungary's borders with Germany or Austria, but individuals and groups identifying as Germans lived practically all over Central Europe, as well as in the Baltic States, Romania, and beyond that in Ukraine and Russia. (Casanova noted that the language spoken in St Petersburg was 'principally' German.[21]) Up until the end of the Second World War, the German cultural influence in the area far outweighed the Russian. Even under communism, in spite of efforts to teach them about Russian and Soviet culture, people continued to be both more familiar and more identified with Western models, often mediated by Germany or Austria.

Wolff forgets the German presence when he writes that 'Prague is north of Vienna, and just slightly to the West, but for Mozart, as for us in the twentieth century, [a journey to Prague] was a voyage into Eastern Europe nevertheless'.²² For Mozart, it almost certainly wasn't. Let another one of Wolff's own entertaining anecdotes illustrate the fact. He notes that Mozart, following the reception of *Don Giovanni*, which premiered in Prague in 1787, was very pleased by the opera's rapturous reception. *Meine Prager verstehen mich* ('My Praguers understand me'), he was supposed to have said.²³ This then became the slogan of the legendry surrounding Mozart's allegedly special relation to the city. Wolff offers the following odd interpretation of the quote: 'It meant that they appreciated his music, but surely Mozart, with his love of wordplay, also enjoyed the irony of the fact that they understood him, while he, from the moment he was among the Czechs, did not understand them'.²⁴

Surely? Prague in 1787 was bilingual, but German was far more at home there than in Casanova's St Petersburg. It was probably the language of the majority of the city's inhabitants. The Estates Theatre, where *Don Giovanni* was played, was only four years old, having been founded by Count Franz Nostitz (who spelled his Slavic surname the German way). The building carried the German name, *Nationaltheater*. Later, in the nineteenth century, increasing numbers of people from the Bohemian provinces moved to the capital, most of them speaking Czech, and they started to identify this linguistic peculiarity with a national identity. Still, it took some decades following Mozart's visit for Czech-speakers to clearly outnumber German-speakers (who included most of Prague's Jews). To imagine that Mozart did not understand 'his Praguers' is quite fanciful.

The complexities of identity in Bohemia and Moravia have been explored in a classic study by Jeremy King of the town České Budějovice, known as Budweis in German. Here, for most of the nineteenth century, townsfolk were quite flexible in their identity. There was a tendency, conditioned by work and family alliances, and to some extent by socioeconomic class, to choose to 'be' Czech, German, or a third, neutral category, simply a 'Budweiser' (the eponymous American beer brand has roots in the town). Emerging Czech and German loyalties were woven around the central pole, at first, of a binational, bilingual *Böhmer* (Bohemian) identification. Only after the Second World War did today's Czech Republic become almost exclusively Czech. Only then, writes King, 'The Bohemian lands became wholly Czech, and part not of Central

Europe [defined to include Germany and Austria] but of a Slavic East separated from the West by a nuclear Cold War.'

The self-declared ethnic composition of the citizens of the Slovak capital is an even better example of the transactional character of ethnolinguistic identity than that of Budweis. Bratislava was a mostly German city (known mainly by its German name, Pressburg) until the 1867 'compromise' creating the Austro-Hungarian 'dual monarchy'. At that point many of the Germans, Slovaks, and Jews began to identify as Hungarians. After the establishment of Czechoslovakia, large numbers declared themselves Slovaks or Czechs. Today, more than 90 per cent say they are Slovaks, a fact that cannot be explained only by the postwar expulsion of many Germans and Hungarians.[25] But until 1918 and even until the expulsion of Germans following Hitler's defeat, Posen (Poznań), Prague, and Pressburg were not, as cities, considered to be culturally different from the West (to the extent that the West included Germany), although the Czechs of Prague, the Poles of Posen, and the small Slovak minority of Pressburg *were* considered and considered themselves culturally different from Germans.

Until the Second World War, the German presence heavily coloured the image of Central Europe in Western popular culture. Arthur Conan Doyle published his first Sherlock Holmes story, 'A Scandal in Bohemia' in 1891. The principal character of Doyle's story is the hereditary king of the country, but he is no Czech. His name, Wilhelm Gottsreich Sigismond von Ormstein, Grand Duke of Cassel-Felstein, is meant to poke fun at the German language and to belittle antiquated German forms of aristocratic behaviour and through them German pretensions of elegance.

Farther East and South, the German presence is murkier, more mysterious. Germans were long imagined by Western Europeans and Germans themselves as the dominant ethnic 'type' of Central Europe – more on that later. In Southeastern Europe, the local Germans become more truly exotic, more heavily immersed among populations who are less fully white than they.

The unfamiliar world of the Balkans, Eastern Orthodox like Russia and unlike most of Central Europe, was fertile ground for the kind of imagination called 'Gothic', a term that strongly invokes Germany. In Bram Stoker's 1897 thriller, *Dracula*, the writer imagines the vampire's castle at the vanishing point of a long train ride, in Transylvania. Such regions are separated in the authors' imagination from the much more familiar landscapes of Central Europe. On Jonathan Hawker's ride to Transylvania, the trains fail to run on time (a stereotypical sign of backwardness or chaos) as soon as he's east of Budapest.[26] In the Belgian artist Hergé's graphic adventure novel, *Ottokar's Sceptre* (1938), Tintin the boy detective travels to Frankfurt and Prague, where he boards a 'special plane' for Syldavia, a kingdom that recalls Bosnia (the signs have Cyrillic letters, the men wear fezzes, and there is at least one minaret), but is a made-up place with no real-world name at all. It is only after Prague that the boy detective flies into fantasy land. Stoker and Hergé locate the Bohemian and Hungarian capitals at the very edge of the familiar, that is, the Western world, but still *within* it. The more mysterious European East begins beyond them.

Neither Stoker nor Hergé use the term 'Eastern Europe'. The identity central as an influence on the region is not Russian (as it would be to an Eastern Europeanist) but German. A close look reveals that Dracula and Tintin are not about Hungarians, Romanians, or Bosnians – or not only. Perhaps the most crucially relevant ethnic presence in these fantasies is German. The German language is used by Dracula and his entourage, but even the pitchfork carrying villagers who finish off Dracula are able to speak it. Tintin travelled to Syldavia to defend it from an invasion by Borduria, an allegory of Nazi Germany. (The artist at first meant to represent Syldavia as Austria, as an allegory of the German occupation of that country, the *Anschluss*. He may have lent it Balkan characteristics only when he learned of another invasion, Albania's occupation by fascist Italy.)[27]

Before national consciousness (national 'revival' or 'awakening' in the nationalists' terms) engulfed Central Europe in the nineteenth century, the German-Slavic distinction was perhaps more of a class than ethnic character. The town dwellers assimilated to the German language and culture brought by settlers from Germany and became 'German', while rural families clung on to their Slavic heritage. This general picture had many variants. Germanization did reach from the cities to the countryside, especially in areas closer to western Germany.

Even across the border in Germany, in the second half of the nineteenth century, a large Slavic population, known as Sorbians,

Lusatians, or *Wenden*, still lived alongside the Germans. Today, only a few thousand are left.

In the Habsburg Empire, a significant push for Germanization was given, unintentionally, by Joseph II, who reigned from 1780 to 1790 (and was served by Mozart). Fancying himself a modern, Enlightenment ruler, he set upon centralizing his government as much as possible. When he declared that German was henceforth to be the uniform language of government in the multilingual empire, he was probably governed by a practical, rather than a German nationalist agenda. His modernizing efforts led to an unprecedented increase in the empire's bureaucracy. Hungarian, Czech, Slovak, and Polish speakers, including those living in rural areas, applied for government jobs and became a visible presence. Nevertheless, it is reasonable to assume that as they spoke German with a foreign accent and maybe exhibited other non-German ways, they hit glass ceilings at the highest levels of government service. In Latin America, frustration with discrimination in the civil service was held by the anthropologist Benedict Anderson to have been the origin of Latin American nationalism, which was then exported to Europe.[28] Whether Anderson's view is correct when it comes to the Americas, it seems to make sense that a similar motivation might have been, at least in part, behind the origins of Slavic and Hungarian nationalisms in the Habsburg Empire. It may have been the same for Poles in the Prussian and Russian ruled areas of their country.

The idea of nationalism as such arrived from Germany. Slavic and Hungarian nationalism mimicked German nationalism. In particular, the influence of Johann Gottfried Herder (1744–1803) has long been recognized. Herder was largely responsible for the view, originating in late eighteenth-century so-called pre-romanticism, that history was a stage on which the main actors are nations. He was an influence on the growing German demands to form a united, national state from the myriad German-speaking principalities of Europe ('Germany' would become the name of a country, rather than a cultural and linguistic space, only in 1871). But Herder, who was born in a small town in what is today Poland, also had a sympathetic view of Slavs and Hungarians. Even the Czech nationalist Emanuel Rádl, in his rather belligerently entitled volume, *The War Between the Czechs and the Germans*, in

1926, would give the German philosopher admiring attention, when he called Herder the John the Baptist of the Czech national revival movement.[29] Herder was fondly referenced by proudly Slav intellectuals even in Russia.[30]

Lonnie Johnson, in his comprehensive book, *Central Europe*, suggests that '[i]f one had to identify a thinker responsible for giving Central European nationalism its peculiar twist, it would be Johann Gottfried Herder'.[31] Johnson's summary of Herder's influence in the area is standard historiography today:

> Herder admired the ancient Slavs as 'charitable, almost extravagantly hospitable, devoted to their mystic independence, yet loyal and law-abiding and contemptuous of pillaging and looting'. However, given the unfortunate position of the Slavs between the Germans and the various threats from the east, Herder observed: 'All of this was no use to them against oppression, it conduced it'. It is one of those quirks of history that a German was one of the most influential figures in the development of Slavic historiography. Herder popularized the idea of peace-loving and protodemocratic Slavs as the victims of the aggressive, warlike, and autocratic Germans. Consequently, he played an essential role in the way the Slavs came to view their own history, as a national struggle against German aggression that culminated in the loss of ancient Slavic freedoms, and he envisioned a day when these 'submerged peoples that were once happy and industrious' would rise from their 'long, languid slumber' and be 'delivered from their chains of bondage.'[32]

Hungarians speak a language that belongs to the Finno-Ugric family, and as such they are not Slavic. This fact goes a long way to explain why German nationalists both in Germany and Austria tended to ally themselves with Hungarians, as a counterweight to Slavic solidarity. But Hungarians, too, were inspired by Herder, who wrote about them – recognizing the multiethnic character of Central Europe – that 'they are now the smallest part of the local inhabitants, among Slavs, Germans, Wallachians and other peoples. After some centuries we may hardly be able to find their language'.[33]

The growing non-German middle classes of Central Europe acquired their education through exposure to German music, literature, and theatre. But Slavs and Hungarians aspired to demonstrate that they did not lag behind in cultural potential if not attainment. Grammars of Slavic languages and Hungarian were written, folk tales and folk songs compiled, plays and operas composed, art encouraged. In Bohemia, infamously, a librarian produced fake Czech-language chronicles from the Middle Ages to demonstrate the cultural greatness of his nation.[34] Competing German and Slavic 'National Theatres' were built in both Posen and Prague. A Hungarian national theatre was erected in Budapest in 1837. While these were built in a competitive and assertive spirit, they were not meant to stress difference from German culture as much as equivalence to it. Slavic Russia was never a model. Several of the theatres and opera houses imitated those of Vienna.

In Central Europe, those who aspired to middle-class and even upper-class status often hoped to do so through acquiring proper bourgeois manners. The craze for building national theatres and museums was part of this process of *embourgeoisement*. In earlier times, social mobility meant individual adaptation to the German language and even adopting a German identity,[35] but as the bourgeoisie grew in Central Europe in the nineteenth century, ascent into it was increasingly happening as a group. Czechs, Poles, and Hungarians wanted to join the *Bildungsbürgertum*, as Germans called the educated bourgeoisie, as Czechs, Poles, and Hungarians, and not as Germans. Later, they were joined by Slovaks.

A survival from this period is the use, in all of the languages of Central Europe including German, of the contrasting pair of words, 'cultured' and 'primitive'. *Primitiv* in German, *primitív* in Hungarian, *primitívny* in Slovak, *primtivní* in Czech, *primitiwny* in Polish: the term associates the class prejudices of modern capitalist society with the racialized prejudices of colonialism, for it was in the colonies that Europeans believed they found 'primitive societies' of 'natives'. In Central Europe, 'primitive' was a synonym, more or less, for 'peasant'. The Russian historian Aleksandr Etkind describes the great divide in Russia between the upper classes and the peasant serfs, speaking of 'internal colonization' in the country.³⁶ The contempt for the peasantry was not quite the same in Central Europe, but it was similar. Every self-respecting person wanted to be 'cultured', a *Kulturmensch*. But also, every ethnic nation wanted to be a 'cultured nation', a *Kulturvolk*.

The content of the labels 'peasant' and 'primitive' (unfashionable, unsophisticated, unintelligent, untrustworthy, and so on) is still levelled by some snobs in Central Europe at the local working and rural population, though illiberal nationalism discourages such overt classism, in part because it needs the support of what in the Introduction I called the white periphery. But ironically, it is also levelled by Eastern Europeanist prejudice, against *all* Eastern Europeans and, interchangeably, all 'Slavs'. According to the Polish scholar Maria Janion, Polish nationalism has, in a subtle way, actually encouraged a distancing of Polish identity from Slavic, bringing it closer, in the imagination, to the West.³⁷ Although this certainly reflects resistance to Russia, which ruled most of divided Poland, it could be read as a bourgeois nationalist effort to be better than a peasant.

Perhaps the desire to attribute peasant characteristics to the Eastern European betrays an anxiety about sliding back into peasant status also among some of the lower middle- and upper working-class people of the West. In the Introduction I suggested that, globally, illiberalism finds strong support not among the lowest socioeconomic strata but among those just above, who struggle to retain their fragile privilege. Not the peasants, but those who want to make sure they're not peasants.

The peasant was, and to a large extent remains, the ever-haunting ancestral figure that the European petty bourgeois struggles to stay different from. To the extent that 'German' and 'Slav' meant anything in premodern times, peasant serfs were 'Slavs' and the traders and artisans of the towns were 'Germans'.³⁸ The distinction was mainly linguistic: it was not that Germans became lords and burghers and peasants became Slavs, as much as that burghers came to speak German and peasants a Slavic language. With the rise of the Slavic petty bourgeoisie and the decline of serfdom, the linguistic switch to German that used to accompany urbanization was less likely to happen. This was an important source of the 'national revival' among the 'Slavs'.

It was only with the defeat of Germany and Austria-Hungary in the First World War, however, that independence from Germans for Slavs began to be considered as a serious, viable option. In order to weaken Germany, the Western allies decided after some hesitation to dismantle Austria-Hungary and to encourage Slavic and Hungarian nationalists, whose demands had (except perhaps for the Poles) generally been more moderate, to choose complete independence. This separation in terms of political sovereignty was met, however, by some on the German side with a desire to literally eject Slavs from territory that was to be occupied by Germans in search of 'living space' or *Lebensraum* for their nation. The German-Slavic difference was now put by extremists in overtly racial terms. German racial policy under Hitler aimed at not only the cultural but ultimately also the physical removal of peoples who were white but not quite.

It was mainly the Polish people who bore the wrath of this racist hatred, with millions of Poles perishing under the brutal German occupation. Wartime Germany did ally itself with fascist puppet regimes in Slavic Slovakia and Croatia. Czechs were given autonomy in a truncated region called 'The Protectorate (using a term often employed for African and Asian semi-colonies) of Bohemia and Moravia', from which the German-identified border areas had been excised. In spite of savage incidents of oppression, however, Czechs, Slovaks, and Croats fared hardly worse than occupied West Europeans such as the French.

A secret Nazi plan called *Generalplan Ost* (General Plan for the East), which aimed to exterminate or exile large numbers of Slavs and to turn others into forced labourers, was only beginning to be implemented during the war.[39] But it revealed that the long-term German policy was what Achille Mbembe calls a necropolitics,[40] aiming to destroy a people physically or at least to rob them of their distinctive culture. In this case the goal was to replace Slavs with Germans. Like the dispossession of Indigenous peoples by white settlers in the Americas, in Africa, and in Australia, the *Generalplan Ost* was also motivated by the thirst for territory to exploit, and used race to strip the Other from the protection of the law and of human sympathy and to make it possible to enslave them. It has been claimed that Germans learned genocide when they brutalized the Indigenous people of their colony, Southwest Africa (which they held until their defeat in the First World War). It has also been suggested that Germany's plans for territorially dispossessing and exterminating Slavs were inspired by the Mussolini regime's policies aiming at settling hundreds of thousands of Italians in Africa, and specifically in Libya.[41]

During the interwar period, German racism was met by 'the Slavs' not so much by rejecting eugenics and other biomedical approaches to race and nationality, but rather by adopting the same approach to advocate for the qualities and future 'improvement' of their own racial stock. In 1932, a year before Hitler became chancellor of Germany, the Slovene author Franc Derganac (1877–1939) wrote that '[t]he united front of Western European eugenics has declared an aggressive, decisive struggle for survival to all small, "depleted, mixed and degenerate nations", above all the Slavs of Central Europe.' He added that the Slavs' historic duty is 'defence', presumably using the same eugenic means.[42]

The logic of racial eugenics leading to violent expulsion turned out, with Germany losing the Second World War, to be fatal for German presence in East Central Europe. The 'Slavs', with the explicit support of the victorious USSR *and* Western powers, put in practice a brutal policy of ethnic cleansing. Millions of Germans were expelled from Poland and Czechoslovakia, and to a lesser extent from Hungary. Instead of the Slavs being moved East, it was the Germans who were pushed out to the West.

Erasing the German presence in Eastern Europe is a logical prerequisite for erasing Central Europe from the mental map of Eastern Europe. It was only as East Central European states became nearly homogeneous ethnically, that it was possible for the first time to imagine East Central Europe as unambiguously 'Eastern European'.

The flip side of pushing Central Europe to the eastern side of a clear, binary divide, was pushing Germany entirely to the West. This happened quickly after the war, but not right away. During the Second World War, Germans had been labelled as 'Huns', a term evoking Eastern marauders ravaging mediaeval Europe. When Winston Churchill introduced the term 'Iron Curtain' into the English language in his famous speech at a Missouri college in 1946, he began not by opposing Western democracy and Eastern communism, but the Anglo-Saxon race with tyranny, including tyranny imposed by Germans. What he called 'the capitals of the ancient states of Central and Eastern Europe' (with the *and* still a meaningful concatenation, mutually excluding Central and Eastern), included not only Warsaw, Prague, and Budapest, but also Berlin and Vienna.[43] These were all cities occupied fully or in part by the Soviets. Their inclusion puts into question Larry Wolff's observation that 'Churchill's demarcation of a boundary line ... followed a line that was drawn and invested with meaning over two centuries, dating back to the age of his most famous ancestor, the warrior duke of Marlborough'.[44] As the Soviets withdrew from Vienna and as West Germany was admitted into the Western alliance during the Cold War, the Iron Curtain, far from representing a centuries old 'invention', was still being formed.

Yalta

It was the so-called Yalta agreement among the United States, the United Kingdom, and the Soviet Union that laid the mental prerequisite for the mass collective punishment and ethnic cleansing of Central Europe's Germans. Roosevelt, Churchill, and Stalin met in February, 1945, at the seaside resort of Yalta in the USSR, to divvy up Europe after the now predictable German defeat. The four Central European countries were assigned, with the exception of some areas in Western Czechoslovakia, to Stalin for postwar control, along with most of the areas of the continent to the East and the South. The rest was to be looked after by the Western allies, including the French. Berlin and all of Austria, were to be divided internally. Within the next years, the Soviets gave up their occupation zone in Austria, but managed with minimal interference from the West to dismantle democratic structures and establish their version of socialism in the other areas under their control.

As Timothy Garton Ash, describes it, the Yalta agreement led to the invention of a new term for the new East–West division of Europe: 'Western Europe implicitly accepted this dichotomy by subsuming under the label "Eastern Europe" all those parts of historic Central, East Central, and Southeastern Europe which after 1945 came under Soviet domination.'[45]

Before the end of the Second World War, the phrase 'Eastern Europe', as a proper name referring to a civilizational as well as a geographic section of the continent, barely existed.⁴⁶ Nor do we often find 'Eastern Europe' with double capitals in most languages of the continent before 1945. In German, the term *Osteuropa* (literally, 'Easteurope') does appear earlier than that, toward the end of the nineteenth century, for reasons that we will come to know soon. But its earliest use contrasted with and did not include *Mitteleuropa* or Central Europe. It was only the Cold War division of Europe, and the expulsion of Central European Germans that accompanied it, that made it possible to imagine a distinct 'Eastern Europe' and to locate Central Europe inside it.

Anti-Slavism provided some of the imagery of Cold War Eastern Europeanism. Russia was still the land of despotism, and the ordinary Eastern European was imagined on the pattern of the Slavic peasant. In popular culture, a good example are Steve Martin and Dan Akroyd's 'Festrunk Brothers', a.k.a. 'Czechoslovakian Brothers', which began in 1977 as a regular skit on the American television comedy show, 'Saturday Night Live'. The pair of visitors or immigrants from Bratislava to New York misuse American slang with an unattractive accent and wear ridiculously out-of-fashion clothes. In every episode they try to pick up American women ('foxes'), but of course they fail to do so. 'We are two wild and crazy guys', they declaim. But no one but they think they are 'wild', though they do seem quite crazy. Essentially, these are hillbillies with a European accent.

There were also relatively attractive representations of Eastern Europeans. When in Peter Sellers' *Party* a troupe of happy Russian ballet dancers bursts into a staidly formal bourgeois get-together at a Hollywood boss' house, the Russians are a breath of fresh air. In 1988, a year before what the Germans call *die Wende* ('the Change'), Jamie Lee Curtis as a lead character in the comedy, *A Fish Called Wanda*, still found John Cleese's barrister character Archie Leach irresistibly sexy when he showed her his ability to speak Russian.

After 1989

Such flattering clichés would seem out of place in Western popular culture after the fall of communism. The changes that happened in the screen representations of Russia and by extension Eastern Europe after 1989, are well illustrated in the developments of the

James Bond franchise. During the Cold War, the enemy in Bond films is not the USSR as such, but criminal organizations staffed by defectors from communism who are seduced by the very capitalist dream of unlimited wealth. In the 1963 film, *From Russia With Love*, the politically non-aligned organization, SPECTRE (Special Executive for Counter-Intelligence, Terrorism, Revenge and Extortion), hopes to steal a valuable encryption device from the Soviets, under the direction of a Czechoslovak chess master and a defector from a Soviet spy agency, named Rosa Klebb. An elegantly sexy Soviet agent, Tatiana Romanova (named after the deposed Tsar's family), desires to defect to the West, and does so although Bond and the audience are at times forced to suspect her sincerity. Throughout the film, SPECTRE and the Soviets remain separated. It is not true that during the Cold War Western cinema represented the USSR and the KGB in uniformly negative ways. Sometimes, the Soviets helped the West to find common enemies.

After communism, however, the pragmatic male and the seductive female officers of the KGB disappeared from the screen. Post-communist Russia came to be depicted as a declining empire with a weak and/or corrupt government easily taken advantage of by gangster oligarchs, often linked to international terrorism. Russian government agents disappeared as a substantial character, except when they defected or even formed oligarchic gangs themselves.

In the first James Bond film of the post-communist period, *Golden Eye* (1995), an untrustworthy Soviet-born Cossack, Alec Trevelyan, who is Bond's fellow British agent, turns out to have betrayed MI6 on a mission to blow up a Soviet chemical weapons facility in 1986, when he faked his own death. A typical Russian gangster-style criminal, he is now acting on his own behalf, having used stolen Soviet machinery to steal from the Bank of England. One of his chief accomplices is a Russian general. The film also introduces Valentin Dimitrovich Zhukovksy, a former KGB officer turned mafia boss. Zhukovsky returns in *The World Is Not Enough* (1999), where Russian nuclear facilities are easy prey for gangsters and their terrorist clients. The pretty villain here is not a Russian spy but an ambitious female gangster called Electra King, whose mother hailed from formerly Soviet, oil rich, and famously corrupt Azerbaijan. Her romance with Bond, unlike that of Romanova, doesn't end well: Zhukovsky kills her.

Essentially, the three-way Cold War era competition among the West, Russia, and the psychotic gangsters has been turned into a dual contest between the West against a Russia that has fused with the criminal oligarchs. Cinematic fiction exploits a reality here: Eastern Europeanism after 1989 became much more intense and much more clear-cut. Now 'Central and Eastern Europe' is portrayed as a backward region of unmitigated squalor and decay. One of the most amusing parodies of this image is Sasha Baron Cohen's comic character, Borat, a Kazakh and therefore not actually a European (but a citizen of a post-Soviet country), who speaks Polish, Russian, and, in a nod to Cohen's own white-but-not-quite, Jewish background, Hebrew – all of them brilliantly offered up to the unknowing audience as 'Kazakh'.

The Cold War, post-Yalta competition between the West and the East was based on the mutual recognition of rights within Europe as codified at Yalta, and was more about dominating the rest of the world together, at a time when the West's colonies were being emancipated, often with Soviet support. The possibility of peaceful collaboration played a significant part in how 'Eastern Europe' was imagined. In contrast, post-1989 Eastern Europeanism is all about competition and domination.

Conclusion

In sum, I have examined here the contention that the radical difference between 'Eastern Europe' and the West are old notions, predating the current phase of Central Europe's relationship to the West and therefore not essentially dependent on it. I hope to have shown, however, that this is only partly true at best. Rather, the notion of an East-West divide in Europe can be traced through four stages. It is only in the last, post-1989 stage, that it takes on fully its current characteristics.

First, in the early phases of capitalism and colonialism, as Manuela Boatcă showed, the demand for certain agricultural products resulted in increased forced labour – serfdom – in Europe to supply the markets of Western Europe.[47] Serfdom increased gradually from West to East, and it only got more severe in that direction even as the Industrial Revolution progressed; but there was no sharp border between free labour in the West and forced labour in the East.

Serfdom sometimes had an ethnic aspect, as when Polish landlords used Ukrainian serfs[48] or Hungarians used Romanians.

Second, during industrial capitalism and the rise of the Northwest European colonial empires, national identities began to be pursued with romantic fervour. This was especially so in Central Europe, where the town dwellers, who in many places identified as Germans, eventually came into conflict as a result of urbanization with people who migrated to the cities from the non-German-speaking countryside. As they competed for the new opportunities created by the expansion on the one hand of business activity and the other of the bureaucracy and educational systems, German-Slav tensions developed. In this German-Slavic conflict, distinct borders were difficult to define, as the two communities lived together side by side in many places. It is only in the late part of this period that, in extreme cases like that of the Nazis, some German nationalists strove not only to acquire overseas colonies but to expand the German state eastward. They wanted to spatialize their domination by eventually expelling some Slavs (especially Poles).

Third, with Germany's defeat in the Second World War, conditions were ripe for the first time for drawing the familiar line between Eastern and Western Europe, in the context of the Cold War, where the East was dominated by the Soviet Union. With the massive ethnic cleansing of the German minority, the Central European countries of the Eastern Bloc might now look much more 'Slavic' and so the East–West division created at Yalta may appear as a continuation of the Slavic-German conflict of old. But 'Eastern Europe' was created at Yalta under very different material conditions than the urbanization and the struggles for land of the nineteenth and early twentieth centuries. Now it was a matter of global rivalry between capitalism and Soviet socialism. Not only did it have a much broader context than the German-Slavic rivalry, but also did not map particularly well onto it. Hungary and Romania, who were also part of the Eastern Bloc, were not Slavic. Unlike the previous periods when areas of the east of Europe were flexibly and indistinctly imagined as marginal, but without fixed borders, Yalta created an Eastern Europe with a deliberately drawn frontier: the 'Iron Curtain'.[49]

Fourth, the post-communist context, which is our main focus, retained the imagined Iron Curtain contrary to the logic of Central

Europe joining the liberal democracies of the West and the EU. Here the context is the need by Western capital to maintain the area as a source of cheap labour and as a captive market, in competition with local capitalists and in defiance of the interests of local labour and consumers.

Each of the four periods provoked a different kind of resistance from the subordinated party. Serfs engaged in small and large-scale peasant rebellions, which, contrary to nationalist historians, were class revolts not associated with a strong national affect. In the second period, the interests of certain parts of the rising middle classes were expressed through genuinely national resistance. This included the 'unification' movements resulting in the founding of modern Germany and Italy, but failed at the time to revive Poland. In the Cold War, the peripheralization of Central Europe as 'Eastern European' was resisted in the area by the 'dissidents'. And finally, resistance to the continued othering of Central Europeans, who had expected to be able to fully 'return' to the West, has become today one of the major sources of the area's illiberal revolt.

While, then, there are recognizable continuities in the way that the centre and east of Europe have been imagined in the last two or three centuries, the historical conditions in which the notion of 'Eastern Europe' functions, and how it does or does not include Central Europe, have taken on a new character since 1989.

As I investigated, in this chapter, the genealogy of 'Eastern Europe' as an idea – not in the Enlightenment, partly in anti-Slavism, largely in the Cold War, and substantially in the post-communist era – I have consistently attempted to show also the crucial relevance, to understanding Central Europe, of the historical presence of German people, the German language, and German ideas in the area. Writing them out of history, which parallels their postwar expulsion, is also, to a large extent, what makes writing Central Europe out of Eastern Europe possible.

Let me therefore bring Germany back, in a small way, at the end of this chapter. The rejection of the hoped-for coming together of East and West after the fall of communism and through the eastward enlargement of the EU, has echoed within reunited Germany also. There is little reason to believe that before 1945 anyone in Germany considered what is now called the 'new federal states' as in any way less German than the rest of the country. Berlin,

Dresden, and Leipzig were at least as focal to German culture as Frankfurt or Hamburg. During the Cold War, East Germans were viewed in the West the same as West Germans, only stranded on the wrong side of the Iron Curtain. But now the East German *Ossi* came to be racialized as culturally different, in much the same way as other 'Eastern Europeans'.[50] As the German sociologist Alexander Yendell has noted, Western Germans view their fellow citizens in the formerly communist East of the country as backward, underdeveloped and disadvantaged, a judgment that expresses Eastern Europeanist racism.[51] In this way, the overlap in the image of Germany and of Central Europe, which disappeared after Yalta, seems to have come back in some small but, to Germans at least, significant way.

3

How Central Europeans Became Central European (Time and Time Again)

If 'Eastern Europe' is an invention, so is 'Central Europe'. It, too covers, if on a lesser scale, different areas, different populations, different cultures. But while Eastern Europe was invented by outsiders, in the West, Central Europe was invented by Central Europeans themselves. In fact, Central Europeans have reinvented themselves several times.

'Central Europe is not a region whose boundaries you can trace on the map—like, say, Central America', wrote Timothy Garton Ash. 'It is a kingdom of the spirit.'[1] But what exactly is that spirit? Marcin Moskalewicz and Wojciech Przybylski, co-editors of an anthology that brings together a number of scholars from the area, ask, 'Is it possible to complete the map of Central European ideas? Is it possible to finally understand the peculiarity of Central Europe?'

Their answer is, 'Definitely not'.[2] In this chapter, I nevertheless attempt to trace the history of Central Europe, as an idea tied to a place between the East and West of Europe, from its initial, nineteenth-century German formulation to Orbán's corrupt illiberal version. What we will find is that, radical as Orbán's notion is, it is not as different from its antecedents as we might have expected.

Since the nineteenth century, the concept of Central Europe has changed form and content repeatedly, yet maintained a surprising continuity. It is this that we, in this chapter, will seek to understand. Before the Central European local patriotism of the Visegrád Alliance, as advocated by Viktor Orbán, we can discern three phases of Central European identity. First, amid the revolutionary fervour in mid-nineteenth-century Europe, Central Europe or *Mitteleuropa* was a German idea, meant to raise the region between Russia and France into a new European force under German leadership. Second, after the First World War, Polish and Czechoslovak versions of Central Europe ironically excluded Germany, and meant to create an alliance that would be politically and culturally located between Germany and Russia. The third incarnation of the Central European idea came in the 1980s. Then, some 'dissidents' under communism, and some of their Western allies, imagined a post-Cold War region in the heart of Europe that would position itself between not only America and Russia but also between heartless capitalism and totalitarian socialism.

The fourth version of Central Europe was reinvented as a part of its illiberal revolt. The dream of representing a serious alternative to standard Western and Eastern models of organizing the world remains and is even more evident than ever in illiberal notions of Central Europe. One difference, however, is that while many of the 'dissidents' liked much in both communist socialism and liberal capitalism, the illiberals despise both.

Before the First World War: the German idea of Central Europe

Mitteleuropa, as the Germans call Central Europe, became a notion in the aftermath of the Napoleonic wars. Many Germans had welcomed the freedoms introduced by Napoleon when he occupied the different states of not-yet-united Germany, but resented the arrogant spirit of French superiority in the way those freedoms were administered. At the same time, many resented the Russian forces who helped to free them from Napoleon but squashed his liberalizing reforms as well. This was a time when poets and philosophers began to see history as a theatre on whose stage ethnic nations or *Völker* were the main actors. The emerging German national movement hoped that, in the next act, Germans, occupying the space between the Atlantic powers and Russia, would play the main role. As a first step, the dozens of independent German states that then existed would have to unite.

Those dreaming of German unity, however, had a serious problem, which came to be known as 'the German question'. Who would lead the united Germany and what would be its borders? Habsburg Austria had long been the major power within the mostly German Holy Roman Empire, which Napoleon forced to dissolve in 1805. Many German nationalists considered the project of uniting Germany to be reviving something like that mediaeval realm, but in a modern context. However, Austrian leadership was controversial for many of them. A major problem was that Austria at the time included territories that are now parts of Poland, Italy, and Romania, and all of what is now the Czech Republic, Slovenia, and Croatia. It also incorporated the Kingdom of Hungary, which in turn comprised today's Slovakia and parts of Romania, Serbia, and Ukraine. The German-identified subjects of the Habsburg Empire were considered to be as genuinely German as anyone in Berlin, Hamburg, or Cologne. But Austria was not entirely, or even mostly, German. How then could it lead a united German nation state?

Austria's chief rival for the leadership of the German lands was the Northeastern German kingdom of Prussia, with its capital in Berlin. Prussia, too, included non-German, Slavic-language populations: Poles and the Sorbians mentioned in the last chapter. But although these minorities were numerous, Prussia unlike the Austrian Empire had an overwhelmingly German majority. So, in order to safeguard the national character of the new Germany, many German nationalists wanted it to be a Prussian-led German state, excluding multi-ethnic Austria. They supported the *kleindeutsche* (Lesser German, literally Little German) solution, which would not unite all of the territory that was under the control of German rulers, but would exclude the Habsburgs and their multinational Austrian (later Austro-Hungarian) realm.

The idea also pleased Protestant Germans who feared that Catholic Austria would add its weight to southern German states like Bavaria, threatening what they envisioned as the Protestant culture of the new Germany and introducing an outside power: the Pope. (Prussia was proudly Protestant.) There were, nevertheless, Catholic proponents of the Lesser German solution, including the

German nationalists of Austria. They felt that the German-majority areas of the Habsburg Empire (which included some in the future Czech Republic) should split from the non-German.

That would mean the dissolution of the Habsburg Empire, which naturally did not sit well with the Habsburg establishment and its supporters. Some Austrian leaders countered the Lesser German argument for an ethnically purer Germany with a culturalist argument for a new association of states, where much of the population would not be German, but the German people, language, and culture would still predominate. It would be a loose confederation, rather than a single realm. This was *Mitteleuropa*.

Such was the vision of the Prime Minister of Habsburg Austria, Prince Felix of Schwarzenberg. The Schwarzenbergs were nobles of Bohemia and maintained an attachment to the Czech language as a marker of their local identity. (Karel, a recent Prince Schwarzenberg and a dual Swiss and Czech citizen, was the chief of staff of President Václav Havel's office, and the runner-up in the Czech presidential elections of 2013.) Affirming the multiethnic, if German-dominated, character of an Austrian-led *Mitteleuropa* accorded with the genuine personal sentiments of the Schwarzenbergs and other members of the high nobility, who served the Habsburgs and who had non-German roots to one degree or another. (One of the most famous among them was the Hungarian Eszterhazy family, employers of the composer Joseph Haydn.)

Proudly multi-ethnic yet also primarily German in culture, the Central Europe that Schwarzenberg and his peers dreamed of would also be a conservative bulwark against the liberal nationalisms, including the German variety, that were sweeping the continent. Schwarzenberg represented the reactionary aristocratic party that crushed the 1848 revolutions in Vienna, Prague, Krakow, and Budapest.

In the meantime, the Prussian rival was developing its industry, army, education, and political administration and becoming a powerful modern state. Competition with Austria increased when Otto von Bismarck became prime minister and foreign minister of Prussia in 1862. Four years later, the animosity between the two 'German' powers escalated into a war. In the bloody battle of Hradec Králové (Königgrätz) in Bohemia, Prussia dealt the Habsburg forces a resounding defeat. Among the concessions that Austria was forced to make was to relinquish most of predominantly German-identified Silesia (historically a part of the Crown of Bohemia and today, of Poland) to Prussia.

Victory in an even more important war, against France in 1871, made the Prussian ascendancy final. Bismarck assembled various German princes and military commanders in the famous Mirror Hall of the Palace of Versailles, the proud residence of French kings since Louis XIV. Here he proclaimed the King of Prussia, Wilhelm I, German Emperor. Locating the ceremony near Paris was meant to make all that much sweeter the Germans' revenge against Napoleon. But also, it declared a shift of power within Europe. For at least two centuries, French cultural influence had dominated Europe, including Germany. German courtiers spoke French when they meant to impress; French scholarship dominated the education of the German nobles. This French supremacy now seemed eclipsed by that of the new German Empire (*Reich*) located between France and Russia. In terms of the racialized terminology used in this book, Germany became fully white.

The Prussian leadership of the new German *Reich* consciously saw itself as a Central European power. Although Austria (which had become Austria-Hungary in 1867) was not included in the 'little-German', Prussian-led Wilhelmine Empire, it was very much included in the idea of a *Mitteleuropa* that was now seen as an association of the German Reich and satellite states to the East. During the First World War, when the old rivals Germany and Austria-Hungary joined forces as the leading 'Central Powers', the *Mitteleuropa* idea gathered momentum in both countries, this time as an ideological prop for the war alliance. For Prussia, a greater *Mitteleuropa* was an imperial strategy. Prussian proponents were eying a very wide alliance, supporting an informal German hegemony in all of Europe between Russia and the West, including even Turkey.[3] But also, the idea appealed to the many non-Germans of Austria-Hungary loyal to the Habsburg dynasty. In such a broad alliance of states, they felt that their national rights would be protected, because Germans, now seeing multiethnic Austria-Hungary as an ally, would lessen their pressure on installing German supremacy there.[4]

Some of the wartime thinking on *Mitteleuropa* prefigured the claims of East Central European leaders of the twenty-first century, such as Viktor Orbán, who suggest that Central Europe has preserved European values better than the West. Arthur Moeller van der Bruck wrote that the Central Powers represented an 'organic' European group that can protect European culture against the 'artificial' conglomeration that was the Allied Powers.[5] Friedrich Naumann was a Saxon Protestant minister, a liberal politician, and a friend of the influential sociologist Max Weber (Weber was himself interested in promoting a postwar, German-centred Central Europe).[6] Naumann's book, *Mitteleuropa*,[7] appeared in late 1915, at a time when the Central Powers seemed to many of their citizens to be poised for victory. The book was a great success even though its concrete political, economic, and military proposals were never implemented. 'Mid-Europe will have a German nucleus, will invariably use the German language', Naumann wrote, and even fantasized about a new type of human being that German leadership would engender: 'a type of Mid-European may be worked out, including all elements of culture and strength, the bearer of a civilization of rich and varied content growing up around the German nationality'.[8]

If such fantasies threatened to be contradicted by the Slavic presence in Central Europe, they may have been assuaged somewhat by the proposition, made by the wildly popular racist 'scholar' Houston Chamberlain, that the Germanic race also included, along with Celts, the Slavs (though Houston could not stop himself from making a remark about the 'typical Czech potato face').[9] Another enthusiast of *Mitteleuropa*, Wilhelm Schwaner, exclaimed, 'Now the new Germany has to emerge! Now the United States of Europe under German leadership must appear!'[10]

For many German-speaking Austrians, the *Mitteleuropa* idea was a reasonable compromise. They would remain in the multinational Habsburg Empire, but in the Central Europe that was envisaged, German domination would be firmly established. One such German-Austrian was Rudolf Steiner (1861–1925), an occultist philosopher and educator, who is now most remembered as the founder of 'Steiner education', championed by the worldwide network of Waldorf Schools. Steiner was strongly influenced in his efforts to unite interfaith 'spirituality' and science by the immensely popular theosophical movement, of which he was initially a member. Theosophy was founded by the Russian occultist, Helena 'Madame' Blavatsky, and at the time of the First World War was led by Annie Besant, an Englishwoman with feminist and socialist sympathies. Besant, like Madame Blavatsky before her, claimed to be in touch with South Asian spiritual leaders and was, among other things, a founder of the Indian National Congress, which advocated autonomy for British India.[11] During the Great War, Besant championed the cause of England and denigrated that of Germany. This confirmed Steiner in wishing to break with theosophy. It also inspired him to reflect on Germany as a *mitteleuropäisch* cultural force, located between Besant's West and Blavatsky's East. The term *Osteuropa* (Eastern Europe), which had seldom if ever before been used in German to refer to a civilization, finds expression in Steiner's writing along with *Mitteleuropa*. *Osteuropa* referred primarily to Russia and, to Steiner, excluded *Mitteleuropa* or Central Europe by definition, including its Germans, Slavs, Hungarians, and Romanians.

Steiner saw history as the unfolding of occult knowledge. Europe experienced, over the centuries, an 'occult development' (*okkulte Entwickelung*). The 'fifth post-Atlantic civilization', as Steiner saw it, began at the end of the fifteenth century, and it was dominated by Anglo-Saxon culture, which is lucidly rational, but so materialistic that it has difficulty understanding the spiritual aspect of the occult. In contrast, Russian culture is thoroughly spiritual, but confused, incapable of clearly expressing the subconscious (*Unterbewußtsein*) which inspires it instinctively. Steiner believed that the German spirit, as expressed in German idealist philosophy, was both lucid and spiritual, and so capable of mediating between West and East.[12] In the upcoming sixth post-Atlantic civilization, Russian spiritual culture will rise in importance as a corrective to Western materialism. However, for that process to be successful, German mediation will be required. 'Central Europe' was a geographic metaphor for this German role of mediation. The non-German peoples of the region, of whom his book has next to nothing to say, hardly interested Steiner at all. He assumed them to be a marginal fixture of a Central Europe built around a clearly German civilizational centre.

Mitteleuropa in the interwar period

Things did not work out as Naumann or Steiner hoped. The Central Powers lost the war, and German ascendancy had to be put aside as an idea, until it came back with a vengeance in National Socialism. In the period following the First World War, *Mitteleuropa* was, however, taken up at least as enthusiastically by many of the non-German Central Europeans.

Long before the First World War, in the Habsburg Empire, the Slavic-speaking groups, and especially the Czechs, had developed the ideology of 'Austro-Slavism', which viewed the Slavs of the empire in an in-between position. If the German ideologists of *Mitteleuropa* saw themselves located, culturally as well as geographically, between Russia and the West, for these Slavs their middle location was between Russia and Germany. František Palacký, the leading Austro-Slav ideologist, was described as a 'mad German' by Karl Marx's collaborator, Friedrich Engels, because he was a self-identified Czech who (like many, perhaps most, other early Czech nationalists) actually had to learn the Slavic language.[13] In Palacký's view, the goal of the Habsburg Empire was 'to be Europe's shield and refuge against Asiatic elements of all kinds ... [with] complete equality of rights and the equality in respect of all nationalities and confessions united under its sceptre'.[14] The 'Asiatic elements of all kinds' included the Ottoman Empire but also Russia, and defending against them could best be achieved by promoting the political and cultural interests of the Slavic nations as equal with the Germans and others in the fold of the empire.

Loyalty to the Habsburgs remained a common characteristic of Czech nationalists even as the original 'Old Czech' Austro-Slavism gave way throughout the nineteenth century to other formulations. However, as the First World War saw German nationalism feature as a public justification for the German-Austrian Axis alliance and, especially, as it was becoming ever clearer that the Axis was losing the war, some of the leaders of the non-German peoples began to work for the dissolution of the Habsburg Empire, and for the establishment of independent nation states. The Czech professor, Tomáš Masaryk, in exile in America, planned, with his Slovak allies and with American support, to establish the new state of Czechoslovakia. A few weeks before declaring Czechoslovak independence, Masaryk made a Declaration of Independence for 'Middle Europe'. The event was held at a meeting of the Democratic Mid-European Union, whose president Masaryk was, at Independence Hall in Philadelphia, the site where American independence from Britain had been proclaimed. Notably, no German or Hungarian delegate was present (Czechs resented the rights given to Hungarians in Austria-Hungary, which were of the sort they had demanded for themselves). On the other hand, in addition to Poland, delegates signed also for 'Jugoslavs', 'Ugro-Ruthones',[15] Ukrainians, 'Rumanians', 'Italia-Irredenta', Greeks, Lithuanians, Albanians, and 'Zionists' (*The New York Times* reported that 'much interest was created by the arrival of a delegate from Jerusalem, representing the Jews in Palestine').[16] Evidently, Masaryk, who would soon become the first president of Czechoslovakia, was hoping for Czechoslovakia to lead a new Central Europe that would help to protect the newly independent countries against the influence and territorial appetites of both Germany and Russia.[17]

Similarly, the newly created, post-First-World-War Polish leadership dreamed of an association referred to as *Intermarium* (*Międzymorze*, 'land between the seas'), which would be an association of nations including Finland, Estonia, Lithuania, Latvia, Belarus, Ukraine, Hungary, Czechoslovakia, Romania, and Yugoslavia. This Polish-led alliance would unite states located between the Baltic and the Adriatic seas. But more importantly, *Intermarium* would unite the space between the two powers, Germany and Russia, from whom, like the Czechoslovak equivalent, it was meant to provide protection.[18]

While the political leaders dreamed impossible dreams, for ordinary people in the newly independent states *Mitteleuropa* was a much less serious matter. It became a means to keep alive the cultural, and perhaps also something of a sentimental, connection among Austria-Hungary's successors. The first European football cup for team competition, for example, was the Central European Cup or *Mitropa Cup* (where *Mitropa* stood for *Mitteleuropa*). It was the brainchild of the Austrian football player and enthusiast, Hugo Meisl, who organized it in 1925. After his death, the competition was called *Meisl's Cup* in his honour, a label eventually retracted by the Nazis because Meisl was Jewish. Early on, the national team of truncated Austria did very well in the Cup, bringing a minor sort of relief to the nostalgics of the Austrian Empire. The *Mitropa Cup* included at its height Austria, Hungary, Czechoslovakia, Italy, and Romania. Tellingly, it did not include Germany, or even Poland.[19]

In spite of its ability to assuage nostalgia for the integrated Central Europe that Austria-Hungary had represented, the interwar notion of 'Central Europe' was not overtly pro-Habsburg. It was cultural, not ideological. As such, it provoked no objection from interwar Czechoslovak, Polish, or Hungarian nationalists. Nor did it raise eyebrows under communism, although it could encode, under the radar, an identity that balanced the region's attachment to the Soviet East. In fact, achievements of socialist construction, such as major bridges or oil refineries, could even be referred to with pride by the communists as 'the largest in Central Europe',[20] suggesting that communist-style socialism could compete with capitalist Austria or West Germany. 'Central Europe' was a term without any controversial substance.

Kundera and the 'dissidents'

Then, in the 1980s, a number of prominent intellectuals, including political émigrés, again injected the phrase 'Central Europe' with ideological content. The focus was on the cultural renaissance experienced in the interwar period in multilingual Central European metropoles such as Krakow, Prague, Budapest, and especially Vienna. There was, to all this, a clear and explicit feeling of nostalgia for the Habsburg monarchy, although ironically its target was the post-Habsburg period in countries that had been founded on the ruins of the Danubian Empire. It was an elegant manoeuvre, having one's *Mitteleuropa* identity along with one's national independence, and celebrating one's Habsburg nostalgia through idealizing the multicultural character of the interwar states, each actually identified with a single ethnic nation. Subtly, memories of German-speaking Jews became almost as important to the image of this Central Europe as those of German idealist philosophers and literati had been earlier. In the words of the Czech, and later French, author Milan Kundera,

Sigmund Freud's parents came from Poland, but young Sigmund spent his childhood in Moravia, in present-day Czechoslovakia. Edmund Husserl and Gustav Mahler also spent their childhoods there. The Viennese novelist Joseph Roth had his roots in Poland. The great Czech poet Julius Zeyer was born in Prague to a German-speaking family; it was his own choice to become Czech. The mother tongue of Hermann Kafka, on the other hand, was Czech, while his son Franz took up German. The key figure in the Hungarian revolt of 1956, the writer Tibor Déry, came from a German-Hungarian family, and my dear friend Danilo Kis, the excellent novelist, is Hungario-Yugoslav. What a tangle of national destinies among even the most representative figures of each country!

And all of the names I've just mentioned are those of Jews. Indeed, no other part of the world has been so deeply marked by the influence of Jewish genius. Aliens everywhere and everywhere at home, lifted above national quarrels, the Jews in the twentieth century were the principal cosmopolitan, integrating element in Central Europe: they were its intellectual cement, a condensed version of its spirit, creators of its spiritual unity. That's why I love the Jewish heritage and cling to it with as much passion and nostalgia as though it were my own.[21]

Like the earlier proponents of *Mitteleuropa*, Kundera placed Central Europe at the core of Western civilization and, like them, he opposed it to the Russian East. In fact, for him and like-minded members of a generation that grew up under communism, 'Central Europe' was ultimately an answer to the insult, as he saw it, of being treated not as a Western but as an Eastern European. The famous essay from which the above quote is taken was published in French in 1983 and amounted to the manifesto of the aggrieved Central European. 'The Tragedy of Central Europe' was written at a time when the communist regimes of Central Europe still seemed unassailable. The original French title was '*Un occident kidnappé ou la tragédie de l'Europe Centrale*', meaning literally, 'A West kidnapped, or the tragedy of Central Europe'.[22] The kidnapping happened when, after the Second World War, Central Europe, in the imaginative geography of postwar Europe, was taken out of the West and placed in Eastern Europe. This mental kidnapping recalls the mythological one that gave the whole continent its name: Europa, a noblewoman of Tyre in today's Lebanon, was snatched away to Crete by Zeus, disguised as a tame bull to trick her. The kidnapping of Central Europe was in the other direction, West to East, and the kidnapper was communist Russia. Its leader, Joseph Stalin, seduced the Western powers into granting him Central Europe but, like the *raptus Europae*, the kidnapping of Central Europe was an act of violence, which took place without the victim's consent.

According to Kundera, Europe was

> always divided into two halves which evolved separately, but these were not Western and Eastern Europe as we now use those terms. Rather, one half was tied to ancient Rome and the Catholic Church, and the other was anchored in Byzantium and the Orthodox Church. After 1945, the border between the two Europes shifted several hundred kilometers to the west. Now several nations that had always considered themselves to be Western woke up to discover that they were suddenly in the East.[23]

Elsewhere in the article, Kundera refers to the 'two Europes' as Europe proper (Western Europe including Central Europe, or simply 'Europe') and Russia: 'Russian communism vigorously reawakened Russia's old anti-Western obsessions and turned it brutally against Europe.'[24] Soviet communism, in other words, was the latest embodiment of the Eastern Orthodox other Europe, the Europe of the East, which had for centuries been led by Russia.

Central Europe, the 'Eastern border of the West',[25] has resented and fought this unjust kidnapping to the East. It has always wanted to be a 'small, arch-European Europe, a reduced model of Europe conceived according to one rule: the greatest variety within the smallest space. How could Central Europe not be horrified facing a Russia founded on the opposite principle: the smallest variety within the greatest space?'.²⁶ Russia was, to Central Europe, an alien civilization with 'another image of space (a space so immense entire nations are swallowed up in it), another sense of time (slow and patient), another way of laughing, living, and dying'.²⁷ Kundera quotes the Polish anti-communist dissident, Czeslaw Milosz, who described the sixteenth- and seventeenth-century Polish view of a Russia that Poland fought militarily as 'only a big void to the east'. (Thus, Milosz and Kundera echoed much of what Edward Said wrote about the West's conceptions of the Arab and Muslim Orient.)

The anti-Soviet rebellions of Central Europe were, as Kundera saw it, more than anything a fight for Central Europe's Western cultural identity. If a people's identity 'is threatened with extinction, cultural life grows correspondingly more intense, more important, until culture itself becomes the living value around which all people rally'.²⁸ And rally they did, in Hungary in 1956, in Czechoslovakia in 1968, and in Poland during numerous revolts begun in 1956 and continued into the time of Kundera's writing and beyond.

> Every single one [of these revolts] was supported by almost the entire population. And, in every case, each regime could not have defended itself for more than three hours if it had not been backed by Russia. That said, we can no longer consider what took place in Prague or Warsaw in its essence as a drama of Eastern Europe, of the Soviet bloc, of communism; it is a drama of the West – a West that, kidnapped, displaced, and brainwashed, nevertheless insists on defending its identity.²⁹

If any passage in Kundera's jeremiad is worth rereading today, it is this. Note that the rebels, whom we have long thought to be fighters for a liberal democracy, are in Kundera's view warriors of 'identity', a concept that has in recent years expanded, along with so many others, from the political left to the right, and is a favourite with illiberal Europeans and Americans, from Orbán to the more 'extremist' groupings who refer to themselves as 'identitarians'.³⁰

To Kundera, identity is based on 'culture'. What he means is the *Kulturmensch* (see Chapter 2), 'cultured' rather than 'primitive'; that is, what he means is high culture: literature, art, and music. Central Europe's unique contribution to the West was, according to Kundera, baroque art. Baroque 'Central Europe (characterized by the predominance of the irrational and the dominant position of the visual arts and especially of music) became the opposite pole of classical France (characterized by the predominance of the rational and the dominant position of literature and philosophy). It is in the baroque period that one finds the origins of the extraordinary development of Central European music, which, from Haydn to Schönberg, from Liszt to Bartók, condensed within itself according to Kundera the evolution of all European music'. In this framework, German-Austrian musicians characteristically belong to Austrian, that is, Central European culture, not German.

Kundera is proud of the fact that, as he sees it, the anti-Soviet rebellions were led by creative artists.

> It was Hungarian writers, in a group named after the Romantic poet Sándor Petöfi, who undertook the powerful critique that led the way to the explosion of 1956. It was the theater, the films, the literature and philosophy that, in the years before 1968, led ultimately to the emancipation of the Prague Spring. And it was the banning of a play by Adam Mickiewicz, the greatest Polish Romantic poet, that triggered the famous revolt of Polish students in 1968. This happy marriage of culture and life, of creative achievement and popular participation, has marked the revolts of Central Europe with an inimitable beauty that will always cast a spell over those who lived through those times.[31]

The tragedy of Central Europe in Kundera's conception includes the fact that while Central Europeans struggled beautifully against their kidnapping to the East, the West in the meantime took it as a *fait accompli*, and indeed seems to have forgotten that Central Europe was ever part of the West: 'In the eyes of its beloved Europe, Central Europe is just a part of the Soviet empire and nothing more, nothing more'.[32] Sadly, the reason the West sees in Central Europe only 'Eastern Europe' is that it cannot understand how important Central European culture is to Western culture. In fact, Western Europe cannot recognize its own Western culture anymore, because 'Europe itself is in the process of losing its own cultural identity'.[33]

Kundera's Central European is the last real European, a tragic figure who means to teach Europe about its own disappearing culture, but does not have the satisfaction of seeing itself recognized as such.

> That's why in Central European revolts there is something conservative, nearly anachronistic: they are desperately trying to restore the past, the past of culture, the past of the modern era. It is only in that period, only in a world that maintains a cultural dimension, that Central Europe can still defend its identity, still be seen for what it is.[34]

The history of national movements in Central Europe is that of 'small nations' that are always faced with extinction, but who have chosen to survive. He notes that the Polish national anthem is 'Poland has not yet perished' and attributes this will to protect a dying culture to Central Europe. But in this case, the dying culture is European culture as a whole.[35]

Sadly the West, instead of recognizing the Central European revolts as a last-ditch fight for its own survival, returns only a half-interested, condescending sympathy for these 'Eastern Europeans'. Kundera's sense of a personal insult is palpable. When he says that the Central European's 'picture of the West ... is of the West in the past', he means it as a criticism not of the Central Europeans but of a West that has lost its soul. He adds, spitefully, that in Central Europe unlike in the West, 'culture had not yet entirely bowed out'.[36] And it is a Western, European culture, not an Eastern, Russian-like one. Kundera is deeply irritated by the 'noisy and empty sentimentality of the "Slavic soul" that is attributed to me from time to time!'.

Kundera was far from the only leading 'dissident' who championed the notion of Central Europe as a counterweight to Soviet domination. Among the many others were the future Czechoslovak and Czech president, Václav Havel, the Hungarian writer and essayist, György (George) Konrád, and the Polish activist and public intellectual, Adam Michnik.[37]

The Central European dissidents' celebration of a *Mitteleuropa* rethought as a brilliant intellectual and artistic centre celebrating multiculturalism *avant la lettre*, connected well with a 1970s' wave of nostalgia, in Western Europe, for the café culture of late Habsburg

Vienna, and by extension of Prague and Budapest as Habsburg-era capitals. This Viennese turn was marked by works in cultural history such as Allan Janik and Steven Toulmin's *Wittgenstein's Vienna*, published in 1973,[38] or Carl Schorske's 1979 work, *Fin-de-siècle Vienna*.[39] There was a mushrooming of art exhibits celebrating Habsburg era *Sezession* (art nouveau), held throughout the Western world in the 1980s.[40] Often stylishly nostalgic, such retrospectives almost completely forgot the German nationalist streak in the original version of *Mitteleuropa*, which, as we have seen, had been particularly strong in Austria. Among other things, this helped the Vienna vogue to supply East Central Europeans with a ready-made claim to some fashionable cultural capital.[41]

Nowhere was the Vienna mania stronger than in Vienna itself. Austrians have long cultivated the image of the city as a multi-ethnic mecca of culture. (Among other things, the image helps Austrians to minimize the impact of their countryman Adolf Hitler on Austria's image in the world.) The famous conductor of the Viennese Philharmonic, Nikolaus Harnoncourt, believed that the music of the King of the Waltz, Johann Strauss, resonated with the 'sadness of the Slavs' and the 'temperamentality of the Hungarians'. Harnoncourt could understand the Polish polka and mazurka as well as the Viennese waltz, he said, because as an Austrian he had these in his 'blood'.[42] Germanness does not even get mentioned in such accounts, though of course – as I argue here – it is really the silent historical deep structure of most Central European patriotism. German-Austrian Vienna is presented as the home of ostensibly universal (but really, European and white) Culture. It generously accepts and feels 'enriched' by the local colour of 'its' Slavs and Hungarians. Or so it pretends to, and so many of them wish.

The rise and fall of the Third Way

To Timothy Garton Ash, the Central Europe that was being discussed by the 'dissidents' was not so much an entity of the past as a project for the future. It was 'an idea. It does not yet exist', he insisted, 'The new Central Europe has yet to be created.'[43]

But what, exactly, was this new Central Europe to be like? Ash respected the moral integrity of the 'dissidents', and the value of integrity is, he believed, what they were most capable of teaching to the West.

> Under the black light of a totalitarian power, most ideas—and words—become deformed, appear grotesque, or simply crumble. Only a very few stand the test, remain rocklike under any pressure; and most of these are not new.
>
> There are things worth suffering for. There are moral absolutes. Not everything is open to discussion.
>
> 'A life with defeat is destructive', writes Michnik, 'but it also produces great cultural values that heal. ... To know how to live with defeat is to know how to stand up to fate, how to express a vote of no confidence in those powers that pretend to be fate.' These qualities and values have emerged from their specific Central European experience—which is the central European experience of our time. But since we can read what they write, perhaps it may even be possible to learn a little from that experience, without having to go through it.[44]

As the Trump presidency drove home in the West, grotesquely deformed ideas, conspiracy theories and fake news were capable of taking root there also, and honest thinkers in the West have learned to contemplate at least the possibility of defeat, as well.

The defence of honesty, like any defence, is not a forward-looking programme but essentially a conservative one. In the case of communist Central Europe in the 1980s, it knew what it wanted to dismantle: the dishonest communist regime that 'kidnapped' Central Europe to the East. But, rather than building a new kind of society, it wanted to simply go back to its alleged heyday. Ash saw little original thinking among the dissidents he was discussing. He was not too disturbed by this. Nor was Jürgen Habermas, the influential German philosopher, who expressed satisfaction with 'the lack of ideas that are either innovative or oriented towards the future' that he saw in the 'rectifying revolutions' of 1989.[45] According to Ivan Krastev and Steven Holmes, Habermas believed – and they agree – that '[f]ar from searching for an untested wonderland or craving anything ingeniously new, the leading figures in these revolutions aimed at overturning one system only in order to copy another'.[46]

But were the liberal dissidents really the main motor of the democracy movement leading to the changes of 1989? One does not want to underestimate the influence of dissident intellectuals celebrated in the West. Yet conversations with people living in the small towns of Czech Silesia, for example, a coal mining area that spun into decline after 1989, show that many barely knew who Havel was.[47] They would have clearly remembered Alexander Dubček, though, who inspired millions in Czechoslovakia and elsewhere to produce a movement of hope that was soon crushed by Soviet tanks, but which briefly flourished during what was known as the Prague Spring of 1968. With all of its differences, the Prague Spring can be considered to have been part of a worldwide mobilization of mainly young people with mainly left-wing ideas. And, contrary to Kundera's recollections, not liberal democrats but reform communists were the main initiators, and remained the most prominent leaders.

James Mark and his team of historians at the University of Essex have argued convincingly that '1989' was far from a revolution of the masses:

> the cameras' focus on ordinary people as agents of historical change hid a far less marketable truth about 1989: contrary to public perceptions in the West, it was mainly reforming Communist elites, rather than popular revolt, that had played the pivotal role in shepherding many countries of the region to a new world.[48]

These were elites not necessarily outside the party, and mostly not in prison, but at the very top of the political leadership and, crucially, of the management of the socialist economy. These elites – in Central Europe and the USSR, but also beyond, in China – at first wanted to find the way to a socialism capable of satisfying the demands of the population for goods matching, in quality and quantity, those of the West.[49] They were encouraged by some of the Soviet communist leadership, who saw Central Europe as an area to experiment with market reforms within a still-recognizable socialist framework and without threatening the political hegemony of the communist parties.

Aleksander Dubček was a communist, the leader first of the Slovak and then the Czechoslovak Party. What he and his enthusiastic supporters most looked for was not a restoration of prewar capitalism, but a compromise, in the best Central European tradition, between Western freedoms and individualism and the communalism of the Russian East. Dubček helped to give the idea its most enduring name: 'socialism with a human face'. Devoted to much the same ideals, the Hungarian rising of 1956 had been similarly led by the head of the country's communist Hungarian Working Peoples' Party, Imre Nagy.

To be sure, Lech Wałęsa, the leader of Poland's rebellious Solidarity movement, was no communist. Yet he was willing to compromise with the communists. Most important of the arrangements he made with the Polish communist government were perhaps the four 'August Understandings' signed in 1980.[50] Seven years later, this achievement was celebrated by the intellectual Leszek Kołakowski, who was a major influence on Solidarity.

> The historical meaning of Solidarity consisted in that it showed how a totalitarian regime might possibly, under strong social pressure, yet peacefully (whatever violence was used all those years was used by the police and the military), assume a new, more humane and economically more reasonable form by allowing some room for pluralism in social life.[51]

Wałęsa disagreed with a Solidarity colleague, Andrzej Gwiazda, that Western capitalist enterprises such as General Electric and General Motors could serve as models for Polish industry. 'We know that we are a socialist state', Wałęsa declared,

> and we want to stay that way. But we know that our systems are non-socialist. We know that everyone should feel needed. We know that hospitals and teachers are perhaps more needed than others, because they heal and educate us. But how do we pay them? In an un-socialist manner (*niesocjalistycznie*).[52]

The problem, in other words, was not socialism as such, but that the Polish communists were not *really* socialist. They did not pursue socialism with a human face.

What most of the leaders of reform in the 1960s and in the 1980s in Central Europe were hoping for, each in their own way, was a Third Way, a democratic socialism faithful to the moral ideals of both liberal democracy and communist socialism, but avoiding the manner in which each was abused in both the West and the East. Kundera himself remained a reform communist during the Prague Spring and for a time after. Havel was always opposed to communism, but even he insisted that the question as to whether socialism or communism are better 'gives me a sense of emerging from the depths of the last century. It seems to me that these thoroughly ideological and often semantically confused categories have long since been beside the point'.[53]

Once again, as in the case of the German-centred *Mitteleuropa* before and during the First World War, this ability to see the problems from both East and West gave Central Europeans the moral claim to proclaim themselves the ultimate carriers of European values. In spite of obvious differences, the promise to match capitalism with socialism even resembled Rudolf Steiner's effort to marry efficient but amoral Western materialism with inefficient Eastern idealism.

The idea was not necessarily just an Eastern, post-communist one. To some on the left in Western Europe, the 1980s' ideal of a Third Way represented by Central Europe was a model for the entire continent, which they wanted to unite against the dictates of both America and Russia. The historian Victoria Harms traces a particular connection between proponents of the Central European idea in Hungary, such as György Konrád and György Dalos, and their West German counterparts, Hanz Magnus Erzensberger and Karl Schlögel. The last-mentioned proclaimed programmatically that '[t]his apparition called Central Europe might undermine the dominance of East-West thinking'. Harms describes Schlögel's *The Centre Lies to the East* as merging 'the wave of nostalgia for the Habsburg Empire with the dissidents' political demands for Central Europe'.

How Western European intellectuals looked toward union with East Central Europe, as a counterweight also to the American domination of Western Europe, was aptly noted by the influential commentator, Tony Judt.

> In a sense what we are seeing here is once again a projection of a Western radical vision onto an imaginary Central European landscape. Where once it was the fantasy of socialism, now it is the dream of 'a united, independent Europe'. If it cannot be achieved in the West because of the presence and interests of the United States, then let it be enacted further East, in some loosely defined Central Europe miraculously released from all historical and geographical constraints.

Judt adds that Western 'theorists and interlocutors' sought out dissidents in Central Europe as 'living evidence of the plausibility of their projects'.[54] They would have been reassured by the propositions of someone like George Konrád, who argued that

> It is an unobservant European who fails to notice that the Iron Curtain is made of explosive material. Western Europe rests its back against a wall of dynamite, while blithely gazing out over the Atlantic. I consider Western Europe's good fortune as uncertain as our misfortune. Caught between the United States and the Soviet Union, we Europeans can assure peace only if we detach ourselves from [each] by mutual agreement, and then go on to draw the two parts of a divided Europe together.[55]

Many of the Western proponents of the Third Way might also have sympathized with Kundera's criticism of the demise of European high culture. At the time at least, most Europeans who agreed with him would have ascribed that to the influence of crass, unsophisticated America.

The long-standing, cautious effort of the communist elites to – *noblesse oblige* – make the people happy through finding a way between the wished-for egalitarianism of the communists and the imagined consumerist paradise of the capitalists, culminated in Mikhail Gorbachev's *perestroika*, which the Soviet communist leader explicitly dubbed 'socialism with a human face'.[56] By then, though, it was beginning to look like the East would never catch up. The Kádár regime in Hungary, installed by the Soviets after they violently suppressed the 1956 uprising there, is the best-known example of communists making compromises with market capitalism and consumerism. As one reminiscing Hungarian put it, 'Under the Kádár regime, we managed just fine up to our necks in tepid water. They always added enough hot water so we wouldn't freeze'.[57] But the partial fixes of moderate communism just weren't enough. Eventually, the politicians and the economists in and around the communist parties gave up and went over to the neoliberal revolution that was sweeping Reagan and Thatcher's West and continued into the twenty-first century. James Mark and his team note how economists active in the late phase of communist rule, who would be of decisive influence in the transition to capitalism, imbibed the neoliberal spirit during their studies in the West.[58] In the words of the author of perhaps the most extensive book on neoliberalism in Hungary, Adam Fabry,

> neoliberal ideas and practices were not simply imported, 'from outside' after the fall of the Berlin Wall in 1989, but emerged 'organically' in the late 1970s and early 1980s, as a response by domestic political and economic elites to the deepening economic and political crisis of Soviet-style state capitalism, in the wake of a mounting debt crisis and increasing geopolitical competition with the 'West', and growing disbelief in the Soviet model amongst local members of the nomenklatura.[59]

The superiority of the neoliberal Western capitalist model appeared incontestable at the time to most experts, including Western professors to whose work some economists in the Soviet bloc were exposed. These included Leszek Balcerowicz in Poland and the future Czech president, Václav Klaus. Although these people were critical of orthodox communists, they were able to work within the system and had the ear of the less doctrinaire members of the leadership. Their trips to the West, where they came in contact with neoliberal economists, were at the same time a characteristic perk that the regimes allowed those whom they considered within the bounds of reliability.

At home, the economists were closely associated with the managers of the state enterprises, many of whom had acquired access to wealth in the last stages of socialism. As James Mark's research team has noted, this experience made it easy for them to further increase their personal wealth in the brutally deregulated, chaotic post-transition economy.[60] Such internal factors may have been even more important than the flotillas of advisers that flooded Central and Eastern Europe from the West,[61] spreading the conviction that the ideal of a Third Way between capitalism and communism was dead, and that neoliberal globalism was the only alternative to Soviet-style socialism.

The Visegrád Alliance

Reflecting on the general demise of the Third Way option between capitalism and communism, Victoria Harms concluded that 'whatever constitutes Central Europe today, it shares little to nothing with the vision ... pronounced by cosmopolitan dissidents in the 1980s'.[62] That may be an exaggeration. 'Central Europe' as an idea is affirmed by the illiberals of the area, if anything with more passion than by any 'dissident' in the 1980s. Nor is the difference between the Central European vision of a Viktor Orbán and that of a Milan Kundera as great as it may appear.

In this chapter, I have focused on three perennial claims made by all proponents of the Central European idea:

1. that Central Europe is of decisive importance to Europe as a whole;
2. that Central Europe is a mediator between East and West; and
3. that, at the same time, Central Europe is part of the West – perhaps even its most authentic part.

These claims remain as much part of the current illiberal notion of Central Europe as they were of the 1980s' dissidents and of all the earlier versions of Central Europe as a moral, political, and cultural value, going back to the pan-German ideologists of more than 100 years ago.

The Visegrád Group, created right after the fall of communism, has remained true to these general features of the Central European idea. The organization saw the light of day on 15 February 1991, when government leaders of the Poles, Hungarians, and Czechoslovaks (as they then were) came together in the hilltop resort of Visegrád in Hungary. The location was symbolic: Visegrád is where a mediaeval alliance had been formed in 1335 among the kings of Hungary, Poland, and Bohemia.

The heritage of these kingdoms was Latin Christian. Poland and Hungary bordered the Orthodox Christian worlds in the Russian and the Ottoman empires, with the latter also representing the 'threat' of Islam. Collectively and individually, the people of the Visegrád Four countries (three before the splitting of Czechoslovakia) generally consider themselves to be more Western than predominantly Orthodox nations like Ukrainians, Russians, Serbs, Romanians, or Bulgarians. This common sentiment was served by the Visegrád Alliance, which distinguished what I call here in a very narrow sense Central Europe, from other post-communist states. At the affective level at least, the Polish anthropologist Michał Buchowski was certainly right to believe that this was the Alliance's major goal. But Buchowski also recognized how this pre-existing feeling of greater Westernness expressed the neoliberal agenda of the post-1989 transformation. The liberal former 'dissidents' who then led Central Europe felt that they could bolster their Western credentials by claiming that they had espoused the credo of installing 'the free market and liberal democracy more enthusiastically and more efficiently than the other, 'real' Eastern Europeans. They believed that this entitled them to push the border of the imagined East 'out onto the Balkans and the former Soviet Union'. Rather than challenging the East–West distinction, and the power relations it embodies, as such, the Visegrád leaders wished to keep it but redefine its borders. In terms of the history of imagined geography that I discussed in Chapter 2, they wished to reset the borders of the East where they had been before communism.

This was not an innocent historical exercise. Buchowski argues that the Visegrád leaders located their countries on the Western side while keeping their eastern and southeastern neighbours in the role of the devalued Other.[63] What we see here is an effort to reverse the rejection, by the West, of a Central European insistence on belonging with the privileged West, and not the stigmatized East. In the terms of this book, this is an instance of the desire – already by the liberal democrats who preceded in power their illiberal opponents – to prove that they are fully, not just partially and conditionally, white.[64]

The use of the Central Europe idea by illiberals departed from its earlier, 'dissident' version in some respects, and did not in others. The views of the 'dissidents', unlike those of the illiberals, were in broad agreement with liberal democratic principles, as they were also with the neoliberal economic policies that appeared unchallenged at the time in the West. The founding declaration of the Visegrád Alliance was drafted by Václav Havel, the new president of Czechoslovakia. The others who signed on were Lech Wałęsa, then President of Poland, and the Hungarian Prime Minister, József Antall. The Declaration described the event as 'a process of creating new foundations and forms of political, economic and cultural cooperation in the changed circumstances of Central Europe', brought about by the demise of the communist regimes. Among its goals, it avowed the 'renewal of … freedom and democracy', the 'construction of parliamentary democracy and the modern legal state, and respect for human rights and basic freedoms'.[65]

> Starting with the most important element of the European heritage – with universal human values and resting on one's own national identity, it is necessary to create a human society characterized by harmonious mutual cooperation, tolerant to individuals and of family, local, regional, and national communities, one that is not burdened by hatred, nationalism, xenophobia, and disputes with neighbours.[66]

Here Havel's voice is clearly discernible. This was the statesman who would make himself odious to local racists when he suggested that getting rid of anti-Roma discrimination would be 'a litmus test' of success for post-communist society.[67]

If anyone in the political mainstream disagreed with such liberal sentiment, their voices were at first muted. One aim of the Visegrád Alliance was to achieve the admission of its members into the EU, and this was a dream shared by almost everyone. The Czech researchers who edited *Central Europe's Culture Wars*, a collection of incisive essays on topics of central importance to this book, suggest that the 'war' between illiberals and their liberal and leftist opponents could begin only after Central Europe's absorption into the Western military and economic alliances, and especially the EU, was accomplished. As a condition for admission, the EU had required adherence to its liberal values. So universal was the yearning to 'return' to the West throughout the area, that even those who did not wholeheartedly agree, or at all, with liberal positions held their peace until admission was secured.[68] This then freed them to subvert Brussels' views of liberty and democracy – from within. We see this change in Orbán and Kaczyński's Central European credo, which surely contradicts the egalitarian, anti-racist parts of the Visegrád Declaration.

And yet, there are other passages in the document that they could hardly have objected to. For example, among the foundations of cooperation within the Visegrád Group, the Declaration mentions a

> system of traditional relations created by historical development, their cultural and spiritual heritage, and the common roots of their religious traditions. The multifarious, rich culture of the nations who live here comprehends also the fundamental richness of European spiritual life. Long-standing mutual spiritual, cultural, and economic influence, founded in natural historical evolution and springing from our proximity as neighbours, may facilitate this cooperation.[69]

The rich culture of the nation within the context of 'European spiritual life': now that's something in the liberal Visegrád Declaration that an 'illiberal democrat' can connect to.

Nationalism that is compatible with Central European solidarity, however, requires avoiding the bitter and often violent antagonisms that characterized the relationship among the four Visegrád nations in the past. The most important features of friction in interwar Central Europe were probably the irredentist claims of Hungary on territory that was taken from it with the so-called Treaty of Trianon in 1920. Trianon is a palace at Versailles, where the powers who defeated Germany and Austria-Hungary decided to dismember the latter, forcing Hungary to cede land, much of it inhabited largely by ethnic Hungarians, to Czechoslovakia, Romania, and Yugoslavia.

These three newly minted nations, fearful of Hungary's response, proceeded to form an anti-Hungarian alliance. (Poland, which also had claims on Czechoslovak territory, tended to side with Hungary.)

For conservative Hungarians, and for many liberal Hungarians as well, mourning what they see as the tragedy of Trianon is an essential part of their patriotism. The phrase 'Central Europe' did not appear once in Orbán's well-known 2014 speech, in which he announced the principles of his 'illiberal democracy'. Symbolically, he chose to make his declaration at the Romanian spa resort of Băile Tușnad, known to its predominantly Hungarian population as Tusnádfürdő.[70] There, Orbán reaffirmed his claim to represent all Hungarians in what he refers to as the 'Carpathian Basin'. His government had already given Hungarians outside the country's borders the right to vote in Hungarian elections, for which they rewarded him handsomely at the polls. Initially, such efforts appeared anything but 'Central European' in character; they smacked much more of Magyar nationalism.

However, as speeches in Romania became more or less an annual ritual for Orbán, their content grew ever more conciliatory, calling for Hungarian rights within a framework of Central European reconciliation. By the time of his 2017 speech, Orbán presented himself as a spokesman for all of Central Europe: 'the spirited Poles, the ever-thoughtful Czechs, the sober Slovaks, and the romantic Hungarians'; 'Warsaw, Prague, Bratislava, and Budapest' all speaking 'with one voice'.[71] Orbán's gallery of stereotypes was a bit cheerier than that of conductor Harnoncourt, with the 'sadness of the Slavs' gone if not the 'temperamentality of the Hungarians'. Perhaps Orbán had given up on the Austrians, too. It was now the post-communist Central Europeans alone that were advancing Central Europe's mission to bring the West back to its true self.

The 100th anniversary of Trianon, in 2020, arrived in the midst of the coronavirus epidemic, sparing Hungarian leaders some of the headache of devising ostentatious commemorations. Nevertheless, the task remained to present an approach to Trianon that, at the same time, stressed the perceived injustice of their country's loss and affirmed Visegrád solidarity. Orbán's ruling Fidesz Party nimbly orchestrated a remembrance day, acrobatically balancing aggrieved memories of the amputations of 1920 with the political imperatives of illiberalism in the Central Europe of 2020.

In the Hungarian Parliament, the job of introducing a commemorative resolution fell to the Speaker, the notoriously sexist and homophobic nationalist, László Kövér. His words are worth quoting for the way they combine radical irredentism with the desire to make common cause with other Central Europeans and to face together what Kövér represents as the Western desire to denationalize Europe.

> As long as Hungarians living outside of Hungary in the Carpathian Basin must wage a bitter existential battle to safeguard the mother tongue, the culture, and the native land that they inherited from their ancestors, the Trianon decision will not be a closed chapter of history, but an open, current, existential issue, alive in our own time.
>
> ... a hundred years ago, it was only the Hungarian nation whose existence was questioned by the victors of the time, while today those who fancy themselves sufficiently strong and as eternal victors, call into question the existence of each and every European nation!
>
> [...]
>
> ... let us not forget: in the past one hundred years it is not just we who were alone; at times each of the other Central European nations has also experienced loneliness. In 1920, to be sure, it was only us that the victorious Western powers threw on the butcher block of history to have us chopped to pieces, but in 1938 they did essentially the same to Czechoslovakia, then to the Baltic States and Poland, until after 1947 the West offered up everyone as prey to Stalin.
>
> [...]
>
> If in this region we do not stand on guard together for our national states, languages, and cultures, then they'll manoeuvre us all out of these. They'll estrange us from our native land, they'll demote our states into imperial tax farms, they'll turn our mother tongues into depraved kitchen dialects, and they'll make us forget our national cultures. The countries of our region can only stand up to this if we are together, if we are united.[72]

Orbán himself did not make a major speech on the occasion, and left the word to his chief of staff, Gergely Gulyás. Gulyás, quoted the poet Gyula Illyés to the effect that 'the state is a worldly power, but Nation and Homeland are from up high'. Gulyás added that 'God the Creator placed the peoples of Central Europe next to each other, tying their destinies to one another' and that the 'solidarity of the Visegrád countries is the best example of how the implementation of national rights is not an obstacle to, but a guarantee of successful coexistence'.[73]

While Orbán's financial and ideological support for friendly ethnic Hungarian parties in neighbouring Slovakia and Romania did raise an occasional eyebrow, on the whole the country's neighbours reciprocated his plea for Central European solidarity. The Prime Minister of Slovakia, Igor Matovič marked the 100th anniversary of Trianon by inviting 100 ethnic Hungarians to a commemoration, held at the historic Bratislava Castle. The motto of the gathering was 'We did not write the past, but the future is in our hands'. Péter Cseh, an ethnic Hungarian member of Matovič's OL'aNO Party, enthused that 'the participants are politicians, artists, professors, scientists, religious leaders, mayors, entrepreneurs, public personalities, and representatives of the media. Never before in the modern history of Slovakia has a Slovak head of government taken on Trianon!'[74] The prime minister's words did give expression to a slow trend in Slovakia to get beyond the still prevalent, official memory of pre-1918 Hungary as one marked by brutal Magyarization, and the dismemberment of the Kingdom of Hungary as marking the liberation of Slovaks from Magyar oppression. For one thing, Matovič recognized that what meant victory for one nationality could justifiably mean tragedy for another, that 'what meant a loss and an injustice to one meant a chance and new opportunities for others'.[75]

Even more transformative was Matovič's valuation of Slovakia's position in the historic Hungarian state that it had been part of for some 1,000 years. 'I think', he said, 'that historic Hungary was ours as well. Slovaks fought alongside Magyars and other nationalities against the Turkish invaders. The kings of Hungary did not only make decisions about the life and fate of Magyars, but also of Slovaks and everyone who lived on the territory of historic Hungary.' Matovič was articulating the old Slovak position, that the Kingdom of Hungary (*Uhorsko*) was, unlike the current state of Hungary (*Mad'arsko*), a multiethnic realm that did not rightfully belong to only the Magyars. But what was new was that Matovič chose to present this past not only as a story of Magyar oppression, but also with pride as a common Central European heritage. It allowed him to conclude, 'Let us build Slovakia together. Let us build cooperation within the V4, let us build a common Europe.'[76]

Matovič's broadening of the vision of cooperation from country to V4 *to Europe* may have been a subtle hint to Orbán that while Slovakia wants to be part of a self-assertive new Central Europe, it does not necessarily want to do this as a means to oppose the EU, the way Orbán was wont to do. Yet, although none of the other three V4 members were as keen on Central European solidarity as a way to fight 'Brussels', all were on board with the Hungarian leader offering Central Europe as a source of wisdom born of its location between the Western core of Europe and its Eastern periphery.

Matovič was deposed during the coronavirus crisis when he bought the Russian Sputnik vaccine without any meaningful consultation with anyone. Most of the public, it turned out, never identified with his very personal leadership. He was unable to push through most of his desired policies, which included large and widely available bonuses for family support.

In that, Matovič was modelling himself on family-friendly policies in Poland and Hungary. The earlier Central European search for a Third Wave between capitalism and socialism finds a distorted echo in twenty-first-century Central European illiberalism, which is open to social welfare policies, though they favour middle-class families more than the down-and-out poor. There is every reason to believe that the illiberal PiS party's family bonus handouts have done more for its popularity than their ideology. The political scientists Bill and Ben Stanley point out that '[i]n the 2020 [parliamentary] election, no opposition party suggested abolishing the popular PiS-initiated family bonuses'.[77] In Hungary, measures intended to encourage the birth rate, including a lifetime tax break for mothers of large families, were accompanied by a whole battery of other welfare regulations by the Orbán government. In that country, too, it is the Jobbik Party, which is often described as an extremist racist organization to the right of Fidesz, that has the most radical social benefit policy, especially vis-à-vis the West. Jobbik politicians would like there to be a 'wage union', with salaries legislated to be the same for comparable work, across the EU.[78]

This does not mean, far from it, that the Third Way ideal of socialism with a human face has continued into the current era. The Hungarian sociologist Dorottya Szikra noted how Orbán's social welfare policies carefully distinguished between the deserving not-so-poor and the not-so-deserving poor, the latter often racialized as Roma.[79] What we see here is a typical mixture of statism and racism reminiscent of the classic fascist regimes.

Viktor Orbán, never a man to mince his words, has always made the racial motivation of his concern with working people abundantly clear. In his infamous 'illiberal democracy' speech of 2014, he refered to the Open Society Foundation, financed by his nemesis, George Soros. Orbán claimed that the Foundation 'published a study not long ago analyzing Western Europe. In this, we could read a sentence which says that Western Europe was so preoccupied with solving the situation of immigrants that it forgot about the white working class'.[80]

It is certain that Soros' Foundation has ever meant to foster this disingenuous, race-based separation between the working class and immigrants. But Orbán does. And to progressive or liberal Europeans, his racist illiberalism is a clear warning: 'in Central Europe we used to believe that Europe was our future; now we feel that we are the future of Europe'.[81]

Through the many transformations of the Central European idea, from German *Mitteleuropa*, through socialism with a human face, to the illiberal rhetoric of the ordinary white man as victim, what has continued is the resurgent desire to make Central Europe central to Europe. Considering the semi-peripheral position of the area, never quite Western, never quite white, however, efforts to make Central Europe the continent's leader might sound somewhat unrealistic. In later chapters I will see them as the expression of an inferiority complex, a desire to lead in a club to which one has not even been fully admitted.

4

Central Europe: Half-Truths and Facts

Throughout the previous chapters, I have alluded to the Eastern Europeanist error of imagining an unbridgeable contrast between Eastern and Western Europe, a trick of the imagination accomplished by leaving out Central Europe in the middle. A major task of this book is to restore Central Europe to the picture.

The restorative surgery that is required commands us to delve in some detail and to some depth into the semi-peripheral area occupied by Central Europe between the West and the East. In this chapter, there will be statistics and figures: I concentrate here on quantitative data. The picture that will emerge consistently is first, that Central Europe is located on many economic and cultural measures somewhere in the middle between West and East, though typically closer to the West; and second, that, at least in Central Europe (but probably also farther East), the things that are said about 'Eastern Europe' are mostly false, even though they may have an element of truth in them. They are half-truths. As Marshall McLuhan once quipped, 'There is a lot of truth in a half-truth'.[1] While a half-truth is not a fact, it raises the question of what makes some, or many, believe that it is. Typically, it is the result of some true facts twisted into a false conclusion by the observer's expectations.

What I will be fact-checking are some of the commonest Eastern Europeanist expectations. Some of them may or may not apply to other parts of Eastern Europe, including Russia, but are at most half-truths when applied to Central Europe. Often, when they do apply to Central Europe, they also apply to semi-peripheral areas in the West. Here is a partial list of them:

- Freedom and democracy failed.
- Corruption is beyond control.
- Poverty is rampant.
- There are gangsters and prostitutes everywhere.
- People are surly and miserable.
- Outmigration is draining the population.

As we examine these common Eastern Europeanist stereotypes, we must insist on avoiding two methodological traps. One is to assume a priori that the facts will differentiate between East and West, and then to arrange them so that this appears to be true. In discussing current affairs, this Eastern Europeanist error can make us view recent European history 'through the lens of the Cold War, more than twenty-five years after it ended'.[2] The Austrian researcher Philipp Ther wrote these words in 2004; as I write it's been much longer since the Cold War, but the lens of Cold War conflict still filters and, I believe, distorts our views of Central Europe, including its illiberal revolt. The other problem with the Eastern Europeanist method is that it limits one's attention to the country level and ignores variation within countries. The most relevant among these is the difference between the large urban centres and the rural areas. Once we drill down to the country-town level, we may find more East–West similarities than differences. In other words, what on a country-by-country comparison seems to oppose East to West, turns out to oppose, even more or instead, city and countryside. This, too, was recognized by Philipp Ther and, as we go on in this chapter, will become crucial to our narrative.

Let me illustrate the first – the a priori assumption of an East–West difference – by a map published by the American Pew Research Center, under the heading, 'Eastern Europeans are more likely to regard their culture as superior to others' (Map 4.1). The data visualized by Pew, contrary to the heading, do not justify such an Eastern Europeanist assumption.

The map's headline does not lie, but it is misleading. If you force an Eastern-vs.-Western Europe divide on the data, the average for this measure of jingoistic nationalism is clearly higher in 'Central

Map 4.1: Which Europeans consider their culture superior to others

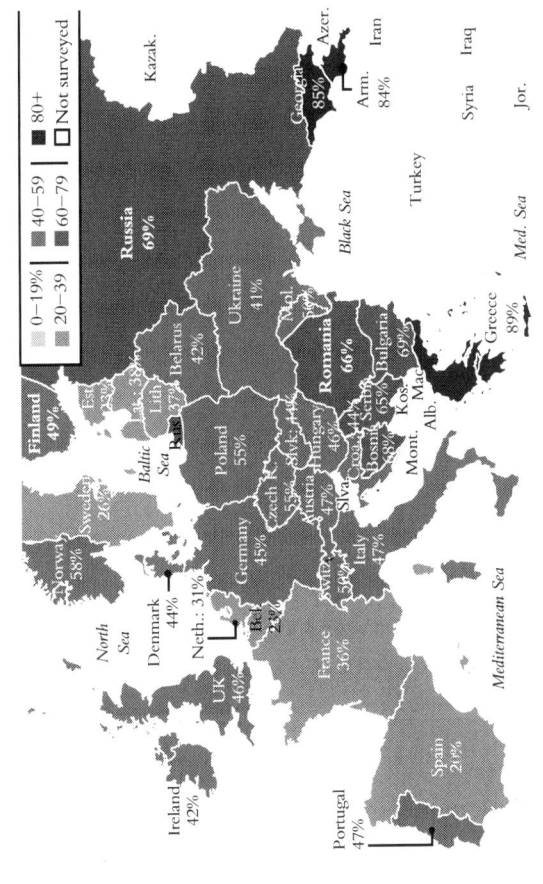

Source: Pew Research Center[3]

and Eastern Europe' than in the West. But actually, an East–West difference is *not* what is most obviously generated by the map, which uses five, not two shades of colour. The dubious distinction of over 80 per cent believing in their own cultural superiority goes to Greece, Georgia, and Armenia, in that order. It may matter that Greece is geographically in the East of Europe, but, not being a post-communist country, it is seldom thought of as 'Eastern Europe' and more often as part of the West. The next most jingoistic group of 60–79 per cent includes Russia. But Russia's companions in this category do not include Central Europe; rather, they are Romania and Bulgaria and parts of the former Yugoslavia – all Balkan countries like Greece and, like Greece and Russia, mostly Eastern Orthodox.

What if countries were grouped by increments of 10 per cent rather than the 20 per cent as is done by the Pew colour code? Then there would be a group of 50 to 59 per cent, and it would include, in order of magnitude:

1. Norway (58 per cent)
2. Poland tied with the Czech Republic (55 per cent)
3. Switzerland tied with Moldova (50 per cent)

The East vs. West split makes little sense when Switzerland is coupled with Moldova.

Nor is the East–West difference so clear-cut within the groups that Pew does shade differently. For example, the 40–59 per cent group includes:

- The United Kingdom
- Portugal
- Finland
- Germany
- Hungary
- Slovakia

Hungary's percentage of 46 per cent is identical to the UK's, but quite different from Russia's or Bulgaria's 69 per cent. So it is not true that 'Eastern Europeans are more likely to regard their culture as superior to others'. Only Eastern Europeanist bias and the desire for a catchy heading could have made the authors see their map as justifying that wording. One is reminded of another saying attributed to Marshall McLuhan: 'I wouldn't have seen it if I didn't believe it'.

The Pew map does not allow us to break down the data to sub-country level, and so to avoid the other methodological fallacy beside prioritizing East–West comparisons: ignoring differences within countries. It is a safe bet, though, that self-satisfied nationalism is greater outside the big cities with their economic and educational elites and relatively multi-ethnic population. Unfortunately, we lack data on that, as a country-by-country comparison has exhausted the curiosity of the researchers. However, we will have occasion to examine that form of bias, later.

Half-Truth 1: Freedom and democracy have failed

Let us now move on to perhaps the most important half-truth when it comes to illiberalism: the alleged failure of Eastern, and by Eastern Europeanist implication, Central, Europe to establish freedom and democracy in the area.

Communism effectively ended in Europe in 1989, when Germans from both sides of the Berlin Wall climbed atop and hacked bricks off together. Soon bulldozers came to finish the job. Like the hated barrier, the entire edifice of Soviet-style socialism came crashing down with barely anything left standing. The Cold War ended with a definitive Western victory: capitalism 1, communism 0. Notoriously, the Stanford University professor, Francis Fukuyama, declared the end of history.[4] In this view, the vast regions emptied of communism became a political, economic, and cultural vacuum, which, when opened up, would naturally suck in capitalism from the West. Rushing in along with capitalism as practised in the West at the time (that is, free-market, neoliberal globalization), expected to bring prosperity, would be liberal democracy, envisaged to bring personal freedom and a feeling of being represented by one's government. Besides the fact that there was no other game in town, isn't that what the peoples of Eastern Europe, as seen in the books, plays, and poems of the pro-democracy 'dissidents', had so long been supposed to be calling for?

Certainly, even the greatest optimists in the West did not expect democracy to take solid root right away in the desolation left by communism. What was to follow 1989 was called 'transition', a term indicating unambiguous direction – a direction toward liberal democratic capitalism as known in the then triumphant West. Expert 'transitologists' came in droves to advise the local neophytes on how to rebuild democracy: some of them sent by governments, others by privately sponsored NGOs; some of them invited, others not, most of them quite welcome at first. Most believed that the transition would end with full capitalist democracy taking solid hold of the East.

There is little agreement on when Western enthusiasm began to fade. Irritation at racist nationalism, now openly expressed after decades of suppression by the communists, surfaced early. Anti-Semitic pronouncements by far-right activists were quickly linked to 'Eastern European' collaboration with the Nazis, which had allegedly not been fully dealt with by the communists. But for some two decades at least, mainstream politics was at first dominated by the dissidents, still celebrated in the West, such as Lech Wałęsa, the Nobel Prize-winning founder of the anti-communist trade union, Solidarity, in Poland, and Václav Havel, the Czech playwright. Each became the first president of their country after communism. In Hungary, József Antall, the first prime minister after communism, was a respected right-of-centre democrat.

It was tiny Slovakia (population 5.3 million) that first saw the rise of a frankly illiberal government, after the country separated from Czechoslovakia at the beginning of 1992. On the Slovak side, the 'velvet divorce' from the Czechs had been negotiated by the former communist (expelled from the Party for his reform views), Vladimír Mečiar. An authoritarian illiberal ahead of his time, Mečiar installed a corrupt regime contemptuous of democratic legalities. Slovaks removed Mečiar in the elections of 1998, though they are still fighting his legacy of lawlessness. It may be that it is the Slovaks' early experience with *mečiarizmus* that now serves as a shield against more extreme forms of illiberalism, and is making Slovakia at the time of writing the most liberal country among the Visegrád Four.

Arguably, one reason Mečiar did not get away with his blatant flaunting of democratic freedoms was that Slovakia, like the rest of post-communist Central Europe, was being watched by the EU. The EU intensely monitored the political, economic, and legal 'transition' in Central European democracies, requiring them to fulfil certain specific conditions before admission. These included adopting the extensive set of European laws known as the *acquis communautaire* as well as a range of capitalist economic practices. In 2004, the European Commission agreed that the process has been accomplished, and the four Central European countries were admitted into the EU (along with the three Baltic States, as well as Slovenia, Malta and Cyprus).

As we have seen, some observers maintain that the alleged slide from democracy began right at this point. They say that the Central Europeans, having adopted EU norms only in letter and not spirit, now felt assured of funds from Brussels and were ready to drop the democratic pretence. Others place the turning point at the global financial crisis of 2008, which revealed to the 'Eastern Europeans' the failings of the previously (allegedly) idolized West. It allowed them to see themselves for the first time as possessing qualities superior to those of the West.[5]

Such analyses are mostly based on hindsight. The quiet chorus of complaints about the East amplified to *forte fortissimo* only when the so-called 'European migration crisis' of 2015–16, propelled illiberal tendencies to the fore in all Visegrád countries. Attention to what was happening in Central Europe increased when Donald Trump won the American presidential elections in 2016, causing some serious handwringing by those (the majority of Western observers) who had thought that Orbán's assault on liberal democracy was limited to 'Central and Eastern Europe', that it recalled Russia but not something that could happen in the West. Now a small industry of books explaining the global emergence of illiberal illiberalism appeared, using Central Europe as an example where democracy has already all but disappeared, and thus as a case study of what happens if illiberalism is left to run unchecked. Two that I mentioned earlier include Anne Applebaum's *The Twilight of Democracy* and Ivan Krastev and Stephen Holmes' *The Light That Failed*.[6] Note how both visualize some form of darkness. Applebaum speaks of the 'twilight' of democracy, a term that can mean the extinguishing of light, but also its rise from darkness. Her concluding message is that both are still possible. Krastev and Holmes' book affords no such ambiguity;

using the past tense, it discusses not light that is failing now, but light that has failed *already*.

Is that really so? Has democracy really died in darkness in Central Europe? The facts do not fully justify such harsh judgement. Reports of the death of liberal democracy in Central Europe are premature.

The Economist

One attempt to measure degrees of democracy across the countries of the world is the periodic review by the Economist Intelligence Unit. The Intelligence Unit does classify all Central European countries as 'flawed democracies'. But, in 2020, this was a category that also included the United States under Donald Trump. Table 4.1

Table 4.1: Degree of democracy in selected states

	Overall score	Political culture	Civil liberties
France	7.99	6.88	8.24
United States of America	7.92	6.25	8.53
Italy	7.74	7.50	7.94
Czech Republic	7.67	7.50	8.53
Cyprus	7.56	7.50	8.53
Slovenia	7.54	6.25	8.24
Belgium	7.51	6.88	8.24
Greece	7.39	7.50	8.53
Slovakia	6.97	5.63	7.65
Argentina	6.95	5.63	7.94
Poland	6.85	5.63	7.06
Bulgaria	6.71	4.38	7.06
Philippines	6.56	4.38	6.47
Hungary	6.56	6.25	6.76
Peru	6.53	5.63	7.35
Croatia	6.50	4.38	6.76
Romania	6.40	3.75	7.06
Serbia	6.22	3.75	7.06
Ukraine	5.81	5.00	5.88
Turkey	4.48	5.63	2.35
Russia	3.31	3.13	4.12
Niger	3.29	4.38	4.71

Source: Economist Intelligence Unit[8]

shows that, as would be expected, Ukraine and Russia ranked below the Czech Republic. But so did Belgium! On the criterion of civil liberties, the Czech Republic equalled the United States and outranked France. To be sure, the other Visegrád countries fell behind; Table 4.1 does not suggest that Central Europe is at the level of the West. But it does show that it is higher than certain other Eastern European countries. And all Central European countries have a score that is much closer to a Western country like France than it is to Russia.

Map 4.2 shows European countries divided into *The Economist*'s four categories, ranging from 'full democracy' to 'authoritarian'. Note that, contrary to Eastern Europeanist assumptions, the border in Europe between democracy and non-democracy puts Central Europe on one side with the West, with Russia and Belarus on the other, described as 'authoritarian'.

Map 4.2: The state of democracy in European countries

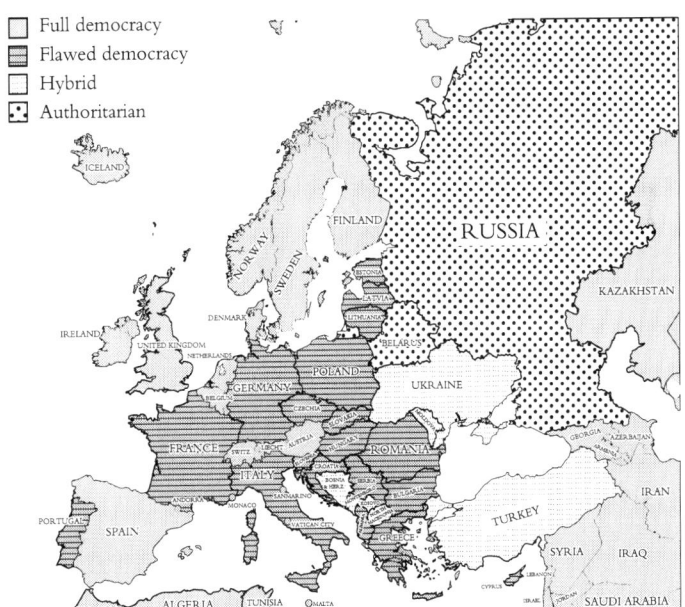

Note: Map created using mapchart.net
Source: Economist Intelligence Unit, 2020[9]

Figure 4.1: Global Freedom scores, 2021 (out of 100)

Country	Score
UK	93
Czech Republic	91
France	90
Italy	90
Slovakia	90
USA	83
Poland	82
Hungary	69
Ukraine	60
Russia	20

Source: Freedom House[10]

Freedom House

Ranking countries on freedom and democracy is also a central preoccupation of the organization Freedom House. Some critics point out that most of this NGO's funding comes from the United States government,[7] a fact that Freedom House insists does not influence its rankings. In fact, the United States does not exactly rank at the top of Freedom House's rankings. Figure 4.1 shows that in 2021 (when Donald Trump was still in power), the Czech Republic and Slovakia both scored higher than the United States, and Poland was only slightly behind. The Czech Republic, in fact, scored higher than France on some measures. Orbán's Hungary's score of 69 was far lower, closer to (pre-Russian-invasion) Ukraine's, but even so much nearer to the US's 83 than to Russia's 20.

Varieties of Democracy

The Varieties of Democracy or V-Dem project at the University of Gothenburg in Sweden produces the largest global dataset on democracy with almost 30 million data points for 202 countries from 1789 to 2020 (Figure 4.2). Here, too, we see the same general picture, except that Poland and especially Hungary under Orbán rank considerably lower. In fact, Hungary's score was about halfway between the UK or France and Russia, and is similar to Ukraine.

Figure 4.2: Liberal Democracy Index, 2020

UK	0.8
France	0.8
Italy	0.78
Slovakia	0.76
USA	0.73
Czech Republic	0.71
Poland	0.49
Hungary	0.37
Ukraine	0.35
Russia	0.1

Source: Varieties of Democracy project[11]

This is still no reason for the Eastern Europeanist lumping Central together with other parts of Eastern Europe. But it is a serious warning that, if the illiberal ascendancy is not reversed, then Eastern Europeanist exaggeration may become a self-fulfilling prophecy.

Reporters Without Borders

If *The Economist* and Freedom House are rightly or wrongly accused of a conservative bias, this is hardly true of Reporters Without Borders, a mostly publicly funded organization, whose efforts on behalf of journalistic freedom enjoy widespread respect. The organization's conclusions about press freedom (Figure 4.3) broadly agree with the findings of *The Economist* and Freedom House. In terms of press freedom, Slovakia and the Czech Republic are comparable to the freest Western countries, and outrank the United States. Although Poland is ranked lower, it is still slightly higher than Greece.

As with *The Economist* and Freedom House rankings, Hungary is the outlier, due to Orbán's much-criticized assault on the country's independent press. (One well-publicized example was the Hungarian authorities' use of the NSO spying software to tap the phones of journalists and others suspected of being critical of the government.)[13] In 2021, Reporters Without Borders classified

Figure 4.3: Press Freedom Index for selected countries

Country	Score
UK	21.59
France	22.6
Slovakia	23.02
Czech Republic	23.38
Italy	23.39
USA	23.93
Poland	28.84
Greece	29.01
Hungary	31.76
Russia	48.71

Note: Higher scores indicate less press freedom
Source: Reporters Without Borders, 2021[12]

Viktor Orbán a 'press predator', alone among EU political leaders. Such activities are just the covert aspect of an open attempt to control the press through the National Media and Info-Communications Authority, a five-member board that is legally empowered according to very vague guidelines to govern the granting of media licences and is authorized even to interfere in media content.

However, according to Reporters Without Borders, even the Hungarian case is not nearly as problematic as that of Russia. What the data suggest is that freedom and democracy in Central Europe, unlike in Russia, still has not quite 'failed' in general, even if one must be anxious lest Hungary's slide toward autocracy under Orbán point the way for others.

Half-Truth 2: Corruption is beyond control

Indispensable to the post-1989 racializing of Central Europeans is a moralizing condemnation of their corrupt society. And indeed, the corrupt ways of post-communist politicians are legend. It was reported, for example, that the average net worth of Hungarian members of parliament increased, under Viktor Orbán, 786 per cent between 2010 and 2021.[14] Péter Új, a journalist and essayist opposed to the Orbán government, mused that Hungarian parliamentarians must be master investors, since their success outstripped NASDAQ and that of Orbán's imagined archenemy, the Hungarian-Jewish-American investor, George Soros.[15]

Of the corruption cases in Central Europe outside Hungary, the affairs of the former Czech Prime Minister Andrej Babiš stand out. As we saw in the Introduction, he was personally accused of embezzling EU funds, as well as engaging in suspicious offshore transactions used to purchase luxury property on the French Riviera.

It is worth recalling, however, that at the same time as Babiš' clandestine business operations contributed to his electoral defeat in 2021, the prime minister of neighbouring, 'Western', Austria, Sebastian Kurz, had to resign on suspicions of corruption.[16] It is not the case that corruption in Central Europe is so different from *all* of the West. It certainly is not as bad as in some other Eastern European areas, including Russia.

Transparency International is an institution that ranks countries according to the perceptions of people doing business there. It is a subjective measure, but the agency's rankings are widely respected. Figure 4.4 is a list of countries ranked by the Transparency International Corruption Perception Index (CPI).

The ranking that emerges from Figure 4.4 accords, at least for the most part, with the pattern we have seen in the other quantitative data discussed above. In this case it is true that the countries at the top are all bona fide Western countries. However, the gap within the Western set of countries is greater than between some of the Central European countries and them. For example, the US score is only 76 per cent of the Danish, while the Czech score is 81 per cent of the American. Similarly, the Polish score is 81 per cent of the French, but the French is only 78 per cent of the Danish. To put it another way, the difference between the Central European and most of the Northwest European countries on the list is smaller than the difference between the latter and Denmark.

It is not the case that the data suggest an East-West difference as primary. While the extent of corruption certainly does vary among different countries, as Adam Fabry points out, one must ask, after the *Panama Papers* affair revealed the great degree of corruption among politicians and business people in the West, how corruption can be attributed particularly to the post-communist East.[18]

Figure 4.4: Corruption Perception Index (CPI) scores of selected countries

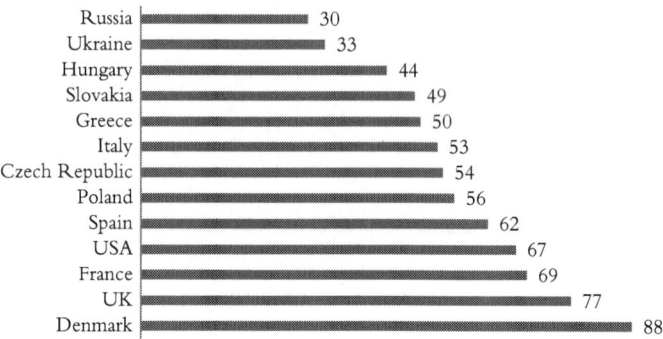

Note: Lower numbers indicate higher corruption rates
Source: Transparency International[17]

One of the most contentious issues when talking about corruption is the justice system. Judges may be corrupted by money or by the pressure of government figures. The Polish PiS government's attacks on the freedom of the judiciary have been well publicized, and similar problems emerged in Orbán's Hungary. However, the public's perceptions of the independence of the justice system do not differ very much between Central and Western Europe. The results of a survey on the subject presented by the European Commission[19] show that only in the Czech Republic did more than half the public express trust in the country's judicial institutions. The Czech result was not appreciably different from that of France or Belgium. In Poland and Hungary the public was indeed more disappointed. Poles were less confident than Hungarians. Slovaks, whose justice system is far less often discussed in the West, were particularly unhappy. Note, however, that the Polish respondents were slightly *less* concerned about their justice system than Italians. Spanish interviewees were also less confident in the independence of their courts than Central Europeans.

On the ground, certainly, there have been well-attested cases of criminal corruption, including by organized gangs connected to personalities in the government or the justice system. Tiny Slovakia (population: 5.3 million) has been particularly vulnerable. Or perhaps we just know more about organized crime there, because of the country's extraordinarily talented investigative journalists and its lively free press.

One such journalist was Ján Kuciak. In the winter of 2018, Kuciak's investigation was zeroing in on the Italian 'Ndrangheta, who were active in Slovakia in agriculture, the drug trade, and tax fraud. One of the mafiosi, Antonio Vadalà, bragged of having the Slovak customs officials in his pocket. Among his suspected operations was hiding drugs in shipments of vegetables produced on farms in Eastern Slovakia, on land he and his cronies bought in part with misappropriated EU funds. Vadalà had an affair with a former nude model and Miss Universe contestant, Mária Trošková. The romance did not last, but the two remained business associates, which some suspect contributed to Trošková's spectacular career success: she became an official adviser to Prime Minister Robert Fico. Kuciak found out that Vadalà's other contacts included several high officials in the Slovak state administration.

Kuciak was also on the trail of Marian Kočner, one of the country's richest businessmen, investigated and later charged by the police in a number of wide-ranging criminal plots, involving people at the highest level of government, the judicial system, and police. Kočner was highly irritated by Kuciak's journalism. In December 2017, he was recorded threatening the journalist, promising to uncover 'dirt' on him and on his father, mother, and siblings. Kuciak was living with his partner, Martina Kušnírová, in a small house near Bratislava. On 21 February 2018, Martina's mother called the police because she had not received her daughter's daily phone call for four days. Upon arrival at the house, the officers found the couple dead, the result of gun shots fired at close range. Kuciak and Kušnírová were both 27 years old. They had not resisted.

The murders shocked the Slovak public. Spontaneously organized into a grassroots movement, 'For a Decent Slovakia', thousands of citizens demonstrated on the streets for justice and for an end to the official corruption in government. The police chief Marek Gajdoš, accused of improper contacts with Kočner, resigned, but replacing him with another supporter of the ruling Smer Party, Milan Lučanský, did not cool the crowd's temper. Eventually the whole Smer government of Robert Fico had to go. Lučanský was himself accused of corruption, and on the second try succeeded in hanging himself in prison.[20] The predictable conspiracy theories began to circulate, but most observers agreed that a genuine effort had begun, under pressure, to cleanse the country's institutions. How wide-ranging the campaign was is illustrated by the fact that among the high officials arrested and placed under investigation were 13 judges.

At the time of my writing, the dust has not yet settled. Judicial proceedings have been of partial success. Kočner remained in jail for his other crimes, but the prosecution was unable to prove that he had ordered Kuciak's murder. His own honey pot, Alena Zsuzsová, known for her erotic correspondence with several influential men, was charged with and convicted of ordering several murders, and was widely held to have ordered Kuciak's, too, on behalf of Kočner. But this, too, remained unproven. Two men, Miroslav Marček, who pulled the trigger, and Tomáš Szabó, who directly assisted the murder, were convicted and received lengthy sentences. As various appeals and judicial reviews continued, it was clear that if the whole truth is ever known, it will be a few years down the line, perhaps when a film or TV series is created of this sordid set of crimes. But while a shadow of doubt lingers on the complete transparency of the investigation, the renewed Slovak state, whatever its shortcomings, must be congratulated on a genuine attempt to rid itself of mafia domination.

The deep penetration of state institutions by criminal crony networks may easily bring to mind the Yeltsin years in Russia, which witnessed the rise of a group of oligarchs with connections to the government. But the Slovak and the Russian cases have led to very different results: in Slovakia more democracy, and in Russia more authoritarianism. The chaos under Yeltsin was muscled into a disciplined system under centralized control by Putin. The Russian opposition figure, Grigory Yavlinsky, describes the 'Putin System' as one in which 'a narrow ruling circle ... has secured a monopolistic control over the pyramid of administrative power while preventing any significant concentration of political resources in the hands of any other group'.[21] Among the businesspeople who tried to defy Putin was Mikhail Khodorkovsky, who used his money to support the opposition. In 2003, Putin's government put him on trial and jailed him, until Putin deigned to pardon him in 2013. Yavlinsky writes that

> From then on, the authorities became more and more determined to curb rich Russians' opportunities to use their personal fortunes toward political activities outside the government's control. In practice, this was pursued primarily through the 'ruling party', United Russia. The party assumed the functions of a vertical supervisory authority, extending from Moscow into the country's periphery. It has been charged with tracking the political activities of regional business owners and integrating them into the unified system of the authoritarian state while resolutely blocking any attempts to organize or to fund social and political projects that have not gained the consent of [the] vertical hierarchy of power.[22]

Nothing approaching such a vertical authoritarian system exists in Slovakia, although the first prime minister after the breakup of Czechoslovakia, Vladimír Mečiar, may have dreamed of it. There seems to be little will to install a 'Putin system' in Slovakia. Slovak economic and political corruption resembles the Italian rather than the Russian model.

In Poland, in spite of the government's consistent assaults on the independence of the justice system, the Supreme Audit Office, mandated by the constitution, has been able to investigate waste and corruption in government spending. Marian Banaś, a former Solidarity activist from the governing PiS party, became a thorn in the side of the government when he insisted on proper audits of its spending on elections and pandemic control. The government tried to turn the tables on him, accusing him among other things of owning a building used as a brothel. Banaś denied the accusation, and no charges were laid.[23]

Although corruption in Central European countries is a significant problem, it is not generally comparable to Russia's and, to return to Italy once more, is generally less pervasive than in that 'Western' country. The one exception where this could not be said with the same confidence is Orbán's Hungary. There, the illiberal leader installed, through his Fidesz party, a form of vertical control reminiscent of One Russia solid enough to survive to a large extent even if he were defeated in a national election.

The story of Lajos Simicska illustrates well how Orbán's largesse required strict obedience. Simicska and Orbán were schoolmates. As prime minister, Orbán favoured Simicska with various important administrative and party positions; he was, for example, at one point the Fidesz treasurer. Orbán encouraged his friend among other things to take control of the media, to ensure that they were friendly to the government. However, after Orbán's re-election in 2014, Simicska had some disagreement with Orbán, the exact nature of which remains unknown. The conflict may have been started by Orbán removing several of Simicska's protégés from office, and reportedly encouraging others to resign from his media corporations. Simicska was heard using a profanity about Orbán, which the prime minister considered to be the last straw. One day Simicska was sitting in a meeting with his media executives, when an assistant brought to him a yellow device, which Simicska promptly put into his briefcase. He explained that it was a tool for measuring ambient radiation. Evidently, the businessman was afraid that Orbán would have him poisoned, Russian style. Two days following Orbán's next triumphant parliamentary election victory on 6 April 2014, Simicska sold all of his media interests, including a leading commercial television station and the paper *Magyar Nemzet*, which promptly returned to its job of spewing Fidesz propaganda.[24]

The Orbán-Simicska conflict shows how close Orbán came to being a Putin-style autocrat. But even Hungary has never become another Russia. Simicska was neither jailed nor poisoned.

In short, on the criminal corruption count, as on others, the Central European situation is *grosso modo* intermediate between the West on one hand and parts of Eastern Europe, especially Russia, on the other. Between the two, Central Europe is closer to some parts of the West.

Half-Truth 3: There are gangsters and prostitutes everywhere

The Eastern Europeanist perception of alleged Central European corruption is based partly on facts, but it is partly a moral judgement that radically inverts the amoral essence of capitalism, and projects it to Europe's ex-socialist East. Money, not ethics, makes the world go round in capitalism. If taken to its dystopic extreme, capitalism produces a man or woman who, stripped of any moral compunction, will do anything at all for money. If we add gender stereotyping to the mix, then we end up with two tropes of the ultimate rule of money over morality: the gangster and the prostitute. The man will kill and rob without restraint, and the woman will sell her body without modesty. We are, of course, talking about unacceptable classic stereotypes, which brutally assert that sex workers are 'whores' who offer their bodies voluntarily. But even recognizing that she is being coerced by a male gangster may just complete the picture by adding unrestrained patriarchy to unrestrained capitalism: the unlimited rule of men to the unlimited rule of money. The gangster and the prostitute are the frightening image, the *Schreckbild*, of the essence of capitalism. It is an act of comfort, of psychological self-defence, to imagine these figures, falsely, as flourishing especially outside the Western liberal form of capitalism, which is supposed to be hemmed in by ethical consideration.

But how many gangsters are there really in Central Europe? We have seen that the presence of gangs in Slovakia, for example, is deeply disturbing. Even so, Slovakia is nothing like the gangster-and-prostitute ridden 'Eastern European' tourist spot portrayed in the horror film *Hostel*. Here Western tourists are lured into a darkly dystopic, hopelessly poor Slovakia, hoping to exploit pretty but desperate local women. They fall victim to sadistic members of the Elite Hunting Club, organized for oligarchs who delight in killing and mutilating tourists.

In reality, visitors to this and other parts of Central Europe will find an area that ranks among the lowest in crime in the world. For peace and security, there is also a country ranking, this time by the Institute for Economics and Peace. Figure 4.5 shows the Global Peace Index (GPI) for various countries: the lower the number the better.

Figure 4.5: Global Peace Index for selected countries

Denmark	1.316
Czech Republic	1.383
Hungary	1.54
Slovakia	1.55
Bulgaria	1.607
Poland	1.654
Spain	1.699
Italy	1.754
UK	1.801
France	1.892
Greece	1.933
USA	2.401
Ukraine	2.95
Russia	3.093

Source: Institute for Economics and Peace[25]

The Index shows the four Central European countries to be among the most peaceful and secure, ahead of most Western European countries and close to Scandinavian Denmark. In fact, illiberal propagandists justified their refusal to accept migrants from outside Europe during the 'migration crisis' of 2015–16, by falsely blaming the higher rates of violence in much of the West on migrants of colour (without commenting on the low rates in Denmark, or on the very much higher rates in Russia).

Sadly, criminal activity in Central Europe does include trafficking of people for forced labour, including sex work.[26] However, there is no justification for the perception that sex work is a particularly common feature of Central Europe. Counting the number of sex workers is notoriously difficult, though it may be slightly easier than counting gangsters. Figure 4.6 compares countries in terms of the number of sex workers per 10,000. It shows Poland and France both to have five, the Czech Republic 12 (one over the UK's 11), and Hungary a much higher 21 but still less than the US at 31. Slovakia's sex workers, 40 per 10,000, are proportionately even more numerous than America's, but no country even remotely approaches Russia's hard-to-believe figure of 208. The Russian data, even if only partly reliable,[27] suggest that the image of widespread prostitution in Central *and* Eastern Europe is amplified by extension, in the Eastern Europeanist imagination, of Russian circumstances onto Central Europe. Among the issues with such figures is that they cover up the extent

Figure 4.6: Number of sex workers per 10,000 population in selected countries in 2018

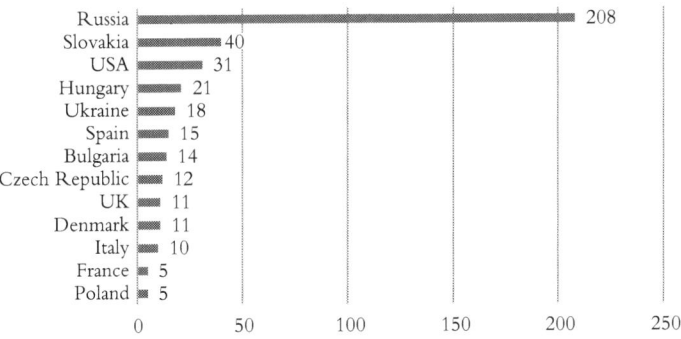

Source: Joint United Nations Program on HIV and AIDS[28]

to which it is poor and racialized women who are forced into sex work, either by economic circumstances or by direct violence and intimidation. One may suspect poverty as well as race to play a factor in the United States and in Russia, which includes a large population of Central Asians. In Slovakia and Hungary, the poor prominently include the Roma.[29]

The Czech actor, Martina Babišová (no relation to Prime Minister Babiš) had to work very hard on acquiring an Irish-English accent before she was able to launch a career in Ireland, at which point she was at last able to declare, 'I no longer belong to the category, "from the East", so I no longer have to portray only prostitutes'.[30] Recall Nasar Meer's test for telling if one is targeted by racism: at the minimum it makes life harder[31] (Chapter 2). Babišová's is an example of how being Eastern European makes life harder.

Half-Truth 4: People are surly and miserable

The gloomy landscape of imagined 'Central and Eastern Europe', infested with gangsters and prostitutes, is not surprisingly inhabited by an assembly of dejected and unfriendly people. Under communism there was little incentive to be friendly to patrons of hotels and restaurants, and so tourist services rightly got a reputation for awfulness. This reputation is amplified by the image of allegedly

Figure 4.7: Human Development Index for selected countries

Norway	0.957
USA	0.926
UK	0.923
France	0.921
Czech Republic	0.9
Italy	0.892
Poland	0.88
Slovakia	0.86
Hungary	0.854
Russia	0.824
Bulgaria	0.816
Ukraine	0.779
Moldova	0.75

Source: United Nations Development Programme[32]

ingrained authoritarianism: being bossed around is not conducive to wearing a smile. Confirmation bias may still seem to fulfil expectations of grey misery for casual tourists to Central Europe, but a quick look at TripAdvisor reveals no more complaints about unfriendliness than in most other places. There is, unfortunately, no Global Grouchiness Index to provide us with anything aspiring to be an objective measure. However, there are two measures, one objective and the other subjective, of life satisfaction that we may use here.

Human Development Index

The Human Development Index intends to provide a measure of well-being that is not entirely based on money. According to its sponsor, the United Nations Development Programme, 'The Human Development Index (HDI) is a summary measure of average achievement in key dimensions of human development: a long and healthy life, being knowledgeable and have a decent standard of living' (see Figure 4.7).[33]

Here we can certainly see a rough West-to-East decrease in the HDI, but as is often the case, the Czech Republic is among the Western countries, with its HDI very close to those of Spain, France, and Italy. But, once again, the divisions *within* the East and the West are as great as those *between* the two. Even if we take Hungary, the country with the lowest HDI of the four Visegrád Group members, it is about equally distant from the lowest-ranking country on our list, Moldova, as it is from the no. 1 ranked country on our list and worldwide, Norway: Norway's index is 112 per cent higher than Hungary's, but Hungary's is 114 per cent higher than Moldova's. So there is no justification here for an Eastern Europeanist lumping together of all of post-communist 'Eastern Europe', any more than there is for considering the East–West divide to be the main determining factor of a country's 'human development'.

Happiness Index

The subjective state of the public – do they feel happy? – is the concern of the World Happiness Report. Subjective attitudes are important to understanding illiberalism. Unhappy people may voice their frustration by rallying to illiberal leaders and their ideas (Figure 4.8).

In this case again, the Czech Republic is the most Western-like, outflanking Spain, France, and Italy; but Slovakia follows Italy closely and Poland and Hungary are not far behind. There is then a major gap between them and the countries of the Balkans (including never-communist Greece) and the ex-USSR, where people appear to be considerably less happy.

We are fortunate in that the 2020 World Happiness Report also ranked cities (Figure 4.9). As I have argued, a country-by-country

Figure 4.8: Happiness Index for selected countries

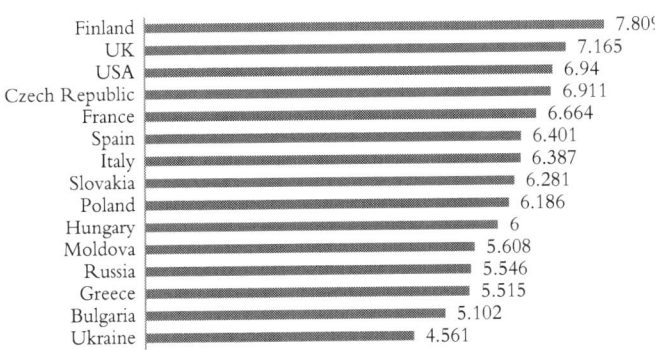

Source: World Happiness Report 2020[34]

Figure 4.9: World Happiness Index for selected cities, 2017–19

Helsinki	7.828
London	6.782
Paris	6.635
Prague	6.62
Madrid	6.5
Bratislava	6.383
Barcelona	6.38
Tokyo	5.989
Lisbon	5.66
Budapest	5.642

Source: World Happiness Report 2020[35]

comparison encourages Eastern Europeanism. It overlooks the similarities between regions in one country and another. Along the East–West dimension, it is blind to the importance of the similarities between the big globally connected cities and 'the West', as well as those between the rural areas and the Western periphery.

Confirming this fact, the Happiness Report ranks Prague right next to Paris. Bratislava came out just a little happier than Barcelona. Even in apparently unhappy Hungary, Budapest was ranked very close to Lisbon. Although Polish cities were not evaluated, there was certainly no East–West divide detectable in the city list at all.

The city ranking further disconfirms the stereotype of 'Eastern European' sulkiness in Central Europe. Poland, the Czech Republic, Slovakia, and Hungary do not necessarily provide today a mental landscape of sunny happiness, but they are not much different on that count from the West.

Half-Truth 5: Poverty is rampant

Many of the Eastern Europeanist stereotypes are connected to the notion that the region is desperately poor. This is the supposed economic backdrop to the alleged unhappiness of its people, of their willingness to resort to crime or to sell themselves into sex work, of their desperate desire to move to the West. Their poverty is taken, implicitly or explicitly, as testimony to their backward cultural characteristics: even when capitalism is gifted to them, they are unable to take advantage of it to become rich. They are congenitally working class, or rather, forever peasants.

Truth be told, to most Central *and* Eastern European citizens, greater prosperity was probably the most personally felt of the many hopes of 1989. Writing about the post-Soviet space, the Belarusian author Svetlana Alexievich voiced one of her characters to say, 'Most people were not anti-Soviet; they only wanted to live well. They really wanted blue jeans, VCRs, and most of all, cars.'[36] In communist Central Europe, people were understandably anti-Soviet, but their frustration with communism was similarly focused on the lack of consumer goods.

If anyone expected then to catch up with West Germany or Britain within a few years, over 30 years later they are still waiting. But the gap has narrowed. Today, Poland has more cars per capita than Germany, and the Czech Republic more than Belgium.[37] Once the Europe-wide trend of biking and bike lanes reaches Western levels in Central Europe, perhaps the gap in car ownership will close. But what's clear is that the era of 'Eastern Europeans' in Central Europe gawking at Western automobiles is long over. So are the shortages and shoddy products of the communist era, which, it is good to remind remote observers, ended decades ago, before most pre-mid-life-crisis Central Europeans were born. In fact, if Central Europeans are fairly happy today, it may be because their economies have improved. As in any capitalist country, the rich have benefited more from economic upturns and suffered less from downturns than the poor, but most people have seen an improvement. The poor cousins aren't as poor as they used to be, which may be why they're starting to talk back.

To discuss the economy of Central Europe, I am going to use a number of common indicators. None of them is perfect, but together they disprove the picture of abject 'Eastern European' poverty.

In suggesting that the Visegrád area is economically far from the most miserable, either in the world or in Europe, I do not mean to defend its governments or its business elites. Later we will see that the economy is indeed a motivator of serious discontent, but that is based not so much on an extreme, 'Eastern European' lack of wealth as on the precarity of people's means of livelihood. Economic insecurity, not poverty is the main cause of dissatisfaction, though poverty certainly is a serious issue as well. Just like in the West.

Figure 4.10: Gross domestic product in selected countries, purchasing power parity dollars, per capita, 2019 (Spain: 2020)

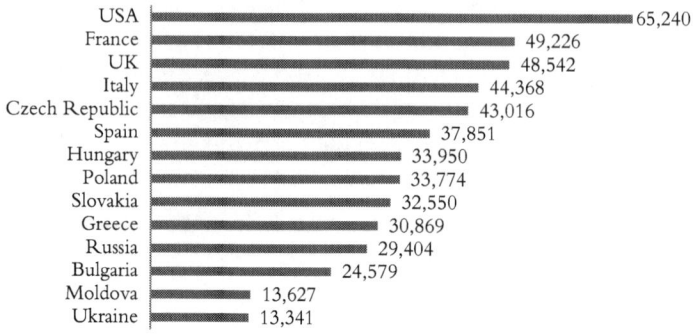

Source: OECD, except for Moldova and Ukraine (World Bank)

Gross domestic product

A very rough measure of an area's wealth is its gross domestic product (GDP). If we look at GDP statistics on a country-by-country basis, then we get the facts shown in Figure 4.10. It is a list based on GDP in US dollars at purchasing power parity (GDP PPP), per capita. Purchasing power parity means that data are adjusted for different price levels in different places. One hundred dollars will go much farther in Budapest than in Paris or New York. GDP PPP is a figure that aims to eliminate such differences, making a fairer estimate of how well you can live if you stay home. (The situation of outmigrants from Central Europe will be discussed later.)

Figure 4.10 suggests no clear difference between West and East. The Czech Republic does better on the GDP PPP measure than Spain and is close to Italy, two southern European countries usually reckoned as part of the West. All the Central European countries do better than Greece. And consider the following facts: The US GDP PPP is 193 per cent of Poland's but also it is 147 per cent of Italy's. In comparison, the Polish GDP is 115 per cent of Russia's, and as much as 253 per cent of pre-invasion Ukraine's! To suggest that the main division in the data is that between the long-time capitalist West and the post-communist East is false. The richest Western countries are at the top, but the divisions within each group are greater than the differences, and there is overlap at the East–West border.

Figure 4.11: Gross domestic product in selected countries, regions, and cities, purchasing power parity dollars, per capita, 2019

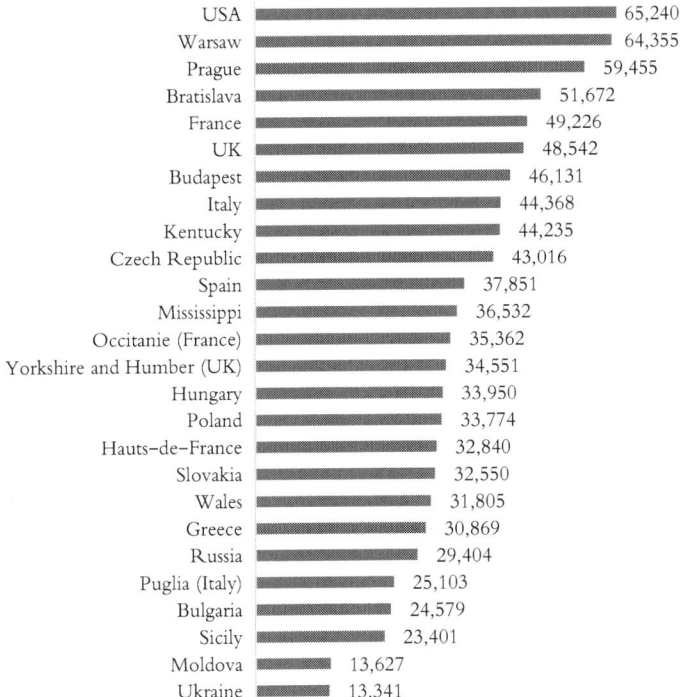

Source: OECD, except for Moldova and Ukraine (World Bank)[38]

Once again, a truer comparison between East and West emerges when we compensate for the fallacy of looking only at country-level data, and include also the regional and urban levels. We will compare some of the more peripheral regions of the West with the 'world-class' capitals of Central Europe; that is, the periphery of the Western core with the core of the Eastern periphery. Though long, Figure 4.11 deserves detailed inspection. It proves a point that is crucial to my argument about illiberalism. Central Europe resembles the peripheral areas of the West (such as the State of Mississippi or the English county of Yorkshire and Humber), in this case in terms of how well (or not) a person can live there. At the same time, some of the big cities of Central Europe resemble the general level of living in the richest countries of the West.[39] This has clear consequences on how people vote in elections. The white periphery tends to vote illiberal, while the prosperous cities support a progressive agenda.

Figure 4.11 shows that GDP PPP in Warsaw is almost at the American level, and far above not only the overall country figure for Poland, but also every Western European country on the list. At the same time, the selected peripheral regions of Western Europe rank roughly the same as the Visegrád countries taken as a whole. Wales does the worst, coming just below the lowest-ranked Central European country, Slovakia.

It could and should be objected that GDP data have problems; I look at some of those next. Here are some of the things to consider that might limit the validity of GDP as a measure of prosperity:

- the amount of wealth produced in the country but transferred outside of it;
- the unequal distribution of the wealth produced in the country;
- the difference between GDP and take-home pay.

Let us now briefly turn to these indicators. Do they present a sharp West-to-East difference, with Central Europe stuck on the impoverished, Eastern side?

Foreign investment

One of the scholars concerned with the drain of profits away from countries that produce it is the celebrated French economist, Thomas Piketty. One of Piketty's regular blogs in the French daily *Le Monde*,[40] made quite a splash when it suggested, contrary to common belief, that Central European countries may be getting a raw deal from the EU. The focus, he suggested, is often on the subventions sent to Central Europe from Brussels, suggesting that 'Eastern Europe' depends on the EU for its prosperity. However, Piketty pointed out, Western European businesses take out much more in the form of profits in Central Europe than the EU puts in in the form of financial support. EU subventions, seen in this light, are actually indirect subsidies to Western business. The East loses more than it gains.

What happened to Piketty's observation is a good example of how left-wing ideas get highjacked by the nationalist right, which is as common an occurrence in Central Europe as it is anywhere. It has endeared Piketty to some nationalist leaders in Central Europe, even though they have no intention of borrowing his many other insights into the economy of the area. The Polish Prime Minister, Mateusz Morawiecki, acknowledged Piketty's influence as he observed that an inordinate amount of money earned by foreign investors in his country was 'transferred every year in the form of dividends or interest on capital, interest on loans, deposits and current accounts'.[41] Viktor Orbán was probably influenced by Piketty's blog when he stated, unequivocally, that '[t]hrough the budget of the European Union, it returns to other Member States a portion of the profits its companies make in the Single Market' and so, in the case of Germany which he was addressing, 'Hungary's membership of the EU does not cost Germany any money; on the contrary, Germany makes money from our membership'.[42]

The leader of the Czech extreme right Party of Direct Democracy (SPD), Tomio Okamura (yes, he was born in Tokyo!), created a poster centred on the portrait of Thomas Piketty. In oversized letters, the poster, published on Okamura's much visited Facebook page, asks, 'Where is money from the Czech Republic escaping to?' This is followed by 'Western Europe lives off us' and: 'Czechs are a defeated nation. They lose the most money with membership in the EU, as the world-renowned economist, Piketty, has clearly stated'.[43]

If indeed the money 'escaping' (*odtéká*, literally leaking out) is significant, then GDP is misleading as a measure of a nation's wealth – because the nation does not keep it. However, in this particular case Piketty's generally brilliant insight is questionable. It compares only what flows in the form of EU subsidies and investments with what flows out as foreign investors' profits. But in the case of profits, what flows out had first flown in. Foreign businesses also make investments in Central Europe, which need to be included, along with EU subventions, as capital *inflows*. You cannot consider EU inflows alone, and then compare them to private funds as outflows. Once inflows from private investors are also taken into account, then the result is that the four Visegrád countries maintain relatively balanced capital flows. Table 4.2, which also includes other countries, shows that in Central Europe in 2019, only the Czech Republic showed a capital flows deficit,

Table 4.2: Capital flows in selected countries

Country	Capital flows (USD million)	Exchange rate	Capital flows period
UK	41,819	32,374 million GBP at currency rate 1.2917455395 on 30/09/2019	09/2019–09/2020
France	20,899	17,091 million EUR at currency rate of 1.2228112197 on 31/12/2020	12/2019–12/2020
Italy	19,447	16,279 million EUR at currency rate of 1.1946333284 on 30/11/2020	11/2019–11/2020
Russia	5,087	USD	09/2019–09/2020
Spain	5,059	4,235 million EUR at currency rate of 1.1946333284 on 30/11/2020	11/2019–11/2020
Poland	2,649	2,217 million EUR at currency rate of 1.1946333284 on 30/11/2020	11/2019–11/2020
Ukraine	2,420	USD	09/2019–09/2020
Hungary	1,611	1,374 million EUR at currency rate of 1.1723775153 on 30/09/2020	09/2019–09/2020
Slovakia	900	753 million EUR at currency rate of 1.1946333284 on 30/11/2020	11/2019–11/2020
Bulgaria	366	306 million EUR at currency rate of 1.1946333284 on 30/11/2020	11/2019–11/2020

Table 4.2: Capital flows in selected countries (continued)

Country	Capital flows (USD million)	Exchange rate	Capital flows period
Czech Republic	−300	−6,594 million CZK at currency rate of 0.0454562371 on 30/11/2020	11/2019–11/2020
Moldova	−380	USD	09/2019–09/2020
USA	−600	USD	12/2019–12/2020
Greece	−767	−642 million EUR at currency rate of 1.1946333284 on 30/11/2020	11/2019–11/2020

Source: Trading Economics[44]

and it was not a particularly serious one. In the other three Visegrád countries, slightly more capital came in than 'escaped' out.

There is much that is wrong with what foreign companies wrought in Central Europe. But bleeding the area of capital is not high on the list.

Inequality

If foreigners don't siphon off more of the GDP in Central Europe than in the West, then how about the rich within the country? Doesn't an inordinate amount of the GDP increase flow into the coffers of the 'oligarchs'?

The notion of 'oligarch' is worth examining. There are not many observers who would deny the connections between the Russian government and oligarchs, both tainted by corruption and often violent crime. Much of the Russian-style pattern of post-communist business corruption is apparent in Central Europe as well. Yet there are also local entrepreneurs who are neither less nor more honest than most in the West. Daniel Křetínský, who was 14 when communism fell in 1989, is one of the Czech Republic's richest people. He was implicated in the Panama Papers scandal, which hardly makes him any more compromised than many major Western investors. Still, when Křetínský acquired a share of the major French newspaper, *Le Monde*, he met with stiff resistance, and was described as an 'oligarch'. The word technically refers to a rich or otherwise well-connected person who exercises power through or over the government. It should not be applied to Křetínský, who is not known to have unduly strong links to either the Czech or any other government. Even so, the label seemed to stick. 'Oligarch' has become a term for any rich person from Russia *or* other parts of Eastern Europe, on the assumption that Eastern European wealth cannot possibly be legitimate. As Jérôme Lefilliâtre, the author of a biography of Křetínský, explained, 'In France there are still many people who automatically connect the Czech Republic with the Russian sphere of influence. And Russia obviously tries to influence media in France. Russia Today broadcasts here, spreads disinformation, we know what Russia can and does do.'[45] Lefilliâtre admits that such Eastern Europeanism 'is a mistake'. But he knows that it remains common in the West, where competition from the East is not welcome, not only if it comes from Russia (or China) but even when it comes from Central Europe, that is, from parts of the EU that had ostensibly been *expected* to become successfully capitalist.

The truth is that wealth inequalities trouble the whole world, and the anger that some are obscenely rich while the rest struggles is rightly listed among the causes of illiberalism everywhere. But in this respect, Central Europe fares relatively well.

A commonly used index of economic inequality is the Gini Index. It is no more free of flaws than any other macroeconomic indicator, but it is the only one we've got where worldwide figures are readily available. Figure 4.12 ranks a number of countries according to this index. Higher numbers mean more inequality. Of the four Visegrád countries, Hungary has the most inequality. But even Hungary's rank is still better than that of France or the United Kingdom. In fact, the Central European countries as a group are among those with the lowest inequality rates as measured by the Gini Index.

The relative equality in the post-communist EU countries is almost certainly due to their communist heritage, and sadly, we may expect it to slip as time goes on. At the same time, they preserved much more of an egalitarian social structure than Russia or Ukraine, which have

Figure 4.12: Gini Index of inequality for selected countries

Slovakia	22.8
Czech Republic	24
Hungary	28
Poland	28.5
France	29.2
Greece	31
Italy	32.8
Spain	33
UK	33.5

Source: Eurostat (2019)[46]

descended to the kind of inequality seen in Italy. So a generalization in any objective terms about 'inequality in Eastern Europe' would be quite wrong. Contrary to the stereotype of the 'Eastern European oligarch' lording it over a population living in abject misery, to find centres of even more extreme social inequality in Europe, one is well advised to start looking either farther East or – to the West.

Wages

Nevertheless, as in any capitalist society, inequality is a central feature of the economy in Central Europe, too. For most people, who live on salary, a high GDP is meaningless if it does not mean bigger paychecks. Table 4.3 shows the average annual wage in selected European countries and regions, both at the nominal, unadjusted level and when adjusted for purchasing power.

Clearly, a lot depends on how far money will go locally. A Warsaw worker can live better at home than in an average Italian town. The proverbial *plombier polonais*[47] might still want to move from Warsaw to France to improve his standard of living, but on that count alone he would not be more motivated than an Italian plumber.

The net wage statistics, nevertheless, do show a clearer difference than GDP (Table 4.10) between Western and even Southern Europe (that is, Spain and Italy, though not Greece) on one hand, and Central Europe on the other. It is obvious that, in spite of what is

Table 4.3: Net annual wage in selected countries and regions in Europe, for a single person without children working full time and earning the medium wage, in euro, 2018[48]

Country/region/city	Yearly net medium wage (PPP)	Yearly net medium wage nominal	Percentage of UK average (PPP)	Percentage of Warsaw region average (PPP)
USA	30,819	35,528	107	149
UK	28,725	34,279	100	139
Yorkshire and Humber (UK)	26,302	31,387	92	127
Wales	25,696	30,664	89	124
Kentucky	24,918	28,726	87	120
France	24,612	28,005	86	119
Occitanie	22,843	25,992	80	110
Hauts-de-France	22,521	25,625	78	109
Spain	21,976	21,198	77	106
Mississippi	21,399	24,668	74	103
Warsaw region	20,689	12,318	72	100
Italy	20,640	21,295	72	100
Prague region	19,131	14,137	67	92
Greece	18,140	15,713	63	88
Puglia	17,935	18,504	62	87
Budapest county	17,459	11,512	61	84
Poland	16,119	9,597	56	78
Sicily	15,627	16,123	54	76
Czech Republic	15,233	11,256	53	74
Bratislava region	14,652	12,341	51	71
Karlovy Vary region (Czech Republic)	13,160	9,724	46	64
Hungary	13,023	8,587	45	63
Slovakia	11,238	9,465	39	54

Table 4.3: Net annual wage in selected countries and regions in Europe, for a single person without children working full time and earning the medium wage, in euro, 2018 (continued)

Country/region/city	Yearly net medium wage (PPP)	Yearly net medium wage nominal	Percentage of UK average (PPP)	Percentage of Warsaw region average (PPP)
Bulgaria	10,531	5,447	37	51
Russia	10,514	5,843	37	51
Szabolcs-Szatmár-Bereg region (Hungary)	9,605	6,333	33	46
Prešov region (Slovakia)	8,876	7,475	31	43
Ukraine	7,807	2,784	27	38
Moldova	6,951	3,140	24	34

Note: PPP = purchasing power parity

still a *relatively* egalitarian distribution of wealth in Central Europe, a highly disproportionate amount of the wealth generated since the return to capitalism has gone to employers and investors, rather than people living off their wages.

The pattern we have seen throughout this chapter still applies, however: on the whole, Central Europe is below Western Europe, but above the rest of Eastern Europe, and on some measures closer to the West than to the East. This is again clearest when differences between the urban centres and the provincial regions are taken into account. The average Warsaw worker makes only 72 per cent of what the average British worker makes, even on the PPP measure; the figure for the average worker in Poland as a whole is 56 per cent. But then, the average Russian or Bulgarian worker makes only 51 per cent of what the Warsaw worker makes (and only 37 per cent of the UK average).

Purchasing power parity statistics never tell the whole story. Internationally priced goods and services will not necessarily be cheaper in places where things like food and accommodation decidedly are. The internationally priced products include high-end clothing and cars, which may explain why Central Europeans might look poorer than people in, for example, parts of the South of Europe, where the overall buying power of wages is actually lower. (Another reason is that visitors' impressions are moulded by the sentiment, expressed in a famous Charles Aznavour song, that poverty is more tolerable in the sun.[49]) But, on the whole, the difference in wages that does exist in nominal terms between Western and Central Europe (otherwise, why would Western and Asian companies locate their manufacturing there?) is not as great in practical purchasing-power terms as might be expected.

Half-Truth 6: Outmigration is depopulating the area

Still, because wages are generally higher in Western Europe, there is pressure on local earners to emigrate. The differences in purchasing power add to the attraction of leaving, and also influence the nature of migration.

In Warsaw you may buy almost the same amount with an average wage as in some parts of France. But you'd be better off earning your euros in France than your złotys in Poland, if you are going to send them home or take them home with you. You would need the higher French pay to maintain an only slightly better lifestyle in France than you have in Warsaw. But your French-earned wages will buy you a lot more in Warsaw, where prices are lower. Consequently, the incentive is less for leaving with your family in search of a better life (as life may not actually be that much better in many parts of the West), as it is to leave temporarily, with a plan to come back with money saved. Although that plan often changes once a worker gets to like life abroad, workers who do not intend to emigrate permanently are now the great majority of out-migrants from Central European countries. Their number is notoriously difficult to count, especially in the EU, considering that it grants free and essentially uncontrolled mobility rights to all its citizens. According to the Polish statistical office, however, almost two and a half million Poles were living outside the country at the end of 2019, excluding permanent emigrants, and it is presumed that most of them were working abroad.⁵⁰ That is more than 6 per cent of the total Polish population of 40 million.

Not all Central Europeans are equally eager to move away, permanently or temporarily. Strictly comparable country-by-country statistics are hard to come by. But the differences within the area appear to be great. The Czech Ministry of Foreign Affairs says that between 200 to 250,000 people with Czech passports live abroad (this figure would include many long-ago emigrants like the author of this book, and their children as well). According to Czech TV, there are also 56,000 people who maintain residence in the country but work across its borders. That would mean at most 3 per cent of Czechs live abroad, including permanent emigrants,⁵¹ a much lower figure than that for Poles. On the other hand, the Slovak Business Association believes that 300,000 Slovaks work abroad, which would be 5.5 per cent of the country, almost the same as in Poland – but almost half of those don't travel very far, and work in the neighbouring Czech Republic, with others crossing daily to work in Austria.⁵² Estimates for Hungary vary widely, from somewhere near the Czech percentage⁵³ to somewhere near the Polish.⁵⁴

Among the many factors that make such figures no more than estimates is that there is a large number of dual nationals in the area, especially Hungarians who are also Romanian or Slovak citizens, and it is not clear how these are included, or not, in the statistics. However that may be, to have between 3 and 6 per cent of the entire population working abroad is worrisome for any country. The situation is worsened by the fact that highly skilled and/or educated people are among those who move away. In Slovakia, for example, there is a major shortage of nurses.⁵⁵

Yet the situation is not necessarily unmanageable, and is not unique to Central Europe. The Fund for Peace is a non-governmental organization focused on the departure of qualified personnel from the world's poorer countries. It's 'Fragile States Index' scores countries among other things along the dimension of 'human flight and brain drain'. It shows that the brain drain is a serious issue in Central Europe (see Figure 4.13). Again, the performance of Central Europe varies significantly within the area, and is somewhere in the middle between the West and East of Europe. It is not demonstrably more different from the West than

Figure 4.13: Human flight and brain drain in selected countries, 2020

Australia	0.7
Spain	1.1
USA	1.8
France	2.2
Italy	2.3
UK	2.5
Ireland	3.1
Japan	3.1
Czech Republic	3.3
Russia	3.5
Greece	3.6
South Korea	3.6
Hungary	3.9
Slovakia	4
Bulgaria	4.5
Poland	4.6
Ukraine	5.5
Moldova	7
El Salvador	8.5

Source: Fund for Peace[56]

from the East. Slovakia's rate is not good, though it is not markedly worse than South Korea's. The Czech Republic is affected only marginally more than Ireland. Its score is about halfway between that of Germany and Poland. (It should be considered, however, that a country like France or Ireland is also a destination for skilled migrants, including from Central Europe.)

These statistics look at people leaving the country, but not at people coming in. In Poland, the vacuum left by people moving West has been filled by workers from the East, many of them escaping local conflicts and a malfunctioning economy. Even before the Russian invasion of Ukraine, the country issued well over 400,000 residence permits to Ukrainians, but the real number of Ukrainian workers was estimated to be about 2 million.[57] Putin's invasion then forced further multitudes into Central Europe. Over 14 per cent of the Czech labour force in 2020 were foreign citizens.[58] A large number of these were Slovaks (adding, incidentally, to Slovakia's outmigration and brain-drain scores). In Slovakia itself, there are proposals to alleviate the shortage of doctors and nurses by attracting professionals from Ukraine and Serbia.[59] If population inflows and outflows are considered together, then the balance for Central Europe, indeed, hardly looks catastrophic.

Nevertheless, a UN agency such as the International Organization for Migration, came up with a generalization like the following, in its 2020 report:

> For most South-Eastern and Eastern European countries, emigration rather than immigration has been the key feature over recent years and decades, with fairly low levels of immigration compared with other subregions of Europe. Due to this and other factors, several countries in Europe are projected to experience very significant population decline by 2050 (including Bosnia and Herzegovina, Bulgaria, Romania, the Republic of Moldova and Ukraine).[60]

The generalization is less of a deduction from the UN data than an induction from the Eastern Europeanist assumption, that there is such a 'subregion' as 'South-Eastern and Eastern European countries'. On that assumption, the quote tells the truth or, more precisely, half the truth. But note that the examples given (Bulgaria, Romania, and so on) do not include the four countries discussed here as Central Europe.

The overall flattening of 'Eastern European' (and South-Eastern European) data is evident in the assessment by Krastev and Holmes (who think that depopulation is a serious cause of illiberal sentiment in post-communist Europe):

> In the period 1989–2017, Latvia haemorrhaged 27 per cent of its population, Lithuania 22.5 per cent, Bulgaria almost 21 per cent. Two million East Germans, or almost 14 per cent of the country's pre-1989 inhabitants, went to West Germany in search of work and a better life. 3.4 million Romanians, a vast majority of them younger than forty, left the country only after the country joined the EU in 2007. [...] [The] fear of nation-killing depopulation is seldom openly voiced, perhaps because publicizing high rates of expatriation

will encourage imitators. But it is nonetheless real and may well be expressed indirectly in the nonsensical claim that migrants from Africa and the Middle East pose a threat to the existence of the nations of the region. According to UN projections, Bulgaria's population will shrink by 27 per cent between now and 2040. Almost one-fifth of the territory of the country is predicted to become a 'demographic desert'. Indeed, 'Bulgaria experienced the largest percentage drop in population not attributable to war or famine for a country in the modern era. Every day, the country was losing 164 people: over a thousand a week, over 50,000 a year.'[61]

Perhaps so in Bulgaria; not so in the Czech Republic or even Hungary. However serious the outmigration from Central Europe is, it is not in itself a reason for the 'unexpressed dread of demographic collapse' for which Krastev and Holmes think the anti-migrant stance of the governments might be some sort of a psychological compensation:

> We might even hypothesize that anti-immigration politics in a region essentially without immigrants is an example of what psychologists call 'displacement', a defence mechanism by which, in this case, minds unconsciously blot out a wholly unacceptable threat and replace it with one still serious but conceivably easier to manage. Hysteria about non-existent immigrants about to overrun the country represents the substitution of an illusory danger (immigration) for the real danger (depopulation and demographic collapse) which cannot speak its name.[62]

There is a dread of demographic developments at play here, certainly, but it is not of a Bulgarian-style collapse of population size, which is simply not happening in Central Europe. Krastev and Holmes themselves recognize that what they consider to be 'a largely unspoken preoccupation with demographic collapse' is 'fomented by a fear that unassimilable foreigners will enter the country, dilute national identity and weaken national cohesion'.[63]

Spoken plainly, the fear is mainly of white nationals being replaced by migrants of colour.

Depopulation is a serious fact also in many parts of the West, especially its rural areas and rust belts, where similar racist fears can emerge. While the demographic issue is serious in Central Europe[64] (and racist arguments against migrants are common), the facts here resemble the others dealt with in this chapter. On almost all the measures we have discussed, stereotypical ideas about Central Europe turn out to be either false or, more often, half-true; they tend to ignore that there is generally a difference between Central and the rest of Eastern Europe, and that undesirable characteristics ascribed to Central Europe are also found in parts of the West.

5

The Last of the White Men: Central Europe's White Innocence

At first sight, *Midsommar*, a horror film set in Scandinavia, seems to have little to do with Central Europe.[1] The title refers to Sweden's traditional mid-summer festival of music, food, and dance. The pagan, cult-like Hårga community lives apart from other humans and only opens up to visitors every 90 years. This time has arrived. Dani, a woman whose sister killed her parents and herself, seeks some relief by accompanying her boyfriend Christian and his fellow graduate students of anthropology, to travel to Sweden and take part in the event. One-by-one, the students are picked off by the Hårga, unaware of what is happening, until only Dani is left. She ends up approving the murder of her boyfriend by the cult, a way for herself to become a member.

The film is made by the American director Ari Aster and was distributed by Amazon Prime. The main actors are an Englishwoman, an American, and a Swede. Other than that, almost all the actors are Hungarians pretending to be Swedes. The location, named as Hålsingland – a real place in Sweden – is actually Hungary.

Why Hungary rather than Sweden? Certainly, economics must have played a role in the producers' choice: lax labour laws, favourable tax treatment. But the work of Anikó Imre, a scholar who has been in the forefront of research on how race and whiteness function in the media produced in Central Europe, suggests that there is much more at play.[2] Focusing on the Netflix series, *The*

Witcher, based on Polish source material and shot mostly in Hungary, Imre notes how Central and Eastern Europe provide a location where the vagaries of racial guilt can be dreamed away, where one can escape race as one of the major problems of contemporary life. Imre refers to Central European nations' claimed lack of responsibility for racialized, colonial exploitation (see Chapters 7–9 in this book), as a fantasy of 'white innocence'. The fantasy is eagerly supported by media producers in the West, and especially in America. It induces them to consider Central Europe as the ideal location for plots that are free of the complications of race and the guilt that historical racial exploitation brings with it.[3] Their 'white innocence' is an imagined condition of pure, undisturbed, and guiltfree whiteness.[4]

This condition of untroubled whiteness is amplified by the fact that Central Europe's population is almost entirely white. There is a tendency to view illiberalism in Central Europe as anti-Western. It is nothing of the sort. Critical of the West *as is*, that is, of the liberal and *multiracial* West, illiberal white Central Europeans see themselves as true to the West's real 'heritage', that is, to its racially white character. They are the real, that is, the purely white, Europeans. And their Western allies couldn't agree more.

Untroubled whiteness is an imagined feature of Central *and* Eastern Europe both; this is one area where the two can rightly be viewed as closely related. The whiteness of Russia (wrongly assumed, as Russia is a multiracial nation) as an ideal for Western racists is the subject of *Russia and the Western Far Right: Tango Noir* by the Ukrainian writer, Anton Shekhovtsov. Shekhovtsov discusses in great detail the present and historical function of Russia for white supremacists as the last bastion of pure white power.[5] But Russia's white innocence is extended also, by illiberal racists both in the West and *in situ*, to Central Europe. While, for the most part, the far-right 'extremists' that Shekhovtsov deals with see little reason to mince their words about their racism, more mainstream illiberals rely on dog-whistles. That can mollify sympathizers who consider overt racism in bad taste, without losing more crudely racist supporters.

As far as the relatively 'moderate' Western illiberals are concerned, Budapest is the new Moscow. The leading American conservative talk show host, Tucker Carlson, spent a week in 2021 broadcasting praises of the Orbán regime, directly from the Hungarian capital.

Here you can proclaim the same racist 'values', disguised a little if need be, as the 'extremists' (who are also quite welcome in Budapest), but without appearing to be too friendly with Russia, which some American patriots even in the right-wing camp may not necessarily appreciate, especially after Putin's Ukraine invasion.

It is from this perspective that we need to view the protestations by Central European illiberal leaders, that 'Brussels' has abandoned these 'values' and that they are there to defend them. They have no intention of leaving the West, either literally through exiting the EU or in their hearts, through no longer imagining themselves as 'European'.[6] On the contrary, they view themselves as the last holdout of genuine (white) European civilization. They are ready to fight for it, together with their confreres of the West.

Illiberal Central Europeans like to complain that the yoke of Russian communism has now been replaced by bondage to the liberal West. Paolo Morawski, the Polish-Italian co-author of *Polonia Mon Amour: From the Indies of Europe to the Indies of America*,[7] is a sensitive observer of Poland's location in global geopolitics. He dubs this attitude 'yesterday Moscow, today Brussels'. According to Morawski,

> Since the 16th century, now and again Poland has been, or believes it is, the West's bastion, outpost, rampart against the barbarianisms coming from Asia. And yet, nowadays there is a strange syntony between the Polish Church and the Russian Orthodox Church in an anti-western key, opposing modernity, secularisation, atheism, materialism, consumerism, the degeneration of customs etc. The narrative outline is a shared one; the East's spiritual purity against the West's decadence. This type of mental and value-based convergence between Poland and Russia should be neither over- nor underestimated. It is, however, an element that exists and must be added to other interpretations of today's Poland. Until recently the West and Europe were a destination that millions of Poles yearned for. Nowadays part of Poland considers that same West/Europe as the kingdom of barbarity, in fact perhaps rather like Sodom and Gomorra.[8]

The vicious attack on progressive values of gender and sexuality, evident in Poland's near-complete ban on abortion and its campaign against LGBT rights, is evidence of this. Morawski rightly points out that it brings Poland closer to its traditional enemy, Russia, whose homophobic policies have served as a model for repressive legislation both in Poland and in Hungary. I will return (in Chapter 6) to the astounding claim by the Polish president, Andrzej Duda, that 'LGBT ideology' is even more destructive than communism,[9] and a similar declaration by Marek Jędraszewski, the Archbishop of Krakow, that there is a new 'plague' ravaging Poland now, 'not red, but rainbow'.[10]

Illiberal leaders see their Central European countries as a bastion of patriarchal, heteronormative conservativism, and their struggle as the last stand of the White Man. Man indeed: they champion a world where, as Jarosław Kaczyński put it, 'a woman is a woman and a man is a man'.[11] The casual observer may well be convinced that Central European illiberals are 'anti-Western' and that they are moving back into the embraces of Russia. There is a degree of veracity in this half-truth. Disdain for Western decadence does go hand-in-hand with understanding for Putin's Russia. But this is hardly a Central European characteristic alone. Illiberal movements in the West – the supporters of Matteo Salvini in Italy, of Marine Le Pen in France, or of Donald Trump in America – have also been friendly toward Russia. In fact, Jarosław Kaczyński, whose anti-Russian sentiments are more overbearing than those of many of his compatriots, let alone his Central European allies, has voiced reservations about an alliance with Western illiberal parties in the European Parliament, citing their cosy relationship with Putin.[12]

Nevertheless, illiberal leaders like Kaczyński and Orbán must surely realize that equating Brussels with Moscow is nothing but vicious hyperbole. Though they suffer approbation from the EU, they are free not only to argue back but to go on running their countries and benefiting from handsome EU subsidies. Their commitment to the West is visceral, though they dislike what they see as the kidnapping of the idea of 'the West' by leftists and liberals. Their flirtation with Russia has a much more transactional character.

True, Russian efforts to build goodwill in Central Europe and to undermine the stability of the EU through a revived 'pan-Slavism' have borne some fruit in the three Slavic countries of Central Europe (Hungary is not Slavic). Pan-Slavism has found some mild interest in the Czech Republic and even traditionally anti-Russian Poland. It may have reached a higher level in Slovakia, where much of the far right, known to receive extensive Russian support, encourages Slavic kinship. (That may be indicated by the fact that, as coronavirus vaccines were being rolled out in 2021, the opinion research firm Globsec found that 15 per cent of Slovaks preferred the Russian Sputnik V variety, compared to only 4 per cent of Hungarians, 3 per cent of Czechs, 1 per cent of Poles, and 2 per cent of Austrians.)[13] But, as had been the case with Central European pan-Slavism in the nineteenth century, this very modest revival is designed more to counterbalance the importance of the West in Europe, than to see any meaningful dissociation from it in favour of Russia.

When a Slovak film production team created, in 2021, a TV series called *Slovania* ('Slavs'), the obvious model was Netflix-style productions and videogames about pagan Vikings and Celts, with no consideration at all of the Russian-style Eurasianist fantasies that a Western viewer might have expected.

Certainly, disagreements and disappointment with 'Brussels' have led to some strategic flirting with Russia and China. There is clear evidence in all four Visegrád countries of at least some of the leadership encouraging what Orbán has dubbed an 'Eastern Opening'. His declaration for illiberal democracy at Băile Tuşnad in 2014 was preceded by a meditation on the failure of Western and the success of Eastern state 'systems'. He expressed a wish to understand

> systems that are not Western, not liberal, not liberal democracies, maybe not even democracies, and yet making nations successful. Today, the stars of international analyses are Singapore, China, India, Turkey, Russia. And I believe that our political community rightly anticipated this challenge. And if we think back on what we did in the last four years, and what we are going to do in the following four years, then it really can be interpreted from this angle. We are searching for (and we are doing our best to find ways of parting with Western European dogmas, making ourselves independent from them) the form of organizing a community, that is capable of making us competitive in this great world-race.[14]

Although Turkey and Russia, at the very least, and possibly India, ceased to be 'the stars of international analyses' soon after these remarks, Orbán remained a supporter of Russian interests in Hungary. He oversaw the secretive expansion of the Russian-built Paks nuclear power plant, which supplies more than 50 per cent of the country's power needs. The University of Debrecen, which Orbán has been building up, in the face of considerable opposition, as a subservient academic institution, has seen fit to award an honorary diploma to Vladimir Putin. Just before Russia invaded Ukraine, Orbán went to Moscow and obtained assurances about Russian deliveries of gas. However, he joined the rest of the EU in approving sanctions following the invasion.

Under Orbán's leadership, Hungary also became perhaps China's best friend in the EU, vetoing, for example, a resolution against China's suppression of protests in Hong Kong.[15] It has been an enthusiastic participant in China's Belt and Road Initiative. Having effectively closed the respected Central European University campus in Budapest because it was financed by George Soros, Orbán moved on to welcome a megaproject for China's prestigious Fudan University to open its first campus in the EU.

It was also on Orbán's watch that fancies about the Magyars' eastern origins became popular. Although the 'Asianization of national fantasies'[16] was more pronounced on the far right, it penetrated Orbán's Fidesz as well.

It got to the point where the liberal opposition – which, to be sure, has been at least as jealous of the whiteness of Central Europe as the right, and possibly more so – even accused Orbán of sliding toward oriental despotism. As a group of opposition leaders stated to the venerable German paper, *Die Zeit*:

> We Hungarians declare our attachment, as we had done already under Founder of the State, St. Stephen [who ruled from about 1000 AD to 1038], to the European community of values. We did not overcome communist one-party rule only to let a corrupt and autocratic regime take the EU as well as Hungary as hostage, and to take away the rights of Hungarian citizens and rob them of their subventions.
>
> With his astonishing demagogy, he likened the EU to the Warsaw Pact, while acting as a Trojan horse of

> Eastern autocratic rulers in Europe, and consistently seeks to become closer to dictators like Alexander Lukashenko and Gurbanguly Berdimuhamedow [the President of Turkmenistan].[17]

Such oppositional voices come largely from the Budapest 'elite', who are certainly not Orbán's favourites. In one survey, Budapest was the only place on the continent whose people felt more attached to Europe than even their own country or region.[18] But the critics were making a mistake if they were interpreting Orbán's *rapprochement* with Russia and its clients as opposition to the West as such, rather than to the West as represented by its current European incarnation or 'Brussels'.

Orbán had made his fame as a young man in the summer of 1989, when the communist regime, which was busily self-destructing, permitted the reinternment of Imre Nagy, Hungary's leader during its 1956 revolution. As Nagy and four of his colleagues were being put to rest, Orbán declared an unqualified desire to follow the Western model.

> Up until this very day, 1956 was the last chance for our nation to create economic prosperity, treading on the Western path of development. The heavy burden of failure weighs upon our shoulders because they [the communists] bloodily suffocated our revolution, and forced us back into that same Asian blind alley that we're now searching a way out of.[19]

We have already seen that describing Russia as 'Asiatic' is an old orientalist, racist epithet that long predates its use by the Nazis. 'Asian' here unambiguously referred to Russia. Coupling his anti-Russian prejudice with a call to follow the West, Orbán was giving vent here to the typical Central European desire to be counted not with the 'Asian' East but with the 'European' West. Such prejudices run deep. They survive strategic alliances needed to balance the influence of a West seen as not valuing its own heritage, so unlike Central European patriots, the Eastern sentries who stand on guard for Europe as they have in the long centuries past.

Even under communism, Central European leaders did not necessarily identify culturally with Russia. Certainly, the last communist leader of Czechoslovakia, Miloš Jakeš, did not. Just before the regime fell, this previously faithful apparatchik expressed indignation against Gorbachev's plans to return land to private farmers. In his characteristically rambling and inarticulate way, Jakeš actually held that Czechoslovakia was too civilized for such a move, suited only to the USSR's culturally underdeveloped countryside! 'The Soviet Union is another story', he said, 'It's dysfunctional over there, it's backward, the situation there is different from ours; our villages are highly cultured, they're similar to the cities; they're not different in their way of life, in their cultural life, home furniture, what have you ... education, from the city.'[20] The illiberal President of the Czech Republic, Miloš Zeman, is possibly the most pro-Russian and pro-Chinese leader in Central Europe. But even he has never declared himself for a cultural identification with the East as part of the strategy to make his country less dependent on the West.

In fact, the entente of some of the illiberal Central European leaders with Russia is best read as part of an overall strategy to lessen their political and economic dependence on just one power, 'Brussels'. Central European leaders of all stripes, wary of limiting their alliances, have also made efforts to build a special friendship with the United States, over the heads of their Western European allies. This was most evident under Donald Trump's presidency, among other things because Trump and the Central European illiberals have had the same attitude to the West: we're part of it, but we want to reverse the way it has developed.

Liz Fekete locates illiberalism in Orbán's Hungary within the context, not of an East–West confrontation, as much as of a 'pan-European culture war'. Orbán preaches 'order and responsibility as the foundational values of a patriarchal Christianity, one that starts from the protection of kith and kin and proceeds to love of country and culture'.[21] Anne Applebaum uses terms like 'restorative nostalgia' and 'cultural despair' for the lament, common among 'authoritarians', that the Western world as a whole, and one's own Western nation in particular, has lost its vigour and its values.[22] Those lachrymose about the cultural decline of Europe, of the West, (or – as among Trump supporters – America), are not anti-European or anti-Western, in any sense other than Orbán's: they are 'restorative nostalgics' who want to bring back a mythical past when their nation, their continent, and especially – though this is seldom said out loud – their race was powerful and respected.

Orbán and his Central European partners and followers rightly feel that they are working with Western allies. On 1 April 2021, Orbán welcomed the Polish Prime Minister, Mateusz Morawiecki, and the leader of the Italian right-wing Lega Party, Matteo Salvini, to Budapest to discuss establishing a formal alliance of their parties in the European Parliament. Salvini called the event the beginning of a 'renaissance' in Europe. Orbán praised Salvini profusely:

> We are accustomed to calling Matteo Salvini simply our hero. As the greatest debates ranged about migration, and several countries defended themselves by saying that it was physically impossible to stop migration, then he, as a member of the Italian government and interior minister, was able to prove the opposite. Just as we Hungarians knew how to stop migration overland, so he knew how to stop migration at sea.[23]

Orbán affirmed the three right-wing leaders' allegiance to the EU and to NATO before explaining how all three of them wanted to reform these Western alliances: 'It is clear that we represent, beyond our Atlantic obligations, the values of freedom, dignity, Christianity, family, and national sovereignty. We say no to censorship, to a Brussels-style European Empire, to communism, to illegal immigration, and to antisemitism. It is obvious that we agree about these values and attitudes.'[24]

If this type of rhetoric is anti-Western, then so is Salvini's, or that of other significant Western right-wing leaders (the opposition to anti-Semitism mentioned here functioned to insist that they are not the *far* right[25]) like France's Marine Le Pen or the Netherlands' Geert Wilders. These leaders, too, have been friendly to Russia and enjoyed active Russian support.[26] That does not make them anti-Western, as opposed to simply championing a 'true', illiberal West, which, among other more important things, would be friendlier to Russia.

As a matter of fact, in Putin's Russia itself one may discern two different attitudes to the West. One may associate each with the name of political philosophers Ivan Ilyin and Aleksandr Dugin.

Both have been described as fascists, and both have been said to inspire Putin's view of a Eurasian political association that would include Europe under Russian leadership.[27] The difference is that Ilyin articulated essentially a universal case for illiberal government, while Dugin infuses the same with anti-European content, calling, for example, for Russia to ally itself with non-European 'Aryan' powers such as Iran. Dugin's Eurasian political union would restore spirituality over Western materialism, because materialism is a feature that he, like Rudolf Steiner (see Chapter 3), sees as essentially alien to the Russian spirit.[28]

Ilyin's critique of the liberal West is anti-Western-liberal; Dugin's is anti-Western *tout court*. It is safe to assume that Orbán, Morawiecki, and Salvini would find inspiration in Ilyin, but Dugin's essentially anti-Western Russian spirit would hardly hold any appeal to them. Although, as Shekhovtsov has noted,[29] Dugin's ideas have found some popularity among the extreme right in Europe and America (who see in Russia the last bulwark of the white race now abandoned by a degenerate liberal West), Russian Eurasianism has only a minuscule following outside Dugin's native country. It is no stronger in Europe's Centre than in its West. Admittedly, illiberal nationalism has breathed some new life into ideas about Hungary's history that focus on the country's non-Indo-European language, in typical nineteenth-century fashion, as proof of the nation's unique racial identity. Ideas ranging from identification with ancient Sumer through Atilla the Hun to kinship with Central Asian Turkic peoples[30] are again becoming quite popular, especially, although not exclusively, with nostalgics who espouse the symbolism of the prewar nationalists including the Hungarian Nazis.[31] But the dominant narrative remains that the Magyar people, emerging from the steppes of the East a thousand years ago, threw in their lot with the Christian West, and ever since have remained steadfastly faithful to that pledge.

Tomasz Zarycki, one of the most acute observers of the Central European perspective on the West, writes that the Polish right 'is in its majority not really anti-Western. The West is seen as far from ideal for Poland, but the main responsibility for the unequal relations between Poland and the West is laid on the liberal camp.'[32] To Central European illiberals, their illiberalism is not meant to move them away from the West; rather, it means to bring the West closer to them.

In his 2017 speech in Romania, Orbán fondly recalled Donald Trump's address in Poland, where the American president referred to 'our struggle for the West'. He said it did not begin on the battlefield, but in our hearts, and that it was a fight for 'family, freedom, country, and God'. The slogan reminds one of Marshal Pétain's motto during his pro-Nazi collaborationist French government: 'work, family, country', which was deliberately meant to replace 'liberty, equality, fraternity'. Nevertheless, Orbán likes to think of his 'struggle' as something new. Although enthusiastic about Trump, who had gained entry to the White House a year earlier, Orbán was jealous of those who gave credit to the orange-haired American.

> There are theories that describe the changes now happening *in the western world* as if it were the emergence of the American president that made recognizable the struggle waged between the so-called global, supranational elite and the patriotic, nationally minded leaders on the stage of world politics. This assessment makes sense in my opinion, there's a lot of truth in it, and if we turn our attention to ourselves then we might say that, well before the American presidential election, in 2010, we were apparently the forerunners of this new, patriotic *western politics*.[33]

While Western Europe has 'failed' because of its migration policy, Orbán has suggested,

> Central Europe works, the Central European economic models work, today Central Europe consists of successful countries; countries that add to the strength of the European Union. We contribute more to the strength of the European Union than anyone would have thought at the time in 2004 when these countries joined the community. ... we reject immigration, and ... we think that strengthening families is important, we believe that the willingness to bear children must be supported, and we are convinced that Europe can be realized [only] through protecting and strengthening Christian European culture.[34]

Such talk is not anti-Western, but it calls out a truth that is inconvenient for the *liberals* of the West. The Western (neo-)liberal project of incorporating post-communist areas was presented as if it extended freedom and democracy, as allegedly Western values, to an 'East' where such values were supposedly alien. Yet unfreedom and inequality have always been inherent in the West. In an essay published in 2013, the Oxford anthropologist Dace Dzenovska discussed the amused 'befuddlement' with which Western observers greeted Latvians' pride in allegedly participating in the colonization, in the eighteenth century, of Tobago and Gambia. Clearly, the Eastern Europeans did not understand that colonialism (and all the racist language and assumptions that accompany it) are now something that one is meant to disassociate oneself from. The West is no longer proud of colonialism, and the East is still trying to be? Dzenovska argues that the amusement of the Western observer stems from an embarrassment. For the Easterners who, as expected, want to join the West, *correctly* though inconveniently understand that the West is deeply imbued with colonial and postcolonial racism.

> And it is precisely this – the affective relationship of Latvians to Europe's colonial history – that seems to suggest to the Western traveller that, indeed, Latvians are not yet European. In the eyes of the Western traveller, they seem to lack the skill to correctly identify those elements of the European past which Europe wants to strategically forget rather than proudly remember. Thus the Latvians' and other not-quite-Europeans' colonial aspirations become yet another site through which the Western traveller or scholar can assert moral superiority, as well as authority to affectively and discursively interpret the situation – by bafflement, bemusement, laughter and thereafter by explanations that locate the source of the colonial aspirations in the national histories of the not-quite-Europeans.[35]

In 2013, Dzenovska was probably right that Latvians were committing a naive faux-pas due to their lack of understanding of what liberal Westerners required of them. Today, after more than ten years of Orbán and after the rise of Trump, it is clear that Central and other Eastern European claims to represent an unrepentant white superiority are a conscious political statement, part of a global, not just Eastern European reaction, against efforts to free the West of its legacy of racial exclusion. In important parts of the West, whiteness is becoming a much more contested gateway to social status. New, increasingly multiracial elites have emerged in the global cities, demanding at least verbal affirmation of equality of race, and of gender and sexual orientation, as a condition of membership. This relative devaluation of whiteness has contributed to the illiberal revolt of much of the white periphery.

That is why the illiberals of Western Europe and America have no problem with Orbán's vision of 'Christian European culture'. His fight is their fight: not against the West, but for the soul of the West. Central European illiberals are not anti-Western. They do not want the exclusive Western club and its global white hegemony to disappear. They just want to make sure that the club survives long enough to at last accept them. And they value greatly the alleged white 'purity' of Central Europe. As one social media commentator put it, using the Nazi-tinged term *entvolkt* (literally de-nationed, unraced), the German people no longer have any pride in their nation as an ethnic group (*Volk*). 'I am moving to Hungary or Poland', she said, 'Austria has too many refugees already, too'.[36]

To return to screen productions made in Central Europe, it is worth noting that among them horror fantasy stories are quite common. Horror films project our fears onto the screen, and this externalization helps us to deal with them. It is a sort of cleansing exercise: we deal with what frightens inside by projecting it outside. Locating horror in an imagined purely white Central Europe works to allay Western anxieties about race and whiteness. It works, by dislodging productions form their Western locations, charged with the political and historical guilt of racial and colonial exploitation, and moving them eastward to where that baggage of guilt is (wrongly) perceived as non-existent.[37]

This is exactly parallel to the projection of one's own racism onto 'Eastern Europeans', such as Eastern Europeanism engages in, as discussed throughout this book.

Midsommar, the film mentioned at the beginning of this chapter, is a so-called 'folk horror' story, a subgenre of which *The Texas Chainsaw Massacre* franchise (with some recent parts filmed in

Bulgaria) is a prototype. Folk horror has urban, often educated protagonists enter a frightening rural world, where they are fatally attacked by strange local folk. The class subtext is obvious, but there may also be a racial one. The 2010 American horror comedy, *Tucker and Dale vs Evil*,[38] is something of a spoof of this subgenre. A small group of white university youth including a token Black student go on a vacation in the woods, where they encounter a pair of local male friends they qualify as 'hillbillies'. From the start, the hillbillies scare them as potentially violent. They are wrong; the two hillbillies are completely harmless, good-natured fellows. The students are doomed not because of the hillbillies but because of their own prejudice against them. The college kids are killed one-by-one in accidents caused by their clumsy attempts to 'free' the one eventual survivor, who they mistakenly think was kidnapped by the locals. In fact, the hillbillies saved her from drowning and were nursing her in their cottage. The racial allusion is not spelled out but is clear. (At one point the main instigator among the college kids is actually discovered to have had a hillbilly father, and is described as 'half hillbilly'.)

There may be a mutual lesson to be learned from studying together the white-on-white racialization of 'Eastern Europeans' and of such marginalized white American groups as the 'hillbillies' or, to use an insufferably racist *and* classist term, 'white trash'.

Whoever such terms refer to are groups that are often accused of supporting right-wing racist tendencies, of which Trumpism is the most recent. That is a half-truth, just like the charge that Central Europeans are necessarily illiberal. The fantasy of the 'Eastern European' as the Last White Man standing, proud and free of guilt, is one of a true White West that is an alternative to 'liberal' multiculturalism and multiracialism. It is an eastward projection that is embraced openly by Western illiberals. White anti-racists should beware of the temptation to embrace it unconsciously, too, which can serve to provide some relief from the unbearable duty to face one's own heritage of racism.

6

'Have Eastern Europeans No Shame?' Anti-Semitism, Racism, and Homophobia in Central Europe

Not all Central Europeans are racist. To recognize this is a moral necessity. But hate in Central Europe is rampant and dangerous. Its open expression has become more common than in much of the West, both among the general public and at the highest levels of political leadership. At the same time, hate there is not entirely different in form from the West, nor does it spring from completely different sources. That also means that, just as in the West, there is hope for overcoming it.

As we have seen earlier, when East Central European states refused, in 2015, a compulsory quota for refugee resettlement, which had been decreed against their objections in Brussels, they were accused of transferring to Muslim migrants an intolerance spawned by centuries of anti-Semitism. The eminent Princeton historian, Jan Gross, asked:

> 'Have Eastern Europeans no sense of shame?' [...] When the war ended, Germany – because of the victors' denazification policies and its responsibility for instigating and carrying out the Holocaust – had no choice but to 'work through' its murderous past. This was a long, difficult process; but German society, mindful of its historical misdeeds, has become capable

of confronting moral and political challenges of the type posed by the influx of refugees today. And Chancellor Angela Merkel has set an example of leadership on migrants that puts all of Eastern Europe's leaders to shame.

Eastern Europe, by contrast, has yet to come to terms with its murderous past. Only when it does will its people be able to recognize their obligation to save those fleeing in the face of evil.[1]

Gross' anger at the inhumane attitudes against the migrants was justified. His outrage was shared by people in Europe and the world. Yet his generalizations about Germany and about the implied difference between Eastern and Western Europe are problematic.

If anyone has the right to comment on the murderous past, it is Gross. It was he who forced the Polish public to take a look at anti-Jewish atrocities committed by Poles during the Holocaust and even after, when survivors returning from the camps to reclaim their property were attacked by Polish mobs. Emblematic of the wartime horrors was the incident at Jedwabne, where a large number of local Jews – estimates range between 350 and 1,600 – were massacred by the local Poles. After a smaller group of victims was killed and buried in a barn, the others were herded into it alive. Their attackers set the barn on fire, burning alive those who were trapped inside. Of the pogroms against returning survivors after the war and liberation, the Kielce massacre is the best known. More than 40 Jews lost their lives in the Polish city, among accusations that included the mediaeval blood libel that they kidnapped Christian children to use their blood for Passover. Although the memory of these incidents had never been entirely suppressed, it was researchers like Gross who, following the fall of the communist regime, provided the evidence to seriously challenge their prevailing interpretation as exceptional. While Gross also detailed the involvement of Poles who tried to save the Jews, he put to rest the thesis that Poles played a negligible role in their persecution, dispossession, and extermination.[2]

In spite of the merits of Gross' work in general, questions remain about four of his contentions stated or implied in the passage quoted at the start of this chapter: first, that the 'murderous past' of the Poles is comparable to that of the Germans; second, that it is an

'Eastern European' past; third, that the past has been adequately dealt with in Germany and the West; and fourth, that the anti-Semitic massacres of the Holocaust and its aftermath are related to the Islamophobic rejection of migrants 70 years later, and to the racism and homophobia now observed in the area.

Horrible as the crimes of Poles against Jews were, they pale in comparison to the crimes of the Germans. German involvement was a precondition for the Polish-perpetrated killings, either because Germans encouraged or assisted them, or because they permitted them under their control. The killings in Poland and in Europe directly organized by Germans were in the millions rather than the hundreds or thousands. Yet by likening Germany's coming to terms with its past to 'Eastern Europe's', Gross is, perhaps unwittingly, suggesting that their responsibilities are comparable. It is regrettable that the Polish government reacted to Gross' and others' inculpation of Poland by proposing a law that makes it a crime to ascribe collective responsibility for the Holocaust to the Polish people. It was a reprehensible response, even if in practice the controversial law has at the time of writing never been applied, having been significantly weakened by the Polish courts.

The law is certainly mean-spirited, but it is also wrong to overlook that it is an expression of justifiably hurt pride. Having suffered the loss of about 3 million Jewish and 3 million non-Jewish people under the brutal German occupation, many Poles are understandably angered by being labelled perpetrators of crimes that were committed by Germans. The expression 'Polish concentration camps' particularly irks Polish sensibilities, because apparently many people in the West interpret it as 'camps run by Poles' rather than 'camps in Poland'.[3] Timothy Garton Ash well understands the sentiment.

> Watching a German television news report on the trial of John Demjanjuk a few weeks ago, I was amazed to hear the announcer describe him as a guard in 'the Polish extermination camp Sobibor'. What times are these, when one of the main German TV channels thinks it can describe Nazi camps as 'Polish'?
>
> In my experience, the automatic equation of Poland with Catholicism, nationalism and antisemitism – and

thence a slide to guilt by association with the Holocaust — is still widespread.[4]

Compare that to how the word 'Germans' has been unconsciously cleansed of its Second World War connotations. In discussing the Holocaust, it is now routine to describe German perpetrators as 'Nazis' rather than 'Germans'. (A Google search for 'German concentration camps' redirects to 'Nazi concentration camps'.) In comparison, Polish perpetrators are routinely referred to simply as 'Poles', rather than, for example, 'Polish collaborators'. Such usage implies that in Germany, contrary to the evidence, only Nazis were responsible for or complicit in deporting and murdering Jews, while in Poland it was, or at least could be, anyone.

How 'Eastern European' were the crimes against the Jews, detailed in the Polish case by Gross and others? The Holocaust took place in different conditions in the different Central European countries. The Czech territory was occupied by the Germans far less brutally than Poland. Slovakia and Hungary were run by collaborating nationalists who perpetrated their own anti-Jewish atrocities, but those became much worse when these countries were occupied by German troops close to the end of the war, when Germany felt that it could no longer trust them. It was during this time, in November 1944, that my own grandparents were murdered near the village of Kremnička, where dozens of other mainly Jewish and Roma victims were shot and buried in anti-tank trenches, by members of the Slovak Emergency Unit of the Hlinka Guard (POHG) and possibly some Germans. Brutal deportations to the German-run camps, which the Slovak government initiated earlier but then stopped, resumed at the same time.[5] Following the war, some of the Slovak perpetrators were convicted in reunited Czechoslovakia.

In the Czech territories, which were given only partial autonomy by the Germans, there is little evidence of independent anti-Jewish action by Czechs, either during or after the war, although the population for the most part followed German directions. That included expelling Jews from their jobs, a process that began already during the brief existence of a nominally independent, collaborationist Czecho-Slovak Republic.[6] Czech police worked efficiently with their German masters, including at the infamous Theresienstadt concentration camp. Yet what we know of Czech complicity with the Germans cannot be compared to the Polish or the Slovak case.

In Hungary, in spite of anti-Semitic measures inspired by Germany and in spite of many Jewish men being interned in brutal work camps, transfers to the German death camps in Poland began only under German occupation. Then, with the vigorous cooperation of the Hungarian police, most of the provincial Jews were deported. In Budapest, many were murdered by Hungarian Nazis, although most were saved, in part famously through the heroic efforts of the Swedish diplomat, Raoul Wallenberg. After the war, anti-Semitism continued, but there was no violence comparable to the Polish pogroms as in Kielce and elsewhere, or to smaller-scale but comparable postwar attacks in Slovakia.[7] Today, nationalist Hungarians attempt to minimize the Hungarian role in the Holocaust. Similarly to the Poles, they try to present a picture of common Jewish and Hungarian suffering at the hands of the Germans. Perhaps the most controversial example is the monument to the victims of the German occupation in Budapest, which includes the Jews as only one of the persecuted groups, and makes no mention of the vicious anti-Semitism of the pre-occupation, collaborationist Horthy regime.[8]

While the enormity of the crimes against the Jews in Central Europe must not be denied, it is unclear that it has any generalizable 'Eastern European' characteristics. The Polish massacres are arguably unique on the territory of what is today the EU, resembling perhaps similar horrors perpetrated in Ukraine. This may be due to the fact that the proportion of Jews was much higher in those countries, providing more targets for violence and dispossession. The demographic factor may also explain why, also intolerably, the Polish government unlike other European governments, including in Central Europe, never declared a universal restitution of Jewish property to its owners or their descendants. In 2021, it shocked its allies and the Jewish world by decreeing that, essentially, property taken from Jews by the Germans and subsequently nationalized by the Poles would no longer be recoverable if its fate had not previously been decided. This ended the hopes of families whose efforts to regain such property had often been endlessly stalled by the authorities. Such manoeuvrings would be inexcusable anywhere, but given the large number of Jews once living in Poland they affect the selfish needs of more people owning stolen Jewish property than in other parts of Central Europe or the EU.

Granted that Poland may have been a special case, however, it would be difficult to argue that Czech, Slovak, or Hungarian anti-Semitism was different in kind from what was practised by collaborationists in Western Europe, in countries such as Italy, Austria, and of course Germany.

Under the communist regimes, anti-Semitism did affect all of Central Europe. It was, however, not necessarily the locally brewed variety; rather, it was deliberately orchestrated from Moscow. Connected to the ageing Stalin's fears that Jewish doctors wanted to poison him,[9] anti-Semitism was encouraged by the Soviets throughout the 'Eastern bloc'. In the early 1950s, there were important show trials against communist leaders falsely accused of disloyalty, in Hungary and Czechoslovakia. Many of the accused were Jewish. In Poland, an anti-Semitic campaign began in 1967, with Israel's victory in the 'Six Day War', and intensified when the government reacted to anti-regime protests in 1968 by blaming them partly on 'Zionists', resulting in thousands of Polish Jews leaving the country under official encouragement and pressure.[10] Many Jews who remained in Central Europe spent most of the communist period fearing real or potential hostility, unmatched in the Western parts of the continent.

After the fall of communism, however, the fear of official persecution dissipated. For various reasons, the governments of Central Europe became close allies of Israel. Local Jewish history was exploited, sometimes controversially, as an attraction for Jewish and non-Jewish tourists. Krakow's 'Jewish district' and its *klezmer* cafés may be the best example of a 'fun' Jewish tourist site, while Prague's Jewish Town appeals to the popular taste for mediaeval mystery. With international and local support, many synagogues and Jewish cemeteries were restored, even though, with the exception of Budapest, there are barely any Jews left to frequent them.

Reluctance – sometimes vocal – to fully acknowledge local complicity in the Holocaust exists in all Central (and other) European countries. However, unlike in Poland and Hungary, where it is arguably the official position, in Slovakia the government and parliament have repeatedly accepted responsibility and apologized.[11] In 2001, the Social Democratic President of Poland,

Aleksander Kwaśniewski, did apologize for the Jedwabne massacre, but Polish complicity in the Holocaust has been vehemently denied by the illiberal PiS government. In the Czech Republic, the full extent of local collaboration is only beginning to be discovered by some historians, to a mixed reception by the public.[12]

On the other hand, it is not necessarily the case that the crimes of collaborationists have been fully acknowledged in the West, either. The Austrian narrative has long been that the Nazis were German occupiers of their country, in spite of Hitler being an Austrian, and contrary to the popular quip that the Austrians were good anti-Semites but bad Nazis, while the Germans were good Nazis but bad anti-Semites. The French, proud of *la résistance*, were shocked to be reminded of the other half of the country collaborating under the Pétain regime, by the famous documentary, *The Sorrow and the Pity*, released in 1969.[13] Postwar stories of Danish and Dutch help to the Jews have only more recently begun to be balanced by the recognition that there were Nazi sympathizers and collaborators in these countries as well. The refusal of the Western allies to act more pre-emptively to save the Jews, and the almost total rejection of Jewish refugees by countries such as Canada,[14] are known but seldom highlighted in the national memories of Western countries.

It is undeniable that at least Germany has indeed, as Gross suggests, 'worked through' its murderous past. West Germany accepted the heavy legal and moral burden of compensating survivors and the relatives of the victims of the Nazi regime. It paid billions in indemnity to Israel as well as to Jewish organizations and individuals. At the same time, East Germany and the communist successors to the collaborator regimes of Central Europe hid behind the fiction that they had themselves been victims of Nazism, and therefore were not responsible for the atrocities perpetrated by Germans, or under German pressure and occupation. (The current official positions in Poland and Hungary perpetuate this fake history, originally written by the communists.)

The most visible signs of German atonement for the past are the many memorials erected across the country to commemorate the victims (though not necessarily to remember the perpetrators) of the Holocaust. The most striking example is perhaps the Memorial to the Murdered Jews of Europe in Berlin, right next to the famous

Brandenburg Gate and the Reichstag. The impressive monument, covering 19,000 square metres, was inaugurated only in 2005, well after unification. That the location of Hitler's bunker, unmarked, is nearby, is symbolic, but perhaps even more so is the fact that the memorial is built over the former border between East and West Berlin. For the monument, along with many other impressive Holocaust memorials and museums, or the bronze pavement plaques marking where deported and murdered Jews once lived, also installed after the Fall of the Wall, are meant to mark that the new, united Germany has conquered the memory of its Nazi history. It's called *Vergangenheitsbewältigung*, 'mastering' but also 'overcoming' the past. This achievement is the precondition for a new post-unification Germany, one that confidently takes up its leading position in Europe, believing to have reassured others that the country's 'historical misdeeds' will not be repeated. As the Russian historian Alexander Etkind observes in another context, 'by building monuments to its former enemies and victims, the state asserts its own transformation'.

> Monuments represent [the nation's] continuing identity as a desired and often mythical unity between the state, the people, and their common history. They work as materialized forms of patriotic sentiment: sites of historical memory, of course, but first and foremost visible and touchable bodies of nationalism, which has created the present by distorting the past.[15]

In this case, the distortion may be to claim that the German nation has completed its mastery of the past, and at the same time to project the remaining anxieties eastward.

Etkind notes that monuments to victims often have a vertical shape, like that of an obelisk (in Berlin, there are concrete slabs), and adds that 'one way to interpret the vertical shape and central location of such monuments is to imagine a wooden stake that nails a mythological vampire to the ground'. We may connect that interpretation to Slavoj Žižek's Lacanian idea that the vampire genre represents the human fear of the dead who have not been properly laid to rest. 'Let us then ask', Žižek proposes, 'a naive and elementary question: why do the dead return? The answer offered by Lacan is the same as that found in popular culture: *because they were not properly buried*, i.e., because something went wrong with their obsequies.'[16]

If the terrible past refuses to rest, properly buried in the ground, in spite of its being recognized in Germany by both monuments and texts, then one may be tempted to look eastward for a reason. The point of the memorial's location on the 'death strip' between East and West Berlin symbolizes that unification has produced a liberal democracy dedicated to freedom and human rights, and that these 'Western values' are now shared also in the East. If this does not always appear to be true, then the blame can be put on the character of East Germans (the *Ossi* or 'Eastie' is subject to a form of Eastern Europeanism within Germany).[17] The greater popularity of the right-extremist Alternative for Germany Party (AFD) in the former East Germany can be treated this way, as can the crimes and misdeeds of Eastern German neo-Nazis, such as the attack on the synagogue of Halle in 2020,[18] although, as the anthropologist Nitzan Shoshan has shown, extremists in the East have depended on financial and moral support from the West.[19] The same eastward projection works with a vengeance when it comes to discussing anti-Semitism farther East in Central Europe.

The claimed distinction between Germany and 'Eastern Europe' – 'German society, mindful of its historical misdeeds, has become capable of confronting moral and political challenges', but 'Eastern Europe, by contrast, has yet to come to terms with its murderous past', in Gross' words – functions to confirm to Germans that they have mastered their shameful heritage. Their success is more gleaming in its chiaroscuro opposition to an East that has not yet thrown light onto its dark past.

But if the truth be told, in contrast to West Germany's willingness to shoulder responsibility for the Holocaust at the state level, its approach to individual Nazi perpetrators (known as 'denazification') has been far from perfect, and it suggests adding some nuance to the standard assertion that the West dealt with its past but the East didn't. Right after the war, Nazis and their collaborators probably had more to fear in Central and Eastern Europe, before and after full communist takeover, than in the countries of the West. War criminals insinuated themselves into 'normal society' and, sometimes, the secret services, on both sides of the Cold War, and prosecution was often sluggish. But, apart from the highly visible Nuremberg Trials (in which the Soviets participated), it was generally swifter and more severe in the East.

If it was West Germany that dealt more resolutely with Germany's Nazi heritage, for a long time it was not the West but the East that addressed the past of individual Nazis. Although the victorious powers instituted denazification processes, on 10 April 1951 the West German *Bundestag* or parliament passed a law that explicitly made it possible for all former Nazis, except those who had been in the highest positions, to return to the civil service.[20] This included professors. In the Soviet occupation zone and later East Germany, punishment was both more severe and more lasting, as it was in Central Europe. Not surprisingly, Nazis and collaborators alike sought refuge in the West, where they sometimes found sympathy for their anti-communist views.[21]

In consequence of my grandparents' murder at Kremnička, the Slovak commander who was most directly responsible, Jozef Nemsila, was given the death penalty by a Czechoslovak court. The sentence could not be carried out, because Nemsila had moved to Canada and, in spite of finally being charged decades later in his old age, he died a free man before his case could be judicially dealt with. Such cases are very far from unusual.[22] Suffice it, however, to mention the fate of one of the most notorious Gestapo butchers in Slovakia, Gustav Hauskrecht, who took refuge in West Germany, where he conducted a successful carpet business, having learned the trade from a Jewish family whom he had dispossessed. He lived out his days surrounded by a loving family and kind neighbours.[23]

Vergangenheitsbewältigung in West Germany really picked up most of its intensity when the generation of Nazis was already beginning to retire and to die. It reached its peak once Germany reunited after the Fall of the Wall. Since then, acknowledging German responsibility for the Holocaust has become a teaching point to address to not only former East Germans but also to immigrants.[24] The anthropologist Esra Özyürek speaks of 'subcontracting guilt' to those populations.[25] Continent-wide, it seems that German, but also, more generally, Western guilt is being subcontracted to 'Central and Eastern Europe'.

Let us return now to Jan Gross' contention that 'Eastern Europeans' are unable to 'recognize their obligation to save those fleeing in the face of evil' – that is, the mainly Muslim, Brown and Black, refugees entering Europe – because they have 'yet to come to terms with [their] murderous past', meaning the Holocaust.

The relationship between anti-Semitism and Islamophobia has extensively been explored by a number of writers, including myself.[26] The connection had indeed been noted by Edward Said, the highly influential author of *Orientalism*.[27] Anti-Semitism provided a set of images and vocabulary ready to be transformed into Islamophobia by the first Christian Islamophobes, going back to the eighth century.[28] Islamophobia resurged in the West with such events as the Iran 'hostage crisis' of 1979–1981 and more recently acts of terrorism in New York, Paris, London, Madrid and elsewhere, and with American military involvement in Iraq and Afghanistan. The virulent anti-Muslim rhetoric, one of whose peaks was President Trump's so-called 'Muslim ban', was often compared to anti-Semitism. Gross was far from the only one attributing what was seen as unusually virulent Islamophobia, to an alleged Eastern European heritage of virulent anti-Semitism.

Let us now examine this alleged connection between Eastern European anti-Semitism and Islamophobia. The American Pew Research Center asked Europeans in 37 countries if they would be willing to accept a Muslim or a Jew, as the case may be, into their family. In Figure 6.1, some of the results are given in terms of percentages of those who are prepared to do so.

The results do not confirm the idea that anti-Semitism is greater in Central Europe than in the West, even though they were obtained during the height of anti-migrant, Islamophobic hysteria in Central Europe following the 'migration crisis' of 2015–16. Slovakia's acceptance of Jews ranks above both Germany's and the UK's, and Poland's and Hungary's are the same as Italy's. The most anti-Semitic on this measure, by far, is Greece. The Eastern European countries outside of Central Europe, Russia and Moldova, are next. Nevertheless, the Pew Research Center decided to headline its widely cited communiqué of these and other results, 'Eastern and Western Europeans Differ on Importance of Religion, Views of Minorities, and Key Social Issues'. The editors choosing this headline were blind to the patterns emerging from the data,

Figure 6.1: Percentage per country of people willing to accept a Muslim or a Jew into their family

Country	Willing to accept Muslim	Willing to accept Jew
Greece	31	35
Moldova	30	40
Russia	34	40
Czech Republic	12	51
Bulgaria	32	55
Hungary	21	57
Poland	33	57
Italy	43	57
UK	53	69
Germany	55	69
Slovakia	47	73
Netherlands	88	96

Source: Pew Research Center, collected 2015–2017[29]

choosing instead to classify them a priori on the basis of Eastern Europeanist assumptions.

Other studies of anti-Semitism tend to show similar Europe-wide results, with Central European anti-Semitism similar to Italy's, and ranked roughly in the middle between the Atlantic West and the Orthodox East. The Pew study is an outlier when it comes to anti-Semitism in the Czech Republic, which other studies consider to be quite low. For example, the Anti-Defamation League's 2014 survey of global anti-Semitism found that in fact Czechs were less anti-Semitic than most Western Europeans. Their anti-Semitism percentage was only 13 per cent in the Czech Republic, 1 per cent *less* than in Canada![30]

In contrast, the Pew data on accepting Muslims are, with the exception of Slovakia, closer to Eastern Europeanist expectations; that is, Central European countries resemble on this account other Eastern European countries more than the West. With the exception of Slovakia, Central European countries are now found at the bottom of the list, below Greece and Moldova. Table 6.1, which ranks the selected countries by their acceptance of each group, shows clearly the shift in Central Europe from generally middling scores on Jews to very negative scores on Muslims.

If 'Eastern European' anti-Semitism were the underlying cause of the indeed shameful rejection of Muslims that Jan Gross points to,

Table 6.1: Selected countries ranked by the percentage of respondents who are willing to accept a Jew or a Muslim into their family

Rank	Most willing to accept	
	Jew	Muslim
1	Netherlands	Netherlands
2	Slovakia	Germany
3	UK	UK
4	Germany	Slovakia
5	Italy, Hungary, Poland (tied)	Italy
6		Russia
7		Poland
8	Bulgaria	Bulgaria
9	Czech Republic	Greece
10	Russia	Moldova
11	Moldova	Hungary
12	Greece	Czech Republic

Source: Pew Research Center, collected 2015–2017[31]

then the discrepancy between attitudes to Jews and Muslims would be far more comparable. In reality, as the Czech researcher Zdeněk Tarant has shown, if anything it is increasing Islamophobia that may lead to more anti-Semitism, rather than the other way around. Tarant found that far-right anti-Muslim demonstrators, generically attracted to conspiracy theories, spread classic and contemporary disinformation about Jews.[32]

Islamophobia without Muslims?

Why then are Islamophobic attitudes so pronounced today in Central Europe?[33] We may begin the search for an answer by turning to the oft-repeated expression: 'Islamophobia without Muslims'.[34] The phrase is a hyperbole: there are Muslims in every Central European country, but not many. According to Pew

Research Center's statistics,[35] in 2016 Muslims made up less than 0.1 per cent of the population in Poland, 0.1 per cent in Slovakia, 0.2 per cent in the Czech Republic, and 0.4 per cent in Hungary. In Germany, by comparison, Muslims made up 6.1 per cent of the population, in the United Kingdom, 6.3 per cent, and in Sweden, 8.1 per cent. So, although there were about 22,000 Muslims in the Czech Republic and around 40,000 in Hungary, that number is low enough to justify using 'without Muslims' as a turn of phrase.

The relative absence of Muslims in the four Central European countries makes it difficult to see Islamophobia there as an issue of conflict and competition among neighbours, similar to the widespread racial prejudice against Roma, or to anti-Semitism before the Holocaust. I suggest that the motivation for it needs to be understood in the context of the Western rejection of the Central European hope, after 1989, to be taken seriously as fully European, or, in the terms used in this book, as fully white.

I have been arguing that Central Europe as a whole shows the characteristics of other semi-peripheral areas of partial privilege, such as the rural, mostly white regions of Western Europe and America. This is also the case with 'Islamophobia without Muslims'. Peripheral parts of the West, too, have few Muslims, and they, too, tend to be more Islamophobic than the core urban areas, both in the West and in the East. The Turkish researchers Kaya and Kayaoglu culled data from the World Values Survey and the European Values Study, two large-scale international projects, to find correlates of Islamophobia. They found the size of town or city where a person resides to be very influential; the smaller the place the greater the likelihood that a resident exhibits Islamophobic prejudice (specifically, not wanting to live next to Muslims).[36]

To explain Islamophobia where there are few Muslims, Kaya and Kayaoglu resort to the so-called 'contact hypothesis', which suggests that familiarity between groups decreases hostility. However, such an explanation flies in the face of experience with other kinds of racism, including against African Americans and, in Europe, against Jews, which tended to be greatest where there were more, not fewer, of the targeted group. A better explanation is that populations of precarious white privilege (including some lower-middle-class white people in cities) tend to defend that privilege by asserting their difference from those they consider beneath them in the racialized class hierarchy.

There were not more Muslims in Central Europe in the years preceding the 'migration crisis' of 2015–16, so on the contact hypothesis one might expect at least as much Islamophobia before than after that landmark event. However, the available research data do not show a steady Central European attitude toward Muslims, but rather a sharp increase in Islamophobia during and after the 'migration crisis'. Central European opinion research agencies do not traditionally research attitudes to Muslims as such. But for both the Czech Republic and Hungary, there is clear evidence that attitudes to 'Arabs' worsened considerably during the 'migration crisis'. In the Czech Republic, hostility to Arabs increased 8 per cent from 2014 to 2015, and more than 10 per cent from 2015 to 2016.[37] Meantime, antipathy to Arabs overtook that toward the main racialized Other in the area, the Roma, also in Poland.[38] Comparable longitudinal data are difficult to find for Slovakia. However, in response to the EU's assignment of refugee quotas in 2015, the opinion research firm POLIS asked Slovaks if they were in favour of receiving refugees from 'the Middle East and North Africa' in their country, and 70.1 per cent said 'no'. Only 23.5 per cent were for admitting refugees, and only 4.2 per cent agreed strongly.[39]

Like the contact hypothesis, explanations of Islamophobia in terms of deep history are of questionable value.[40] Admittedly, Islam and Muslims have had mostly negative press in the history books and popular fiction in the area, due to the Ottoman Empire's encroachment on that of the Habsburgs. The struggle between the two powers was widely interpreted at the time, and is now, as one between Islam and Christianity. The tide of Ottoman expansion was stopped in 1683 at the gates of Vienna largely by troops commanded by the Polish king, John III Sobieski. (Memory of the event was dusted off by Polish provocateurs who scribbled the date, 1683, next to anti-Muslim graffiti in 2016 on the walls of the Krakow mosque.)[41]

The subsequent retelling of the complex relationship between the Ottomans and Central Europe has left the indelible impression on its peoples, of a neat division between Christians on one side of a struggle and Muslims on the other, even though in fact this was not so. (The Hungarian Protestant nobility who ruled Transylvania under Ottoman tutelage, for example, were allied with their Muslim overlords against the Catholic supporters of the Habsburg court.) The racialization of religion, which was taking place in Spain and Portugal, has its counterpart in the East, in the development of Central European national feeling as a form of Christian solidarity in opposition to Muslims, racialized in Iberia as 'Moors' and here as 'Turks'.

But the sharp rise in Islamophobia connected to the 2015–16 'migrant crisis' was not the result of memories of the Ottoman enemy, any more than it was in Germany, where also the Christian character of the nation was being given racial overtones in response to the Muslim migrants.[42] At most, what 'traditional' Islamophobia contributed was a ready-made reference to efforts at 'invasion' by an alien power. Comparisons between a Muslim invasion then and the migrant 'wave' now were made in Central as in Western Europe. In France, it had long been a particularly popular rhetorical device for the far-right *Rassemblement* (previously *Front*) *National*. The sharp increase in Islamophobia in Central Europe during and after the 'migration crisis', however, shows that it was not memories of Turkish scimitars that stimulated Islamophobia in the twenty-first century.

Islamophobia provided, more than anything perhaps, a politically exploitable means to show the West that Central Europeans will no longer accept the need for moral tutelage. This happened just at the moment that Central Europeans were gathering sufficient confidence to finally confront the preachy paternalism of the liberal West, whose prestige was weakened by the fiasco of the 2008 financial crisis. Rejecting the demands of Western 'political correctness' proved to be a perfect vehicle to express injured spite. In countries with almost no Muslims, provocative Islamophobia was a politically safe means to stand up to the liberals of 'Brussels' and their perceived lackeys among the local intellectual and business elites. For in a country 'without Muslims', politicians don't have to worry about the votes of Muslims, or of those who marry or befriend them.

As with any complex issue, there are other important factors that increase the wrongheaded appeal of Islamophobia. In Central Europe, as elsewhere, citizens have lived through decades of ever increasing insecurity. I have focused on the economic insecurity introduced by neoliberalism. Since the dismantling of the welfare state in the West and of socialism in the East, precarious work without job security has been steadily increasing. Feelings of insecurity increase in proportion to the build-up of the 'security' environment online, where we must provide personal information, of potential commercial value, to log in. The incessant demands for 'secure' passwords heighten our sense of living in an insecure world. Such feelings of insecurity are experienced in a larger emotional universe that includes the security threats from terrorism, which every now and then strikes almost any part of the world. In a few cases, sometimes spectacular, the terrorists are Muslim (although not as often as they are anti-Muslim), and this provides fodder for the frightened imagination of people who feel threatened already.

Add to this the even more consequential threats of unprecedented natural disasters caused by climate change, which is also partly responsible for the appearance of devastating pandemics. In the face of a radically unpredictable world, it is no wonder that people turn to the comforts of a closeness based in familiarity, such as can be provided by the objectively mistaken but emotionally comforting feeling of sameness and steadiness expressed by ethnoracial identity. The nation, conceived in racialized terms as a community of common descent, expands, to nationalists at least, the notion of family by referring to real or imagined kinship among its members. Nation and family are both bulwarks against the feelings of impersonality produced by capitalism. The illiberal misuse of these solidarities provided the political potential to allow the Visegrád Alliance to unite in defiant opposition to 'Brussels' and its 'elitist' support base in the West and at home.

Illiberal politicians have been able to capitalize on the opportunity provided by the 2015–16 migration crisis especially in areas, such as Central Europe, where there were few Muslims, to depict the Muslim migration as yet another massive threat to the closeness and sameness of their communities. Widely described as 'flooding' Europe, the migrants, some of whose friends and relatives had indeed perished during their perilous seaborne journey, could be dehumanized as just another natural disaster.

From Islamophobia to homophobia

How Islamophobia functioned as only one item in the toolkit of racist politics, however, and how it intersects with other hatreds and prejudices, was well illustrated in Central Europe by what happened when the 'migration crisis' subsided somewhat. The power of the 'Muslim' as a figure to represent an ongoing threat to national cohesiveness decreased to an extent, and the potential of the Muslim to be the figure animating the politics of racial exclusion decreased. Viktor Orbán was wrong that his government stopped the migration wave of 2015–16 by erecting his border fence. Much more effective was the EU's deal with Turkey, whereby Brussels paid Ankara to keep refugees stuck there. But Orbán may have been right in that it was his spirit of rejection that led to that deal. After the German chancellor's memorable declaration that 'we will manage' the mass influx of refugees, Western Europe, too, chose the path of 'protecting' itself from the largely Muslim migrants of colour. The EU signed the Turkey deal on 18 March 2016, less than two years after Orbán built his fence. That Western Europe had decided to sing from Orbán's hymn book became glaringly obvious in 2021, when, encouraged by the Belarusian dictator Alexander Lukashenko, large numbers of Middle Eastern migrants attempted to enter Poland and the EU from his country. Polish border guards made a practice of returning the would-be refugees without a hearing to the frigid no-man's land between Poland and Belarus. The rest of the EU made barely a noise. (The silence contrasted with the open-arms policy towards refugees from the Russian invasion of Ukraine, deemed white enough to deserve the full solidarity of Europeans.)

So while Orbán continued to raise the spectre of brown migration at every possible occasion, the fact that now fewer migrants arrived in Europe, and practically none of those braved the brutal detention that was offered them in Hungary, robbed Islamophobes and colour racists of live news to exploit. They needed another target. This proved to be the LGBTQ+ community.

Orbán, who had made hate against Muslim and other migrants an important part of his campaign in the elections of 2018, arranged a referendum on a law 'protecting children' against LGBTQ 'propaganda' to be administered together with the parliamentary poll in 2022. But it was the Polish government who initiated the 'culture wars' against homosexuality. The Polish LGBTQ+ community has never been given its rights, but a movement to fight for them does exist, and it has had a certain amount of success among the liberal and left-wing public. Activists may have taken some satisfaction from the fact that a supporter of both migrant and LGBTQ+ rights, Paweł Adamowicz, was able to hold the office of mayor of the city of Gdańsk from 1998 until 2019. But then he was, tragically, assassinated by an apparently deranged former criminal. That the killer was enabled by the illiberal rhetoric of the ruling PiS party was widely suspected. The openly gay mayor of a smaller city, Słupsk, Robert Biedroń, founded his own party and ran for president in 2020. He gained an underwhelming 2.29 per cent of the vote in the first round, which disqualified him from the second. The winner, Andrzej Duda of PiS, had exploited homophobia with at least the same energy that Beata Szydło (like Duda, a mouthpiece of strongman Jarosław Kaczyński) had used to exploit 'migration wave' Islamophobia in the 2014 elections, to wrest the Polish government from the centrist, liberal Civic Platform Party of the future president of the European Council, Donald Tusk.

Perhaps eager to recreate the hysteria of 2014, but this time with homosexuals, trans, and gender-fluid people the target, Duda suggested that homosexuality was an 'ideology' and that it was worse than communism. His parents' generation fought communism for 40 years, he said, and 'they didn't fight for this so that a new ideology would appear that is even more destructive'.[43] The president's office in all four Visegrád countries is mainly ceremonial, but carries moral authority. Soon after Duda's election, the PiS government passed legislation making it impossible for same-sex couples to adopt. The measure elicited a large amount of protest, but it prevailed.

The reference to LGBT 'ideology' is part of a rhetoric encouraged by some at the highest levels of the Polish Catholic Church. Marek Jedraszewski is the Archbishop of Krakow, the country's cultural capital. Jedraszewski condemned same-sex 'ideology' as a 'rainbow plague', worse than Bolshevism. He blames it for trying 'to take away our Poland, our land that has been Christian for over 1,050 years'.[44] The concerted homophobic campaign of both the Church and the government has enabled over 100 Polish towns to declare 'LGBT ideology-free zones', though most eventually relented under EU pressure.

LGBT 'ideology' (that would be texts or visual material or speeches with a positive attitude to sexual orientation) appears from the perspective of the homophobes to be part of a broader 'gender ideology', now often referred in Polish (as well as in Hungarian) simply with the English word 'gender'. What is meant is any attack on the traditional heteronormative, patriarchal 'family values' that illiberals aim to defend. The super-conservative Catholic orientation of the government has led to the law, passed in October 2020 and provoking widespread street demonstrations, that limits abortion to cases where the woman's life or health is in danger.

The *Gazeta Wyborcza* ironized that 'Poland will fight gender in all EU documents. Europe probably does not understand this noble enthusiasm. Only in Poland do we know how dangerous the gender devil can be.' The occasion was the EU's attempt to give official approval to a document regarding artificial intelligence. The Polish objection was not to anything of substance, but to the fact that the word 'gender' appeared in the text.[45]

Orbán's government picked up the issue with a vengeance in the summer of 2021, when Fidesz proposed and passed in parliament a law against 'homosexual propaganda' modelled on similar legislation in Russia. It was henceforth forbidden to make available to people younger than 18 any item that 'popularizes or invokes' homosexuality. Because of the international (and domestic) uproar about the law, Orbán decided not to attend Hungary's EuroCup football match against Germany in Munich, apparently afraid that the crowd would boo him and challenge, for Hungarian TV viewers, his desired image of 'Europe's strongman'. Organizers had, indeed, threatened to light up the stands with the rainbow colours symbolic of LGBT rights.

Noting these events, the Hungarian journalist Péter Magyari argued that the anti-LGBT 'propaganda' law was a deliberate attempt by Orbán to whip up domestic passions, in order to distract the public from the fact that, for the first time in a long time, the opposition had just achieved a victory over the government: it forced it to rethink its plans to build a campus of China's Fudan University in Budapest, and to promise to hold a referendum on the subject.[46]

Magyari notes that the government's expectation that gay-bashing would be popular in the country was a gamble; the 'propaganda' law was certainly the subject of heavy domestic criticism. Across Central Europe, opinions on LGBTQ+ rights vary greatly, but there is considerable support for such LGBT-friendly projects as same-sex marriage. The Pew Research Center studied the percentage of respondents in various European countries who favour same-sex marriage, and some of the results appear in Figure 6.2.

The results confirm the pattern we have seen previously in Chapter 4, when surveying quantitative research regarding East–West differences, and to a lesser extent in the data on anti-Semitism and Islamophobia:

- There is not a clear border between East and West.
- Central European countries tend to rank between the West and (the rest of) the East, but there are major differences among them.
- The quantities (here, percentages) show a greater difference between (the rest of the) East and Centre than between Centre and West.

The Czech Republic resembles, on this measure, Ireland and Finland, and is more favourable to same-sex marriage than Italy and

Figure 6.2: Percentage of people who said they 'favoured' or 'strongly favoured' legalizing same-sex marriage

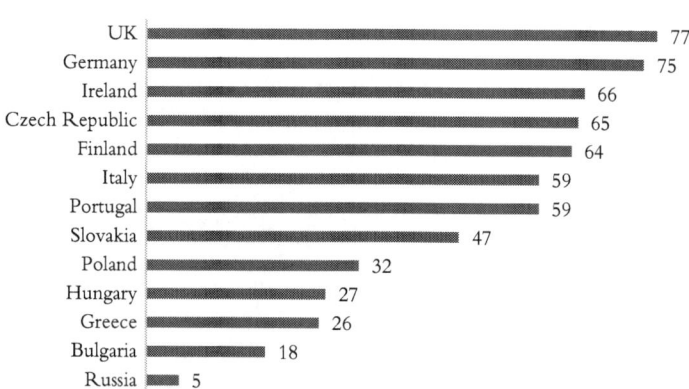

Source: Pew Research Center, collected 2015–2017[47]

Portugal. Poland and Hungary are very negative about same-sex marriage, but still much less so than Bulgaria and, especially, Russia. Such data hardly justify the Pew Research communiqué's gross generalization that the 'Iron Curtain that once divided Europe may be long gone, but the continent today is split by stark differences in public attitudes'.[48] Moreover, it is very likely that if we had data about opinions on same-sex marriage in rural America and Western Europe – the peripheries of the West – as we did for some of the other 'Eastern European' data discussed in Chapter 4, then we would find once again a great deal of overlap between those areas and the overall figures for Central Europe, while we might expect the big cities of Central Europe to be closer to the West.

Like Islamophobia, homophobia in Central Europe has long foundations in history. These are common European and Christian foundations, rather than 'Eastern European'. Do 'Eastern Europeans' have no shame? Many don't. But if, shamefully, racist and homophobic sentiment continues to increase, however unevenly, across Central Europe, then this must not be viewed as an exclusive, ingrained cultural characteristic of the East.

There is the desire, mentioned earlier, to locate racism and similar prejudice in the East, in order to deal with the unpleasant fact that they are also very much part of the West, thus undermining attempts at keeping the two separate.[49] But racism and homophobia are not unique to Central or even Eastern Europe. They are partly a warning sign of alienation from liberal and humanitarian values, common in all areas negatively impacted by neoliberal globalization. Illiberal social conservativism provides some partially privileged groups of people, including in Central Europe, a tragically misguided way to fight back. Resentment does not in the least excuse racism or homophobia. But the Western role in causing resentment through self-serving rhetoric, meant to fight hate in the East but implicitly exonerating it in the West, should also be examined. That is what I do next.

7

Imitators Spurned: Why the West Needs Central Europe to Stay in its Eastern European Place

The excitement when the barriers came crashing down – the actual wall in Berlin and the imagined Iron Curtain across Europe – soon cooled. The Westerners were disappointed with the Easterners, and the Easterners were disappointed with their disappointment. In this chapter, I elaborate on how accepting the East Central Europeans as full members of the Western club was actually never really intended. There was the usual scorn with which the privileged view those who are less rich and powerful, and who, as the more fortunate see it, have only themselves to blame. But, more importantly, full acceptance of East Central Europe was never in the interest of Western business. Western multinational corporations were not out to take on new partners. They were looking for new markets and cheap labour in Europe's East, much as they had always done in the Global South.

As we have seen earlier, the universal contempt for a culturally and economically backward East in Europe is replicated in every place, along the way from England to the borders of Russia. Historically, the English felt it for the French and together the English and the French felt it for the Germans; now western Germans feel it for eastern Germans, who may feel it for Poles and Czechs the way they in turn feel it for Ukrainians and Russians. (While also western Ukrainians may feel it not only for Russians but also for eastern Ukrainians.) This transitive Orientalism is for the most part unreflecting and unexamined by those infected by it. They include not only the right-wing illiberals but, perhaps even more so, the left and liberal *Bildungsbürgertum*, the educated classes or 'intelligentsia', who in each area see themselves as mediators between the local population and the prestigious culture of the West. The cultural capital they possess in the form of their familiarity with Western cultural trends and languages (now mainly English), earns them at times the respect, and at other times the resentment of their compatriots, who may see them as betraying their native roots. At the same time, it makes them feel entitled to be taken seriously as intellectual equals in the West. That is exactly what they hoped would happen once the communist regimes fell and released them from their Cold War confinement in the Eastern Bloc.

Sometime back in the mid-1970s, Milan Kundera walked the streets of Prague, still quietly splendid in spite of the baroque and art nouveau façades greying due to neglect by the incompetent and impoverished communist government. He and his walking companion agreed that, in the West, '[c]ulture no longer existed as a realm in which supreme values were enacted'.[1] His suspicions were confirmed when he arrived in Paris in 1975, in his mid-forties, a refugee from communist Czechoslovakia. His French friends looked at him 'indulgently' and 'with an embarrassment' as he lamented the 'tragedy' of the communist regime closing all literary and cultural reviews. 'In Paris, even in a completely cultivated milieu, during dinner parties people discuss television programs, not reviews', he complained, feeling indignantly that even if 'all the reviews in France or England disappeared, no one would notice it, not even their editors'. Kundera concluded that, in the West, culture 'has already bowed out'.[2]

Perhaps. But there is another explanation, which surely at some level must have occurred to Kundera. It could be that it's not that the cultivated diners of Paris or London had become uncaring about literary reviews, but rather, that they did not really care much about literary reviews published in Prague. Or, that they did not care about overtly self-important declarations by writers about their work as an actualization of 'supreme values', especially when contrasted with the dreadful low culture of 'television programmes'. They may have dismissed that as something typical of the earnest *intelligentsia* of Eastern Europe. Indeed, Kundera's sentiments were reminiscent of how Russia's most famous dissident writer, Aleksandr Solzhenitsyn, lambasted Western 'mass living habits, introduced by the revolting invasion of publicity, by TV stupor, and by intolerable music'.[3]

Viktor Orbán arrived at Pembroke College, Oxford, in September 1989, in his mid-twenties. His project was to study the idea of civil society in European political philosophy, a topic close to the hearts of dissidents such as Václav Havel, who thought that civil society had been destroyed by the communists. He arrived with a scholarship from the Open Society Foundation, funded by his future nemesis, George Soros. Orbán barely stayed at Oxford for four of his intended nine months. He does not talk much today about his experience there; his reasons for cutting the visit remain for future biographers to investigate. There was an obvious practical reason for an ambitious young politician: the communists agreed to the demand for free elections, and he probably felt a path to a political career opening up. It would be interesting to know, however, more about his feelings upon arrival in England and during his stay there: was he, like Kundera, disappointed in the West he saw, compared to the West he had hoped to see? What was his reception as a fresh-off-the-plane 'Eastern European'?

In the event, all we know from the little that Orbán has revealed is that, as he put it, 'Oxford was a very good experience, but I felt all along that, for me, this is not my place.'[4] Being out of place was the common sensation on their first major experience with the West, for both Kundera, who chose to become a Frenchman, and for Orbán, who returned to a Central Europe that was itself now collectively experiencing an unprecedented encounter with the West. In 2017, Orbán described his disillusionment in terms that betray, many years later, something of the same sense of personal injury and shattered illusions.

> Recall how back then, at the beginning of the nineties, most people – not only in Hungary but in all of Central Europe – considered it to be evident that what we needed was complete assimilation, a complete assimilation, adjustment, a kind of molting: the shedding of old skin in order to grow a new, fashionable, Western

one. In a political sense, what followed from this was that quite simply we needed to do what they [the West] were doing. And then ... we got together here and we reflected that we, the freedom fighters on this side of the iron curtain, might perhaps have something of value to say to that Europe which had lived for forty years already in peace, freedom, and prosperity.[5]

Thus does Orbán reject the wish of the early post-communist leadership, many of whom had been prominent dissidents under communism, to adopt the then current standards of a Western liberal democracy. To them, this did not mean mimicking a foreign standard. It meant returning Central Europe to its historical home, the democratic West. To Orbán, now, they appeared as nothing but pathetic, failed imitators of a foreign model.

The 'Imitation Imperative'

The idea of post-communist Central Europe as failed imitators has been raised to the level of an academic theory by Ivan Krastev and Stephen Holmes. Indeed, the two political scientists take an even more radical view than Orbán. I have argued (in Chapter 5) that the Hungarian leader objects to imitating the specific form of 'the West' represented by neoliberal globalization and the liberal elites. He does not mean at all to dissociate himself from the West; rather, he would very much like to lead the EU's East and West on the way to a Europe remade according to his ideal of an 'illiberal democracy'. Krastev and Holmes, on the other hand, interpret Central European illiberals as believing that any attempt to make the East be like the West is, to them, a priori a misguided imitation. In fact, they seem to believe this themselves.

Krastev and Holmes' analysis deserves attention, and I will discuss it next. Ultimately, however, I believe that it misses the point. For, to the extent that Central European countries have indeed failed to cut the grade as Western democracies, they did not do so necessarily because of their inherent incapacity to successfully imitate the West. It was in the Western interest, and it was part of Western practice, to reject local efforts to build democracy as a poor imitation. To bring into the focus the Western role, after discussing Krastev and

Holmes I will turn to an illuminating essay from the 1990s by the social critic Homi Bhabha, and to his notion of 'colonial mimicry'. Reading Krastev and Holmes together with Bhabha should permit us to build a fuller picture of why the West needs Central Europe to be, to borrow a phrase from Bhabha, 'the same, but not quite'. Which in our case means white, but not quite.

In *The Light That Failed: A Reckoning*,[6] Krastev and Holmes, a Bulgarian and an American political scientist, interpret the illiberal turn in Central and Eastern Europe as a misguided reaction against the post-1989 'transition' from communism, which tried to adopt everything Western and abandon everything that was not. As they put it,

> according to the illiberals, the Western-inspired Imitation Imperative made it seem like destiny for countries to shed their hallowed pasts and adopt a new liberal-democratic identity which, if truth be told, would never be fully theirs. Shame at reshaping one's preferences to conform to the value hierarchies of foreigners, doing so in the name of freedom, and being looked down upon for the supposed inadequacy of the attempt – these are the emotions and experiences that have fuelled the anti-liberal counter-revolution that began in post-communist Europe, specifically in Hungary, and that has now metastasized worldwide.[7]

The Light That Failed is one of the worthiest analyses of the foundations of illiberalism in 'Central and Eastern Europe'. The introduction of affect, of shame in this instance, as key to understanding illiberalism is particularly valuable. Nevertheless, an ingrained Eastern Europeanism appears to prevent the authors from fully following up on their often-brilliant insights. In the quote above, for example, they speak of how the post-communist, Hungarian case 'metastasized worldwide'. The idea that the worldwide 'anti-liberal counter-revolution' began in Hungary is hardly meant seriously and the authors do not take it up again. But then they also miss the opportunity to more fully locate Central

European illiberalism in its global context, not as much an export to as an import from the outside world.

Krastev and Holmes' geopolitical perspective is reduced largely to the impact of what seemed like the crushing victory of Western capitalism over communism in the Cold War. The triumph of the West, which Krastev and Holmes sum up under the label 'liberalism', seemed so spectacular that 'liberalism' had no alternative. Certainly, the peoples of formerly communist Europe had no alternative of their own. So they had no choice but to imitate the Western model.

> 1989 heralded the onset of a thirty-year Age of Imitation. The Western-dominated unipolar order made liberalism seem unchallengeable in the realm of moral ideals. This ideological supremacy, in turn, conferred such normative legitimacy on Western institutional forms as to make copying them, for those able to do so, seem obligatory.[8]

At least the Russians, as Krastev and Holmes see it, know that Eastern Europe is not the West; that it is not fertile ground for Western democracy and liberalism. From the beginning when the ex-communist apparatchik, Boris Yeltsin, made sure he had his own country to be president of, by splitting Russia from Gorbachev's shipwrecked Soviet Union, Russian imitation was always but a show. To get Western support during the initial years of the 'transition' from communism, Russian rulers pretended that they were about to adopt liberal democracy. But that was all theatre, designed to fool the unsuspecting West while Russia's oligarchic structures were being developed under its noses. Russian elites had no sincere desire to adopt liberal democracy, say Krastev and Holmes: 'most of them found faking democracy perfectly natural since they had been faking communism for at least two decades before 1991'.[9] The turn to an illiberal, authoritarian Russia was, therefore, in a sense less striking, less radical than in Central Europe. All it required was abandoning its superficial liberal rhetoric once, under Vladimir Putin, kleptocratic autocracy was firmly established. Russia turned from diffidence to defiance toward the West, and the Russian government stopped most of the liberal democratic charade.

In contrast with Russian fakery, or East Asian utilitarianism (the Japanese, and later the Chinese, copied Western technologies and practices, but to adapt them to non-Western goals), Krastev and Holmes see Central Europeans as having honestly pursued not only the 'technical instruments' but also the 'targets, objectives, goals and ways of life' of the West. Central European 'elites', Krastev and Holmes suggest, earnestly accepted that Western-style liberal capitalism was the 'normal' state of society. They felt that 'copying' the West as a model would be the only way to restore health to their societies, after what they regarded as the moral, political, and economic deformities of communism. Their self-respect was damaged when they found that the West did not accept their imitation liberalism as the genuine article. 'The wave of anti-liberalism sweeping over Central Europe reflects widespread popular resentment at the perceived slights to national and personal dignity that this palpably sincere reform-by-imitation project entailed.'[10]

Clearly, Krastev and Holmes do realize that Western rejection played a role in the failure of East Central European 'imitation'. But they do not attribute this to Western motives, and certainly not to any self-serving economic or political ones. Rather, they suggest that *all* imitation, by its very nature, leads to insult and social strife. Citing the French philosopher René Girard (1923–2015), they propose that conflict is inevitable given that imitation damages the imitator's self-respect.[11] It is for this reason that '[e]ven the best intentioned' among the Western advisers who guided the East Central European imitators 'were unable to conceal the implied superiority of the model over the mimic'.[12]

Krastev and Holmes add that there are two types of imitation. One is where you want something and you copy someone else's ends for getting it (an imitation of means), and another where you did not originally want it, but learn to do so. In this case, you're imitating not just the means but the end; you imitate your model's desires. Krastev and Holmes explain that

> [t]he form of imitation most likely to generate resentment and conflict, according to Girard, is the imitation of desires. We imitate not just means but also ends, not just technical instruments but also targets, objectives, goals and ways of life. This, in our opinion,

is the inherently stressful and contentious form of emulation that has helped trigger the current sweeping anti-liberal revolt.[13]

The authors suggest that Central Europeans feel a particularly acute sense of injury, because their sincere attempts at emulating the West were an imitation of desires themselves ('targets, objectives, goals and ways of life') and not just, as with East Asians, the means to achieve them.

Krastev and Holmes' analysis places the alleged imitators-of-desire in the role of a child learning from an adult. The child learner is, in fact, an important character in Girard's drama of imitation. His theory of mimicry was not developed to explain the imitation of the West by Central Europe – that is an adaptation by Krastev and Holmes. In the following original passage from Girard, however, I put [the East] and [the West] in square brackets in places where he speaks of children and adults, respectively.

> All the grown-up voices [the West] around him [the East], beginning with those of the father and mother (voices which, in our society at least, speak for the culture with the force of established authority [the West]) exclaim in a variety of accents, 'Imitate us!' 'Imitate me!' 'I bear the secret of life, of true being!' The more attentive the child [the East] is to these seductive words, and the more earnestly he responds to the suggestions emanating from all sides, the more devastating will be the eventual conflicts. The child [the East] possesses no perspective that will allow him to see things as they are. He has no basis for reasoned judgements, no means of foreseeing the metamorphosis of his model [the West] into a rival. This model's [the West's] opposition reverberates in his [the East's] mind like a terrible condemnation; he can only regard it as an act of excommunication. [...]
>
> The unchanneled mimetic impulse hurls itself blindly against the obstacle of a conflicting desire. It invites its own rebuffs and these rebuffs will in turn strengthen the mimetic inclination. We have, then, a self-perpetuating

> process, constantly increasing in simplicity and fervor. Whenever the disciple [the East] borrows from his model [the West] what he believes to be the 'true' object, he [the East] tries to possess that truth by desiring precisely what this model [the West] desires. Whenever he sees himself closest to the supreme goal, he comes into violent conflict with a rival.[14]

The way that Krastev and Holmes substitute East and West for child and adult reveals the extent to which their concept of 'imitating desire' infantilizes Central Europe. Since they believe that Central Europeans had to learn to desire Western 'goals and ways of life' from scratch, like a child learning appropriate behaviour from an adult, it is not surprising that they view Central Europeans' encounter with reinstated capitalism as 'veering close to a "conversion experience"'.[15] 'The core complaint motivating anti-liberal politics in the region today', they suggest, 'is that the attempt to democratize formerly communist countries was aiming at a kind of cultural conversion to values, habits and attitudes considered "normal" in the West'.[16] 'Central European elites' were 'hopeful converts who wished to lure their societies into a collective conversion experience'.[17]

Converts? Did either the elites or the 'societies' of Central Europe really need to 'convert' in order to have the same desires as people in the West? Krastev and Holmes do not spell out what Western 'values, habits and attitudes' in the West may be, or why they should be considered uniformly present in the West and not at all in the East. They simply assume an East–West cultural border along East Europeanist lines.

They are mistaken. To be sure, before and after 1989 many, and almost certainly most, Central Europeans did desire what the West had and they did not. This is most true in the literal sense of *having*: Central Europeans wanted high-quality material goods and the material signs of a good life that were so much more common in the West. But wanting what someone else has does not necessarily mean having to be 'converted' to new desires. When a large shiny Mercedes sign was erected on the western side of the Berlin Wall in 1965, the 'capitalists' in the West didn't have to do any missionary work to appeal to East Berliners' desire for a fancy ride.

To be fair, Krastev and Holmes focus on conversion not to material goods as much as to the ideals of liberal democracy. But here their approach is just as problematic. We may overlook perhaps that Girard was interested in conversion, not *to* any particular mimetic desire, but *from* mimetic desire as such. When they speak of conversion, they mean it in the everyday, common sense, rather than specifically Girard's. They mean that Central Europeans, who did not previously desire to have a liberal democracy, 'converted' to desiring it circa 1989 through imitating the West.

Certainly, not everyone in Central Europe has wanted a meaningful democracy – but does everyone in the West? However, Central Europeans did not have to imitate West Europeans to want liberal democracy. To those many Central Europeans who wanted and want a democracy based on the rule of law, it is not a Western European ideal but a general European, and indeed a universal human one. Kundera, Konrád, Michnik, and Havel would no doubt take some offence at the suggestion that they needed to convert to Western 'values, habits and attitudes'. Arguably (though here, too, caution is required), there is less of a history of the democratic ideal in Russia and the other predominantly Eastern Orthodox post-communist countries, which may go some way toward explaining why Central European 'imitation' would appear sincere compared to the Russian. But certainly for Central Europeans, the change from communist socialism to liberal democracy did not entail learning new desires.

The roots of democracy in Central Europe

Generally speaking, liberal democracy in the area has historical roots as deep as among its Western neighbours (which means not very deep), and the legacy of liberal democracy has just as much had its ups and downs. The liberal constitution passed by the Polish parliament, the Sejm, in 1791 was the first written constitution in Europe. It established a constitutional monarchy along the general principles of Enlightenment liberalism, and on the model of the Constitution of the United States, a country in whose revolutionary war of independence the Polish military commanders Tadeusz Kościusko and Casimir Pulaski played an important part. Also in the New World, Polish soldiers sent to fight by Napoleon against

Haitian rebels joined the Black slaves, earning them the honourable epithet, 'white Blacks of Europe', by the first head of state of the first Black republic in modern times, Jean-Jacques Dessalines.[18] The Hungarian national movements in the mid-nineteenth century were part of Europe-wide romantic liberalism. The revolutionary leader of the country, Lajos Kossuth, was widely admired in Europe and the United States as a freedom fighter. Karl Marx's close collaborator, Friedrich Engels, likened Kossuth to the great figures of the French Revolution, Danton and Carnot. No nineteenth-century writers contrasted the Hungarian and French rebels along East–West lines; Eastern Europeanism had not yet been born. The revolutionary year 1848 also saw revolts in the future capital of the Czech Republic, Prague, which, as we have seen, was then an Austrian provincial capital with a large German-speaking presence. The demands of the uprising included full civil liberties, along with national rights within the Austrian Empire for both Czechs and Germans. The Free City of Krakow, too, rose to arms.

East and West, the demands of the liberal revolutionaries were often unsuccessful, and their revolt was suppressed. However, liberal political tendencies struggled on into the period between the two World Wars. The mixed record of interwar democracy in East Central Europe was hardly worse than that of countries in West Central and Southern Europe. Poland and Hungary succumbed to authoritarianism, but in that they were no worse than, and were largely inspired by, Mussolini's Italian fascism. Austria's Catholic-tinged fascism, too, had great appeal in both Poland and Slovakia. And, of course, it was not in East Central Europe but in Germany that the most vicious form of fascism triumphed.

Interwar Czechoslovakia was, arguably, no less democratic than France. Neither country was able to hold on to its democratic system once Hitler's troops marched in. Then the Vichy government in France, led by the war hero Marshal Philippe Pétain, replaced the liberal Republic with a regime remarkably similar to those run in Central Europe by authoritarian leaders such as Hungary's Miklós Horthy and Slovakia's Jozef Tiso.

No one would argue that communism rather than liberal democracy would have been chosen by Central Europeans if the Soviet Union did not impose it. Czechoslovakia was the only Central European country with a strong communist party capable of winning elections, which is something that one saw after the war also in France and especially Italy. It is not unreasonable to assume that if the Soviet Union had not occupied East Central Europe, liberal democracy might possibly have flourished there as much as in the West.

Even Krastev and Holmes recognize, intermittently, that Central European reformers were not taking on Western values as something new, but as a heritage to return to. The authors refer approvingly to the German philosopher, Jürgen Habermas, who understood the changes of 1989 as 'rectifying revolutions' or 'catch-up revolutions'. In their view, Habermas saw these 'revolutions' as having the goal to '*return* Central and Eastern European societies to the mainstream of Western modernity, allowing the Central and East Europeans to gain what the West Europeans already possessed'.[19] Elsewhere, Krastev and Holmes suggest that, in East Central Europe, '[i]mitation was *justified* as a "return to Europe", and that meant a return to the region's authentic self'.[20] But how can you *return* to something that others, but not you, 'already' possess? The implication is clearly that, yes, many and perhaps most East Central Europeans did think of 1989 as a return to their previous status as citizens of the West, but that they were deluding themselves. For their version of acting Western was, in fact, nothing but a risible imitation. Here Krastev and Holmes themselves reproduce the act of exclusion that provokes the injured pride of Central Europeans; they, too, reject them as wannabes. In general, their 'imitation' thesis suffers from not seeing what things look like to the Central Europeans themselves: a major defect in the practice of social science, which is called upon to 'recognize' the groups it studies.[21]

An even greater problem is that Krastev and Holmes focus only on what Central Europeans did, thought, and felt. But neither the 'transition' to capitalism nor the turn to illiberalism was a tango for one. To understand these developments, we must also look at the lead partner: the West.

Mimicry rejected: on capitalism and exclusion

A classic essay by Homi Bhabha on 'colonial mimicry', 'On Mimicry and Man', provides us with the tools we need to admit Western power among the factors that enter into what might appear as Central Europe's desire to imitate, or as Bhabha puts it, 'mimic' the West.[22] Bhabha speaks perhaps from the position of the postcolonial intellectuals, who acquire the culture and many of the credentials of the white elite, but not its full acceptance. Instead, their acculturation is rejected as mimicry. Colonial mimicry in general, writes Bhabha, is

> the desire for a reformed, recognizable Other, as *a subject of a difference that is almost the same, but not quite.* Which is to say, that the discourse of mimicry is constructed around an *ambivalence*; in order to be effective, mimicry must continually produce its slippage, its excess, its difference.[23]

Bhabha shows how Western supremacy in the colonial and postcolonial contexts hinges on non-Western elites becoming *almost* an integral part of the West, but at the same time depends on maintaining the difference between East and West. Equality is promised, but delayed forever.

It is worth looking at this pattern in some detail, because it is possible to apply the way that Bhabha grasps the imitation/mimicry relationship between the West and postcoloniality, also to the relationship between the West and the post-communist space.

In the Central European as in the postcolonial context, it is not the non-Western (or not-Western-enough) others that see themselves as a mimic. 'Mimicry' stems from the logic of the dominant, which bars the Other from becoming 'quite' the same. 'Mimicry emerges as one of the most elusive and effective strategies of colonial power and knowledge', writes Bhabha.[24] Psychologically, colonial power emerges as 'the twin figures of narcissism and paranoia that repeat furiously'.[25] What is narcissistic is the colonizer's belief that they have reached the pinnacle of human development and as such must serve as the example to all. This leads to a missionary zeal to convert the Other to one's own civilizational standards. What is paranoid is the fear that permitting complete sameness will end a privilege that is based on immutable difference.

Bhabha illustrates the tension between the narcissistic and the paranoid with the example of Charles Grant's *Observations on the State of Society among the Asiatic Subjects of Great Britain* (1792).[26]

One dimension along which the West wished the colonial world to assimilate to it, but not quite, is the religious one. The *mission civilisatrice* of the Northwest European colonizers was often also a Christian mission.

> Grant's dream of an evangelical system of mission education conducted uncompromisingly in English was partly a belief in political reform along Christian lines and partly an awareness that the expansion of company rule in India required a system of 'interpellation' – a reform of manners, as Grant put it, that would provide the colonial with 'a sense of personal identity as we know it.' Caught between the desire for religious reform and the fear that the Indians might become turbulent for liberty, Grant implies that it is, in fact the 'partial' diffusion of Christianity, and the 'partial' influence of moral improvements which will construct a particularly appropriate form of colonial subjectivity. What is suggested is a process of reform through which Christian doctrines might collude with divisive caste practices to prevent dangerous political alliances. Inadvertently, Grant produces a knowledge of Christianity as a form of social control which conflicts with the enunciatory assumptions which authorize his discourse. In suggesting, finally, that 'partial reform' will produce an empty form of 'the imitation of English manners which will induce them [the colonial subjects] to remain under our protection', Grant mocks his moral project.

Bhabha is quoting Grant from the papers of the East India Company,[27] which hold an earlier version of the *Observations* than the more widely available 1813 issue, published by the House of Commons. In the latter, Grant speaks of the 'imitation of English manners' as the best option for Indians among European options to mimic. 'Hindoos ... now subject to Great Britain must, in their supposed new circumstances ... continue to need the supply of many wants from that country', says Grant, describing an acute insight into the effect of developing colonial markets as an export of consumer 'needs' along with the goods to supply them. He continues to say that if, as is to be expected, the 'Hindoos' will want British goods, then they must be protected by the most powerful 'maritime power', that is, Britain, from other colonial navies that would disrupt the supply. Consequently, '[i]t is rather to be expected that their own interest, and the preference which their *imitation of our manners* have given us over other European nations, will jointly induce them to remain safe under our protection'.[28]

This portrayal of what Indians adopting British ways means for British power, both political and economic, is as clear as it is frank. Grant advocates for an 'assimilation' of the Indian subjects that knows its limits. In Bhabha's words, 'The ambivalence of colonial authority repeatedly turns from *mimicry* – a difference that is almost nothing but not quite – to *menace* – a difference that is almost total but not quite'.[29] Mimicry brings the colonial subject close enough to desire the goods and protection of the colonizers but creates, from the colonizer's point of view, the menace of a closeness that abolishes economic and political privilege.

I have discussed (in Chapter 1 and elsewhere in this book) the close connection between race and capitalism, referring to Stuart Hall's insight that capitalism 'has always advanced as much by way of the production and negotiation of difference as it has through enforcing sameness, standardization, and homogenization'.[30] Racial difference is one of capitalism's products. In capitalism, while the total amount of wealth is not a zero-sum game – competition is not a matter always of competing for a slice of the same pie – the winner is one who outperforms the competition. Capitalists seek new markets and new sources of cheap labour; they do not seek new competition. This is the underlying logic of capital expansion, whether by an enterprise, a country, or the 'globalized' system of regulated competition, dominated by US and West European capital and their established allies, and flourishing at the end of the twentieth and at the beginning of the twenty-first century.

Perhaps the saddest irony of the history of liberal democracy is that the states where liberal democracy has been most secure are the saltwater imperial powers on both sides of the North Atlantic, who have combined the increasing democratic empowerment of their own public with the domination of territories where democratic freedoms were denied to a population seen mainly as a source of cheap labour and a market for its cheap products. This two-faced character of Western imperial power, that it grants democracy to its own but denies it to those under its economic and/or political sway, survives, as many observers have noted, into the postcolonial period.[31]

The expansion of Western business requires the population to assimilate to Western ways in order to promote new markets and to efficiently organize new workers, but it also requires them to keep just enough of a distance so they do not become competitors. Imitation is encouraged, so to speak, on condition that it fails. This self-contradictory pattern has been transferred, with the end of communism, to the 'emerging markets' of Central Europe.

After all that has been said in this book, I believe it requires little comment to see how Bhabha's analysis of the West's relationship to the colony and postcolony applies here. Yet there are also crucial differences. In the next chapter, I discuss how Central Europe, a partially privileged region of global geopolitics, has been and continues to also function in ways that take part in the Global North's exploitation of the South. I will argue that, contrary to common belief, Central Europe did historically benefit as a white European region from the West's colonial adventure, and that it continues to profit from its postcolonial privilege. On almost all the measures discussed in Chapter 4, Central Europe places somewhere in the middle between Europe's East and West, and arguably closer to the former colonizers than to most of the formerly colonized.

The Central European version of being 'the same but not quite' is white, but not quite. White but not quite is, still, white. I have already stressed (in the Introduction) that Eastern Europeanism as a racism of degree does not compare in intensity and pervasiveness with colour racism. This provides Central Europeans aspiring to full acceptance in the white racial hierarchy with the opportunity to espouse the discourses of white racism in a way that is obviously not available to people who are not white (at all).

The desire to be among the beneficiaries and not among the victims of white privilege goes a long way toward explaining the success of racist rhetoric among many Central Europeans.[32] The work of the Prague political scientist Pavel Barša allows us to connect this insight to what we have seen earlier about the hidden similarities between the liberal former 'dissidents' and their illiberal successors in the leadership of Central European political life. In a brilliant Czech-language essay, Barša discusses the 'dissidents' like Milan Kundera, who, as we have seen earlier, saw liberation from communism as a means to 'return' Central Europe to its rightful place in the West.

> Central Europeans were returning to 'their' Western civilization, which by the fact of their return proved that it was the centre of the world. [...] the imperative of assimilating to Western norms and accepting neoliberalism was often justified by the contention that they were a necessary condition to ensure that we didn't fall to the level of a 'developing country'. The erstwhile 'second' world was to be split between those who would succeed in joining the 'first' and those who, declassed, are become part of the 'third'. The premier task of Central European nations was to acquire a place in the first group and, at all costs, prevent possible demotion to the third. [...]
> When the President of the European Commission, Jean-Claude Juncker, tried in September 2015 to awaken in the countries of the Visegrád Four a consciousness of moral obligation to non-European refugees, and pointed to the fact that Western Europe had welcomed *their* refugees with open arms, he hit a wall of incomprehension. From the Central European point of view, Western Europeans had an obligation of hospitality towards these refugees who belonged to European civilization, which they compared with a far lesser obligation, if any, that we have towards fleeing adherents of Islamic civilization.[33]

'The effect of mimicry on the authority of colonial discourse is profound and disturbing', Bhabha suggests.[34] Central European applicants to the Western club belittle other applicants' credentials by stressing their own 'European' racial privilege. The pitifulness of their position becomes obvious once their claim for full member privileges is rejected, condemning them as bad imitators, as eternally unsuccessful mimics.

8

'We Will Not Be a Colony!'

Contemporary illiberalism has been able to adapt and turn into easy clichés the terminology of progressive politics. 'Alternative', 'identity', even 'revolution' have all been 'borrowed' by the illiberal phrasebook, though in a form hardly recognizable by their involuntary lenders on the Left. 'Colony' and 'colonialism' are in this category of perverted parlance also, including when they are used to describe the condition of Central Europe vis-à-vis the West.

Facing hundreds of thousands of applauding Hungarians clad in coats on a mid-March day in 2012, Viktor Orbán declared defiantly, 'We will not be a colony!'. Orbán was then only two years into his second mandate as prime minister, after an election that he had won by promising that the country would abandon the liberal democratic course that, he believed, had led it from the slavery of Russian-dictated communism to the false freedom of free-market neoliberalism dictated from 'Brussels'. 'We will not live according to the commands of foreign powers', he promised. 'We are more than familiar with the character of unsolicited assistance, even if it comes wearing a finely tailored suit and not a uniform with shoulder patches.'[1]

This was three years before the 'migrant crisis' and the high-profile resistance to refugee quotas that Orbán would organize in Central Europe. In 2012, the issue was essentially economic, although Orbán was already being accused of authoritarian practices toward the judiciary and the central bank. The EU was threatening to withhold 495 million euros of transfers, because Hungary was projected to have an annual deficit of 3.6 per cent, more than the required limit of 3 per cent set in Brussels in the spirit of neoliberal discipline. The punishment was unprecedented. Never in the history of the EU had a state been refused funds because of breaking deficit targets. Spain had just increased its deficit forecast to 5.6 per cent. But Spain was not punished, prompting even Austria to note that the EU was applying double standards.[2]

In this chapter, we will see that with the cry, 'we will not be a colony', the illiberals of Central Europe recognize the real problem of the quasi-colonial takeover of Central Europe by the West, even, at times, correctly analysing its economic foundations, though giving it the wrong response. I will examine here in more detail the parallels between Central Europe and the former colonies in their political, and mainly their economic, relationship to the West. My contention is that, since the fall of communism, such parallels have been strong. Yet the analogy is not complete: I return to the point that Central Europe is a partially privileged semi-periphery, somewhere in-between the former colonizers and the former colonized.

The illiberals' cry, 'we are not a colony!' is far from a proclamation of solidarity with the Global South and its colonial past, or a declaration that the post-communist condition should be compared with the postcolonial. Rather, it is the expression of injured pride for being compared to non-Europeans. It is meant to legitimate Central Europeans' claims on hereditary status as whites.

Comparing post-communist Europe to a colony of the West did not yet come to almost anybody's mind when the Iron Curtain fell in late 1989, or in the years immediately following. In 2005, a group of specialists of 'the post-Soviet space' asked to debate with one of the founders of postcolonial studies, Gayatri Chakravorty Spivak. The main question was not if the West was colonizing the East of Europe, as it had the Global South. Rather, the colonizer was identified as the Soviet Union, and the debate centred on whether it was right to consider as colonial the area's earlier subjection to the Soviet 'empire'. Yes, said Spivak: 'When an alien nation-state establishes itself as ruler, impressing its own laws and systems of education and rearranging the mode of production for its own economic benefit, "colonizer" and "colonized" can be used.'[3] There was only one participant, the American cultural studies scholar Nancy Condee, who wondered aloud if it were not the EU that has become the new colonial power over Central and Eastern Europe.[4]

Yet by 2005 there were already observers, not present at the Washington, DC conference, who gave a postcolonial reading to the power of 'Brussels' over Central Europe. The critique of quasi-colonial power by the West over Central Europe was then still firmly situated on the left of the political spectrum. Of particular note is a volume edited by József Böröcz and Melinda Kovács, as early as 2001. Böröcz proposed that 'we must proceed with sharp attention to the fact that the major West European societies that control most of the politics within the European Union have been historically – that is, in the past, as well as with deep and meaningful continuities into the present – imperial and colonial centers'.[5] He recognized four 'mechanisms of control' that, for him, defined the exercise of classic colonial power:

- unequal exchange: sustained centripetal funneling of economic value;
- coloniality: cognitive mapping of the empire's populations, creating a fixed system of interiorized otherness;
- export of governmentality: through the launching of the normalizing, standardizing and control mechanisms of modern statehood; and
- geopolitics: fitting all of the above into of [sic] a long-term global strategy of projecting the central state's power to its external environment.[6]

All of these highlights of the 'imperial order' were, as Böröcz argues, present also in the 'eastern enlargement' plans of the EU (and, we would have to agree today, remain visible years after it accepted its post-communist members). Unequal exchange, in particular, is evident in the 'siphoning off' of much of the national product of the 'applicant societies'. Coloniality is apparent in the negative stereotyping of 'Eastern Europe' (what we call 'Eastern Europeanism' in this book). The export of governmental practices was a fact even before enlargement, in the requirements placed on the applicants' legal and economic systems. Finally, EU membership was only one phase of integrating Central Europe in the West's existing geopolitical strategies (an example is the EU applicants' prior adhesion to NATO).

Writing in 2001, Böröcz may not yet have witnessed the full extent of multinationals outsourcing manufacturing to Central Europe. The classic Czech Škoda automobile factory was soon acquired by Volkswagen. Other multinationals founded car assembly plants in Slovakia and Hungary, accounting for a very significant portion of its economic production and employment. Western multinationals acquired a large and even dominant share of all productive assets.[7]

The acquisition of assets, the locating of outsourced production, and the founding of new markets in Central Europe by mainly Western multinationals was aided in the 1990s by the almost unimpeded triumph of the ideology of neoliberal globalization. The 'end of history' infamously declared by Francis Fukuyama was widely seen to be marked by the collapse of communism in its Cold War competition with capitalism, and capitalism was seen as having reached its proper expression in neoliberalism. Philipp Ther speaks of the former communist countries as 'experimentation sites for neoliberal policy'.[8]

National governments loosened protection of their own economies, in the belief that a more relaxed international system of production and trade would be to everyone's benefit. The first Central European governments welcomed Western business and capital with open arms. The postcolonial relationship – Central Europe serving as a destination for outsourced labour and for market expansion – was taking place with the active support of liberal, globally minded local leaders, who saw it as a temporary measure. They expected the free market to do its work uplifting their country eventually to Western levels. Their hopes were made to seem more realistic by the fact that they saw the East–West barrier as an artificial one that would disappear with the fall of the communist regimes that put it in place; they visualized Europe as one common space and, at least potentially, one market. They did not expect the capitalists to treat their region as a perpetually different, Eastern dominion.

Certainly, there were warning voices from the start. Petr Pithart, who was the first Czech prime minister following the collapse of the communist government, recalls early disagreements between his own party of liberal 'dissidents' headed by Havel, and the party of

Václav Klaus, who had been an official of the Czechoslovak State Bank. As Pithart recalls, in the early days of post-communism,

> we started seeing crude slogans of [Klaus' party] such as 'We won't sell the country to foreigners!', 'Pithart sold the family silver for a kiss to the Germans' (the reference is to the Mladá Boleslav Škoda concern). [...] In the end, as our mandate was shortened, we were unable to complete agreed deals with other previously selected interested investors (with Mercedes on Tatra Kopřivnice, with Siemens on Škoda Plzeň, with Renault on Karosa, and likewise ČKD [a classic Czech engineering firm] or Poldi Kladno).

This is a list of some of the longest-established, most prestigious Czech companies. Tatra was a luxury car maker that had inspired the design of Porsche automobiles. Poldi was a firm founded at the end of the nineteenth century by Karl Wittgenstein, the father of the famous philosopher, Ludwig. Pithart adds that the political leadership around Klaus rejected the Western bidders and distributed the companies to what Pithart contemptuously called 'captains of Czech industry'.[9]

In 1992, Klaus replaced Pithart as Prime Minister of the Czech Republic, when it was still an autonomous part of Czechoslovakia. Having been instrumental to the breakup of the country, he then succeeded Václav Havel as president of the now independent country, in 2003, and held that office until 2010. Klaus admired Margaret Thatcher, whom Stuart Hall saw as implementing a new form of capitalist system ('Thatcherism'), which permitted the resurgence of authoritarianism in a liberal democratic setting.[10] Klaus evidently admired Thatcher's capitalist nationalism, including her Euroscepticism. His ascent represented the victory, not just in the Czech Republic but in Central Europe as a whole, of more locally grounded economic interests over the tendency to uncritically integrate with the Western-dominated global capital flows.

Effects of the 2008 financial crisis

Foreign capital, with which the 'dissidents' were, not without foundation, associated in the public's mind, included financial capital introduced via the foreign banks who entered the area soon after 1989. They widely promoted the use of private loans, which had been far less prevalent under the communist regimes. Few people in Central Europe then owned anything of much worth. Borrowing enabled many to quickly acquire the goods they had craved under communism, to start a small business, or to purchase a home. As neither the banks nor the borrowers were quite sure yet about the local currencies, the lending was often done in foreign currency. This was particularly common in Hungary, where people borrowed loans denominated in Swiss francs.

In effect, lending to people without serious assets in Central Europe was very similar to lending to poor people in the US.[11] The consequences were also the same. After enjoying some prosperity, many borrowers were unable to make their payments, speeding up the domino effects of the 2008 financial crisis. Even those who did not borrow, or borrowed but managed to avoid the particularly brutal repossessions (called *exekuce*, 'executions', in the Czech Republic), now developed doubts about the superiority of the neoliberal system as zealously adopted by the leaders of the 'transition'. The latter's international connections, often going back to their 'dissident' times, now began to be a political liability rather than an asset.

Nevertheless, the leadership in place continued with their neoliberal policies unabated. Adam Fabry, who discusses the process in Hungary, writes that

> [c]apitalists responded to the downturn in familiar fashion, raising the exploitation of workers. As a result, Hungary was rapidly turning into one of the worst places to work in the EU. Weekly working hours for full-time employees in 2009 stood at 40.1 hours, higher than the EU-27 and EU-15 averages of 39.3 and 38.9 hours, respectively. ... Meanwhile, real wages fell by 7.3 percent between 2007 and 2009 (the third steepest decrease in CEE, after Latvia and Lithuania). ... Yet, those at the top of Hungarian society came out relatively unscathed from the crisis; in 2009 the wealth of the ten richest Hungarians grew by 124 billion forint (approximately US$ 557.5 million).[12]

The illiberal revolt was born of the disappointment and dissatisfaction such a state of affairs engendered among people who now saw 'the crash' as the logical consequence of the neoliberal style of capitalism pursued by the liberal leadership throughout the post-communist 'transition'. It was in this context that Orbán, who might have appeared to support the liberal consensus earlier, broke with it, and installed a new kind of regime after his resounding electoral victory in 2010. That year, in his speech to the ethnic Hungarian community in neighbouring Romania, he set out with great clarity the view that was taking hold of many minds not only in his country but in Central Europe and beyond in the post-communist space.

> You have probably heard that the Chinese economy is taking flight, that the Western world is in a crisis while India and China are experiencing growth of 5–10 percent. [...] If we want to understand why all this is happening, then it's worth our while to bring up that it is indeed Western style capitalism that has run into a crisis during the last ten years. This is something that the politicians don't like to say out loud, and business people even less so. But in fact we're dealing here not with temporary financial troubles, but with a very serious crisis of a system under whose aegis Europe has lived these past hundred or hundred and fifty years. What happened was that the speculative financial manipulations were given an advantage over work and the creation of values. Instead of productive capitalism, a speculative capitalism materialized as a result of the past few decades, and we are now facing its consequences. The way of thinking in Europe that the market will on its own bring about prosperity and justice as well, and that the state will do best to keep a distance from the economy – this way of thinking has ruined Western civilization. Just think that a year ago [under the previous government] it would have been heretical to question the almighty power of the market, and now it is no longer taboo to talk about how the state must take on a greater role. Indeed, now everyone can

see that it is in reality the states, the governments, and the politicians who saved the collapsing West-European and American economies.[13]

As I have argued in Chapter 5, Orbán's praise for Asian economies was not meant to make Hungary non-Western, any more than he had meant here to make Hungary non-capitalist. What he had in mind was a different kind of capitalism. The state, as he saw it, was there to protect the interests of 'productive' domestic capitalists, not international finance. In practice, this has often meant capitalists close to his regime. At the same time, as in Poland, in Hungary the anti-financialization approach allowed the government to zero in on foreign banks rather than on the multinationals who built assembly factories in the country, providing tax revenues for the state, as well as contracts for local entrepreneurs. These local capitalists, who included Orbán's friends and relatives and presumably himself, were the main economic beneficiaries of a Hungarian capitalism that maintained neoliberal style market policies (balanced budget, flat tax system, regressive taxation) for their profit, while buying off the low-paid workforce with slogans against the alleged enemies of the nation.[14]

National capitalism

Iván Szelényi[15] and Agnes Gagyi have cogently discussed this development in Hungary, where it is the most advanced in Central Europe. Gagyi contrasts the 'democratic anti-illiberalism' of modernization through Western integration embraced by one segment of the economic elite, versus the 'anti-democratic illiberalism' advocated by another part of the elite, allied with the Orbán government, which wants to protect 'national' wealth from Western capital and its local allies.[16] The pro-Western elite initially consisted of managers of the former socialist enterprises, allied with the former dissidents. The 'national capitalists', as Gagyi calls them, came from outside these ranks (although there was some overlap), and saw themselves connected symbolically to the pre-communist bourgeoisie. This group initially had far less access to capital than the manager–dissident alliance, who were in charge of selling, distributing, and reviving the former state enterprises, and who also had much better connections personally, to economic decision makers abroad. The 'national capitalists' needed to seize the reins of government in order to get their hands on EU transfer funds. The tools to alleviate their cash and connections problem

> included a domestic concentration of property in non-tradable goods in the domestic market (banking, utilities, media, retail, telecommunication). On the other hand, they included means to attract some of the new wave of industrial relocation (mainly from Germany) due to market pressure under the crisis. Such means included the reorganization of the education system, and a new labor code to create a flexible, cheap labor force.[17]

The 'national capitalists' were mostly ordinary folks from families who had learned to wheel and deal under the communist shortages, when a sort of grassroots business acumen was needed to get some of the goods you needed and most of those you wanted. The skills required had less to do with rational management science, and more with finding the right people who could get you a pair of genuine Levi's jeans or a bottle of Courvoisier at the foreign currency shop. The communist societies never quite recovered from the wartime and postwar shortages that had been spectacularly overcome in Western Europe. Money couldn't buy you everything, because much was available only through connections.

During the 'transition' years from 1989, connections meant money. Most of the state-owned enterprises, from ageing bakeries to giant steel works, were to be had if you knew how to get them. The managers were at an advantage, because they were in a position to use sophisticated schemes, called *tunelování* (tunnelling) in Czech, to dismantle and acquire or sell parts of socialist companies. Not everyone had access to such opportunities. But if you knew the right people then you could find the golden business opportunities that existed during those 'Wild East' years, known locally as the Wild Nineties.

It helped enormously if you knew the politicians who made decisions on who gets to 'privatize' a business and how they get to run it. Through legal, semi-legal, and illegal means, networks of the new 'national capitalists' became more and more visible in the economy, at the same time as much of it was being given over to the multinationals. The multinationals themselves built relationships with politicians, sometimes by covert illegal means, such as using bribe brokers.[18] Their networks were more likely to include the better educated, internationally connected professional elites. The 'national capitalists'' connections, on the other hand, in some very consequential cases included violent criminal gangs, who helped to protect both their economic and their political interests.

To understand illiberalism in Central Europe, it is crucial to understand that in all four Central European countries, the 'national capitalists' have come to compete with the multinationals.[19] For government support and protection, the national capitalists depend on the national government, while the multinationals depend also on international economic and political structures, and above all, in this area, the EU. 'Illiberalism vs. Liberal Democracy' is a formula that tells a lot about Central Europe's frictions with the West and more specifically 'Brussels'. But if we follow the money, we uncover here the same clash between global neoliberal structures and the national capitalisms that are everywhere, and not just in Central Europe, the economic home base of the illiberals. The conflict is as much between the multinationals and more locally based capital as about the ideologies of liberalism and nationalism.

That conflict, however, cannot in Central Europe do without compromise, because the national capitalists there cannot do without either the EU (who support the multinationals but also inject funds into the local, neighbourhood and rural level economy where the national capitalists' interests lie) or the multinationals (who invest their money in the assembly plants crucial to creating local markets). As a result, Central European governments create conditions for the colonial-style outsourcing of labour by Western (and some Asian) companies in the area. This is why the Central European illiberals' resistance to Western economic 'colonialism' is not nearly as loud as to the political 'colonialism' of 'Brussels' and the West in general.[20]

The 'national capitalists' are generally constrained to spreading their networks in the more locally based sectors of the economy, and actively enticing the multinationals to bring their factories and, with them, also the funds required by the local entrepreneurs.

The atrocious record of the Visegrád area in controlling the later waves of the COVID-19 pandemic was blamed, at least in the Czech Republic, on the government's wish to keep the *montovny* (assembly factories) open.[21] The situation was aggravated by the fact that, as noted by the sociologist Daniel Prokop, in the Czech Republic the number of industrial workers, and therefore people who could not work from a home office, was much higher than in a country like the United Kingdom.[22] Government in Central Europe seems generally more interested in keeping local labour (and taxes) cheap in order to attract much needed foreign capital, than in developing and reproducing a highly qualified national labour force. 'Increasingly, we are lagging behind in digitization, artificial intelligence, augmented reality, bioengineering, the green economy, advanced services and infrastructure', says Peter Mrázik, a trade union official at a Slovak plant of Jaguar Land Rover. 'Slovakia is one of the most endangered countries.'[23]

Russia, China, and Central Europe

The need for the national capitalists to rely in part on the multinationals is one of the main differences between Central Europe and Russia that must be kept in mind if we are to fully understand each. I have mentioned earlier the case of Mikhail Khodorovsky, imprisoned under Putin essentially for political disobedience. The Western press did not spare him the moniker 'oligarch', though an oligarch is supposed to be part of a ruling network, not an outcast sleeping on a prison bed. As we have seen, 'oligarch' became a term used indiscriminately to describe Eastern European businesspeople, whose success is automatically deemed to be illegitimate. Western investors, who rely on the political structures of the EU, the military umbrella of NATO, and the influence of governments such as Germany's to further their interests, show signs of being oligarchs, but because they are considered legitimate they are not labelled so.

A clash between Russian 'oligarchs' obedient to Putin's commands and Western oligarchs moving their operations into the post-communist space goes a long way toward explaining the origins and nature of the 'new Cold War' between Russia and the West. In Central Europe, the political and military support structures of the EU, which favour Western European business, had an easy entry under the umbrella of the EU, as did American influence in the form of NATO. Both the EU and NATO were sincerely welcome by most of the public, eager to share in the freedoms and consumer goods of what they thought of as their natural home in a Europe led by the West. Russia did not join these organizations. Consequently, there was much less of a political or military underpinning to the activities in the country of Western-controlled 'global' capital. The 'Russian gangsters', as the 'oligarchs' were initially called in the West (often but not always with justification), were comparatively free to create large concentrations of capital, in everything from services to banks to the all-important natural resources sector, independently from, and often in opposition to, Western business interests.

In this respect, Russia resembled a much more important player, China, whose neo-capitalist economy at first gladly offered cheap and servile labour to fill Western orders. Once that resulted in the spectacular growth of the East Asian giant's national wealth and a sizeable class of Chinese capitalists, the ruling 'Communist' Party (a 'vertical' control structure à la Yavlinsky, resembling Putin's One Russia – see Chapter 4) was emboldened to stand up to the existing, Western-controlled, global structures of production, trade, and finance.

In 2017, the large Swiss bank, Credit Suisse, headlined their annual report on the world economy 'Getting Over Globalization'. It was becoming obvious that what had been called 'global' was really centred in North America, Western Europe, and Japan, the former colonial powers, with some role played by 'Asian tigers' such as Hong Kong and South Korea. Now cracks were opening within the Western system, while at the same time other players, such as China and Russia, were creating a new, 'multipolar' world of regional blocs. 'Although globalization is unlikely to come to a halt entirely,' the bank's research team predicted, 'we will not return to the kind of globalized world we have become used to. It is being replaced by multipolarity, characterized by the rise of regionally distinct approaches to economics, law and governance.' Academic observers such as Giuseppe Montalbano have also noted that 'transnational hegemonic projects' are undertaken not by a single alliance of 'transnational capitalist classes', but by 'regional historical blocs' in competition with one another. Montalbano recognizes, too, that the US-dominated network of capital has always only been one 'regional bloc' even though its sway was and remains so much greater than that of the others that it had appeared to be global.[24] This fact became more obvious in the second decade of the century.

Analysing the World Input-Output Database and the Trade in Value Added Database, the economists Richard Baldwin and Javier Lopez-Gonzalez noted as early as 2013 that 'the global production network is marked by regional blocks, what could be called Factory Asia, Factory North America, and Factory Europe'.[25] Within most if not all of the regional blocks, core–periphery relations, resembling those between colonizer and colonized, exist between the dominant economic networks and the areas providing cheap labour to make goods and additional markets to sell them. As Chinese business moves to producing higher value-added goods and services, and moves cheap workshop production to countries such as Vietnam, Factory Asia increasingly produces for China and the surrounding region, and a little less for the world market.[26] Mexico produces for the United States in Factory North America. Regionalization is helped by the advantages of easier delivery costs due to shorter distances, and by tariff protection patterns. The USMCA (United States-Mexico-Canada Agreement) eases the movement of goods, and to a far smaller extent labour, among three countries. It includes one peripheral country, Mexico, and two core countries, although, as I mentioned in the Introduction, mainly because Canada depends on supplying natural resources to the US, Immanuel Wallerstein called it a 'semi-periphery'.[27]

The clear core of 'Factory Europe' is Germany, in close alliance with France. In fact, the former Greek finance minister, Yanis Varoufakis, opines simply that 'The Franco-German axis is the European Union'.[28] Presumably, the UK was strong enough to escape such domination by exiting the EU. Within the EU, a number of smaller economies enjoy a Canada-like status of close and profitable dependence on Germany. The Low Countries and Scandinavia are more or less in this position, adding enough breadth to the EU's core to make Varoufakis' complaint a hyperbole. Then there are the southern members, more peripheral, but collectively less so than the eastern, post-communist states, where factory work based on cheap labour is mostly located. The east of the EU is, in this sense, its Mexico.

This colonial-style core–periphery relationship has existed in Central Europe right from the collapse of communism, encouraged by the absence of tariff barriers, and by the speed of transporting goods to nearby major markets. In a report on such developments, entitled 'Globalization in Transition', the leading consulting firm, McKinsey & Co., notes that 'The intraregional share of global goods trade has increased by 2.7 percentage points since 2013, partially reflecting the rise of emerging-market consumption', and adds that '[t]his development is most noticeable for Asia and the EU-28 countries'.[29] In the EU, that means more goods produced in Central European and other post-communist member states for consumption in Western Europe, but also in their own 'emerging' markets.

A Chinese solution – to aggressively pursue global sweatshop orders until local capital increases to the point where it begins to dominate its own international and global networks – is not available to the 'national capitalists' of Central Europe. Central European workers, whose baseline is a far more prosperous condition than that of the average Chinese at the beginning of Deng Xiao-Ping's economic reforms in the 1980s, cannot be compelled in democratic conditions, however flawed, to intense labour in the brutal conditions then and even now seen in China. But also, the broader industrial-military complex in which Central Europe labours is ultimately not under its own control. It is dominated from the West. There is not a powerful independent state in Central Europe, as is China, to concentrate its resources on furthering the global and local interests of its own rising bourgeoisie. No country in the east of the EU has nearly the resources required that China and even Russia possess, to erect fully independent political, military, and economic structures to protect its own business interests. Central European businesspeople still lack the capital to compete with their Western equivalents on the global scale. No Central European is listed by *Forbes* among the world's one hundred richest people, and only one, the Czech financier and telecommunications owner Petr Kellner, is among the next hundred, at number 110.[30] Lőrinc Mészáros, Orbán's protégé, ranks a respectable 2,035, but is nowhere near the company of Jeff Bezos or Bill Gates, or even the richest of the Russian 'oligarchs'. The 'national capitalists' continue to rely partly on injections of funds from the EU, and the governments that support them depend on tax income from the multinationals that employ much of the workforce.

It is possible that their heart is not in it. The Hungarian Fidesz politician, János Lázár, shocked observers by supporting the German Continental tyre company's workers in their strike in Hungary.[31] Criticizing the opposition coalition against Orbán as agents of George Soros and global capital, the Orbán mouthpiece, *Magyar Nemzet*, declared that the opposition 'Democratic Coalition unequivocally embodies the politics of the left-wing, pre-2010 order. It continues a political approach that oppresses Hungarian people and prioritizes the expectations of the multinational corporations and of international political actors.'[32]

Such criticism may represent the real thoughts of the national capitalists of Central Europe. If it were possible, they would probably like very much to transfer most wealth to domestic capital, as in Russia. Orbán's Hungary has developed the farthest in that direction, even, as we have seen in the case of Lajos Simicska (Chapter 4), sanctioning among the national capitalists those who refuse to humbly comply with and support the head of the government. Dorit Geva, a founding dean of the Central European University booted out of Budapest by Orbán, speaks of the Hungarian leader as a 'Bonapartist', aiming to embody the aspirations of the nation personally and weakening the power of institutions in favour of his personal influence. Geva calls Orbán's 'post-neoliberal regime' *ordonationalist*: it *orders* the economy and politics to serve his and his party's interests, and packages this in nationalist language. His policies favour, according to Geva, consumerism over the reproduction of labour, and tend to please broad swaths of the nation, including much of the middle class and the farming population, while excluding Roma and the very poor from the nation that is ostensibly the beneficiary of this new political system. Ordonationalism is, Geva feels, far from limited to Hungary, and is symptomatic of a general trend in the latest stage of capitalism.[33]

The 'System of National Cooperation', as Orbán calls his style of government, appeals to national and 'European' (white Christian) solidarity as a means to counteract the inferiorization of the East within the EU. Promoting the inclusive symbols of national pride along with exclusionary racist and homophobic rhetoric, the strategy includes alleviating the condition of some working people through carefully selected social policies that superficially resemble those of a welfare state, but in fact exclude vulnerable populations such as single-parent families and the Roma.[34] Nationalist rhetoric is presented as resistance to globalization, and the limited welfare-state policies, to neoliberalism. The illiberals provide, in this respect, a critique of the global political and economic system that resembles left-wing critiques, and even use what, on the surface, may appear like left-wing language. As we have seen, that includes the language of anti-colonialism.

Illiberals declaim against Western 'colonialism'

As the Polish sociologist Jan Sowa has argued, postcolonialism itself is, by nature, open to a 'conservative' interpretation, especially in the conditions of Central Europe.[35] Indeed, a postcolonial analysis of post-communist Central Europe has become perhaps more common on the right than on the left.

Orbán may have been early to sound the clarion of a Central European fight against being 'colonized', but the expression is now ubiquitous among illiberal critics of the EU. Often, they use their would-be anti-colonialism in a would-be anti-capitalist context, pointing to the social welfare policies that they, as we have just seen, present as a counterweight to the multinational companies, who only want to find in Central Europe a nearshore source of low-cost labour. A few months after Orbán's 'we will not be a colony' speech in 2012, Slovakia's Robert Fico protested the proposed hike in gas prices by the local multinational utility company: 'I want to say to the owners of 49 percent of SPP [the utility]'s shares from Germany and France, that the colonial period is over. Slovakia is not a colony, where they just come, set their prices, make money, and leave.'[36] The Polish illiberal leader, Jerzy Kaczyński, proudly declared that the social welfare policies he advocated put an end to the 'post-colonial concept of Poland as a source of cheap labor'.[37] The Czech Premier Andrej Babiš, investigated for misusing EU funds to build a country home, furiously responded: 'We here are not a colony of Brussels.'[38] By the time in 2014 that the Hungarian deputy, Krisztina

Morvai, raised a banner in the European Parliament proclaiming, 'We Are Not a Colony', the phrase had become a stock phrase of illiberal rhetoric in all of Central Europe.[39]

The illiberals usually mean by 'We are not a colony' simply to protest that they are exploited by the West. They are not interested in precise models of economic exploitation. Still, their distaste for the multinational corporations (whether or not they are able to act on it) in fact makes it less than fully useful to speak of them as 'right wing', if 'right wing' means leaving the economy to the free market. The right–left political contrast becomes even less precise if we consider that nationalism and other forms of social conservativism characterize to some extent also the self-described centre-left in Central Europe, such as the social democrats of the Czech Republic, Slovakia, and Hungary. A combination of anti-neoliberal economic analysis and illiberal nationalism is simply something that may represent a large consensus among Central Europeans, and survive the tenure of this or that illiberal leader or political party.

One example is the Czech economist, Ilona Švihlíková. In her book, *How We Became a Colony*, Švihlíková argues that, after communism, the leadership put blind faith in the neoliberal fiction of a neutral market. As she puts it, 'the countries of the Eastern Bloc were not integrating into some world of perfect competition free of power relations, but on the contrary into a very concentrated corporate milieu characterized by a profound division of labor'.[40] The global division of labour is one, she suggests, where production and profits are dominated by some countries, while others are made to specialize in contributing to parts of the process through low-paid labour, and are unable to keep a significant amount of the profits, or to upgrade to producing more value-added products. Alluding to the nineteenth-century German economist Friedrich List, Švihlíková adds, 'Deregulation, like liberalization, is a tool of the victors'.[41] This essentially progressive analysis, very compatible with that of Thomas Piketty's[42] (not cited in Švihlíková's book), is then followed by a suggestion that the nation should follow a somewhat more protectionist path, as well as providing greatly increased social services. But also, Švihlíková wants Czechs to become more nationalistic. She complains: 'We are without a national idea.'[43] Salvation, in her view, will come from all Czech people pulling together, as during the nineteenth-century 'national revival', through the efforts of 'an enormous number of "ordinary" people, without whom it would not have succeeded'.[44]

This kind of usurpation of anti-colonialism by the right is by no means unique to the post-communist space. Nigel Farage, then the leader of the United Kingdom Independence Party, declared that Greece, which had run into trouble for not paying its debts, became 'no more than a colony of the EU'. As with the Central European illiberals, being a colony was to Farage something beneath the dignity of a European country; he added that it was something 'even I wondered if they could stoop to'.[45] Even American white supremacists such as David Duke, founder of the National Association for the Advancement of White People, claim now to be for 'decolonization' – as long as the 'colonized' include the white race.[46] It appears that the illiberal rage against the 'colonizing' elites is seen throughout the entire periphery of the Western world.

In the end, the illiberals' cry of being 'colonized' is deliberately ironic; it does not mean what it says. The last thing the illiberals want is to be seriously compared to the racialized populations in or from the former colonies. (This is true not only of illiberal Central Europeans at home, but also of people who move abroad. In the United Kingdom, Polish migrants often chose to deflect racism against themselves by turning to racism against local people of colonial backgrounds.[47]) Complaining about being 'colonized' is meant to accomplish two things. First, it is intended to show the illiberals as victims of the Western liberals, by attacking their soft spot: their guilt for colonialism and racism. Second, it is designed to reject any such guilt on one's own part. That includes rejecting any responsibility, or even empathy, by Central Europeans for the millions of racialized people living in, or migrating from, the former colonies. To accomplish this, the exclamation, 'We will not be a colony!' is amplified by 'We've never been colonizers!'.

'We've never been colonizers!'

According to Mária Schmidt, an ideologist close to Viktor Orbán, Western Europe is feeling rightly guilty toward its former colonies, and this guilt is leading it to admit migrants contrary to its own best interests. But Central Europeans don't need to feel guilty since they have never been colonizers.[48] Hungarian children now read in their history books at school a speech made by the prime minister in 2015, where he argued the same point. At the end of the text, students are asked, 'What do you think, why do the former colonizing countries relate differently to the migration question?'[49]

Lubomír Zaorálek, the erstwhile foreign minister of the Czech Republic, justified his country's noncompliance with EU directives to admit a quota of mostly Muslim migrants, with a searing critique of Western – and Russian – colonialism, referring to their atrocities against Muslims, including in Algeria, Afghanistan, and Iraq. These were, he said, transgressions 'comparable in scale to the Nazi war crimes'. He added: 'Long-suppressed political memories are fuelling a large sudden and explosive awakening energised by Islamist extremists in the Middle East.' European countries that had not had colonies were not responsible for this, and should not allow themselves to be endangered by accepting migrants who may include disruptive radicals.[50]

According to Petr Přeučil, writing in the regional Czech paper, *Krajské Listy*: 'We don't need to apologize for the colonial politics of a number of Western countries and certainly not for the racial segregation that was common until recently in the US.'[51]

In Slovakia, it has been reported that the followers of Milan Kotleba's neo-fascist party were spreading false rumours that Slovaks will be asked to compensate Black people for slavery, which was, of course, meant to shock a public who is convinced that Slovaks had nothing to do with that injustice.[52] Another right-wing activist, Róbert Švec, an activist with a strong pro-Russian attitude, issued a particularly impassioned rebuttal to a Swedish politician who suggested that all EU members must help to resettle refugees.

> Wrong! The Slovak Republic bears no responsibility for accepting asylum seekers. Not a political responsibility, and certainly not a moral one. We did not have colonies, unlike our 'friends' in the West. We do not feel any pangs of conscience towards the countries that people are running from because of the aggressive and irresponsible politics of the 'advanced' Western world. [...] We prefer to be, in the eyes of the 'developed' Western world, a conservative and 'backward-looking' country, rather than allow into our national territory

more than 163 thousand migrants, like the Swedish political elites have done.[53]

In the Polish Catholic magazine *Więź*, Jerzy Sosnowski writes: 'POLAND NEVER HAD COLONIES. We have not to date had any reason to reflect on issues related to colonialism, and we heard about *Murzyny* [a controversial term for Black people][54] ... only as much as the Germans, French, English, or Belgians told us.'[55] Likewise, on a government-friendly Polish news and opinion site, Piotr Lisewicz opines: 'Obviously we're part of Western culture. Yet not only did we not persecute *Murzyny*, but we were ourselves, often at the same time, persecuted by murderous regimes, Western and Eastern.'[56]

The refusal to accept responsibility for colonialism is not unique to Central Europe; it is also a feature of nationalist rhetoric in parts of the West. In Switzerland, the argument that the country owned no colonies is commonly used to reject any moral obligation to empathize with migrants from the former colonies, or to accept more. Doris Leuthard, who served as President of Switzerland in 2006 and again in 2017, said on a visit to Benin that colonialism was a tragic part of the African country's history, and added, standing at a memorial to the deported slaves, 'I am happy that Switzerland has never taken part in these events of slavery and colonialism'.[57] In Belgium, a member of parliament for the Flemish-nationalist party Vlaams Belang, Wouter Vermeersch, claimed that '[t]he Flemish people had nothing to do with Belgium's colonial history. It was the royal family and the French-speaking *haute finance* who were responsible. If someone has to pay for mistakes in the past, it's them.'[58]

What is different is that in Central Europe public opinion appears to be much more broadly behind the denial of responsibility for colonialism and its effects. The quotes just listed from Poland, the Czech Republic, Slovakia, and Hungary range from the illiberal centre to the far right. But unlike in Switzerland or Flanders,[59] not much is being done, even on the left, to counter them. During the Czech presidential election of 2018, President Miloš Zeman, one of Europe's leading Islamophobes, was facing a challenge by the liberal scientist, Jiří Drahoš. Unfortunately for Drahoš, he had put his name to a proclamation, signed by 3,509 Czech intellectuals, asking to make sure that all who seek shelter in Europe 'are offered safety and dignified treatment'. The letter warned against describing migrants as 'harmful wildlife and parasites'. Dreading Zeman's label of him as a *vítač* (welcomer), however, Drahoš decided to eat his words, claiming unconvincingly that he had opposed admitting migrants 'from the start'. This desperate turnaround fooled no one, and soon Zeman was able to toast a narrow but convincing victory: 51.4 per cent against Drahoš' 48.6.

Even before the post-communist applicants were admitted to the EU, and while for the most part the liberals were still in power in Central Europe, József Böröcz had astutely observed that

> a remarkably unreconstructed notion of 'whiteness' is rampant in the identity work performed by the societies of eastern and east-central Europe, under the silence or outright cynical guidance of some surprisingly large segments of their political and cultural elites [...] – the central and east European applicants' current desire for EU membership ends up producing an implicit and unarticulated nostalgia for the contemporary advantages an identity designs originating in somebody else's colonial-imperial past.[60]

The vehement declarations of not being responsible for colonialism are coupled with an unspoken desire, 'but we would like to share in its privileges'.

The Polish analyst Tomasz Zarycki recognizes a 'dominant fear of decreasing one's own "Europeanness" by being associated with non-European colonies of the Western worlds'.[61] The Czech political scientist, Ondřej Slačálek, couples an excellent survey of the literature comparing the postcolonial condition with that of post-communist Central Europe, with noting that, for many there, such a comparison has only strengthened the motivation to show that Central Europe is fully 'Western' (I would say, fully white) and *not* like the former colonies. 'The "authenticity" of Central Europe', Slačálek suggests, 'has been constructed by the dominant Central European spokespeople in opposition to the "subaltern empires" of Germany and Russia as "more Western than the West"'.[62] A similar idea appears in Salman Sayyid's article on the 'Europeanness of the Other Europe'.⁶³ The illiberal analysis of Central Europe as a 'colony', for this reason, generally rejects any serious consideration of detailed correspondences between the Western relationship to Central Europe and its relationship to the Global South.⁶⁴

I return here to the incisive work of the Czech political scientist Pavel Barša, whom I have cited repeatedly in this book. In his article, 'Zero Degree of Decolonialization', Barša, writing as a member, himself, of the dissident generation around Václav Havel, recalls:

> Subjectively, we felt like cosmopolitans let out of the communist prison. In reality, we were heading for the Western metropoles. Some of us were unpleasantly surprised that these were full of immigrants of colour from the former colonies.
>
> … the necessity of assimilating Western norms and of adopting neoliberalism was often justified by the contention that they were the necessary condition for us not to sink to the level of a 'developing country'.⁶⁵

Central Europeans demand that Western European solidarity with them be given a preference over solidarity with non-Europeans.⁶⁶ Barša opposes such a rejectionist position with the notion that joining the West must come with also taking on the obligations of the West:

> If we now share in the enormous advantages that had been brought to Western Europe by the centuries of direct and indirect rule over non-European populations, then we cannot avoid our obligations to them. By succeeding to take our longed-for place among the erstwhile colonizers, we've lost the excuse of the colonized.⁶⁷

The Prague scholar adds, hopefully, 'Decolonialization of our thought may begin at last'.⁶⁸

Barša's sentiments second those north of the Czech border, of the Polish scholar Claudia Snochowska-Gonzalez, who was among the first to examine the issue of coloniality and Central Europe from a progressive perspective. She wrote in 2012 that insisting on Poland as a postcolonial victim of the Soviet 'eastern empire' obscures 'the present comfortable position of Poland in the world of global capital and relieves it of its responsibility for participation in modern acts of (neo)imperialism and (neo)colonialism'.[69]

So, is Central Europe responsible for colonialism?

There is more to the issue still. Barša and Snochowska-Gonzalez suggest that joining the West comes with responsibilities to the South; but they appear to agree with the contention that Central Europe was not involved in the colonial enterprise. In their view, those responsibilities are the result of current membership in the Western geopolitical system, not also from participating in it during the period of colonialism itself. Yet, in addition, Central Europe as a semi-peripheral region between Germany and Russia should be seen as in fact having participated, if somewhat marginally, in Western imperialism, and partially benefiting from it.

In Chapter 2, we examined Manuela Boatcă's observation that serf labour, whose agricultural products were mobilized primarily for the benefit of the colonizing powers, relegated the East of Europe to a condition of coloniality similar to the plantation economies of the Americas. But we saw also that the severity of this condition increased considerably east of Central Europe. While in Russia the burdens of serfdom only intensified during the Industrial Revolution, and severely affected even the freed serfs after emancipation, in Central Europe the Industrial Revolution largely eliminated forced agricultural labour.

True, the Industrial Revolution progressed slowly across the continent from England to Russia. In most places in between, the western regions were more affected than those in the east; this was so also in Central Europe, whose western areas (what is now the Czech Republic, Western Poland, Western Slovakia, Western Hungary) were far more industrialized than its eastern ones. The rural areas throughout Europe were less industrialized than the cities, to which even in imperial Russia country folk streamed in search of employment and a better future. In the Yiddish-language original stories by Sholem Aleichem that inspired the classic American musical, *Fiddler on the Roof*, for example, the family that in the musical leaves for New York just leaves for another city in imperial Russia.[70] The choice for migrants was often: Kiev or New York, Warsaw or Paris, Budapest or Vienna.

Colonial exploitation was one of the engines driving the Industrial Revolution that created the unprecedented rise of wealth observed in the rapidly urbanizing societies of Europe, both in countries that had colonies and those who did not. It was a prosperity that greatly favoured the rich, yet also reached the middle classes by the turn of the twentieth century. It depended on the import of cheap commodities from the colonies and the investment, direct or indirect, of the profits raised by companies under colonial protection.

Austria-Hungary, while not quite as industrialized or prosperous on the whole as England, France, or even Germany, was nevertheless a major economic power. It has been described as having the world's fourth largest machine-building industry,[71] and a considerable part of the manufacturing took place on the territory of today's Czech Republic and, to a lesser extent, Hungary. Consequently, although many of the owners lived or spent much of their money in Vienna, Budapest and Prague rivalled the Austrian capital's glamour and prosperity, along with the urban blight seen in all industrialized regions in the nineteenth century.

The standard of living that was achieved thanks to the Industrial Revolution and its use to advantage the European core of the colonial world-system, did also advantage the more peripheral regions of the continent; the more so the closer they were to the West, but everywhere in stark contrast to the abject poverty that colonizing Europe was exploiting in the Global South. The efforts made by 'Slavs' and Hungarians, following similar efforts by Germans (see Chapter 2), to be a 'cultured people' comparable to the English and the French, the schools, the operas, the libraries, should be understood as undertakings by a rising middle class enabled to access such things through their share of the colonial exploitation that asserted white privilege across the world.

German and Austro-Hungarian imperialism was, in many ways, a part of this effort to gain full Western (white) status. The ambitions of both empires to own overseas colonies came late and enjoyed limited success. Germany did acquire its first colonies, in New

Guinea and Southwest Africa, in 1884, and its last, German West Africa, in 1896. Austria-Hungary, which, let us recall, included some of Poland and all of the other three now Visegrád countries, never managed to get any.

An incident that came somewhat close to establishing a foothold for Austria in the world being 'explored' by the West, were the exploits of the Austro-Hungarian North Pole expedition co-led by Commander Julius Payer. Payer was a native of Šanov in what is now the Czech Republic, a village that has since fused with the warm-water spa, Teplice. Due to various mishaps, Payer was forced to seek shelter for several days in the icy, open landscape of an uninhabited island that he and his team 'discovered'. Nevertheless, he managed to return and, before that, to raise the Austro-Hungarian flag on the island, which to this day bears the name of the Habsburg Emperor: Franz-Joseph Land. Unfortunately, when Payer returned his reports were doubted by many. It took a while for the government to accept that Payer did not make everything up and recompense him with a knighthood. Franz-Joseph Land, however, became part of Russia.[72]

If Austria-Hungary was not a colonial power on a definition that requires colonies to be remote territory, it did resemble Russia in its efforts to expand overland into areas inhabited by foreign ethnic groups. So, if Soviet Russia was a colonizer, then so was Austria-Hungary. But while Poles, who had no political existence under the Habsburgs, can justifiably complain of having been 'colonized' by the Habsburgs, that is much harder to say, unequivocally, about the Czechs, whose territories enjoyed at least limited autonomy as the provinces of Bohemia and Moravia (even if these included millions of Germans and were not recognized as exclusively Czech), and more so about the Hungarians, who in 1867 became, at least on paper, equal to Austria. (Slovakia remained part of Hungary then, and the Magyar government vigorously opposed Slovaks within their territory who demanded their own national rights.)

All of the peoples of the multinational Austro-Hungarian Empire participated in both the benefits and the burdens of its imperial status (including military service), even though some nationalities, such as the Italians or the Serbs and to a large extent the Poles, were clearly unhappy with what they saw as living under the Habsburg yoke. A Czech book on the Czech officers in the revolutionary wars of

1848–49 takes for its title a telling expression used by the soldiers themselves: 'With God, for Emperor and Country', meaning for the Emperor of Austria and the Czech homeland.[73] The men who fought for Francis Joseph I to successfully occupy Bosnia and Herzegovina (which were declared a joint Austrian-Hungarian territory), were for the most part loyal to the emperor, and so were even those, from all nationalities of the Habsburg Empire, who fought for him in the First World War. Many Czech and Slovak soldiers deserted to the Russian side, but a large proportion chose that path only after capture by the Russians, as the fortunes of Germany and Austria-Hungary were clearly on the wane.

As soon as Czechoslovakia and Poland were established under the prodding and assistance of the victorious Western allies at the end of the First World War, there were requests by both countries that some of the colonies taken from defeated Germany be assigned to them. Vilém Němec, a Czech who lived in Africa for almost 25 years, produced a short booklet in 1923, advocating that Ethiopia highly suited Czechoslovakia's needs for colonization.[74] In Poland, plans to acquire a colony, specifically Cameroon, began even before the Polish state was revived.[75] These plans were never seriously discussed by government but Poland did reimpose its rule over mostly Ukrainian-inhabited territory on its East. In an interview in 2015, the future Nobel Prize-winning author Olga Tokarczuk said, 'I think we will have to face our own history and try to rewrite it a little, without hiding all the terrible things we did as colonizers, a national majority who suppressed minorities, as slave owners or murderers of Jews'.[76] By 'colonizers' she meant Poles in their role governing Lithuanians, Belarusians, and Ukrainians not only during the interwar period, but also much farther back in the country's history.[77] If the Soviets, and before them imperial Russia, were 'colonizers' of Poland, then Poland was in its turn a colonizer as well.

Another largely Ukrainian area, now known as the Transcarpathian Region of Ukraine, became part of Czechoslovakia after the First World War. The Prague government immediately instituted governmental policies that resembled those imposed by 'civilized' Western powers in the 'uncivilized' South, ranging from education to efforts to eugenically improve the race.[78] In many ways, Czechoslovakia treated Slovakia as a Czech quasi-colony also, creating considerable resentment among a people who had just been freed from Hungarian domination. And although Hungary lost Romanian-majority Transylvania (briefly reassigned to it by Hitler and Mussolini), Magyar rule there is also viewed today by some scholars as quasi-colonial.[79]

The manufacturing economy of interwar Central Europe continued to depend on cheap raw materials from the Global South, and to some extent also on exports to the colonized world. The Bata Shoe Company of Czechoslovakia built its fortunes on outsourcing labour to, and finding new markets in, the colonies. A promotional video, made by Bata in the 1930s, showed barefoot 'natives' in the Sahara, and promised that the company would make sure that no human would go without shoes. During the postcolonial period, when Bata had been forced out of its home country by the communists, the company became a major outsourcer of labour to places such as Sri Lanka.[80]

Under communism, and with the Soviet Union competing quite successfully for influence in the newly freed colonial nations, Central European communist governments fostered friendly relations with the postcolony. Among the effects of those relations was that an appreciable number of African and Asian students came to study in the area's universities, a pattern that continues today to an extent. Some of the students would marry and remain in Central Europe. As James Mark has noted, also, the 'earlier Eastern European migration to western European imperial settler colonialisms, socialist-era migration from Africa and Asia to the region, and the presence [during communism] of the region's troops in destabilising conflicts in the Middle East' had helped to prepare the region's reaction to the infamous 'migration crisis'.[81]

In short, Central Europe has benefited, and continues to benefit, from being part of the historically colonizing part of the globe – contrary to official and popular opinion. Within the geopolitical relationship of the ex-colonizers and the ex-colonized, it has some characteristics of both.

The level of prosperity in Central Europe, as we discussed in Chapter 4, resembles that of Western Europe more than most other places in Eastern Europe, let alone that of the poor countries of the 'Third World'. Central Europeans may travel freely for work and pleasure to the Western member countries of the EU. They hold voting power and as such are able to affect decision making in the EU, where they have begun, also, to exercise political influence unavailable to a (post)colony. Their economic clout is also, in spite of the many hurdles, increasing. Nor is racism against them – Eastern Europeanism – the same in either intensity or in nature as against people of colour, against Roma, or against Muslims, including racism perpetrated by Central Europeans themselves. The brutal attacks on Eastern European migrants discussed at the beginning of the book are reprehensible but rare, unlike on these other groups. If you're not *too* Eastern European, if you speak excellent English, dress and eat like a Westerner, if you are able to share topics and opinions in a way that fits the expectations of Western society, then you have a fair chance of being accepted, personally, as an equal. Your children born in the West will in most cases pass without even having to try. Whether such an automatic pass will ever also be given to the ordinary 'Eastern Europeans' who stay home, remains to be seen. But, as I have often said in this book, Central Europeans have partial white privilege. It is safe to say that if Central Europeans are colonized, then they are not quite.

The real, if partial, similarities between the postcolonial and the post-communist condition do, however, offer an opportunity for Central Europeans to understand, empathize, and cultivate solidarity with people in and from the Global South.[82] Few have answered the call.

9

Slavia Prague v. Glasgow Rangers: Lessons from a Football Match

'Why should we kneel? We're not England, who colonized half the world and carries the burden of slavery stemming from its history. We need not apologize to anyone.' So said a fan of the Czech soccer champions, Slavia Prague.[1] He was commenting on Slavia's refusal to kneel before their match against London's Arsenal, on 8 April 2021. A few days earlier, an irate Polish commentator demanded, 'Let Russian and German footballers kneel before Poles, to ask their forgiveness!' Piotr Lisiewicz added that while 'the British had colonies, Poles were in Russian and German servitude'.[2] His reference was to a game that pitted Poland against England. In both matches, the English side took the knee as a gesture in support of the Black Lives Matter movement. Athletes were especially honouring the memory of George Floyd, the Black American murdered the year before by a white Minneapolis policeman. (The symbolic gesture dates back to 2016, with American football player Colin Kaepernick taking the knee during the playing of the US national anthem.) Previously, the Czechs had no problem kneeling also. In fact, the Czech national team had knelt during the anthems when they faced the Scottish nationals just a few months earlier, on 14 October 2020. But something had changed drastically on 18 March, when Prague Slavia beat Glasgow Rangers 2–0, on the Scottish team's own turf.

Tensions were high at the Ibrox Stadium. The winner was to proceed into the quarter finals of the Europa Cup. As they have many times, Rangers had recently again qualified as Scottish champions, and had not lost a game at home for a year. At least to their own fans, they were the favourites. But Slavia came to Glasgow after a streak of 18 games without a loss, and could not be easily written off. Fourteen minutes into the game, Slavia's forward Peter Oliyanka, a Black player from Nigeria, scored a header that travelled over the Rangers' defence into goalie McGregor's net. The Scottish team was frustrated by several missed scoring opportunities. They fumed that the referee refused to call a penalty when, as the Scots saw it, Slavia's Abdallah Sima (also a Black footballer) committed a serious foul. After the break, at minute 61, Glasgow's Kemar Roofe attempted to kick a high ball and the Czech goalie, Ondřej Kolář, jumped to catch it. Video available on YouTube appears to show that Roofe allowed his foot to meet Kolář's face with full force, in what some of the international press described as a 'kung-fu' kick.[3] Kolář was taken off the pitch with a fractured skull, and will have to wear a protective brace for the rest of his career. Roofe got a red card, removing him from the game.

Most of the British commentators insisted that the high kick was an accident, while Czechs agreed with the referee that it was a deliberate foul. At any rate, the altercation did nothing to cool Glasgow's tempers. A little over 10 minutes later, another Ranger, Leon Balogun, also had to leave the game with a red card. With the Scottish team down two players, Slavia's Nicolae Stanciu scored with a free kick in the 74th minute.

That sealed Rangers' fate in the championship: they were out. But before the game was over, the Czech player Ondřej Kúdela ran directly at Glasgow's Finnish footballer, Glen Kamara, and, covering his mouth with his hand, whispered something in Kamara's ear. Kamara, who is Black, started off furiously at the Czech team, and a melee ensued. So upset was Kamara that he physically assaulted Kúdela in the tunnel leading to the dressing rooms. After the game the reason for Kamara's anger became clear. What Kúdela said to him, according to Kamara, was 'You're a f—king monkey, you know you are'. Kúdela denied that he made a racist remark, saying that what he said was 'You're a f—king guy'. The European football association, UEFA, believed Kamara, not surprisingly – at least one Glasgow player said he heard the remark and, anyway, why if he was simply swearing would Kúdela need to cover his mouth? The

Czech got a 10-game suspension, very severe in terms of precedent, though insufficient in the eyes of Kamara and his team. The Glasgow player got three games off for attacking Kúdela.

A three-game penalty for assault, and ten games for some words you said? Many Czechs just couldn't comprehend, or, insensitive to the campaign to stamp out racism in football, pretended not to.

The British press, on the other hand, was full of unqualified condemnation for the racist 'Eastern Europeans'. Among the many examples was the response to the incident in *The Scottish Sun*. Journalist Davie Provan opened his commentary with a quote from Kevin Harper, a former forward of Scotland's Hibernian F.C. Harper described his long experience with racial harassment in his own country. This was followed by other examples of football racism in Scotland and the admission, 'In Scotland, we like to think it's not as bad or that we're better than other nations, but we're not'. And yet Provan went on to exhibit a textbook example of Eastern Europeanism. 'Black players have been abused for years in Russia', he wrote,

> but Fifa still gave them the 2018 World Cup.
>
> When the Russian government set up a committee to oversee preparations for the event, it included supporters' union chief Alexander Shprygin. Previously he'd been photographed promoting Neo-Nazi causes. Vladimir Putin crony Sepp Blatter turned a blind eye to Russia's antics.
>
> Slavia player Kudela is a product of Eastern Europe's intolerance.

No explanation required to explain what Russian racism had to do with the behaviour of Czechs, or why the intolerance shown by Kúdela was, in spite of all Provan writes about the Scottish football racism, specifically 'Eastern European'.

Meanwhile this case of perceived Western liberal hypocrisy convulsed the Czech people like no other event. 'If the Rangers didn't play against a team from Central – or as they say, Eastern – Europe; if they played against a German or a French team,' said Jiří Hošek, a Czech sports journalist, 'then they wouldn't behave like this, like Neanderthals.'[4] Here was a prime example of Central

European anger at being classed with the East – which means as occupying a lower rung of the civilizational ladder than the West – when really it's the West who, in their mistreatment of Central Europeans, was behaving like primitive pre-humans.[5]

The American CNN's Czech outlet featured a commentator, Lukáš Hron, who also had 'civilization' on his mind, when he pointed to what he saw as non-Western behaviour among those who condemned the Czechs

> [w]ithout regards to the absurdity of collective guilt. Without regards to the fact that the presumption of innocence is one of the pillars of civilized Western society. Without regards to the fact that the continuing xenophobic attack on Eastern Europeans is perhaps just a slightly better smelling form of racism. [...] Less aggressive British moralizers on social media sometimes do not speak of Czechs as brutes, but do with condescending indulgence instead point out that we as a nation have obviously not yet matured to a sufficiently self-reflective phase in order to deal with our own racism.[6]

'We will not kneel before you'

Even the head of state, President Miloš Zeman, could not stay out of the fray. The presidential website published a letter by Zeman's staff secretary, Vratislav Mynář, addressed to the UEFA in protest against its decision to punish Kúdela for racism.

> You make it impossible for an athlete to fulfill his dream in the European League. And all that just to satisfy the perverted expectations of a narrow group of activists and of a club that is unable to win in the field, but [tries to do so through] shouting empty and injured phrases about racism. [...] Your efforts might lead to … a situation where a person whose skin colour is other than black is discriminated against, oppressed, and robbed of their rights. [...] I value highly the fact that Czech society does not identify with your verdict,

and this is true across [our] entire society. [...] We will not kneel before you, and no threats against Czech fans will succeed.[7]

That last sentence was deliberately calculated to increase the provocation, by interpreting kneeling against racism as kneeling before UEFA and, by extension, Western liberal opinion. The Czech president is on record telling the US ambassador, during Trump's presidency, that '"Black Lives Matter" is a racist slogan because all lives matter'.[8]

Zeman was just the highest placed among the many enablers who encouraged the Czech national team to refuse to kneel before their game against Wales.[9] Slavia repeated the non-gesture in its game on 15 April against London's Arsenal.[10]

Support from another Central European national team was not long in coming. Just one day after the Czech Republic–England match, the Polish national team remained standing as they faced the kneeling players of Wales. The veteran Polish goalie, Jan Tomaszewski, approved. 'I would not kneel. 'Cause I have the eagle [Polish national symbol] on my chest, [...] in our history [...] we never had a situation [of confrontations] with black players, or against blacks [...] we did not exploit them.' The Polish radio station Polska 24.pl interpreted Tomaszewski to mean that the 'protesting about racial inequality and former colonial politics is not applicable to Poland'.[11] In Hungary, the pro-Orbán *Magyar Nemzet* happily picked up the story, quoting Tomaszewski with warm approval. The author of the article called the refusal to kneel 'Visegrád gymnastics'.[12]

Not long before the Glasgow fiasco, the Hungarian football world had itself been embroiled in a controversy, this time concerning the homophobia of goal-keeping coach Zsolt Petry, a Hungarian hired by the Berlin club, Hertha. Petry put his foot in his mouth as he was being interviewed by *Magyar Nemzet*, perhaps not expecting the Hungarian-language conversation to reach the West. His comments regarded a younger Hungarian footballer engaged in Germany, RB Leipzig's goalie Péter Gulácsi. Gulácsi had objected to the Orbán government's ban on adoption by gay couples. 'Family is family,' he wrote in Hungarian, using the slogan of a Hungarian movement supporting same-sex adoption, 'every child has the right to grow up in a happy family, be that family composed of any number of people of any gender, any colour, any religion.' Gulácsi connected this belief to his life in the West:

> I have been living abroad for more than 14 years. As much in my private life as in pro sport, I have met a huge number of different people, be it in terms of their nationality, culture, religion, philosophy of life, or anything else. The more time you spend abroad or among different people, the more you find out that the fact that not everyone is the same just makes the world more colourful and that the main thing is the love, acceptance, and tolerance of others.[13]

Though surely not intended that way, Gulácsi's intervention may have been seen as packaged in the language of someone with Western experience, teaching the inexperienced East. But it was certain to boost the case of the Hungarian protesters, who were under considerable pressure. For example, a former national team member, János Hrutka, appeared to have been fired from his job as a TV commentator when he stood up for Gulácsi.[14]

In his remarks condemning Gulácsi, Petry borrowed from Orbán's favourite anti-migrant phraseology:

> I can't even understand how Europe is capable of sinking to the moral depths where it now finds itself. To me, migrant policy expresses a moral decline. Let's go on living in Europe with the values that we have learned over many years. Europe is a Christian part of the world, and I am not pleased to watch the moral decline that is sweeping the continent. The liberals spread the opposing opinion: if you don't think that migration is a good thing, because an enormous number of criminals have overwhelmed Europe, then they hit you right away with the charge that you're a racist.[15]

His Berlin club, shocked by his harangue, refused to be placated by Petry's subsequent apology. Stating that his views were 'not compatible with the values of Hertha BSC', they let the coach go.

Against this disturbing background of racism, it was hardly surprising that, before a Hungary–Ireland match in Budapest on 8 June, the Irish knelt and the Hungarians stood. This time no less than Viktor Orbán called the Irish action a 'provocation'. He took up the theme of how Hungary, unlike the West, was not responsible for slavery, and so did not carry the burden of the racism protested by Black Lives Matter. 'We as Hungarians do not see this burden, [...] In the carrying of these burdens, we, who were not slave-owners, cannot help them [the Western countries where the kneeling demonstration began], it is futile of them to bring this burden onto football fields.' Evidently, Orbán has little knowledge of Roma slavery in his land, or of the fact that if any European nation failed to benefit from the global economy of slavery, then it was – as we saw in Chapter 2 – the Irish!

These incidents were far from the only examples of racism and other prejudice in Central European football. At various times in the Czech national league itself, Black players have suffered insults, including monkey calls.[16] The Slovak team Slovan Bratislava was fined 3,000 euros after ultras displayed a large 'White Lives Matter' banner.[17] In 2018, Polish fans took their racism abroad when Poland faced Italy in a World Cup qualifier in Bologna. For yelling racist insults, the Poles were fined 2,000 euros.[18] The Hungarian national team was accused of yelling racist abuse by the Romanian captain, who said the Hungarians called the Romanians 'Gypsies'. It is unclear if any of the Romanians were actually Roma.[19] (Ironically, the incident recalls another context in which non-Roma Romanian migrants to Britain have chosen to counter Eastern Europeanist racism against them, by attempting to transfer it to those among them who are Roma.[20])

Such incidents are not rare. Racism in Central European football has been abundantly demonstrated (even if a player like Ghana-born Prince Ofori, who had played for a Slovak provincial team and then after an injury settled in the country, remembers no racist attacks or insults on the football field).[21] So does this not confirm the Eastern Europeanist prejudice, that Central Europeans have a unique predisposition for racism?

Not necessarily. Football racism in Central Europe is absolutely appalling. But is there more of it there than in the West? After Arsenal defeated Slavia 2–1, fan Zachary Stevens made a blog post with the headline, 'Arsenal kick Slavia Prague and racism out of Europa League'.[22] If only it were so simple. All you have to do to rid the League of racism is to kick out the Eastern Europeans? Such a projection of racism out of Western Europe and unto the East is another attempt to cleanse the self-image of Western Europe by ejecting evidence of its own undemocratic, illiberal impulses toward its post-communist neighbours – to subcontract guilt. As I have argued, this psychological (and political) process is fundamental to Eastern Europeanism.

Between September 2011 and August 2019, football teams in the following countries have received sanctions for racism from UEFA:

- four sanctions: Croatia, Russia
- three sanctions: Romania, Serbia, Spain
- two sanctions: Italy, Ukraine
- one sanction: France, Georgia, Greece, Hungary, Montenegro, Poland, Portugal, Slovakia, Slovenia, United Kingdom[23]

No sanctions were levelled at the Czech Republic. On an Eastern Europeanist assumption that what happens in one part of 'Eastern Europe' also holds for another, football racism is shown here to be greater in 'Eastern Europe'. But if we refuse lumping all Eastern European countries together, then what is revealed is that there is no evidence that any Central European country shows more football racism than, say, France or the United Kingdom. Results from Russia or Romania should not be automatically taken to be evidence for what happens in Slovakia or Poland.

There is, sadly, plenty of racism in Western European football. Following England's loss to Italy in the 2021 Euro Cup final match the vitriol of racist abuse by some English fans against their own players of colour caused a shock.[24] As *The Guardian* recognized in a headline, 'English football is consumed by racism and hatred'. Here is one of the many incidents quoted.

> Last season Haringey Borough in north London were the victims of racist abuse from Yeovil Town fans during an FA Cup qualifying game. Their goalkeeper Valery Pajetat was spat at, pelted with stones and called a 'black c★★t'. After the game was stopped for several minutes,

manager Tom Loizou decided that there was only one course of action. 'My players were getting racially abused', he says now. 'The referee had no control. So I decided to take them off. The FA Cup don't mean that much to me. I said to the Yeovil manager: "Good luck in the next round".'[25]

Both before and after the Kúdela–Kamara scandal, there occurred what seem like comparable incidents of abuse by players in the Spanish and French leagues. But unlike in the Slavia–Rangers case, they led to no conviction. And no one held these incidents to be indicative of racism, specifically, in Western or Southern Europe.

On 13 September 2020, Paris Saint Germain (PSG) met Olympique of Marseilles (OM) in a vicious game that saw 17 penalty cards, including five red cards (which remove the player from the game) before Olympique left the field with a 1–0 victory. One of those expelled was PSG's star Brazilian player Neymar, who had delivered a kick to the back of the head of OM's Álvaro Gonzalez. According to Philippe Sanfourche writing for the broadcasting network RTL, Neymar

> affirmed repeatedly that he was acting in response to the racist insults that he had received from the Spaniard. While nothing seems to lead to proving these allegations, new evidence has appeared that argues in favour of the attacker. Three Brazilian experts invited by the media organization *Globo* identified 'without any doubt' the words *mierda de mono* ['monkey shit'], pronounced by Alvaro Gonzalez.
>
> If the Brazilian chain may be perceived as partisan, the information has been quickly confirmed by a Spanish expert questioned by [the magazine] *Le Parisien*. Thus the League will be able to use this new evidence for this case under investigation, which threatens a 10-game suspension for the OM defender.[26]

Neymar is said to have used a homophobic phrase in his response to Gonzalez. Worse, the Brazilian star had been accused of calling the Japanese footballer Hiroki Sakai, a *chino de mierda* ('Chinese shit').

No one was punished on the basis of any of these allegations, though the evidence certainly equalled that against the Czech Kúdela.

There was no punishment, either, for an incident that happened *after* the Rangers–Slavia game, in Spain. *The Guardian* reported that 'Valencia walked off the pitch in protest at alleged racist abuse directed at defender Mouctar Diakhaby by Cádiz's Juan Cala'. After a physical clash, Cala turned around and started out at Diakhaby, in an action resembling Kúdela's provocation against Kamara. Valencia's Gabriel Paulista was caught on camera saying, as he attended to Diahkaby, 'You can't say *negro de mierda* [shitty black man]'. Valencia's captain José Luis Gayà also heard the racist remark. *The Guardian* concludes with the Spanish La Liga federation promising, 'We take any allegation of racism seriously and will work with the clubs and refereeing establishment to do whatever is necessary. La Liga condemns racism in all shapes and forms.'[27]

In spite of Diakhaby's claim having been heard by witnesses, as in Kamara's case against Kúdela, however, La Liga declared five days later that it had found no evidence that Cádiz's Juan Cala insulted Valencia's Mouctar Diakhaby 'in the alleged terms'.[28] Given such a lax attitude toward fighting football racism in Spain, it is perhaps not surprising that the Spanish football federation reacted to an anti-kneeling campaign in the country's social media by declaring that the national team would not kneel before matches during the Eurocup games.[29]

It is difficult to see what makes Gonzalez and Cala's egregious racist remarks less so than Kúdela's, or their cases less fully confirmed by the evidence. But it is clear what made passions so much more enflamed against the Czech footballer. Eastern Europeanism assumes that what is true of one Eastern European is true of all. Gonzalez and Cala are seen as acting on their own. But when a Czech commits a racist provocation, the public in the West sees behind it all the other awful acts ever committed in Russia, Bulgaria, or Serbia, and none of the ones that occur regularly in England, France, or Spain.

The spectacle of a team sport is an important arena of togetherness in capitalist society, a sort of an antidote to the unimpeded market's depersonalization and segmentation of human interaction. A team is an 'imagined community', to use a term that the anthropologist Benedict Anderson used mainly to describe a nation.[30] Both team and nation are extensions, as ordinary language about them often shows, of the family, which remains the basic unit of human cooperation and solidarity. The inclusions and exclusions that manifest themselves in football fandom should not be considered to be a frivolous matter, unrelated to more 'serious' aspects of social life.

Football racism holds important lessons about the nature of racism overall, and of the illiberal orientation that builds on it, in Central Europe. It is not necessarily the case that racism in Central Europe is more common or more intense than in the West. In Central Europe, however, it is perhaps more openly and less controversially expressed. Why?

One relevant, football-specific fact is that Central European football is a peripheral affair compared to the major leagues of England, France, or Germany. Few people in the West are interested in Poland's Ekstraklasa or the Czech Fortuna Liga. Even in Central Europe itself, attendance at matches is nothing like in the West. There, it may be a battle to get a ticket for a top-flight game, but a sold-out game is rare in Warsaw or Prague. The amount of sponsorship money riding on Central European games is practically negligible compared to the major Western European leagues, whose matches are regularly broadcast to millions all over the world. Slavia's president, Jaroslav Tvrdík, apologizing for a racist banner held up by 'unknown ultras' supporting Slavia, cited the club's desire for 'international sponsors' to propel his Chinese-owned club into the position of a 'multicultural international team capable of being the hegemon of Central and Eastern Europe, for example'.[31] Once 'international sponsors' support Slavia, Tvrdík was implying, they will put pressure on the teams and the fans to prevent expressions of racism, which can hurt the image of the brand.

Eastern Europeanist complaints from the West give the impression that anti-racism in the West is the result of a higher moral standard among Western white people than 'Eastern European' white people. What this ignores is that the anti-racist struggle stems from and depends on protests and civil disobedience by racialized people themselves. In Central Europe that would be the Roma,[32] but they are as of yet very weekly organized as a poltical pressure group, and there are too few Black or Muslim residents to mount a visible enough movement to fight back against racism.

There is little political pressure to protest against racism in Central Europe, where people of colour do not, unlike in some parts of the West, form a voter base that can influence elections. There have been cases of people of colour being elected to parliament.³³ They received their mandate from white voters. But there is not a large enough concentration of people of colour for them to be considered as a demographic in electoral calculations. This explains why politicians can exploit racism, like Islamophobia, relatively free of challenge, compared to the West. And even liberals are less compelled by personal emotion to speak up against racism: they do not see racialized people among their families and neighbours, as they would in the multi-ethnic areas of the West. (Again, this generalization loses some power when one speaks of the big cities of Central Europe or the rural areas of the West.)

The progressive Slovak columnist Peter Schutz asked if people in Prague even know why 'f★★cking monkey' is worse than 'f★★cking guy'.³⁴ It is certainly a symptom of racism to not know the difference. Ignorance of the role race plays in Central Europe, not only in the subtle case of the colonial heritage but also in the obvious case of anti-Roma discrimination, is astounding. There is little understanding of the systemic character of racism. Individual cases when a racialized person succeeds are vaunted as proof that racism does not exist (during the communist regime, one of the mantras was that 'anti-Semitism does not exist in our country'). The fact that Czech teams have African players can be misused in this way, as can be the Black members of parliament just mentioned, or the shows of racial acceptance such as naming a Black Czech, Benny Cristo, to represent the country at the 2021 Eurovision contest.

'Political correctness', as sensitivity to offensive symbols is often derided, is a necessary tool in the fight against racism, and it prevents personal hurt when people of different races interact. The major difference between racism in the West and in Central Europe is that Central Europe is less politically correct. This may influence the responses of people to opinion surveys. It is known that even in anonymous surveys people are sensitive to what is expected.³⁵ (The bias depends on how sensitive the interviewees are to the topic, such as racism.) But political correctness can in some cases deteriorate from an anti-racist tool into a cosmetic cover for racism. Symbolic anti-racism then becomes a false alibi for systemic racism. In some ways, that is exactly what happens when the racism that infests football in the West is ejected in the imagination to the East ('kick out Slavia, kick out racism'), where it is more readily allowed to erupt without the symbolic restraints of gesture and language.

To be sure, Slavia did propose an anti-racist gesture of sorts. When its players refused to kneel at the start of the match against Arsenal, they formed a semicircle, arms around shoulders. The team included footballers of different origins, including a few people of colour. Slavia presented the group embrace as a substitute anti-racist gesture, in place of kneeling. Before the World Cup qualifier against Wales, the Czech national team chose another allegedly equivalent demonstration of their stand against racism.

> The national team will take a neutral apolitical stance to certain topics that have been resonating in the sports environment.
>
> This namely concerns the Black Lives Matter (BLM) initiative, in which some players kneel before football matches.
>
> To express their support for the fight against racism and other displays of discrimination, xenophobia and antisemitism, the Czech national team will point to the UEFA Respect inscription on the left sleeve of their jerseys, referring to the UEFA campaign of the same name, before the match in Wales.[36]

That 'Black Lives Matter' should be uncontroversial. To say that it is political is unacceptable. Seeking alternative expressions of anti-racism is as suspect as the disingenuous response, 'All Lives Matter', espoused by enablers of racism such as Miloš Zeman and Donald Trump. But the emotional motivation for not kneeling here is not only hate or, which is not much better, obliviousness to hate. It is also spite.

'We are not racists, but we won't let *you* tell us how we should fight racism.' That is almost literally what Central European footballers were saying. Anyone saying 'I am not a racist' should automatically be suspected of the opposite, as the phrase is usually followed by 'but'. One cannot accept the genuineness of 'an 'anti-racism' that questions the credentials of Black Lives Matter and acts to oppose, rather than advance, its global campaign. But it may be that the spite part plays an important part in this manifestation of Central European racism along with the hate part. Had the Western public not so uncritically levelled the charge of racism at 'Eastern European football' rather than, also, their own, then there is a chance that Czech and Polish footballers might possibly have knelt together with those from the West.

The uproar about the Slavia–Rangers racism incident engulfed Central Europe at the same time as the area was recording some of the world's highest rates of coronavirus infection, hospitalization, and death. The world is entering an era of global challenges. Pandemics and climate change are among these, but so are the global racialized inequalities that fuel migration. All require resolute, joint action by a united humanity. The multipolar capitalism that encourages friction rather than cooperation among large blocs, however, fuels competition rather than cooperation. Twenty-first-century illiberalism relies on a politicized hinterland of racists, anti-vaxxers, and climate-change deniers, producing a noxious ideological mix that fosters division and mutual suspicion. It is a worldwide scourge, seen East, West, North and South. The specific semi-peripheral condition of Central Europe – 'white but not quite' – shapes the content of illiberalism there. But to blame Central Europe's illiberalism, including its racism, exclusively on 'Eastern European' culture and history, is itself racist. It's the last thing we need if we are to fight together the assault on liberty and democracy that neither begins nor ends in the four countries surveyed here.

Conclusion: When the Migrants Come

Let us stay with football for a moment longer. I would like to begin the Conclusion as I have the Introduction, with an allusion to the best-known Central European illiberal leader's penchant for the game. The Hungarian journalist, Pál Dániel Rényi, wrote a whole book on it, claiming that Orbán's view of football was the same as his vision of politics. 'Orbán has never been a fan in the traditional sense', writes Rényi,

> but he knew well the emotional world of a fan. That sort of commitment is built not on rational pondering but on events, beliefs, heroes, and memories. Shared symbols, convictions, and goals connect to one another the team and its followers. Identification is unconditional, requires no explanation, and resists time. The team: it's eternal. And for the loyal fan, victory is not simply important; it's the only thing that counts.[1]

This was not Orbán's own world, as Rényi makes clear; it was the world he created for his fans. With this kind of mentality, every victory by the leader is cheered by his followers, with little thought given to how it benefits *them*. He plays the strings of their beliefs and memories; he offers a community of affect at a time of great dislocation. Orbán became a master at this political game, unlike any in Central Europe or even Europe as a whole. But the false consciousness that illiberalism creates is systemic, not personal. In the end, the shared symbols, the unconditional, unthinking, seemingly eternal loyalty are to, as Liz Fekete put it, one's own kith and kin, more than any charismatic leader who can facilitate it. The focus in this book has been on the triumphant rise of illiberalism in Central Europe, between the 'European migration ciris' of 2015–16, and the efforts of the opposition that gained visibility in late 2021. The illiberal revolt that Orbán and Kaczynski helped to unleash will, however, likely remain a powerful force for much of this century, and long after they are gone, because in the end illiberalism responds to global and local forces that are much more consequential than the personal whims of any individual, no matter how influential.

Liberal, 'free-market' capitalism, which by its very nature creates the pseudo-kinship of race, spawns illiberalism as its not-quite-opposite; the process does not necessarily require a powerful leader. If you exploit people as a group, racial or otherwise, you can expect them to fight back as a group. There is nothing wrong with that as far as it goes. Black solidarity has been a necessary feature of fighting for racial equality, as has been women's solidarity in that for the equality of gender. The trouble is that when illiberal Central Europeans fight back, then instead of the intersectional solidarity of one disadvantaged group with another, which would propose solidarity with the Global South for Central Europeans, they act from a position of limited white privilege. They respond with a struggle for more privilege within the system of disempowerment, rather than for the end to disempowerment itself. In this, I have argued, Central European illiberalism resembles the similar illiberalisms of what I have called the white periphery, including in the West.

In both Central European and Western illiberalism, the real fear and anger sets in not at the hierarchy of white privilege, but at the 'elites' who are willing to let the whole hierarchy go, in the eyes of the white illiberals, if not in reality. This is why the presidency of Barrack Obama caused an increase in the heat of white racist illiberal rhetoric, not only in the United States but everywhere, making Donald Trump the saviour of not only 'real' America but also, as far as European illiberals go, of 'real' Europe. That a Black man was president was unacceptable to them, but so was the fact that he had been elected in part by white voters, including many who were highly educated and economically privileged. To put it another way, illiberals accuse the 'elites' of abandoning, out of weakness and/or naivety, the solidarity of race that has maintained the limited privileges of the semi-peripheral whites in the deeply ingrained system of inequalities inherited from the colonial era.

Is white illiberalism then the same in Central Europe as in the West? Largely yes, if we are thinking of its rhetoric and even of its structural characteristics. In both cases, illiberalism is a misguided protest against the same neoliberal globalism that has exploited groups of working people, and forced them into an alliance with local capital, who also want their nation's protection against the multinationals. But no, white illiberalism is not the same in Central Europe in terms of its influence on society, and especially politics. In spite of significant opposition to it, it has seen more, and more enduring, political success there.

One reason many voters in Central Europe like illiberal party platforms is that the impact of neoliberal globalism in the area was far more brutal than in most of the West, due to the disruptions of the 'transition' from communism. There are others. Limitations on the freedom of vote played a role, for example, especially in Orbán's Hungary – although we have seen in Chapter 4 that in the other countries voters still enjoyed a degree of freedom comparable to much of the West.

It may be also that, as the Czech liberal Catholic Msgr. Tomáš Halík has said, post-communist society has not been 'immunized' against anti-democratic authoritarianism and racism.[2] The question is, who is to administer the vaccine? We have encountered earlier the opinion that racism in 'Eastern Europe' is due to the fact that the area missed the anti-racist education the public underwent in the West. But, however important and impactful predominantly white society's efforts to cleanse itself of undemocratic tendencies, including racism and homophobia, may be, it is unlikely that what the African-American writer Danzy Senna calls 'anti-racist self-help'[3] was or ever will be ultimately effective on its own.

One thing that is objectionable about the view that Central and other Eastern Europeans are racist because under the communists they missed out on the soul-searching and anti-racism programmes in the West, is the self-satisfied assumption that, if racism has become more restricted in official forums in the West than in Central Europe, then that is the achievement of Western liberalism as such. That ignores the fact that there are few people of colour, other than the weakly organized Roma, in Central Europe, which necessarily decreases the power of the anti-racist resistance. Without taking anything away from anti-racist organizations among liberal-minded white people (which do actively fight racism in Central Europe), it is obvious that progress has had to be fought for by racialized people themselves. The American civil rights marches, but also the Black riots that followed the murder of Martin Luther King, are a good example. In the UK, France, and other Western countries with a sizeable population of colour, both peaceful and violent activism have made sure that at least the more obvious signs of racism became unacceptable in much of polite society.

Even the small number of people of colour in Central Europe can have an impact that white allies cannot easily duplicate. Baloji Bolagun and Konrad Pędziwiatr have studied the great uproar that a YouTube video posted by four Black Polish women, in Polish, had in the country. The women entitled their video, 'Do not call me *Murzyn*', a term that the authors compare to 'Negro', and which derives from Renaissance depictions of the North African Muslim 'Moors'. The intervention by the four women alone had a major impact on *Murzyn* becoming ostracized in the country, in what was perhaps the first attempt to cleanse the Polish language of vocabulary with racist implications. The women succeeded in calling Poles' attention to the fact that racism, in Poland, is not a foreign issue, but must be fought within the country itself.[4] In response to their protest, the official council charged with advising on standard language usage in Poland, *Rada Języka Polskiego*, decreed that the term *Murzyn* should henceforth 'be avoided in the media, official administration, and the schools'.[5]

It is impossible to predict, in a world gripped by uncertainty, which way illiberalism and which way Central Europe will go. With Western-dominated neoliberal globalism challenged by a multipolar capitalism of assertively competing powers, it is difficult to be completely sure that Central Europe will remain in the Western orbit. China is making strong efforts to increase its influence in the post-communist parts of the EU. Russia, even, may convince some people that it provides the right antidote to the 'dictates of Brussels', making Central Europe's imagined connection to Russia a self-fulfilling prophecy. Authoritarian capitalist regimes such as Russia's or China's (though the latter pretends to still be 'communist') may conceivably be the real victors if the illiberal revolt in Central Europe keeps up.

There is hope, however, for the survival (or revival, where necessary) of democracy in Central Europe. Vigorous engagement by citizens would be the best guarantee of that, but there may also be some objective factors that will destroy illiberalism as they work themselves out.

Once the 'national capitalists' discussed in Chapter 8 acquire enough capital they will continue to increase their international clout, as many have done already, through foreign investments and collaboration with Western capital. At that point, the national-level false alliance between the very rich and the not-so-poor, which supports illiberalism, may be weakened. Perhaps then, the understandable and legitimate desire of people for community in the face of depersonalizing economic forces and the threats of climate change and pandemics will be satisfied, no longer by racist jingoism but rather by a careful slowing down and rethinking of globalization, with policies that do not favour the requirements of global capital over local needs – yet maintain the international cooperation needed to address the overwhelming challenges of climate change, epidemics, and the nuclear arms race.

As for anti-migrant rhetoric, it is very possible that it will, in the long term, be ineffective anyway. A combination of rising incomes (hopefully) and an ageing population (certainly) will make the need for immigrants in Central Europe simply irresistible. Eventually, the powerful influx of migrants from Ukraine and Belarus, will be supplemented by people from outside Europe. Already a trickle of migrants from the Global South have begun to settle in Central Europe, seeing opportunities for classic migration-driven small businesses like corner stores and kebab shops. There is also a small number of medical and other professionals. It is utterly self-defeating for Central European governments to keep out migrants who will take necessary jobs and pay into social security banks, but also bring in fresh perspectives that are essential to economic growth through new ideas and new global connections. Measures encouraging the local birthrate cannot be expected to have more than very limited success.

If, so far, migration to Central Europe from outside the continent has been limited, it is actually not so much due to restrictive regulations as to the fact that, with Central Europe offering lower wages and little local migrant community organization, most migrants have just not really wanted to go there. Yet, as the few who had already come have realized, there are opportunities there, too. EU cross-border mobility rights will ensure that more will come, and in time will build the grassroots economic and social structures to welcome yet others. Once migrants of colour reach a critical mass, it is likely that they will mount a defence of their rights, as they have earlier in the West, when non-European migration began to be significant decades ago, and provoked similar debates about whether or not Europe is 'immigration country' (*Einwanderungsland*).[6] Migrants of colour might energize also the resistance of the long-discriminated Roma.

Of course, a completely contrary course of events is also possible. As the example of Putin's Russia and Lukashenko's Belarus shows, it is possible for countries to be totally 'captured' by selfish rulers. But, much as one may complain about the weakness of the EU, it is highly unlikely that authoritarianism with arbitrary jail detentions, torture, and executions will take place in any of its member states. A good example of what the EU can accomplish is the way in which Polish regions that had proclaimed themselves to be 'LGBT-ideology-free zones' chose, rather than lose EU money, to drop the resolution, one region even voting to label itself an area 'of established tolerance'.[7] Such events provide a very good reason not to think of expelling illiberal regimes from the EU. That would only deepen the racist rejection of 'Eastern Europeans' that provokes, though does not excuse, the illiberal revolt of Central Europe. And it would needlessly encourage the sense of being the victims of 'Brussels' that fuels the illiberal movement both in the East and in the West of the EU.

The illiberalism that rose to prominence in the twenty-first century in different forms with an Orbán or a Kaczyński, and also with a Trump, a Putin, an Erdogan, a Bolsonaro, a Dutarte, is a force to reckon with, capable of surviving all of these individuals. As long as a semblance of democracy remains, which it should as long as countries remain members of the European Union, illiberal leaders can be removed. It may be harder to remove their legacy. Illiberalism is, I have argued, one of the major reactions to the crisis of the neoliberal globalism that was dominant until the Great Recession of 2008. That crisis exposed not only its festering built-in flaws, but also the power of the opposition it engendered in Russia and China. The result was the beginning of a 'multipolar' world, with serious challenges to the world's political and economic order, no longer as easily controlled by 'multinational' corporations that were really centred around a US–West European core (even if with the participation of some Japanese and South Korean capital).

Unfortunately, rather than creating more equality in the world, multipolarity has continued to increase inequality, both within and among countries and continents. The greatest challenges facing the world, such as climate change and the arms race, all require effective worldwide cooperation. The COVID-19 pandemic showed how, instead, a world based on national sovereignty and the primacy of national interests fails miserably to rise to the challenge. The exercise of material privilege resulted in most people being vaccinated in the richer countries (including the semi-periphery of Central Europe) just as in the poor countries of the Global South death rates rose and intensive-care units were bursting at the seams with unvaccinated patients. At the same time, beggar-thy-neighbour competition set in even among the rich countries. They all tried to reserve vaccine production for themselves, and later used travel bans as a means to further petty economic and political squabbles. The Credit Suisse bank's prediction, that the multipolar world economy will even within the West pit against one another the US, the UK, and the EU,[8] appeared to be coming true with a vengeance.

In all the competing poles of the multipolar world, there are significant core–periphery contrasts and tensions; in the EU perhaps more so than elsewhere. Here Central Europe's illiberal revolt led the internal resistance to 'Brussels', expressing the same racially tinged nationalism that was, also elsewhere, dividing the world in its tragically misconceived response to globalization.

A temporary show of Western unity was provoked in the winter of 2022. The Russian invasion of Ukraine rudely awakened Europe and the world to the fact that a people between Germany and Russia was once again targeted by an international bully. People in the four Central European countries each remember the brutal crushing of their democracy, or their hopes for one, by Hitler in Czechoslovakia in 1938 and by Stalin in Poland in 1945. During the Cold War, Soviet Russia subjugated Hungary in 1956 and Czechoslovakia in 1968. Each of these attacks not only destroyed a nation's aspirations for a just society, but also for recognition by the world that their country belongs to 'Europe', to the West, and not Russia.

Each also reminds Central Europeans that the West did not come to their aid with sufficient force to prevent the victory of a foe who was not only their enemy but also the West's. The Russian attack on Ukraine added 2022 to the list of dates when the West failed to rescue an allied nation in Europe from the aggressor. I am not at all suggesting that the West should go to war with nuclear-armed Russia over Ukraine. The point is that it most likely would, if a 'real' Western country like France or Italy were attacked. Perhaps now it would also do so over Poland, the Czech Republic, Slovakia, or Hungary, who are members of the NATO alliance, but can we be quite sure? Surely the full solidarity of the Western alliance is meant to be extended to its Central European members. But it is hard to be certain that it would not, in a moment of ultimate crisis, once again be reserved only for the most fully white.

And why, indeed, is Ukraine not a member of NATO? It is hard to resist the thought that the imagined hierarchy of whiteness, with each nation located on a roughly West-to-East axis deemed more white than the next (see Chapter 2), has something very deep-seated to do with Ukraine's fate. Certainly, it was too late to admit Ukraine in 2022. But was it only pressure by Russia that kept the country out of NATO earlier, when other Central European and Baltic states were admitted? Or was it also that Ukraine was imagined as even less Western, even less white, tainted by its linguistic, cultural, and religious affinity to the least white of the white: 'semi-Asiatic' Russia?

The process that divides the acquisitive core from the exploitable periphery is entrenched in the logic of capitalism. I have argued that it is this process that creates the noxious divisions between and within racialized groups: between whites and others, and within groups of differentially privileged whites. This logic of exploitation will probably lead the West to both protect Central Europe against the designs of the Russian rival, and yet to continue distancing Central Europe from the core centres of Western privilege. It will go on creating the paradoxical situation where Central Europe is at the same time within and without the Western sphere, compared to both Russia and the postcolonial world.

It is unlikely that mere sentiment can reverse such divisions and create the unity needed for humanity to fight the global challenges of environmental degradation, pandemics, and a looming nuclear holocaust. To be sure, I did suggest in this book that the role of emotion is significant, including in the illiberal revolt. If sentiment did cause change, though, it would likely not be the sentiment expressed by Jean-Claude Juncker, then President of the European Commission, in one of his State of the Union speeches. Meaning to argue for unity, Juncker said, 'East to West: Europe must breathe with both lungs. Otherwise our continent will struggle for air.'[9] But separate-but-equal formulas have never led to equality; quite the contrary. Juncker's lung allegory establishes a dual view of Europe, enshrining division at the same time as he means to overcome it. Another organ metaphor would better highlight the needed unity, emotional solidarity, and empathy with outsiders. It would be better to imagine a Europe, and a world, that beats with one heart.

For now at least, unfortunately, that is no more than a pious wish.

Postscript: Confessions of a Canadian Central European

I wrote this book because I am a Central European, and in spite of its severe faults I love Central Europe.

To be precise, I am a Central European, but not quite. I was born in Prague, by coincidence. I am not quite a Czech, though I do hold a Czech passport (as well as Canadian). My parents survived the Holocaust in Budapest, using false names and forged documents to convince police and collaborators that they were not Jewish. Neither my father nor my mother was quite a Hungarian. He was born in Slovakia, where Jews were not considered quite Slovak. She was a Budapest girl, but her father came from some place in the Habsburg province of Galicia that no one remembers. The family called it Poland, though today it may well be Ukraine. Although my grandfather was not quite Polish, his origins caused problems for my mother's folks. They suffered discrimination by Hungarians, including Budapest Jews. The 'modern' Jews there had contempt for the 'Eastern Jews', as they called the Orthodox Jews from the eastern regions of the Habsburg Empire. They would have been surprised to hear, in what I say in this book is postwar terminology, that they themselves were 'Eastern European'. My father, who had studied medicine in Bratislava before being expelled as a Jew, married my mother when the war was over, and they moved to continue his studies in Prague. He graduated after I was born there, and was drafted into the Czechoslovak army. On the whim of a chance military regulation, they sent him to where he was born: the largely Hungarian-speaking border town of Komárno, in Slovakia. In fact, my father had grown up in a more purely Slovak environment, in another town some 50 miles to the north. But to be sent to Komárno pleased my parents, as it gave my mother a chance to speak Hungarian, and for all of us to travel to the exciting big city of Budapest, whenever the communist authorities allowed us to cross the bridge over the Danube into Hungary.

Having barely escaped annihilation during the Holocaust, my parents decided that we must keep our Jewishness to ourselves. My papers said that my nationality was Slovak, though as a Jew and a half-Hungarian, I wasn't quite. But because I was taught next to nothing about Judaism and we seldom practised Jewish religion or customs, I was not quite a Jew, either. That is a feeling that has never left me, even though I became much more Jewish once we landed, first in Italy and then in the United States, and once I arrived on my own in Canada. Here I married and here my children were born; I became a happy Canadian. But not quite. I have never stopped being interested in Europe, and have travelled to the continent most years all my life. I feel that I am very much the European, but in a way that no one living in Europe can be, because they are first of all English, German, Polish, Hungarian, or Russian, whereas I fancy myself a European first – proving that I am not quite.

I find this not-quite position to be quite comfortable. Not-quite can be not-only. It can teach empathy, with others who are also in one way or another marginalized. For Central Europe, too, not-quite is a potential, even not-quite-white. The potential is for insight, a critique of the condition of a world in which racial and economic inequality puts many others at an even greater disadvantage. As I believe to have shown, the potential for empathy with the postcolonial world has been lost in Central European illiberalism, but it remains there for everyone who calls themselves Central European.

I love Central Europe, but I hate its illiberalism. I ask myself: is my hate for illiberalism not a good enough reason to give up on Central Europe? A difficult question, but I still say no. Central Europe is a troubled and troubling region, when has it not been? But good people doing good things go on living there, as in the rest of the world, and give reason for hope.

I do not deny that many things are extremely bad in Central Europe or even that they are better in the West. But what I really wanted to say is that things are not *that* much better in the West, and that if they are worse in Central Europe then it's partly the West's fault.

Notes

Introduction

1. Király, 'Kiderült'.
2. Keller-Alant, Racz, and Simon, 'In Hungary, Viktor Orban's Favorite Mayor'.
3. I am referring to personalities that at one time were very widely known, especially in the Western world. Americans may also remember Hollywood figures ranging from the famous 'Dracula', Bela Lugosi, and the director George Cukor, to the actor Zsa Zsa Gabor. Football fans might recall Ferenc Puskás. And Béla Bartók is as well known to the audience of modern concert music as Liszt.
4. Dolan, Peterson-Withorn, and Wang, 'The Forbes 400 2020'.
5. Kalmar, ' "The Battlefield Is in Brussels" '.
6. Buckley and Foy, 'Poland's New Government'.
7. Radio Prague International, 'Zeman Describes Orban as "Genuine Leader"'.
8. nextQuotidiano, 'Ma Salvini e Meloni che difendono'.
9. It seems that Orbán missed the gender of *fratello* (masculine), although he may have been trying to pun on the name of Meloni's party. Orbán, 'Due Fratelli. Találkozó Giorgia Melonival'.
10. BFMTV interview with Jean-Jacques Bourdin, 24 September 2015.
11. Caulcott and Bayer, 'Viktor Orbán Rolls Out'.
12. Elfer, ' "Proud of You": Trump Writes'.
13. Anderson, *Imagined Communities*; Hall, Mercer, and Gates, *The Fateful Triangle*.
14. I am drawing here in part on literature about 'racial capitalism'. The recent impetus for this field of study is largely from Bhattacharyya, *Rethinking Racial Capitalism*. The history of racial capitalism is explored among other places in Jenkins and Leroy, *Histories of Racial Capitalism*. The intention is to focus on the racial character

of capitalism as inherent to all capitalism; not, as the term may suggest, to one special kind of capitalism.

15 'Neoliberalism' is notoriously difficult to define. Among progressive critics, it has sometimes become little more than an 'academic f-word' (Springer, 'Fuck Neoliberalism'). On the other hand, it is probably less ambiguous than other common terms about the political economy, such as 'capitalism', 'socialism', and especially 'communism', or indeed indispensable labels for understanding social life, such as 'culture' or 'society'. I mean by it essentially the renewed emphasis in social thought and policy on the alleged ability of the market to regulate itself and to produce wealth, with the implication that government interference in the market, while it may be necessary, should be minimal because it may cause more trouble than good. It can rightly be associated with global as well as state-level deregulation and the attendant rise of the super-rich. As we will see repeatedly in this book, some observers feel that neoliberalism has been replaced since the rise of illiberalism, while others think that it was its main impetus. The difference of opinion is often semantic. Most people agree that whatever capitalism looked like in the 1990s has found some resistance from those who foster a combination of capitalism with illiberal, ethno-racially defined rhetorics. The resistance transformed but did not necessarily dispense with the character of neoliberalism. In particular, illiberal forms of neoliberalism in Central Europe favour the accumulation of capital by the rich; it's just the rich at home rather than the 'globalist' rich outside (see Chapter 8).

16 Laclau, *On Populist Reason*; Mudde and Rovira Kaltwasser, *Populism in Europe and the Americas*; Müller, *What Is Populism?*; Stanley, 'The Thin Ideology of Populism'.

17 Applebaum, *Twilight of Democracy*. *Autoritarismus* is a favourite term in the German-language literature, which sometimes stresses the 'authoritarian personality' as the source of support for what I call illiberalism. Maćków, *Autoritarismus in Mittel- und Osteuropa*; Decker, Brähler, and Baier, *Flucht Ins Autoritäre*.

18 Mondon and Winter, *Reactionary Democracy*.
19 Kubicek and Erişen, 'Majoritarian Democracy in Turkey'.
20 Barša, Hesová, and Slačálek, 'How Does Post-Communism End?'.
21 Tansel, *States of Discipline*; Bruff, 'The Rise of Authoritarian Neoliberalism'.
22 Fabry, *The Political Economy of Hungary*.
23 V-Dem Institute, 'Autocratization Turns Viral'.
24 See Eco, 'Ur-Fascism'.

25 Wittgenstein, *Philosophical Investigations*.
26 Christiaens, Mark, and Faraldo, 'Entangled Transitions'. This is an introduction to a special journal issue where parallels between different relatively peripheral areas of Europe are taken up.
27 Todorova, 'The Balkans'; Todorova, *Imagining the Balkans*; Goldsworthy, *Inventing Ruritania*; Bakić-Hayden, 'Nesting Orientalisms'.
28 Kim, *Bitter Fruit*.
29 Holt, *The Problem of Race*, 100.
30 Moïsi, 'Racisme et violences policières'.
31 Holt, *The Problem of Race*, 17. For studies of the relationship between race and nation, see Meer, *Whiteness and Nationalism*.
32 Zakaria, 'The Rise of Illiberal Democracy'.
33 Hall and Ross, 'Affective Politics after 9/11'.
34 Or, as Mondon and Winter, in *Reactionary Democracy*, put it, 'reactionary democracy' is the new phase of liberal democracy.
35 Hall, 'Popular Democratic vs. Authoritarian Populism'; Fabry, *The Political Economy of Hungary*, 132.
36 Davidson, 'Crisis Neoliberalism and Regimes of Permanent Exception'.
37 Austria does, perhaps, too, but as it was not part of the Eastern Bloc during the Cold War, its international relations and their effect on illiberalism are quite different.
38 'Orbán Viktor Beszéde a XXVIII. Bálványosi Nyári Szabadegyetem és Diáktáborban'. All translations in this book are by the author, unless otherwise indicated.
39 Wallerstein, 'Semi-Peripheral Countries'; Wallerstein, *Capitalist Agriculture*; Wallerstein, *Mercantilism*; Wallerstein, *Centrist Liberalism Triumphant*.
40 Wallerstein, 'Semi-Peripheral Countries', 462–63.
41 Wallerstein, 463.
42 Parvulescu, 'European Racial Triangulation', 37.
43 See Krivonos, 'Racial Capitalism'.
44 Mondon and Winter, 'Whiteness, Populism and the Racialisation of the Working Class in the United Kingdom and the United States'. Mondon and Winter also warn against perceptions of an illiberal groundswell, which ignores the fact that in most places where illiberals win elections a large proportion of the potential voters stay home. Orbán's famed super-majority gained in 2018, for example, when his Fidesz Party won, in coalition with its traditional partner, the Christian Democrats, 49.27 per cent of the popular vote, was still slightly short of a majority of the votes

cast. And when the absence of 29.78 per cent of the voters is taken into account, his expressed support amounted to only 35 per cent. Hungary Office of Elections, '2018'.
45. 'Wybory parlamentarne'.
46. Pawłowska and Dudzik, 'Wybory 2019'.
47. Snyder, *The Road to Unfreedom*.
48. Applebaum, *Twilight of Democracy*, 14.
49. Ther, *Europe since 1989*.
50. Krastev and Holmes, *The Light That Failed*.
51. Moffitt, *Populism*.
52. 'DEMOS'.
53. Populism in Central and Eastern Europe, 'Populism in Central and Eastern Europe'.
54. See, for example, Varoufakis, 'Techno-Feudalism Is Taking Over'.
55. Barša, Hesová, and Slačálek, 'How Does Post-Communism End'.
56. Rupnik, 'The Crisis of Liberalism', 36.
57. Fabry, *The Political Economy of Hungary*, 112.
58. Kalmar, 'The Struggle for Whiteness'.
59. Wolff, *Inventing Eastern Europe*. See Chapter 2.
60. Deák, 'The Danger of Antisemitism in Hungary', 54.
61. 'The Worst Choice for "Greatest Slovak"'.
62. For example, in a 2016 speech he chastised the influence of 'Brussels' and said, 'We shall not import to Hungary crime, terrorism, homophobia and synagogue-burning anti-Semitism.' Orbán, 'Orban's Great Speech'.
63. Walker, 'Hungarian Leader Says Europe'.
64. For various reasons, Romania was not quite fully included.
65. 'Zeman o muslimech'.
66. Kulka, 'History and Historical Progress', 9.
67. BBC News, 'Polish Election: Andrzej Duda Says LGBT'.
68. Luxmoore, 'Church in Poland Continues Confrontation'.
69. Żuk, Pluciński, and Żuk, 'The Dialectic of Neoliberal Exploitation'; Stanley, 'Defenders of the Cross: Populist Politics and Religion in Post-Communist Poland'.
70. 'Hungary's Anti-LGBT Law Is a "shame" Says Ursula von Der Leyen'.
71. Fekete, 'Hungary', 43.
72. Pető, 'Feminist Stories from an Illiberal State', 47.
73. Fekete, 'Hungary', 47; Szikra, 'Interpreting Social Policy Change'.
74. Magyari, 'Az orrunk előtt rövidítik meg Magyarországot'.
75. In Slovak, there is the phrase *odrodilec*, which roughly means 'one distancing oneself from their birth'; more menacing is

the Nazi-German *entvolkt*, which can mean 'devoid of national (*völkisch*) identity', but also 'depopulated'.
76 Gabrizova, 'Hungary Misappropriated V4 Brand, Says Slovak Justice Minister'.
77 Janáková, 'Kvůli vyšetřování Babiše mi vyhrožují'.
78 Applebaum, 'Il Donald'.
79 Orbán, 'Orbán Viktor'.

Chapter 1
1 The Slovak Spectator, 'Slovakia Summoned Belgian Ambassador'.
2 BBC News, 'Belgium Custody Death'.
3 Kentish, 'Polish Angler Suing'.
4 Rzepnikowska, 'Racism and Xenophobia Experienced by Polish Migrants'.
5 Rzepnikowska, 72.
6 Rzepnikowska, 68.
7 Aleksandra Lewicki, forthcoming.
8 Böröcz and Sarkar, 'The Unbearable Whiteness'.
9 Rzepnikowska, 'Racism and Xenophobia Experienced by Polish Migrants', 72.
10 An excellent discussion of anti-Roma racism in Central Europe, today and from a historical perspective, is Shmidt and Jaworsky, *Historicizing Roma in Central Europe*. See also van Baar, 'Socio-Economic Mobility'; van Baar, 'The Production of Irregular Citizenship'.
11 Wachtel, 'Zadie Smith's Latest Book'. See Smith, *Intimations: Six Essays*, Postscript: 'Contempt as a virus'.
12 Often but not always, the subordinated group is located, or made to locate, in a separate space. In Żuk, Pluciński, and Żuk, 'The Dialectic of Neoliberal Exploitation', the authors propose that the LGBT-free zones in Poland, like the special economic zones for cheap labour, but also the ghettos and concentration camps for Jews during the Second World War, show how exploitation through othering is spatialized. On the other hand, Červinková, Buchowski, and Uherek, in 'Introduction: On Rethinking Ethnography', note that discrimination against Eastern Europeans is geographically flexible.
13 'I wish it to be distinctly understood that by "white" races I mean those usually comprised under the name of Caucasian, Shemitic, Japhetic; by "black," the Hamitic, African, etc.; by "yellow," the

Altaic, Mongolian, Finnic, and Tartar.' Gobineau, *The Moral and Intellectual Diversity of Races* Kindle Edition, Location 2798.

14. Gualtieri, 'Becoming "White"'.
15. Alshammari, 'Why Is There No MENA Category on the 2020 US Census?'
16. Green, 'Are Jews White?', emphasis original.
17. Ignatiev, *How the Irish Became White*.
18. Brodkin, *How Jews Became White Folks*. See also Duneier, *Ghetto*.
19. Scott, 'How French Canadians Became White'; Gollner, 'How Mennonites Became White'. Along somewhat different lines of reasoning, there is: Loveman and Muniz, 'How Puerto Rico Became White' and Erkulwater, 'How the Nation's Largest Minority Became White', and even Chapman and Brunsma, *Beer and Racism*.
20. Allen, *The Invention of the White Race*.
21. Handlin, 'Origins of the Southern Labor System'.
22. Ignatiev, *How the Irish Became White*, 2.
23. Heng, *The Invention of Race*, 27.
24. See, for example, Sweet, 'The Iberian Roots'.
25. Kalmar, 'Race by the Grace of God'. Gil Anidjar stresses the positive qualities of Christian blood in the concept of *limpieza de sangre*, as it represented 'the pure and glorious blood of Christ'. He feels that this means that the matter 'cannot be reduced to "the invention of racism"'. That is true, but 'white' also has aspects, including ones present in Christianity – as in the representations of the Virgin Mary – that are positive, so that white racism is not just a matter of excluding the Other. In fact, competition for 'whiteness' is a central theme of this book. Anidjar, *Blood*, 41.
26. Virdee, 'Racialized Capitalism', 3.
27. Hall, Mercer, and Gates, *The Fateful Triangle*, 118–19. Quoted in Virdee, 'Racialized Capitalism', 9.
28. Lowe, *Immigrant Acts*, 27. Quoted in Virdee, 'Racialized Capitalism', 9.
29. Gilman, 'The Jewish Nose', 372.
30. de Buffon, *Barr's Buffon*, 4:262. Quoted and discussed in HaCohen, 'The "Jewish Blackness" Thesis Revisited'.
31. Ignatiev, *How the Irish Became White*, 49.
32. Constable, *Ireland*.
33. Letter dated 30 July 1862. Marx and Engels, *Collected Works. Vol. 41*, 388.
34. Chamberlain, *Foundations of the Nineteenth Century* Chapter 5. 'The Entrance of the Jews Into the History of the West'.
35. Allen, Theodore. *The Invention of the White Race*.

Chapter 2

1. Gleig, *Germany, Bohemia, and Hungary*, 291–92, 294–99, 333.
2. Said, *Orientalism*. However, Said's focus was on the Arab world, which does not include Turkey, while for the East of Europe, the most important and nearest Muslim rival was the Turkish-dominated Ottoman Empire.
3. Wolff, *Inventing Eastern Europe*, 107.
4. Mozart to von Joacquin, 14 January 1787. Mozart, *Briefe*, 368–72.
5. Hobsbawm and Ranger, *The Invention of Tradition*, 1.
6. Eddie, *Freedom's Price*; Okey, *Eastern Europe 1740–1985*.
7. Boatcă, 'Coloniality of Labor in the Global Periphery'.
8. Wolff, *Inventing Eastern Europe*, 52, quoting Palmer and Coulton, 'The Transformation of Eastern Europe, 1648–1740', 174.
9. See also the discussion of Central Europe and the postcolonial condition, in Chapter 8.
10. Boatcă cites, among others, Dobrogeanu-Gherea, *Neoiobăgia*; Makkai, 'Neo-Serfdom'.
11. Kalmar, *Early Orientalism*.
12. Schneider, *Italy's 'Southern Question'*.
13. Todorova, 'The Balkans'; Todorova, *Imagining the Balkans*; Goldsworthy, *Inventing Ruritania*; Bakić-Hayden, 'Nesting Orientalisms'.
14. Žižek, *The Puppet and the Dwarf*, 3–4.
15. A more detailed sketch might perhaps put Ukraine in between Central Europe and Russia. Such changes would reflect better the imagined West-to-East dimension today. The figure is meant primarily to represent, in a simplified fashion, the situation before the Second World War, when Ukraine as an independent country was 'not on the map'.
16. Holt, *The Problem of Race*, 17.
17. Quora, 'What Are Eastern European Facial Features?'
18. Quora.
19. Wittfogel, *Oriental Despotism*. Wittfogel saw the Stalinist Soviet economy as an example of what Marx called the 'Asiatic mode of production'.
20. Franzos, *Vom Don Zur Donau*.
21. Casanova, *The Memoires*, 150 Chapter 19.
22. Wolff, *Inventing Eastern Europe*, 8.
23. Mozart's declaration that 'his Praguers' understood him is the stuff of legend. It, however, is entirely apocryphal. Freeman, *Mozart in Prague*, 258.
24. Wolff, *Inventing Eastern Europe*, 109–10.
25. Salner, 'Ethnic Polarisation'.

26. Stoker and Hindle, *Dracula*, 7.
27. Assouline, *Hergé*, 62.
28. Anderson, *Imagined Communities*, but see also Holt, 'The First New Nations'; Appelbaum, Macpherson, and Rosemblatt, *Race and Nation*, vii–xvi.
29. Rádl, *Válka Čechů s Němci*, 120, 135. Jaromí Loužil discusses Rádl as one of the Czech modernizers of the Hegelian idea of the nation, preceded by the first president of Czechoslovakia, Tomáš Garigue Masaryk, and followed by the philosopher Jan Patočka: Loužil, 'K zápasu o J. G. Herdera u nás'.
30. Dowler, 'Herder in Russia'.
31. Johnson, *Central Europe*, 130. See also Sundhaussen, *Der Einfluss der Herderschen Ideen*.
32. Johnson, *Central Europe*, 132.
33. Herder, *Ideen zur Philosophie der Geschichte*, book 16, chapter 2.
34. Lass, 'Romantic Documents and Political Monuments'.
35. Even then, the class distinction between German and other was, however, not complete. Polish landlords ruled over Ukrainian serfs, causing considerable resentment, as did Hungarian landlords ruling over Slovak and Romanian peasants. In fact, Hungarian supremacy paralleled the German in Slovakia and Transylvania. Czech landlords were often proud of their Czech origins in spite of their German linguistic and cultural habits.
36. Etkind, *Internal Colonization*.
37. Janion, *Niesamowita Słowiańszczyzna*; Narkowicz, 'Janion, Maria'.
38. In this period, there was an important ethnolinguistic differentiation between landlords and peasants as well, during and after serfdom. German or Germanized landlords owned much of the land in the Western parts of Central Europe, as they did in the Baltic region, while the peasants spoke mostly Slavic languages. In Hungarian-ruled Slovakia and Transylvania, Hungarian landlords governed largely Slovak and Romanian-speaking peasants, respectively. In Ukraine, Polish nobility owned land worked by Ukrainian peasants. The Jews, in the meantime, functioned as traders and artisans in the towns and cities, and in Poland and Hungary often as administrators of the landowners' estates. In the West of Central Europe they spoke mainly German, although often with a recognizably Jewish inflection, while in the East their home language was Yiddish. Roma spoke their own language, and interacted with the non-Roma in the local languages.
39. Wasser, *Himmlers Raumplanung Im Osten*.
40. Mbembe, *Necropolitics*.

41 Bernhard, 'Hitler's Africa in the East'.
42 Turda, *The History of East-Central European Eugenics*, 379. The work of Victoria Shmidt is important to understanding how racial segregation, especially of the Roma, has worked in Central Europe, especially from after the First World War until our own day, partly through employing the philosophy and practices of eugenics. A recent work, in collaboration with Nadya Jaworsky, is *Historicizing Roma in Central Europe*.
43 Churchill, 'The Sinews of Peace'.
44 Wolff, *Inventing Eastern Europe*, 4.
45 Ash, 'Does Central Europe Exist?'
46 Lewis Bernstein Namier, who discussed the First World War as a conflict between the German and the Slavic ethnicities of Europe, wrote one of the few works where 'eastern Europe' figured as a geopolitical fact, but he spelled 'eastern', in keeping with custom, with a small 'e'. (Namier, *Germany and Eastern Europe*.) On the other hand, on the two occasions that Bram Stoker mentions 'Eastern Europe' or 'Eastern European' in *Dracula* (1897), he does use capitals.
47 Boatcă, 'Coloniality of Labor in the Global Periphery'.
48 The family of the major nineteenth-century writer, Joseph Conrad, is an example of how Polish landowners, unlike their Ukrainian serfs, were well connected with the West. Coming from a patriotic Polish landowner family in what is now Western Ukraine, Conrad was sent to France to join the merchant marine, and served on British ships. Remaining deeply attached to Poland, he showed little affinity for things Ukrainian. A traditional view is that landlords had a pre-existing, essential Polish identity, and that peasants were Ukrainian. While the language background of the family was clearly important, however, it is at least equally true that being a landowner made one more Polish, while being a serf made one more Ukrainian (or Little Russian, as Ukrainians were often called).
49 More precisely, it permitted the eventual drawing of East–West frontiers. Czechoslovakia was divided between the Soviets and the West, but the West quickly gave up its part. In Austria, a division lasted longer, until the USSR gave up its control in exchange for Austria's neutrality. Germany was divided until 1989.
50 Kalmar, 'The East Is Just Like the West'.
51 Yendell, 'Jammer-Ossis'.

Chapter 3
1 Ash, 'Does Central Europe Exist?'

2. Moskalewicz and Przybylski, 'Making Sense of Central Europe'.
3. Vermeiren, *The First World War*.
4. For a contemporary Czech view, see 'Střední Evropa a učitelstvo'.
5. Moeller van den Bruck, 'Schicksal Ist Stärker Als Staatskunst', 165.
6. Peschel, *Friedrich Naumanns und Max Webers 'Mitteleuropa'*.
7. Naumann, *Mitteleuropa*.
8. Naumann, *Central Europe*. Quoted by Roe, 'Central Europe'.
9. Chamberlain, *Foundations of the Nineteenth Century*, 505–06.
10. Schwaner, 'Das Alte Und Das Neue Deutschland', 139. Quoted by Vermeiren, *The First World War*, 146.
11. Among the works on Annie Besant are Chandra, *Annie Besant*; Dinnage, *Annie Besant*.
12. Steiner, *Mitteleuropa zwischen Ost und West*.
13. Dabrowski and Troebst, 'Uses and Abuses of the Past', 477.
14. Palacký, *Gedenkblätter*, 149–55. Translation: Palacký, 'Palacky's Famous Letter'.
15. This was one of the many terms used for the majority ethnic group of what is now commonly called Transcarpathian Ukraine but was then part of Austria-Hungary.
16. *The New York Times*, 'Free Vote Demanded for Subject Peoples'. On plans to involve the Zionist movement in the construction of a new Central Europe, see Halasi, 'The Ghost of Judeopolonia'.
17. Hayashi, 'Masaryk's "Zone of Small Nations"', 5, 7, 10.
18. Ištok, Kozárová, and Polačková, 'The Intermarium'.
19. It also did not include Poland.
20. This is my personal recollection.
21. Kundera, 'The Tragedy of Central Europe'.
22. Krastev and Holmes, *The Light That Failed*; Kundera, 'The Tragedy of Central Europe'.
23. Kundera, 'The Tragedy of Central Europe', 33.
24. Kundera, 34.
25. Kundera, 'The Tragedy of Central Europe'.
26. Kundera, 33.
27. Kundera, 34.
28. Kundera, 33.
29. Kundera, 33.
30. On identitarian movements, see, for example, Zúquete, *The Identitarians*.
31. Kundera, 'The Tragedy of Central Europe', 33.
32. Kundera, 37.
33. Kundera, 37.
34. Kundera, 38.

NOTES

35 Kundera, who pays very little attention to Slovaks as a Central European nation, fails to note that the Slovak national anthem ends with the words, 'Slovaks shall revive', or that the national anthem of Ukraine, which as largely Eastern Orthodox is presumably a truly Eastern European country, is known as 'Ukraine has not yet perished'.
36 Kundera, 'The Tragedy of Central Europe', 37.
37 Ash, 'Does Central Europe Exist?', 1.
38 Janik and Toulmin, *Wittgenstein's Vienna*.
39 Schorske, *Fin-de-Siècle Vienna*. For an appreciation of the impact of this book, see Ross, 'The Schorske Century'.
40 Steven Beller mentions the exhibitions Vienna 1900: Vienna, Scotland, and the European Avant-Guarde, Le arti a Vienna, Traum und Wirklichkeit: Wien 1870–1930, Vienne 1880–1938: L'apocalypse joyeuse, and Vienna 1900: Art, Architecture, and Design. Beller, 'Introduction', 24 n.8.
41 Jacques Rupnik's use of the phrase 'Habsburg factor' takes into account both the fashion for Habsburg nostalgia and the objective traces in Central Europe of the Austro-Hungarian state, which was not 'liberal, but neither was it an autocracy like Czarist Russia. It was a *Rechtsstaat*, that is, a state run by the rule of law.' Rupnik, 'Eastern Europe a Decade Later', 59.
42 van Zijl, 'De Nikolaus Harnoncourt-Week'.
43 Ash, 'Does Central Europe Exist?'
44 Ash.
45 Habermas, 'What Does Socialism Mean Today?', 5, 7.
46 Krastev and Holmes, *The Light That Failed*, 24.
47 I am planning to publish, separately, the result of field work in Central Europe where we asked older respondents, among other things, about their memories of communism and its demise.
48 Mark et al., *1989: A Global History of Eastern Europe*, 1–2.
49 Mark et al., *1989: A Global History of Eastern Europe*. See also Ther, *Europe since 1989*, 21.
50 Biuro prasowe rzadu, *Porozumienia sierpniowe*.
51 Kolakowski, 'Two Prescriptions for Socialism'.
52 'Wałęsa przed laty'.
53 Havel, *Václav Havel: Living in Truth*, 149.
54 Judt, 'The Rediscovery of Central Europe', 39.
55 Konrád, *Antipolitics*, 10.
56 Dahlburg, 'Gorbachev'.
57 Kovács, 'Baloldali Rémálmok Aggasztják a Magyarokat'.
58 Mark et al., *1989: A Global History of Eastern Europe*, 59–60.

59 Fabry, *The Political Economy of Hungary*, 3. Chapter 3 of Fabry's book is particularly revealing of these facts.
60 Mark et al., *1989: A Global History of Eastern Europe*, 54.
61 Mark et al., 59–61.
62 Harms, 'Living *Mitteleuropa* in the 1980s', 681, 682.
63 Buchowski, 'Social Thought & Commentary', 465. Buchowski discusses the East–West distinction here in terms of a broader geopolitical discourse in the West about the 'Orient' as discussed in Said, *Orientalism*. See also Červinková, Buchowski, and Uherek, 'Introduction: On Rethinking Ethnography'. The Polish literary scholar Maria Janion also referred as Orientalist to the Polish desire to distance the nation from other Slavs and Slavdom as a historical identity. Janion, *Niesamowita Słowiańszczyzna*; Narkowicz, 'Janion, Maria'.
64 I am, in much of this book, myself demonstrating the difference between Central and the rest of Eastern Europe. That is one of the major goals, for example, of Chapters 2 and 4. I am aware that this may make me, too, seem to reproduce the same attempt to move the border of 'Eastern Europe' eastward, so that it does not include Central Europe. But that is a false equation. It is important when critiquing the Western concept of Eastern Europe to point out that differences do exist within that area. Orientalism, which Buchowski rightly considers to be the larger envelope in which what I call Eastern Europeanism functions, cannot be fought by accepting its flattening of all difference in the 'Orient'; quite the contrary. Similarly, Eastern Europeanism can only be strengthened, not resisted, by denying differences within 'Eastern Europe'. The rescuing of difference can, however, have different agendas. The liberal 'dissidents' meant to demonstrate their whiteness rather than challenge the concept of race, as I am hoping to do in this book. Moreover, they were blind to the fact that the very neoliberal, globalist practices whose adoption they thought would make them more Western, were in fact the main factor recreating the contrast that separated them from the West. My goal in discussing the differences between Central and Eastern Europe is to show how negating those differences has served the interests of Western-based global neoliberalism at the time of the capitalist restoration and since, and how that has contributed to the misguided illiberal revolt.
65 Translated from the Czech version pdf available at: 'The Visegrad Group'.
66 'The Visegrad Group'.
67 Kamm, 'Havel Calls Gypsies "Litmus Test"'.

68. Barša, Hesová, and Slačálek, 'How Does Post-Communism End?'.
69. Translated from the Czech version pdf available at: 'The Visegrad Group'.
70. Orbán, 'Full Text of Viktor Orbán's Speech'.
71. Orbán, 'Orbán Viktor beszéde a XXVIII'.
72. Kövér, 'Kövér Lászlónak'.
73. Magyar Nemzet, 'Gergely Gulyás: A nemzet'.
74. Sarkadi, '100 felvidéki magyart hívott'.
75. Matovič, 'Igor Matovič trianoni beszéde'.
76. Matovič.
77. Bill and Stanley, 'Whose Poland Is It to Be?', 9.
78. 'Jobbik's Wage Union Initiative'.
79. Szikra, 'Interpreting Social Policy Change'.
80. Orbán, 'Full Text of Viktor Orbán's Speech'.
81. Orbán, 'Orbán Viktor beszéde a XXVIII'. Orbán used the same formula in his speech on the anniversary of the Czechoslovak Velvet Revolution, in November, 2019: Orbán, 'Közép-Európa lesz Európa jövője'.

Chapter 4

1. Media Education Centre, 'Aphorisms'.
2. Ther, *Europe since 1989*, 163.
3. Pew Research Center, 'Eastern Europeans Are More Likely'.
4. Fukuyama, *The End of History and the Last Man*; Menand, 'Francis Fukuyama Postpones the End of History'.
5. One of the most cogent accounts of how this happened is Fabry, *The Political Economy of Hungary*.
6. Applebaum, *Twilight of Democracy*; Krastev and Holmes, *The Light That Failed*.
7. Herman and Chomsky, *Manufacturing Consent*, 28.
8. 'Democracy Index 2020'.
9. 'Democracy Index 2020'.
10. 'Countries and Territories'.
11. V-Dem Institute, 'Autocratization Turns Viral', Table 4.
12. Reporters Without Borders, '2021 World Press Freedom Index'.
13. Bayer, 'Hungarian Spyware Scandal'.
14. Kitti, 'Tíz Év Alatt 786 Százalékkal Nőtt'.
15. Új, '444.Hu Blog', 17 February 2021.
16. Murphy, 'Austria's Kurz Steps Down Over Corruption Probe to Save Coalition'.
17. 'Corruption Perceptions Index 2020'.
18. Fabry, *The Political Economy of Hungary*, 131.

19. European Commission, 'The 2020 EU Justice Scoreboard'. Figure 44, p 41.
20. The News, 'Slovakia's Ex-Police Chief'.
21. Yavlinsky, *The Putin System*, 66.
22. Yavlinsky, 68.
23. Wilczek, '"Armored Marian"'.
24. Pethő and Szabó, 'Feltárul Simicska Bukásának Titkos Története'.
25. 'Global Peace Index 2020'.
26. See the data and discussion published by the European Commission at European Commission, 'Together Against Trafficking'.
27. A report published by Amnesty International suggests that there are between one and three million sex workers in Russia. Maslova, 'Irina Maslova, Saint Petersburg'.
28. Numbers obtained via UNAIDS, 'Key Populations Atlas'.
29. One must be cautious, however, in speaking of Roma sex workers, lest one feed into popular prejudice. In one highly publicized case, a Canadian anthropologist who studied the prevalence of sex work among Slovak Roma was jailed for sexually exploiting the girls and women he was working with. The Slovak Spectator, 'A Canadian Professor Accused'. Scheffel and Mušinka, '"Third-class" Slovak Roma and Inclusion'.
30. Niček, 'Nespadám už do kategorie ‚z Východu"'.
31. See the Introduction.
32. United Nations Development Programme, 'Human Development Report 2020'.
33. United Nations Development Programme, 'Human Development Index (HDI)'.
34. Helliwell et al., 'World Happiness Report 2020'.
35. Helliwell et al.
36. Alexievich, *Secondhand Time*, 20.
37. European Automobile Manufacturers Association, 'Vehicles in Use: Europe'.
38. Country GDP data are from 2019 and regional/city data are from 2018.
39. For some of the detail, the reader is advised to consult Ther, *Europe since 1989*. In chapter 6, 'Capital Cities Compared' he discusses the evolution of Central Europe's major cities, along with Berlin and Kiev.
40. Piketty, '2018, the Year of Europe'. See also Bershidsky, 'Piketty Thinks the EU Is Bad'.
41. Bershidsky, 'Poland's Economic Experiment'.
42. Orbán, 'Reply to Martin Schulz'.

43 Okamura, 'Češi na členství v EU prodělali'.
44 Trading Economics, 'Capital Flows'.
45 Břešťan, 'Daniel Křetínský'.
46 Eurostat, 'Gini Coefficient'.
47 Böröcz and Sarkar, 'The Unbearable Whiteness'.
48 The purchasing-parity numbers for EU states and the UK and the USA are taken directly from Eurostat, while the other numbers come from the respective national offices for statistics. Some numbers had to be inferred from the official numbers in order to be compared, such as non-PPP wages for Western European and US American regions, and for Russia, Moldova, and Ukraine. The PPP numbers for all regions were directly inferred on the basis of the ratio between their respective national Eurostat PPP versus non-PPP numbers, except for Russia, Moldova, and Ukraine, where inference was based on World Bank numbers and Eurostat numbers. Eurostat, 'Data Browser – Annual Net Earnings'; World Bank, 'GDP per Capita, PPP (Current International $)'; Český statistický úřad, 'Průměrné hrubé měsíční mzdy'; Główny Urząd Statystyczny, 'Bank Danych Lokalnych'; Štatistický úrad Slovenskej republiky, 'Mzdy podľa ekonomickej činnosti'; Központi Statisztikai Hivatal, 'Average Gross Earnings'; U.S. Bureau of Labor Statistics, 'Quarterly Census of Employment and Wages'; Office for National Statistics, 'Median Full-Time Gross Weekly Earnings'; Institut national de la statistique et des études économiques, 'Chiffres détaillés – Salaires et revenus d'activité'; Istituto nazionale di statistica, 'Reddito Netto: Regioni e Tipo Di Comune'; Federal′naia sluzhba gosudarstvennoi statistiki, 'Srednemesiachnaia Nominal′naia Nachislennaia Zarabotnaia Plata'; Biroul Național de Statistică, 'Monthly Gross and Net Average Earnings'; Derzhavna sluzhba statistiki Ukraïni, 'Average Monthly Wages'.
49 Emmenez-moi / Au pays des merveilles / Il la misère / Serait moins pénible au soleil.
50 Główny Urząd Statystyczny, 'Demographic Situation in Poland', 97, Table 10.
51 Ministerstvo zahraničních věcí České republiky, 'Počet českých krajanů v zahraničí'.
52 Kremský, 'Talenty pre Slovensko'.
53 *Budapest Business Journal*, 'Hungarians Working Abroad'.
54 Spike, 'More than 600,000 Hungarians'.
55 Dobré ráno | Denný podcast denníka SME, 'Exodus zdravotníkov spôsobí kolaps'.
56 Fragile States Index, 'Global Data (2020)'.

[57] Fedyuk and Kindler, *Ukrainian Migration to the European Union*; Pędziwiatr, 'Imigranci w Polsce'; Walker, '"A Whole Generation Has Gone"'.
[58] Český statistický úřad, 'Bez cizinců by zaměstnanost'; Le Courrier d'Europe centrale, 'La part des travailleurs étrangers'.
[59] Mathia, 'Ako zas spraviť zdravotníctvo atraktívne'.
[60] McAuliffe, Khadria, and Bauloz, 'World Migration Report 2020'.
[61] Krastev and Holmes, *The Light That Failed*, 37–38.
[62] Krastev and Holmes, 38.
[63] Krastev and Holmes, 37.
[64] As in the West, demographic issues in Central Europe include an aging population.

Chapter 5

[1] Aster et al., *Midsommar*.
[2] Imre, 'Race and Diversity Illiberal Style'. I thank Anikó Imre for her stimulating comments and suggestions, although she is not responsible for the contents of this chapter. The example of *Midsommar* was brought to my attention by her.
[3] Imre.
[4] The term had been used in a different context, referring to the feigned ignorance of racism in Holland, by Wekker, *White Innocence*.
[5] Shekhovtsov, *Russia and the Western Far Right*.
[6] See also Drulák, 'The West, the Centre and the East'.
[7] Morawski and Morawski, *Polonia mon amour*. Unfortunately, the book at the time of my writing exists only in Italian.
[8] Tacconi, 'Kaczynski's Poland vs Europe'.
[9] BBC News, 'Polish Election: Andrzej Duda Says LGBT'.
[10] Chadwick, 'Archbishop Warns of "Rainbow Plague"'.
[11] Tilles, 'LGBT "Ideology Weakens the West'.
[12] de la Beaume, 'Orbán, Le Pen, Salvini Join Forces'.
[13] Hajdu, Klingová, and Sawiris, 'Vaccination Trends'.
[14] Orbán, 'Full Text of Viktor Orbán's Speech'.
[15] Sarkadi, 'Magyarország megint megakadályozta'.
[16] Moreh, 'The Asianization of National Fantasies in Hungary'.
[17] Dobrev et al., 'Umgang mit Viktor Orbán'.
[18] Charron, Lapuente, and Bauhr, 'Sub-National Quality of Government'.
[19] Orbán, 'Orbán Viktor beszéde Nagy Imre'.
[20] iDNES.cz, 'Perly Miloše Jakeše'.
[21] Fekete, 'Hungary', 49, 43.
[22] Applebaum, *Twilight of Democracy*, 75.

23. Orbán, 'Orbán Viktor sajtónyilatkozata Mateusz Morawieckivel'.
24. Orbán.
25. Kalmar, 'Islamophobia and Anti-Antisemitism'.
26. Shekhovtsov, *Russia and the Western Far Right*.
27. On Ilyin's influence on Putin, see Snyder, *The Road to Unfreedom*. On Dugin's influence, see Shekhovtsov, 'Putin's Brain?'.
28. The reference is to the geopolitical stance of Finland during the Cold War, the price the country paid to avoid direct Soviet domination or annexation to the USSR. Dugin, *Osnovy geopolitiki*, 369.
29. Shekhovtsov, *Russia and the Western Far Right*.
30. Makk, *A turulmadártól a kettőskeresztig*; Switzer, 'Nationalism and the Myth of Hungarian Origin'.
31. Pieiller, 'Hungary Looks to the Past for Its Future'; Inotal, 'Dark Family Secrets'.
32. Zarycki, *Ideologies of Eastness*, 94.
33. Orbán, 'Orbán Viktor beszéde a XXVIII', emphasis added.
34. Nagy, 'Orbán: Közép-Európa működik'.
35. Dzenovska, 'Historical Agency', 410.
36. Rieboldt, 'Entvolkt!' The comment appeared on the interactive website run by the Austrian journalist Christian Ortner, *Ornter Online*, which calls itself the 'Central Organ of Neoliberalism'.
37. Imre, 'Race and Diversity Illiberal Style'.
38. Craig et al., *Tucker and Dale vs Evil*.

Chapter 6

1. Gross, 'Eastern Europe's Crisis of Shame'.
2. In Polish, essays detailing the fate of Jews in Poland during the Holocaust were explored among other places in Engelking, Grabowski, and Stowarzyszenie Centrum Badań nad Zagładą Żydów, *Dalej Jest Noc*. The editors were unsuccessfully taken to court for alleged inaccuracies by Poles who felt that the historians were engaging in libel.
3. Hackmann, 'Defending the "Good Name" of the Polish Nation'.
4. Ash, 'As at Auschwitz'.
5. One of my father's sisters and one of his brothers had been deported by Slovaks before the occupation, and died in Auschwitz, as did another sister, who was deported from the Protectorate of Bohemia and Moravia.
6. Procházka, *The Second Republic*.
7. Kubátová, 'Now or Never'.
8. Inotal, 'Dark Family Secrets'.

9. Rapoport, *Stalin's War against the Jews*.
10. Stola, *Kampania antysyjonistyczna*.
11. i24NEWS, 'Slovakia Apologizes For Anti-Jewish'.
12. Frommer, 'The Holocaust in Bohemia and Moravia'.
13. Greene, *Landscapes of Loss*.
14. Abella and Troper, *None Is Too Many*.
15. Etkind, *Warped Mourning*, 182–83.
16. Žižek, *Looking Awry*, 23, emphasis original.
17. Kalmar, 'The East Is Just Like the West'.
18. Chazan, 'German Police Criticised'.
19. Shoshan, *The Management of Hate*.
20. The proceedings of the German Parliament: Deutscher Bundestag, Plenarprotokoll, 5110.
21. Schenk, *Auf Dem Rechten Auge Blind* discusses how ex-Nazis were welcomed into the West German criminal investigative bureau (*Bundeskriminalamt*).
22. CBS, 'Canada's Dark Secret'.
23. Gyarfašová, 'Odkrývanie: Bratislavský nacista'.
24. Brown, '"Our National Feeling Is a Broken One"'.
25. Özyürek, 'Subcontracting Guilt'.
26. Renton and Gidley, *Antisemitism and Islamophobia in Europe: A Shared Story?*; Kalmar, 'Anti-Semitism and Islamophobia'; Kalmar and Penslar, 'Orientalism and the Jews: An Introduction'; Kalmar and Ramadan, 'Antisemitism and Islamophobia'; Zia-Ebrahimi, *Antisémitisme et islamophobie*.
27. Said, *Orientalism*, 27–28, 286.
28. Kalmar, *Early Orientalism*, chapter 3.
29. Pew Research Center, 'Eastern and Western Europeans Differ'.
30. For a discussion of some of the relevant research data, see also Kalmar 2018. At the time of writing, the 2014 data from the Anti-Defamation League is the latest.
31. Pew Research Center, 'Eastern and Western Europeans Differ'.
32. Tarant, *Czech Antisemitic Movements*.
33. See the Special Issue of the journal *Patterns of Prejudice* 52(2), 2018, 'Islamophobia in the East of the European Union', guest-edited by Ivan Kalmar.
34. For a discussion of this issue and a survey of the literature, see Górak-Sosnowska, 'Islamophobia without Muslims?' and my essay, Kalmar, 'Islamophobia Without Muslims'.
35. Hackett et al., 'Europe's Growing Muslim Population'.
36. Kaya and Kayaoglu, 'Individual Determinants of Anti-Muslim'.

37. Tuček, 'Vztah české veřejnosti', 1. For Hungary, see Glied and Pap, 'The "Christian Fortress of Hungary"', 146.
38. Centrum Badania Opinii Społecznej, 'Stosunek do innych narodów'.
39. Pravda.sk, 'Prieskum: Slováci odmietajú prijať utečencov'.
40. See, for example, Glied and Pap, 'The Hungarian Border Barrier and Islam'.
41. Pędziwiatr, 'Islamophobia in Poland'. See also Pędziwiatr, 'The Catholic Church in Poland on Muslims and Islam'.
42. Lewicki, 'The Christian Politics of Identity'; Lewicki and Shooman, 'Building a New Nation'.
43. BBC News, 'Polish Election: Andrzej Duda Says LGBT'.
44. Easton, 'LGBT Rights'.
45. Wroński, 'Jak MSZ ratuje Europę'.
46. Magyari, 'Orbán a kommunista-ellenes röpiratokból'.
47. Pew Research Center, 'Eastern and Western Europeans Differ'.
48. Pew Research Center.
49. Dzenovska, 'Historical Agency', 398.

Chapter 7

1. Kundera, 'The Tragedy of Central Europe'.
2. Kundera, 'The Tragedy of Central Europe'.
3. Solzhenitsyn, 'A World Split Apart'.
4. Kéri, *Orbán Viktor*.
5. Orbán, 'Orbán Viktor beszéde a XXVIII'.
6. Krastev and Holmes, *The Light That Failed*.
7. Krastev and Holmes, 12.
8. Krastev and Holmes, 5.
9. Krastev and Holmes, 15.
10. Krastev and Holmes, 26.
11. Doran, 'René Girard's Concept of Conversion'.
12. Krastev and Holmes, *The Light That Failed*, 11.
13. Krastev and Holmes, 12.
14. Girard, *Violence and the Sacred*, 156–57.
15. Krastev and Holmes, *The Light That Failed*, 9.
16. Krastev and Holmes, 10.
17. Krastev and Holmes, 25.
18. Pachoński and Wilson, *Poland's Caribbean Tragedy*, 213.
19. Krastev and Holmes, *The Light That Failed*, 24. See also Krastev and Holmes' discussion of 'return' on pages 32 and 47.
20. Krastev and Holmes, 11, emphasis added.
21. Tariq Modood rejects studies of British Muslims that focus only on how they are 'othered' by the white Christian majority, without

recognizing the positive content of the Islamic heritage as it appears to British Muslims themselves: Modood, *Essays on Secularism and Multiculturalism*, chapter 4.
22. Bhabha, 'Of Mimicry and Man'.
23. Bhabha, 126.
24. Bhabha, 126.
25. Bhabha, 132.
26. Grant, 'Observations on the State of Society'.
27. East India Company, 'Sessional Papers 1812–13', chapter 4, p 104.
28. Grant, 'Observations on the State of Society', 100, emphasis added.
29. Bhabha, 'Of Mimicry and Man', 132.
30. Hall, Mercer, and Gates, *The Fateful Triangle*, 118–19. Quoted in Virdee, 'Racialized Capitalism', 9.
31. See, for example, Mbembe, *On the Postcolony*; Mondon and Winter, *Reactionary Democracy*.
32. See also: Hasmath and Kay-Reid, 'What Salience Does White Privilege'.
33. Barša, 'Nulový stupeň dekolonizace', 4.
34. Bhabha, 'Of Mimicry and Man', 126.

Chapter 8
1. Taylor, 'Orbán Accuses EU of Colonialism'.
2. BBC News, 'Hungarian PM Viktor Orban Denounces'.
3. Chernetsky et al., 'Forum', 829.
4. Chernetsky et al., 'Forum'.
5. Böröcz, 'Introduction', 14–15.
6. Böröcz, 18.
7. Mark et al., *1989: A Global History of Eastern Europe*, 278.
8. Ther, *Europe since 1989*, 20.
9. Pithart, '"Tak co, Václave, rozhodni se konečně!"'.
10. Hall, 'Thatcherism: A New Stage'.
11. Dale and Hardy, 'Conclusion: The "Crash"', 152; Fabry, *The Political Economy of Hungary*, 106.
12. Fabry, *The Political Economy of Hungary*, 113.
13. Orbán, 'Orbán Viktor beszéde a XXVIII'.
14. Fabry, *The Political Economy of Hungary*, 127.
15. Szelényi, 'Weber's Theory of Domination'.
16. Gagyi, '"Coloniality of Power" in East Central Europe'.
17. Gagyi, 354.
18. I have personally been told by an executive of a major multinational oil company, of the company's use of Czech bribe brokers in the 1990s, who made it difficult to trace the bribe to the company.

19. There have been non-economic factors at play as well, as shown by Varga, 'No Power Grab in Hungary'.
20. Toplišek, 'The Political Economy of Populist Rule', 396.
21. Král, 'Matematik Levínský: Pokud se nezavřou továrny'.
22. Prokop, 'Proč podle nesmíme zapomínat na pracoviště?'
23. Mathiesen and Oroschakoff, 'Leaving No One Behind'.
24. Montalbano, 'Geopolitical Economy and Competing Capitalist Blocs'.
25. Baldwin and Lopez-Gonzalez, 'Supply-chain Trade'.
26. Wang and Sun, 'From Globalization to Regionalization'.
27. Wallerstein, 'Semi-Peripheral Countries'.
28. Varoufakis, *And the Weak Suffer*.
29. Lund et al., 'Globalization in Transition'.
30. Dolan, Wang, and Peterson-Withorn, 'Forbes Billionaires 2021'.
31. Dénes, 'A Sztrájk'.
32. Magyar Nemzet, 'Milyen is valójában'.
33. Geva, 'Orbán's Ordonationalism'.
34. Szikra, 'Interpreting Social Policy Change'.
35. Sowa, 'Forget Postcolonialism'.
36. finweb, 'Fico plynárom: Nie sme kolónia'.
37. Santora, 'In Poland, Nationalism'.
38. Nádoba, '"Kolonie Bruselu"?'
39. Morvai, 'Hungary Is Not a Colony'.
40. Švihlíková, *Jak jsme se stali kolonií*, 31.
41. Švihlíková, 39.
42. Piketty, *Capital in the Twenty-First Century*; Piketty, *Capital and Ideology*.
43. Švihlíková, *Jak jsme se stali kolonií*, 214.
44. Švihlíková, 215.
45. Farage, 'Greece Is Now No More'.
46. Mondon and Winter, *Reactionary Democracy*, 35.
47. Fox and Mogilnicka, 'Pathological Integration'. Narkowicz, 'White Enough, Not White Enough'.
48. Sarnyai, 'Schmidt: Western Countries Want to "Civilize" Central Europe'.
49. Népszava, 'Orbán Viktor tananyag lett!'
50. Wintour, 'Growing Awareness of Colonial Past'.
51. Přeučil, 'Rasismus je svinstvo'.
52. Kernová, 'Kotlebovci v predvolebnom spote klamú'.
53. Švec, 'Švédsky predseda vlády'.
54. See the Conclusion, where I discuss Bolagun and Pędziwiatr, '"Stop Calling Me Murzyn"'.

55 Sosnowski, 'W pustyni, w puszczy'. Emphasis original.
56 Lisiewicz, 'Lisiewicz: Niech rosyjscy i niemieccy'. Murzyny is a controversial term in Poland, though like 'Negroes' it was once uncontroversially accepted to refer to Black people. See Bolagun and Pędziwiatr, ' "Stop Calling Me Murzyn" '.
57 Sommaruga, 'Sklaverei und Kolonialismus. Hat der Bundesrat nichts gelernt?'
58 Mondon and Winter, *Reactionary Democracy*.
59 For examples of criticism in the Swiss and Belgian parliaments, respectively, of claims that the country has no responsibility for colonialism, see Sommaruga, 'Sklaverei und Kolonialismus. Hat der Bundesrat nichts gelernt?' and Meuleman, Bex, and Annouri, 'Voorstel van resolutie over het opnemen van de kolonisatie en het dekolonisatieproces in de eindtermen van het Vlaamse basis- en secundair onderwijs'. See also a discussion of this issue in Dzenovska, 'Historical Agency', 407.
60 Böröcz, 'Introduction', 29–30.
61 Zarycki, *Ideologies of Eastness*, 93.
62 Slačálek, 'The Postcolonial Hypothesis', 27.
63 Sayyid, 'Islamophobia and the Europeanness of the Other Europe'.
64 Progressive academics generally examine the parallels between the postsocialist and the postcolonial experience as a critique of racial capitalism, and suggest solidarity between Eastern Europe and the Global South. More conservative academics, like illiberal leaders, focus more on 'coloniality' as a condition of helpless subordination, and as a solution suggest simply a more muscled self-assertion by Central and/or Eastern Europeans. They are fond of designating 'Brussels' or 'Washington' as the new colonial powers, having replaced 'Moscow'. A sophisticated example is the work of the Polish-American Slavic studies specialist, Ewa Thompson. Thompson believes that Poland suffers from a kind of post-colonial syndrome, never being able to fully exit from a slavish attitude to others that demands a master. Having freed itself of the Soviet suzerain, the Polish elite (especially the liberals) needed a substitute and so found itself a new master: the West. (On this reading, the West is not a real colonial exploiter, but rather Polish liberals make it so. See Thompson, 'A Jednak Kolonializm'.)
65 Barša, 'Nulový stupeň dekolonizace', 3–4.
66 Barša, 4.
67 Barša, 4.
68 Barša, 4.
69 Snochowska-Gonzalez, 'Post-Colonial Poland', 716.

70. See Kalmár, *The Trotskys, Freuds and Woody Allens*, 168.
71. Schulze, *Engineering and Economic Growth*, 295.
72. Ortová, *Julius Payer: Z Čech až k severnímu pólu*.
73. Hlavačka and Munzar, *S Bohem za císaře a vlasť!*
74. Lemmen, 'The "Return to Europe"', 614.
75. Borkowska-Arciuch, 'Polskie Doświadczenie Kolonialne'.
76. Santora and Berendt, 'For Poland, Nobel Prize'.
77. Zarycki, *Ideologies of Eastness*, chapter 6.
78. Shmidt, 'Public Health'.
79. Popa, "Ethnicity as a Category of Imperial Racialization."
80. Bata Shoe Company, 'Bata Shoe Company Papers'.
81. Mark et al., *1989: A Global History of Eastern Europe*, 287.
82. This is not to say that there are not dedicated and effective organizations in the area, for example for helping refugees. For Hungary, see Bernát, 'Solidarity Powered via Social Media'. For Poland, Szałańska, 'Uneasy Mission of NGOs'. For the Czech Republic, iDobrovolník, 'National Database of Volunteers for Refugees'.

Chapter 9

1. The quote is from a comment on the Facebook page of iDnes, a leading Czech paper: iDnes.cz, 'Fotbalový svět zase řeší'.
2. Lisiewicz, 'Lisiewicz: Niech rosyjscy i niemieccy'.
3. Jackson, 'Kolar Left with Horrific Eye'.
4. Štechrová and Urbanová, 'Od Kúdely to byla obrovská taktická chyba'.
5. Štechrová and Urbanová.
6. Hron, 'KOMENTÁŘ: Slávisté na Arsenalu nepoklekli'.
7. Mynář, 'Dopis disciplinární komisi UEFA'.
8. Prague Morning, 'President Zeman Calls "Black Lives Matter"'.
9. Prague Morning, 'Czech Football Players Refused to Kneel'.
10. Fraser, 'Lacazette in Powerful Anti-Racism'.
11. Polskie Radio 24, 'Jan Tomaszewski o Klękaniu Przed Meczem'.
12. Novák, 'Visegrádi gimnasztika'.
13. Deutsche Welle, 'Borussia Dortmund Announce Management'.
14. Borbély, 'Ezért távozik Hrutka János a Spíler Tv-től'. Spíler TV, Hrutka's employer, denied that it fired him.
15. Magyar Nemzet, 'Dárdai magyar segítője nem ért'.
16. Česká televize, 'Další trest za rasismus fanoušků'.
17. Sportnet, 'Slovan spoznal trest'.
18. TVP Sport, 'Liga Narodów: rasizm i race'.
19. Makszimov, 'Romanian Football Captain Complains'.
20. Moroşanu and Fox, '"No Smoke without Fire"'.

21. Mičúch, 'Obrovská smola ho pripravila'.
22. Stevens, 'Arsenal Kick Slavia Prague'.
23. Finnis, 'The Full (and Farcical) List'.
24. Dickson, 'UK's Tech Clampdown'.
25. Liew, 'English Football Is Consumed by Racism'.
26. Sanfourche and Goury-Laffont, 'PSG-OM: Neymar, Alvaro, Sakai'.
27. Lowe, 'Valencia Walk off against Cádiz'.
28. LaLiga, 'Nota informativa'.
29. Castañeda, 'España se posiciona'.
30. Anderson, *Imagined Communities*.
31. Walker, 'Slavia Chief Alleges Rangers'.
32. van Baar, 'Socio-Economic Mobility'; Hegburg, 'Aftermath'.
33. John Abraham Godson in Poland, Dominik Feri in the Czech Republic, and Olivio Kocsis-Cake in Hungary.
34. Schutz, 'Kollárov sabatical je sabotážou'.
35. Krumpal, 'Determinants of Social Desirability Bias'.
36. BBC Sport, 'Wales Players Rail against Racism'. The Hungarian national team that faced the kneeling Irish also chose to point to their Respect badge.

Conclusion

1. Rényi, *Győzelmi kényszer*, quote from the book cover jacket.
2. Luptáková and Senková, 'Tomáš Halík: Kdo se bojí uprchlíků'.
3. Senna, 'White Progressives in Pursuit'.
4. Bolagun and Pędziwiatr, '"Stop Calling Me Murzyn"'.
5. Ferfecki, '"Murzyn" oficjalnie odradzany'.
6. Eibl-Eibesfeldt and Eder, *Einwanderungsland Europa?*
7. Kość, 'Polish Regions Beat a Retreat on Anti-LGBTQ+ Resolutions'.
8. Credit Suisse Research Institute, 'Getting Over Globalization'.
9. Juncker, 'State of the Union Address 2017'.

References

Abella, Irving M., and Harold Martin Troper. *None Is Too Many: Canada and the Jews of Europe, 1933–1948*. Toronto: University of Toronto Press, 2012.

Adam, Christopher. 'University of Debrecen Bestows Highest Honour on Vladimir Putin'. *Hungarian Free Press* (blog), 27 August 2017. https://hungarianfreepress.com/2017/08/27/university-of-debrecen-bestows-highest-honour-on-vladimir-putin/.

Alexievich, Svetlana. *Secondhand Time: The Last of the Soviets*. London: Penguin, 2017.

Allen, Theodore. *The Invention of the White Race*. 2 vols. Haymarket Series. London: Verso, 1994.

Alshammari, Yousef H. 'Why Is There No MENA Category on the 2020 US Census?' Al Jazeera, 1 April 2020. www.aljazeera.com/news/2020/4/1/why-is-there-no-mena-category-on-the-2020-us-census.

Anderson, Benedict. *Imagined Communities: Reflections on the Origin and Spread of Nationalism*. London; New York: Verso, 1991.

Anidjar, Gil. *Blood: A Critique of Christianity*. Religion, Culture, and Public Life. New York: Columbia University Press, 2014.

Applebaum, Anne. 'Il Donald'. *The Atlantic*, 6 October 2020. www.theatlantic.com/ideas/archive/2020/10/trump-pays-mussolini-like-attention-his-own-image/616626/.

Applebaum, Anne. *Twilight of Democracy: The Seductive Lure of the Authoritarian State*. Kindle edition. London: Penguin, 2020.

Appelbaum, Nancy P., Anne S. Macpherson, and Karin Alejandra Rosemblatt. *Race and Nation in Modern Latin America*. University of North Carolina Press, 2003.

Ash, Timothy Garton. 'As at Auschwitz, the Gates of Hell Are Built and Torn Down by Human Hearts'. *The Guardian*, 23 December 2009, sec. Opinion. www.theguardian.com/commentisfree/2009/dec/23/poland-catholicism-nazis-difficult-past.

Ash, Timothy Garton. 'Does Central Europe Exist?' *The New York Review of Books*, 9 October 1986. www.nybooks.com/articles/1986/10/09/does-central-europe-exist/.

Assouline, Pierre. *Hergé: The Man Who Created Tintin*. Oxford; New York: Oxford University Press, 2009.

Aster, Ari, Florence Pugh, Jack Reynor, and Vilhelm Blomgren. *Midsommar*. Drama, Horror, Mystery. A24, B-Reel Films, Nordisk Film, 2019.

Baar, Huub van. 'Socio-Economic Mobility and Neoliberal Governmentality in Post-Socialist Europe: Activation and the Dehumanisation of the Roma'. *Journal of Ethnic and Migration Studies* 38, no. 8 (September 2012): 1289–1304. https://doi.org/10.1080/1369183X.2012.689189.

Baar, Huub van. 'The Production of Irregular Citizenship through Mobile Governmentalities: Racism against Roma at the Security-Mobility Nexus'. *Mobilities*, 1 April 2021, 1–15. https://doi.org/10.1080/17450101.2021.1902241.

Babiš, Andrej. *Sdílejte, než to zakážou!* Prague: ANO 2021, 2021.

Bakić-Hayden, Milica. 'Nesting Orientalisms: The Case of Former Yugoslavia'. *Slavic Review* 54, no. 4 (1995): 917–31. https://doi.org/10.2307/2501399.

Baldwin, Richard, and Javier Lopez-Gonzalez. 'Supply-chain Trade: A Portrait of Global Patterns and Several Testable Hypotheses'. *National Bureau of Economic Research*, NBER Working Paper, no. 18957 (2013). www.nber.org/papers/w18957.

Barša, Pavel, Zora Hesová, and Ondřej Slačálek, eds. *Central European Culture Wars: Beyond Post-Communism and Populism*. Prague: Filosofická Fakulta, Univerzita Karlova, 2021.

Barša, Pavel, Zora Hesová, and Ondřej Slačálek. 'Introduction: How Does Post-Communism End? Central European Culture Wars in the 2010s'. In *Central European Culture Wars: Beyond Post-Communism and Populism*, edited by Pavel Barša, Zora Hesová, and Ondřej Slačálek, 7–27, 2021.

Barša, Pavel. 'Nulový stupeň dekolonizace'. *Artalk*, Winter 2020 (2020): 1–4.

Bata Shoe Company. 'Bata Shoe Company Papers', 2014. University of Toronto. Thomas Fisher Rare Book Library.

Bayer, Lili. 'Hungarian Spyware Scandal Bolsters Fears of Orbán Critics'. POLITICO, 19 July 2021. www.politico.eu/article/hungarian-spyware-scandal-bolsters-fears-of-orban-critics/.

BBC News. 'Belgium Custody Death: "Shocked" Police Chief Steps Aside'. BBC News, 21 August 2020. www.bbc.com/news/world-europe-53864100.

BBC News. 'Hungarian PM Viktor Orban Denounces EU's "Colonialism"'. BBC News, 16 March 2012. www.bbc.com/news/business-17394894.

BBC News. 'Polish Election: Andrzej Duda Says LGBT "ideology" Worse than Communism', 14 June 2020. www.bbc.com/news/world-europe-53039864.

BBC Sport. 'Wales Players Rail against Racism with T-Shirts Ahead of Czech Republic Game', 30 March 2021. www.bbc.co.uk/sport/football/56584845.

Beaume, Maïa de la. 'Orbán, Le Pen, Salvini Join Forces to Blast EU Integration'. POLITICO, 2 July 2021. www.politico.eu/article/viktor-orban-marine-le-pen-matteo-salvini-eu-integration-european-superstate-radical-forces/.

Beller, Steven. 'Introduction'. In *Rethinking Vienna 1900*, edited by Steven Beller. New York: Berghahn Books, 2012.

Bernát, Anikó. 'Solidarity Powered via Social Media: Migrant Solidarity Grassroots Groups in Hungary', 2019. http://sharingandcaring.eu/node/396.

Bernhard, Patrick. 'Hitler's Africa in the East: Italian Colonialism as a Model for German Planning in Eastern Europe'. *Journal of Contemporary History* 51, no. 1 (2016): 61–90. http://www.jstor.org/stable/43697412.

Bershidsky, Leonid. 'A Strike in Slovakia Exposes a European Divide'. Bloomberg.com, 21 June 2017. www.bloomberg.com/opinion/articles/2017-06-21/a-strike-in-slovakia-exposes-a-european-divide.

Bershidsky, Leonid. 'Piketty Thinks the EU Is Bad for Eastern Europe. He's Half Right'. Bloomberg.com, 9 February 2018. www.bloomberg.com/opinion/articles/2018-02-09/piketty-thinks-the-eu-is-bad-for-eastern-europe-he-s-half-right.

Bershidsky, Leonid. 'Poland's Economic Experiment, Starring Thomas Piketty'. Bloomberg Quint, 23 February 2018. www.bloombergquint.com/view/poland-s-economic-experiment-starring-thomas-piketty.

Bhabha, Homi. 'Of Mimicry and Man: The Ambivalence of Colonial Discourse'. *October* 28 (1984): 125–33. https://doi.org/10.2307/778467.

Bhattacharyya, Gargi. *Rethinking Racial Capitalism: Questions of Reproduction and Survival*. Cultural Studies and Marxism. Lanham, MD: Rowman & Littlefield Publishers, 2018.

Bill, Stanley, and Ben Stanley. 'Whose Poland Is It to Be? PiS and the Struggle between Monism and Pluralism'. *East European Politics* 36, no. 3 (2020): 378–94. https://doi.org/10.1080/21599165.2020.1787161.

Biroul Național de Statistică. 'Monthly Gross and Net Average Earnings by Economic Activities, Sectors and Sex, 2013–2019'. Accessed 10 September 2021. https://statbank.statistica.md/PxWeb/pxweb/en/30%20Statistica%20sociala/30%20Statistica%20sociala__03%20FM__SAL010__serii%20anuale/SAL010100.px/table/tableViewLayout1/?rxid=4eec3dd5-755a-4e4e-92de-3dc2d391f3a9.

Biuro prasowe rzadu. *Porozumienia sierpniowe: nadzieje realia perspektywy*. Warsaw, 1983.

Blesk.cz. 'Zeman o muslimech: Když se nepřizpůsobí, deportujte je!' Accessed 30 August 2021. www.blesk.cz/clanek/zpravy-udalosti/295407/zeman-o-muslimech-kdyz-se-neprizpusobi-deportujte-je.html.

Boatcă, Manuela. 'Coloniality of Labor in the Global Periphery: Latin America and Eastern Europe in the World-System'. *Review (Fernand Braudel Center)* 36, no. 3–4 (2013): 287–314. http://www.jstor.org/stable/90000019.

Bolagun, Bolaji, and Konrad Pędziwiatr. '"Stop Calling Me Murzyn" – How Black Lives Matter in Poland'. *Journal of Ethnic and Migration Studies*, Forthcoming.

Borbély László. 'Ezért távozik Hrutka János a Spíler Tv-től'. Index, 19 March 2021. https://index.hu/sport/futball/2021/03/19/ezert-tavozik-hrutka-janos-a-spiler-tv-tol/.

Borkowska-Arciuch, Grażyna. 'Polskie Doświadczenie Kolonialne'. *Teksty Drugie*, no. 4 (2007): 15–24.

Böröcz, József. 'Introduction'. In *Empire's New Clothes: Unveiling EU Enlargement*, edited by József Böröcz and Melinda Kovács, 4–51. Telford: Central European Review, 2001.

Böröcz, József, and Mahua Sarkar. 'The Unbearable Whiteness of the Polish Plumber and the Hungarian Peacock Dance around "Race"'. *Slavic Review* 76, no. 2 (2017): 307–14. https://doi.org/10.1017/slr.2017.79.

Boubínová, Markéta. 'Rezoluce proti Orbánovu zákonu rozdělila zástupce stran Spolu, europoslanci ANO ji podpořili'. Deník N, 9 July 2021. https://denikn.cz/662149/rezoluce-proti-orbanovu-zakonu-rozdelila-zastupce-stran-spolu-europoslanci-ano-ji-podporili/.

Břešťan, Robert. 'Daniel Křetínský je pro nás pan Neznámý z Východu, přiznává francouzský novinář'. Hlídací Pes, 2 October 2019. https://hlidacipes.org/daniel-kretinsky-je-pro-nas-pan-neznamy-z-vychodu-priznava-francouzsky-novinar/?fbclid=IwAR2dnc7ALrMFI4Nu6TWi9sTNmuIHmMawXR--DaCZJY8ctWw3USDwH6HkwRw.

Brodkin, K. *How Jews Became White Folks and What That Says about Race in America*. New Brunswick, NJ: Rutgers University Press, 1998.

Brown, Jessica Autumn. '"Our National Feeling Is a Broken One:" Civic Emotion and the Holocaust in German Citizenship Education'. *Qualitative Sociology* 37, no. 4 (1 December 2014): 425–42. https://doi.org/10.1007/s11133-014-9286-8.

Bruff, Ian. 'The Rise of Authoritarian Neoliberalism'. *Rethinking Marxism* 26, no. 1 (2 January 2014): 113–29. https://doi.org/10.1080/08935696.2013.843250.

Buchowski, Michał. 'Social Thought & Commentary: The Specter of Orientalism in Europe: From Exotic Other to Stigmatized Brother'. *Anthropological Quarterly* 79, no. 3 (2006): 463–82. http://www.jstor.org/stable/4150874.

Buckley, Neil, and Henry Foy. 'Poland's New Government Finds a Model in Orban's Hungary'. *Financial Times*, 6 January 2016. www.ft.com/content/0a3c7d44-b48e-11e5-8358-9a82b43f6b2f.

Budapest Business Journal. 'Hungarians Working Abroad above EU Average', 29 May 2018. https://bbj.hu/politics/foreign-affairs/eu/foreign-affairs/eu/hungarians-working-abroad-above-eu-average-.

Buffon, George Louis Leclerc de. *Barr's Buffon. Buffon's Natural History, Containing a Theory of the Earth, a General History of Man, of the Brute Creation, and of Vegetables, Minerals, &c. From the French. With Notes by the Translator*. Vol. 4. London: Barr, 1792.

Casanova, Giacomo. *The Memoires of Jacques Casanova de Seingalt, 1725–1798*. Translated by Arthur Machen. The Gutenberg Project, n.d.

Castañeda, Ángela. 'España se posiciona en la Eurocopa: ningún jugador de la Selección se arrodilla contra el racismo'. El Español, 14 June 2021. www.elespanol.com/deportes/futbol/20210614/espana-posiciona-eurocopa-jugador-seleccion-arrodilla-racismo/588942502_0.html.

Caulcott, Clea, and Lili Bayer. 'Viktor Orbán Rolls out the Red Carpet for Marine Le Pen's Firebrand Rival'. POLITICO, 24 September 2021. www.politico.eu/article/viktor-orban-meeting-eric-zemmour/.

CBS. 'Canada's Dark Secret'. *60 Minutes*, 2 February 1997. https://thetvdb.com/series/60-minutes/episodes/5685009.

Centrum Badania Opinii Społecznej. 'Stosunek do innych narodów'. Komunikat z badań, March 2018. www.cbos.pl/SPISKOM.POL/2018/K_037_18.PDF.

Červinková, Hana, Michał Buchowski, and Zdenek Uherek. 'Introduction: On Rethinking Ethnography in Central Europe: Toward Cosmopolitan Anthropologies in the "Peripheries"'.

In *Rethinking Ethnography in Central Europe*, 1–20. London: Palgrave Macmillan, 2015.

Česká televize. 'Další trest za rasismus fanoušků. Sparta musí zaplatit pokutu 160 tisíc', 25 June 2020. https://sport.ceskatelevize.cz/cla nek/fotbal/1-liga/dalsi-trest-za-rasismus-fanousku-sparta-musi-zapla tit-pokutu-160-tisic/5ef4c7713d136f1e23523a3a.

Český statistický úřad. 'Bez cizinců by zaměstnanost dlouhodobě nerostla', 26 January 2021. www.czso.cz/csu/czso/bez-cizincu-by-zamestnanost-dlouhodobe-nerostla.

Český statistický úřad. 'Průměrné hrubé měsíční mzdy podle klasifikace zaměstnání – mezikrajské srovnání'. Accessed 10 September 2021. https://vdb.czso.cz/vdbvo2/faces/cs/index. jsf?page=vystup-objekt&pvo=MZD08&z=T&f=TABULKA&filtr= G%7EF_M%7ET_Z%7EF_R%7EF_P%7E_S%7E_null_null_&kata log=30852&c=v3~8__RP2018.

Chadwick, Lauren. 'Archbishop Warns of "Rainbow Plague" amid LGBT Tensions in Poland'. euronews, 2 August 2019. www.euronews. com/2019/08/02/archbishop-warns-of-rainbow-plague-amid-lgbt-tensions-in-poland.

Chamberlain, Houston Stewart. *Foundations of the Nineteenth Century*. New York: H. Fertig, 1968.

Chandra, Jyoti. *Annie Besant: From Theosophy to Nationalism*. Delhi: K.K. Publications, 2001.

Chapman, Nathaniel G., and David L. Brunsma. *Beer and Racism: How Beer Became White, Why It Matters, and the Movements to Change It*. Bristol: Bristol University Press, 2020.

Charron, Nicholas, Victor Lapuente, and Monika Bauhr. 'Sub-National Quality of Government in EU Member States: Presenting the 2021 European Quality of Government Index and Its Relationship with Covid-19 Indicators'. *The Quality of Government Institute*, Working Paper Series, 4 (April 2021). https://gupea.ub.gu.se/bitstream/2077/68410/1/gupea_2077_68410_1.pdf.

Chazan, Guy. 'German Police Criticised over Halle Synagogue Shootings'. *FT.Com*. 10 October 2019. www.proquest.com/docview/2303479128/citation/65808ECBED164022PQ/1.

Chernetsky, Vitaly, Nancy Condee, Harsha Ram, and Gayatri Chakravorty Spivak. 'Are We Postcolonial? Post-Soviet Space'. *PMLA*, Forum: Conference Debates, 121, no. 3 (1 May 2006): 819–36. https://doi.org/10.1632/pmla.2006.121.3.819.

Christiaens, Kim, James Mark, and José M. Faraldo. 'Entangled Transitions: Eastern and Southern European Convergence or Alternative Europes? 1960s–2000s'. *Contemporary European History*

26, no. 4 (November 2017): 577–99. https://doi.org/10.1017/S0960777317000261.

Churchill, Winston. 'The Sinews of Peace ("Iron Curtain Speech")'. International Churchill Society. Accessed 18 August 2021. https://winstonchurchill.org/resources/speeches/1946-1963-elder-statesman/the-sinews-of-peace/.

Constable, H. S. *Ireland from One Or Two Neglected Points of View*. Hatchards, 1888.

Craig, Eli, Tyler Labine, Alan Tudyk, and Katrina Bowden. *Tucker and Dale vs Evil*. Comedy, Horror. Reliance Big Pictures, Loubyloo Productions, Eden Rock Media, 2010.

Credit Suisse Research Institute. 'Getting Over Globalization', January 2017.

Dabrowski, Patrice M., and Stefan Troebst. 'Uses and Abuses of the Past'. In *The Routledge History of East Central Europe Since 1700*, edited by Irina Livezeanu and Árpád von Klimó, 465–506. London: Routledge, 2017.

Dahlburg, John-Thor. 'Gorbachev: Socialism Must Have a "Human Face"'. AP NEWS, 26 November 1989. https://apnews.com/4af0c8eb2eebd3c3ceeca9db4ba63b27.

Dale, Gareth, and Jane Hardy. 'Conclusion: The "Crash" in Central and Eastern Europe'. In *First the Transition, Then the Crash: Eastern Europe in the 2000s*, edited by Gareth Dale, 251–64. London: Pluto Press, 2011.

Davidson, Neil. 'Crisis Neoliberalism and Regimes of Permanent Exception'. *Critical Sociology* 43, no. 4–5 (July 2017): 615–34. https://doi.org/10.1177/0896920516655386.

Deák, István. 'The Danger of Antisemitism in Hungary'. In *The Danger of Antisemitism in Central and Eastern Europe in the Wake of 1989–1990*, edited by Yehuda Bauer, 57–61. Jerusalem: Vidal Sassoon International Centre for the Study of Antisemitism, Hebrew University of Jerusalem, 1991.

Decker, Oliver, E. Brähler, and Dirk Baier, eds. *Flucht Ins Autoritäre: Rechtsextreme Dynamiken in Der Mitte Der Gesellschaft: Die Leipziger Autoritarismus-Studie 2018*. Originalausgabe. Giessen: Psychosozial-Verlag, 2018.

'Democracy Index 2020: In Sickness and in Health?' The Economist Intelligence Unit, 2021. www.eiu.com/n/campaigns/democracy-index-2020/.

'DEMOS – Democratic Efficacy and the Varieties of Populism in Europe'. Accessed 10 September 2021. https://demos-h2020.eu/en/about-demos.

Dénes, Csurgó. 'A Sztrájk, Amiben Még a Fidesz Is a Német Autóipari Multi Ellen Fordult'. 444.hu, 4 March 2021. https://444.hu/2021/03/04/a-sztrajk-amiben-meg-a-fidesz-is-a-nemet-autoipari-multi-ellen-fordult.

Derzhavna sluzhba statistiki Ukraïni. 'Average Monthly Wages of Regular Employees by Region (1995–2020)', n.d. www.ukrstat.gov.ua/operativ/operativ2021/gdn/szpshp/szpshp_reg_rik.xlsx.

Deutsche Welle. 'Borussia Dortmund Announce Management for New Women's Team', 23 February 2021. www.dw.com/en/borussia-dortmund-announce-management-for-new-womens-team/a-56577764.

Deutscher Bundestag. Plenarprotokoll (n.d.).

Dickson, Annabelle. 'UK's Tech Clampdown Could Miss Goal after Football Racism'. POLITICO, 12 July 2021. www.politico.eu/article/uk-social-media-big-tech-clampdown-football-racism-online-hate/.

Dinnage, Rosemary. *Annie Besant*. Lives of Modern Women. Harmondsworth, Middlesex: Penguin Books, 1986.

Dobré ráno | Denný podcast denníka SME. 'Exodus zdravotníkov spôsobí kolaps'. Accessed 10 September 2021. https://domov.sme.sk/c/22665826/dobre-rano-exodus-zdravotnikov-sposobi-kolaps.html.

Dobrev, Klara, Márton Gyöngyösi, Attila Ara-Kovács, Csaba Molnár, Sándor Rónai, and István Ujhelyi. 'Umgang mit Viktor Orbán: Das Trojanische Pferd von Europa'. *Die Zeit*, 23 November 2020. www.zeit.de/politik/ausland/2020-11/viktor-orban-ungarn-eu-haushalt-alan-posener.

Dobrogeanu-Gherea, Constantin. *Neoiobăgia: Studiu Economico-Sociologic al Problemei Noastre Agrare*. Bucharest: Socec, 1910.

Dolan, Kerry A., Chase Peterson-Withorn, and Jennifer Wang. 'The Forbes 400 2020: The Richest People in America'. Forbes. Accessed 3 August 2021. www.forbes.com/forbes-400/.

Dolan, Kerry A., Jennifer Wang, and Chase Peterson-Withorn. 'Forbes Billionaires 2021: The Richest People in the World'. Forbes. Accessed 14 September 2021. www.forbes.com/billionaires/.

Doran, Robert. 'René Girard's Concept of Conversion and the "via Negativa": Revisiting "Deceit, Desire, and the Novel".' *Religion & Literature* 43, no. 3 (2011): 170–79.

Dowler, Wayne. 'Herder in Russia: A. A. Grigor'ev and "Progressivist-Traditionalism"'. *Canadian Slavonic Papers/Revue Canadienne Des Slavistes* 19, no. 2 (1977): 167–80. http://www.jstor.org/stable/40867542.

Drulák, Petr. 'The West, the Centre and the East: Assessing the Strategic Options of Central Europe'. *Global Affairs* 3, no. 1 (January 2017): 5–15. https://doi.org/10.1080/23340460.2017.1294312.

Dugin, Aleksandr Gel′evič. *Osnovy geopolitiki: geopolitičeskoe buduščee Rossii*. 4th edition. Serija: Bol′šoe prostranstvo. Moscow: Arktogeja-Centr, 2000.

Duneier, Mitchell. *Ghetto: The Invention of a Place, the History of an Idea*. First edition. New York: Farrar, Straus and Giroux, 2016.

Dzenovska, Dace. 'Historical Agency and the Coloniality of Power in Postsocialist Europe'. *Anthropological Theory* 13, no. 4 (December 2013): 394–416. https://doi.org/10.1177/1463499613502185.

East India Company. 'Sessional Papers 1812–13', 1813.

Easton, Adam. 'LGBT Rights: New Threat for Poland's "Rainbow Families"'. BBC News, 17 March 2021. www.bbc.com/news/world-europe-56412782.

Eco, Umberto. 'Ur-Fascism'. *New York Review of Books*, 22 June 1995. www.nybooks.com/articles/1995/06/22/ur-fascism/.

Eddie, Sean A. *Freedom's Price: Serfdom, Subjection, and Reform in Prussia, 1648–1848*. Oxford: Oxford University Press, 2013.

Eibl-Eibesfeldt, Irenäus, and Rudolf Eder, eds. *Einwanderungsland Europa?* 2nd edition. Graz, Stuttgart: Stocker, 1994.

Elfer, Helen. '"Proud of You": Trump Writes Gushing Letter to Hungary's Authoritarian Leader Viktor Orbán'. *The Independent*, 31 August 2021. www.independent.co.uk/news/world/americas/us-politics/donald-trump-letter-viktor-orban-b1912030.html.

Engelking, Barbara, Jan Grabowski, and Stowarzyszenie Centrum Badań nad Zagładą Żydów, eds. *Dalej Jest Noc: Losy Żydów w Wybranych Powiatach Okupowanej Polski*. Wydanie pierwsze. Warszawa: Stowarzyszenie Centrum Badań nad Zagładą Żydów, 2018.

Erkulwater, Jennifer L. 'How the Nation's Largest Minority Became White: Race Politics and the Disability Rights Movement, 1970–1980'. *Journal of Policy History* 30, no. 3 (July 2018): 367–99. https://doi.org/10.1017/S0898030618000143.

Etkind, Alexander. *Internal Colonization: Russia's Imperial Experience*. Reprinted. Cambridge: Polity Press, 2011.

Etkind, Alexander. *Warped Mourning: Stories of the Undead in the Land of the Unburied*. Cultural Memory in the Present. Stanford, CA: Stanford University Press, 2013.

euronews. 'Hungary's Anti-LGBT Law Is a "Shame" Says Ursula von Der Leyen', 23 June 2021. www.euronews.com/2021/06/23/hungary-s-anti-lgbt-law-is-a-shame-says-ursula-von-der-leyen.

European Automobile Manufacturers Association. 'Vehicles in Use: Europe', January 2021. www.acea.auto/files/report-vehicles-in-use-europe-january-2021-1.pdf.

European Commission. 'Together Against Trafficking in Human Beings – Member States'. Text, 11 October 2016. https://ec.europa.eu/anti-trafficking/member-states_en.

European Commission. 'The 2020 EU Justice Scoreboard'. Luxembourg, 2020. https://op.europa.eu/en/publication-detail/-/publication/14a9d17e-f245-11ea-991b-01aa75ed71a1.

Eurostat. 'Data Browser – Annual Net Earnings', 9 March 2021. https://ec.europa.eu/eurostat/databrowser/view/EARN_NT_NET/default/table?lang=en.

Eurostat. 'Gini Coefficient of Equivalised Disposable Income – EU-SILC Survey'. Accessed 24 September 2021. https://ec.europa.eu/eurostat/databrowser/view/ilc_di12/default/table?lang=en.

Fabry, Adam. *The Political Economy of Hungary: From State Capitalism to Authoritarian Neoliberalism*. New York: Springer Berlin Heidelberg, 2019.

Fakt. 'Wałęsa przed laty: Chcemy socjalizmu!', 13 December 2010. www.fakt.pl/wydarzenia/polityka/walesa-przed-laty-chcemy-socjalizmu/sztfxg2.

Farage, Nigel. 'Greece Is Now No More than a Colony of the EU: Something Even I Wondered If They Could Stoop to'. Tweet. @Nigel_Farage, 2 February 2012. https://twitter.com/Nigel_Farage/status/164862222307299328.

Federal'naia sluzhba gosudarstvennoi statistiki. 'Srednemesiachnaia Nominal'naia Nachislennaia Zarabotnaia Plata Rabotnikov Po Polnomu Krugu Organizatsii v Tselom Po Ėkonomike Po Sub'ektam Rossiiskoi Federatsii s 2018 Goda, Rublei'. Accessed 16 November 2021. https://rosstat.gov.ru/storage/mediabank/tab4.xlsx

Fedyuk, Olena, and Marta Kindler. *Ukrainian Migration to the European Union: Lessons from Migration Studies*. New York: Springer Berlin Heidelberg, 2016.

Fekete, Liz. 'Hungary: Power, Punishment and the "Christian-National Idea"'. *Race & Class* 57, no. 4 (April 2016): 39–53. https://doi.org/10.1177/0306396815624607.

Ferfecki, Wiktor. '"Murzyn" oficjalnie odradzany przez Radę Języka Polskiego'. Rzeczpospolita, 5 March 2021. www.rp.pl/spoleczenstwo/art246621-murzyn-oficjalnie-odradzany-przez-rade-jezyka-polskiego.

Finnis. 'The Full (and Farcical) List of UEFA Fines and Sanctions for Racist Abuse'. inews.co.uk, 15 October 2019. https://inews.co.uk/sport/football/uefa-racism-protocol-sanctions-punishments-full-list-clubs-fa-3-point-system-350721.

finweb. 'Fico plynárom: Nie sme kolónia', 2 July 2012. https://finweb.hnonline.sk/ekonomika/407344-fico-plynarom-nie-sme-kolonia.

Fox, Jon E., and Magda Mogilnicka. 'Pathological Integration, or, How East Europeans Use Racism to Become British'. *The British Journal of Sociology* 70, no. 1 (2019): 5–23. https://doi.org/10.1111/1468-4446.12337.

Fragile States Index. 'Global Data (2020)'. Accessed 10 September 2021. https://fragilestatesindex.org/data/.

Franzos, Karl Emil. *Vom Don Zur Donau: Neue Kulturbilder Aus Halb-Asien*. Stuttgart: J.G. Cotta, 1912.

Fraser, Dave. 'Lacazette in Powerful Anti-Racism Stance by ladeing in Front of Slavia Stars'. *The Sun*, 15 April 2021. www.thesun.co.uk/sport/football/14664069/arsenal-lacazette-racism-kneel-slavia-prague/.

Freedom House. 'Countries and Territories'. Accessed 19 August 2021. https://freedomhouse.org/countries/freedom-world/scores.

Freeman, Daniel E. *Mozart in Prague*. Minneapolis: Bearclaw Publishers, 2013.

Frommer, Benjamin. 'The Holocaust in Bohemia and Moravia'. In *Prague and Beyond*, edited by Kateřina Čapková and Hillel J. Kieval, 196–234. Jews in the Bohemian Lands. Philadelphia: University of Pennsylvania Press, 2021.

Fukuyama, Francis. *The End of History and the Last Man*. New York: The Free Press, 1992.

Gabrizova, Zuzana. 'Hungary Misappropriated V4 Brand, Says Slovak Justice Minister'. www.Euractiv.Com (blog), 5 November 2020. www.euractiv.com/section/politics/short_news/hungary-misappropriated-v4-brand-says-slovak-justice-minister/.

Gagyi, Agnes. '"Coloniality of Power" in East Central Europe: External Penetration as Internal Force in Post-Socialist Hungarian Politics'. *Journal of World-Systems Research* 22, no. 2 (16 August 2016): 349–72. https://doi.org/10.5195/jwsr.2016.626.

Geva, Dorit. 'Orbán's Ordonationalism as Post-Neoliberal Hegemony'. *Theory, Culture & Society*, 24 April 2021. https://doi.org/10.1177/0263276421999435.

Gilman, Sander L. 'The Jewish Nose: Are Jews White? Or, the History of the Nose Job'. In *The Other in Jewish Thought and History: Constructions of Jewish Culture and Identity*, edited by Laurence

J. Silberstein and Robert L. Cohn, 2: 364–401. New York: New York University Press, 1994.

Girard, René. *Violence and the Sacred*. Durham, NC: Duke University Press, 2007.

Gleig, George Robert. *Germany, Bohemia, and Hungary, Visited in 1837*. Vol. II. London: John W. Parker, 1839. www.gutenberg.org/ebooks/24419.

Glied, Viktor, and Norbert Pap. 'The "Christian Fortress of Hungary"– The Anatomy of the Migration Crisis in Hungary'. *Yearbook of Polish European Studies*, no. 19 (2016): 133–50. www.ce.uw.edu.pl/pliki/pw/Glied%20YPES%202016.pdf.

Glied, Viktor, and Norbert Pap. 'The Hungarian Border Barrier and Islam'. *Journal of Muslims in Europe* 6, no. 1 (9 March 2017): 104–31. https://doi.org/10.1163/22117954-12341339.

'Global Peace Index 2020'. Sydney: Institute for Economics & Peace, June 2020. www.visionofhumanity.org/wp-content/uploads/2020/10/GPI_2020_web.pdf.

Główny Urząd Statystyczny. 'Bank Danych Lokalnych'. Accessed 10 September 2021. https://bdl.stat.gov.pl/BDL/dane/podgrup/temat.

Główny Urząd Statystyczny. 'Demographic Situation in Poland up to 2019. International Migration of Population in 2000–2019'. Warsaw, 2020. https://stat.gov.pl/download/gfx/portalinformacyjny/en/defaultaktualnosci/3289/6/1/1/demographic_situation_in_poland_up_to_2019.pdf.

Gobineau, Arthur. *The Moral and Intellectual Diversity of Races/With Particular Reference to Their Respective Influence in the Civil and Political History of Mankind*. Project Gutenberg, 2011.

Goldsworthy, Vesna. *Inventing Ruritania: The Imperialism of the Imagination*. New Haven, CT: Yale University Press, 1998.

Gollner, Philipp. 'How Mennonites Became White: Religious Activism, Cultural Power, and the City'. *The Mennonite Quarterly Review* 90, no. 2 (2016): 165–93.

Górak-Sosnowska, Katarzyna. 'Islamophobia without Muslims? The Case of Poland'. *Journal of Muslims in Europe* 5, no. 2 (28 October 2016): 190–204. https://doi.org/10.1163/22117954-12341326.

Grant, Charles. 'Observations on the State of Society among the Asiatic Subjects of Great Britain, Particularly with Respect to Morals; and on the Means of Improving It. Written Chiefly in the Year 1792.' London: House of Commons, 15 June 1813.

Green, Emma. 'Are Jews White? Reactions to The Atlantic's Article – The Atlantic'. Accessed 5 May 2021. www.theatlantic.com/notes/2016/12/jews-whiteness/509606/.

Greene, Naomi. *Landscapes of Loss: The National Past in Postwar French Cinema*. Princeton, NJ: Princeton University Press, 1999.

Gross, Jan T. 'Eastern Europe's Crisis of Shame'. Project Syndicate, 13 September 2015. www.project-syndicate.org/commentary/eastern-europe-refugee-crisis-xenophobia-by-jan-gross-2015-09.

Gualtieri, Sarah. 'Becoming "White": Race, Religion and the Foundations of Syrian/Lebanese Ethnicity in the United States'. *Journal of American Ethnic History* 20, no. 4 (2001): 29–58. http://www.jstor.org/stable/27502745.

Gyarfašová, Soňa. 'Odkrývanie: Bratislavský nacista na Edlovej ulici mučil a vraždil'. SME.sk, 18 November 2020. https://domov.sme.sk/c/22537024/odkryvanie-bratislavsky-nacista-edlovej-ulice-video.html.

Habermas, Jürgen. 'What Does Socialism Mean Today? The Rectifying Revolution and the Need for New Thinking on the Left'. *New Left Review* 183, no. 1 (1990): 3–22.

Hackett, Conrad, Philip Connor, Marcin Stonawski, and Michaela Potančoková. 'Europe's Growing Muslim Population'. Pew Research Center, 29 November 2017. www.pewforum.org/wp-content/uploads/sites/7/2017/11/FULL-REPORT-FOR-WEB-POSTING.pdf.

Hackmann, Jörg. 'Defending the "Good Name" of the Polish Nation: Politics of History as a Battlefield in Poland, 2015–18'. *Journal of Genocide Research* 20, no. 4 (2 October 2018): 587–606. https://doi.org/10.1080/14623528.2018.1528742.

HaCohen, Ran. 'The "Jewish Blackness" Thesis Revisited'. *Religions* 9, no. 7 (22 July 2018): 222. https://doi.org/10.3390/rel9070222.

Hajdu, Dominika, Katarína Klingová, and Miroslava Sawiris. 'Vaccination Trends: Perceptions from Central and Eastern Europe'. Bratislava: GLOBSEC, 27 April 2021. www.globsec.org/wp-content/uploads/2021/04/GLOBSEC-Vaccination-Trends.pdf.

Halasi, Zoltán. 'The Ghost of Judeopolonia or the Never-Existing Eastern European Confederation'. In *Understanding Central Europe*, edited by Marcin Moskalewicz and Wojciech Przybylski, 229–37. London; New York: Routledge, 2017.

Hall, Stuart. 'Popular Democratic vs. Authoritarian Populism: Two Ways of Taking Democracy Seriously'. In *Marxism and Democracy*, edited by Alan Hunt 160–1. London: Lawrence and Wishart, 1980.

Hall, Stuart. 'Thatcherism: A New Stage'. *Marxism Today* 24, no. 2 (1980): 26–28.

Hall, Stuart, Kobena Mercer, and Henry Louis Gates. *The Fateful Triangle: Race, Ethnicity, Nation*, Cambridge, MA: Harvard University Press, 2017.

Hall, Todd H., and Andrew A.G. Ross. 'Affective Politics after 9/11'. *International Organization* 69, no. 4 (2015): 847–79. https://doi.org/10.1017/S0020818315000144.

Handlin, Oscar and Mary F. 'Origins of the Southern Labor System'. *The William and Mary Quarterly* 7, no. 2 (1950): 199–222. https://doi.org/10.2307/1917157.

Harms, Victoria. 'Living *Mitteleuropa* in the 1980s: A Network of Hungarian and West German Intellectuals'. *European Review of History: Revue Européenne d'histoire* 19, no. 5 (October 2012): 669–92. https://doi.org/10.1080/13507486.2012.719005.

Hasmath, Reza, and Solomon Kay-Reid. 'What Salience Does White Privilege Have in Non-Diverse Societies?' In *American Sociological Association Annual Meeting, August 6–10*, 2021.

Havel, Václav. *Václav Havel: Living in Truth; Twenty-Two Essays Published on the Occasion of the Award of the Erasmus Prize to Václav Havel*. London: Faber and Faber, 1989.

Hayashi, Tadayuki. 'Masaryk's "Zone of Small Nations" in His Discourse during World War I'. In *Regions in Central and Eastern Europe, Past and Present*, edited by Tadayuki Hayashi and Hiroshi Fukuda. Sapporo: Slavic Research Center, Hokkaido University, 2007.

Hegburg, Krista. 'Aftermath: Accounting for the Holocaust in the Czech Republic'. Columbia University, 2013.

Helliwell, John F., Richard Layard, Jeffrey D. Sachs, and Jan-Emmanuel De Neve. 'World Happiness Report 2020'. Sustainable Development Solutions Network, 2020. https://happiness-report.s3.amazonaws.com/2020/WHR20.pdf.

Heng, Geraldine. *The Invention of Race in the European Middle Ages*. Cambridge, UK: Cambridge University Press, 2018.

Herder, J. G. *Ideen zur Philosophie der Geschichte der Menschheit*. Vol. 16. Riga; Leipzig: Bei Johann Friedrich Hartknoch, 1784.

Herman, Edward S., and Noam Chomsky. *Manufacturing Consent: The Political Economy of the Mass Media*. New York: Pantheon Books, 1988.

Hlavačka, Milan, and Zdeněk Munzar. *S Bohem za císaře a vlasť! Čeští důstojníci ve válkách let 1848–1849*. Vydání 1. Praha: Academia: Ministerstvo obrany České republiky – Vojenský historický ústav Praha, 2018.

Hobsbawm, E. J., and T. O. Ranger, eds. *The Invention of Tradition*. Cambridge; New York: Cambridge University Press, 1983.

Holt, Thomas C. *The Problem of Race in the Twenty-First Century*. The Nathan I. Huggins Lectures. Cambridge, MA: Harvard University Press, 2000.

Holt, Thomas C. 'The First New Nations'. Foreword in *Race and Nation in Modern Latin America*, edited by Nancy Appelbaum, Anne S. Macpherson, and Karin Alejandra Rosemblatt, vii–xvi. Chapel Hill: The University of North Carolina, 2003.

Hron, Lukáš. 'KOMENTÁŘ: Slávisté na Arsenalu nepoklekli. A přestože se Británie zlobí, bylo to správné'. CNN Prima News, 9 April 2021. https://cnn.iprima.cz/komentar-slaviste-nepoklekli-a-prestoze-se-britanie-zlobi-bylo-to-spravne-22798.

Hungary Office of Elections. '2018'. Nemzeti Választási Iroda. Accessed 21 September 2021. www.valasztas.hu/ogy2018.

i24NEWS. 'Slovakia Apologizes for Anti-Jewish Laws During World War II'. Accessed 23 September 2021. www.i24news.tv/en/news/international/europe/1631132662-slovakia-apologizes-for-anti-jewish-laws-during-world-war-ii.

iDnes.cz. 'Fotbalový svět zase řeší, že hráči českého týmu #Slavia před zápasem v Anglii na podporu hnutí #BlackLivesMatter nepoklekli.' *Facebook*, 9 April 2021. www.facebook.com/iDNES.cz/posts/10158382925901314.

iDnes.cz. 'Perly Miloše Jakeše z Červeného hrádku po 20 letech', 3 July 2009. www.idnes.cz/zpravy/domaci/audio-perly-milose-jakese-z-cerveneho-hradku-po-20-letech.A090702_105621_domaci_jw.

iDobrovolník. 'National Database of Volunteers for Refugees'. Accessed 21 September 2021. www.idobrovolnik.cz/en.

Ignatiev, Noel. *How the Irish Became White*. New York; London: Routledge, 2009.

Imre, Anikó. 'Race and Diversity Illiberal Style'. *Journal of Ethnic and Migration Studies*, Forthcoming.

Inotal, Edit. 'Dark Family Secrets Expose Hungary's History Problem'. *Balkan Insight* (blog), 13 February 2020. https://balkaninsight.com/2020/02/13/dark-family-secrets-expose-hungarys-history-problem/.

Institut national de la statistique et des études économiques. 'Chiffres détaillés – Salaires et revenus d'activité'. Accessed 10 September 2021. www.insee.fr/fr/statistiques/fichier/2021266/base-cc-dads-2018.zip.

Istituto nazionale di statistica. 'Reddito Netto: Regioni e Tipo Di Comune'. Accessed 10 September 2021. http://dati.istat.it/Index.aspx?QueryId=22919.

Ištok, Robert, Irina Kozárová, and Anna Polačková. 'The Intermarium as a Polish Geopolitical Concept in History and in the Present'. *Geopolitics* 26, no. 1 (2021): 314–41.

Jackson, Kieran. 'Kolar Left with Horrific Eye Cuts after Roofe's "Kung-Fu Tackle"'. Mail Online, 18 March 2021. www.dailymail.co.uk/sport/football/article-9378755/Slavia-Prague-keeper-Ondrej-Kolar-left-HORRIFIC-eye-cuts-Kemar-Roofes-kung-fu-tackle.html.

Janáková, Barbora. 'Kvůli vyšetřování Babiše mi vyhrožují smrtí, říká europoslankyně. Obrátila se na německou policii'. Deník N, 4 March 2020. https://denikn.cz/305855/kvuli-vysetrovani-babise-mi-vyhrozuji-smrti-rika-europoslankyne-obratila-se-na-nemeckou-policii/.

Janik, Allan, and Stephen Toulmin. *Wittgenstein's Vienna*. New York: Simon and Schuster, 1973.

Janion, Maria. *Niesamowita Słowiańszczyzna: Fantazmaty Literatury*. Cracow: Wydawn. Literackie, 2006.

Jenkins, Destin, and Justin Leroy, eds. *Histories of Racial Capitalism*. Columbia Studies in the History of U.S. Capitalism. New York: Columbia University Press, 2021.

Jobbik. 'Jobbik's Wage Union Initiative to Create Eastern Central European Cooperation', 25 February 2017. www.jobbik.com/jobbiks_wage_union_initiative_to_create_eastern_central_european_cooperation.

Johnson, Lonnie R. *Central Europe: Enemies, Neighbors, Friends*. New York: Oxford University Press USA, 1996.

Judt, Tony. 'The Rediscovery of Central Europe'. *Daedalus* 119, no. 1 (1990): 23–54. www.jstor.org/stable/20025283.

Juncker, Jean-Claude. 'State of the Union Address 2017'. European Commission, 13 September 2017. https://ec.europa.eu/commission/presscorner/detail/en/SPEECH_17_3165.

Kalmar, Ivan. '"The Battlefield Is in Brussels": Islamophobia in the Visegrád Four in Its Global Context'. *Patterns of Prejudice*, 9 November 2018, 1–14. https://doi.org/10.1080/0031322X.2018.1512473.

Kalmar, Ivan. 'Anti-Semitism and Islamophobia: The Formation of a Secret'. *Human Architecture: Journal of the Sociology of Self-Knowledge* 7, no. 2 (2009): 135–44.

Kalmar, Ivan. 'Islamophobia and Anti-Antisemitism: The Case of Hungary and the "Soros Plot"'. *Patterns of Prejudice* 54, no. 1–2 (14 March 2020): 182–98. https://doi.org/10.1080/0031322X.2019.1705014.

Kalmar, Ivan. 'Race by the Grace of God: Race, Religion, and the Construction of "Jew" and "Arab"'. In *Jews Color Race: Rethinking Jewish Identities*, edited by Efraim Sicher, 482–509. London: Berghahn Press, 2013.

Kalmar, Ivan. *Early Orientalism: Imagined Islam and the Notion of Sublime Power*. London: Routledge, 2011.

Kalmar, Ivan. *The Trotskys, Freuds and Woody Allens: Portrait of a Culture*. Toronto: Viking, 1993.

Kalmar, Ivan. 'Islamophobia Without Muslims'. In *Global Islamophobia in an Era of Populism*, edited by Sahar Aziz and John L. Esposito. New York: Oxford University Press, 2022.

Kalmar, Ivan. 'The East Is Just Like the West, Only More So: Islamophobia and Populism in Eastern Germany and the East of the European Union'. *Journal of Contemporary European Studies*, 2 October 2019, 1–15. https://doi.org/10.1080/14782804.2019.1673704.

Kalmar, Ivan. 'The Struggle for Whiteness and East-West Relations in the European Union: An Introduction'. *Journal of Ethnic and Migration Studies*, Forthcoming.

Kalmar, Ivan, and Derek J. Penslar. 'Orientalism and the Jews: An Introduction'. In *Orientalism and the Jews*, edited by Ivan Kalmar and Derek Penslar, xiii–xl. Hanover, NH: University Press of New England, 2005.

Kalmar, Ivan, and Tariq Ramadan. 'Antisemitism and Islamophobia'. In *Routledge Handbook of Muslim-Jewish Relations*, 351–71. New York and London: Routledge, 2016.

Kamm, Henry. 'Havel Calls Gypsies "Litmus Test"'. *The New York Times*, 10 December 1993, sec. A.

Kaya, Ayhan, and Ayşegül Kayaoglu. 'Individual Determinants of Anti-Muslim Prejudice in the EU-15'. *Uluslararası İlişkiler/International Relations* 14, no. 53 (2017): 45–68. http://www.jstor.org/stable/26406839.

Keller-Alant, Akos, Tibor Racz, and Krisztian Simon. 'In Hungary, Viktor Orban's Favorite Mayor Goes on a Shopping Spree'. Deutsche Welle, 25 October 2017. www.dw.com/en/in-hungary-viktor-orbans-favorite-mayor-goes-on-a-shopping-spree/a-41099347.

Kentish, Benjamin. 'Polish Angler Suing Oxfordshire Fishery over "No Eastern Europeans" Sign'. *The Independent*, 19 December 2017. www.independent.co.uk/news/uk/home-news/oxfordshire-fishery-no-eastern-europeans-sign-legal-action-racism-brexit-field-farm-fisheries-bicester-a8118791.html.

Kéri, László. *Orbán Viktor*. Budapest: Századvég Kiadó, 1994.

Kernová, Miroslava. 'Kotlebovci v predvolebnom spote klamú: Šíria, že Slováci majú odškodňovať černochov za otroctvo'. Deník N, 3 April 2019. https://dennikn.sk/blog/1431761/kotlebovci-v-predvolebnom-spote-klamu-siria-ze-slovaci-maju-odskodnovat-cernochov-za-otroctvo/.

Kim, Claire Jean. *Bitter Fruit: The Politics of Black-Korean Conflict in New York City*. New Haven, CT: Yale University Press, 2000.

Király, András. 'Kiderült, hogy mi az Istenre tudott még 2,4 milliárd forint Tao-támogatást kérni Orbán Felcsúti fociakadémiája'. 444.hu, 10 December 2020. https://444.hu/2020/12/10/kiderult-hogy-mi-az-istenre-tudott-meg-24-milliard-forint-tao-tamogatast-kerni-orban-felcsuti-fociakademiaja.

Kitti, Fődi. 'Tíz év alatt 786 százalékkal nőtt a parlamenti képviselők átlagvagyona'. 444.hu, 15 February 2021. https://444.hu/2021/02/15/tiz-ev-alatt-786-szazalekkal-nott-a-parlamenti-kepviselok-atlag vagyona.

Kolakowski, Leszek. 'Two Prescriptions for Socialism'. *The New York Times*, 13 December 1987. www.nytimes.com/1987/12/13/books/two-prescriptions-for-socialism.html.

Konrád, György. *Antipolitics: An Essay*. London: Quartet, 1984.

Kormányzat. 'Orbán Viktor Beszéde a XXVIII. Bálványosi Nyári Szabadegyetem És Diáktáborban'. Accessed 10 July 2020. www.kormany.hu/hu/a-miniszterelnok/beszedek-publikaciok-interjuk/orban-viktor-beszede-a-xxviii-balvanyosi-nyari-szabadegyetem-es-diaktaborban.

Kość, Wojciech. 'Polish Regions Beat a Retreat on Anti-LGBTQ\+ Resolutions'. POLITICO, 28 September 2021. www.politico.eu/article/polish-regions-retract-anti-lgbt-resolutions-after-threat-eu-funding/.

Kovács, Ildikó. 'Baloldali rémálmok aggasztják a Magyarokat'. 24.hu, 14 June 2018. https://24.hu/kozelet/2018/06/14/magyar-rema lom-kutatas/.

Kövér, László. 'Kövér Lászlónak, a Nemzeti önazonosság védelméről szóló politikai nyilatkozat előterjesztőjének nyitóbeszéde'. Magyarország Európai Unió Brüsszel EU, 4 June 2020. https://eu-brusszel.mfa.gov.hu/aut/news/koever-laszlonak-a-nemzeti-oenaz onossag-vedelmerol-szolo-politikai-nyilatkozat-eloterjesztojenek-nyitobeszede.

Központi Statisztikai Hivatal. 'Average Gross Earnings of Full-Time Employees by Location of the Employer's Head Office'. Accessed 10 September 2021. www.ksh.hu/docs/eng/xstadat/xstadat_infra/e_qli029b.html.

Král, Petr. 'Matematik Levínský: Pokud se nezavřou továrny jako před rokem, tak se nám nepodaří stlačit epidemii'. iROZHLAS, 27 February 2021. www.irozhlas.cz/zpravy-domov/koronavirus-v-cesku-levinsky-tovarny_2102271530_pj.

Krastev, Ivan, and Stephen Holmes. *The Light That Failed: A Reckoning*. Kindle edition. London: Allen Lane, 2019.

Kremský, Peter. 'Talenty pre Slovensko'. Podnikateľská aliancia Slovenska, December 2015. alianciapas.sk/wp-content/uploads/2015/12/Talenty-pre-Slovensko.pdf.

Krivonos, Daria. 'Racial Capitalism and the Production of Racialised Difference in Europe: Young Post-Soviet Migrants in Helsinki and Warsaw'. *Journal of Ethnic and Migration Studies*, Forthcoming.

Krumpal, Ivar. 'Determinants of Social Desirability Bias in Sensitive Surveys: A Literature Review'. *Quality & Quantity* 47, no. 4 (2013): 2025–47.

Kubátová, Hana. 'Now or Never: Post-War Anti-Jewish Violence and Majority Society in Slovakia'. *Soudobé Dějiny* 23, no. 3 (1 September 2016): 321–46. https://doi.org/10.51134/sod.2016.020.

Kubicek, Paul, and Cengiz Erişen. 'Majoritarian Democracy in Turkey'. In *Democratic Consolidation in Turkey: Micro and Macro Challenges*, edited by Cengiz Erişen and Paul Kubicek, 123–43. Routledge Studies in Middle Eastern Politics 82. London; New York: Routledge, 2016.

Kulka, Otto Dov. 'History and Historical Progress'. In *The Danger of Antisemitism in Central and Eastern Europe in the Wake of 1989–1990*, edited by Yehuda Bauer, 9–16. Jerusalem: Vidal Sassoon International Centre for the Study of Antisemitism, Hebrew University of Jerusalem, 1991.

Kundera, Milan. 'The Tragedy of Central Europe'. *New York Review of Books*, 26 April 1984.

Laclau, Ernesto. *On Populist Reason*. Paperback edition. London: Verso, 2018.

LaLiga. 'Nota informativa. Informe de LaLiga sobre el Cádiz CF- Valencia CF', 9 April 2021. www.laliga.com/noticias/nota-informativa-cadiz-valenci.

Lass, Andrew. 'Romantic Documents and Political Monuments: The Meaning-Fulfillment of History in 19th-Century Czech Nationalism'. *American Ethnologist* 15, no. 3 (1988): 456–71. www.jstor.org/stable/645751.

Le Courrier d'Europe centrale. 'La part des travailleurs étrangers en République tchèque a triplé en une décennie'. Le Courrier d'Europe centrale, 4 February 2021. https://courrierdeuropecentrale.fr/la-part-des-travailleurs-etrangers-en-republique-tcheque-a-triple-en-une-decennie/.

Lemmen, Sarah. 'The "Return to Europe": Intellectual Debates on the Global Place of Czechoslovakia in the Interwar Period'. *European Review of History: Revue Européenne d'histoire* 23, no. 4 (2016): 610–22.

Lewicki, Aleksandra. 'The Christian Politics of Identity and the Making of Race in the German Welfare State'. *Sociology*, April 2021. https://doi.org/10.1177/00380385211008368.

Lewicki, Aleksandra. Forthcoming. 'East-West inequalities and the ambiguous racialization of 'Eastern Europeans'. *Journal of Ethnic and Migration Studies*.

Lewicki, Aleksandra, and Yasemin Shooman. 'Building a New Nation: Anti-Muslim Racism in Post-Unification Germany'. *Journal of Contemporary European Studies* 28, no. 1 (2 January 2020): 30–43. https://doi.org/10.1080/14782804.2019.1647515.

Liew, Jonathan. 'English Football Is Consumed by Racism and Hatred. Can the Cycle Be Broken?' *The Guardian*, 8 February 2021. www.theguardian.com/football/2021/feb/08/english-football-is-consumed-by-racism-and-hatred-can-the-cycle-be-broken.

Lisiewicz, Piotr. 'Lisiewicz: Niech rosyjscy i niemieccy piłkarze klęczą przed meczami, by przeprosić Polaków!' Niezależna, 2 April 2021. https://niezalezna.pl/388626-lisiewicz-niech-rosyjscy-i-niemieccy-pilkarze-klecza-przed-meczami-by-przeprosic-polakow.

Loužil, Jaromír. 'K zápasu o J. G. Herdera u nás'. *Česká literatura* 53, no. 5 (2005): 637–53. www.jstor.org/stable/42687091.

Loveman, Mara, and Jeronimo O. Muniz. 'How Puerto Rico Became White: Boundary Dynamics and Intercensus Racial Reclassification'. *American Sociological Review* 72, no. 6 (December 2007): 915–39. https://doi.org/10.1177/000312240707200604.

Lowe, Lisa. *Immigrant Acts: On Asian American Cultural Politics*. Durham, NC: Duke University Press, 1996.

Lowe, Sid. 'Valencia Walk Off against Cádiz after Diakhaby Accuses Cala of Racist Abuse'. *The Guardian*, 4 April 2021. www.theguardian.com/football/2021/apr/04/valencia-walk-off-against-cadiz-after-diakhaby-accuses-opponent-of-racist-abuse.

Lund, Susan, James Manyika, Jonathan Woetzel, Jacques Bughin, Mekala Krishnan, Jeongmin Seong, and Mac Muir. 'Globalization in Transition: The Future of Trade and Global Value Chains'. McKinsey & Company, 16 January 2019. www.mckinsey.com/featured-insights/innovation-and-growth/globalization-in-transition-the-future-of-trade-and-value-chains#.

Luptáková, Věra, and Zita Senková. 'Tomáš Halík: Kdo se bojí uprchlíků, není rasista a xenofob'. Dvojka, 18 May 2016. https://dvojka.rozhlas.cz/tomas-halik-kdo-se-boji-uprchliku-neni-rasista-a-xenofob-7466855.

Luxmoore, Jonathan. 'Church in Poland Continues Confrontation with the LGBTQ Community'. National Catholic Reporter, 19 August 2019. www.ncronline.org/news/justice/church-poland-continues-confrontation-lgbtq-community.

Maćków, Jerzy, ed. *Autoritarismus in Mittel- und Osteuropa*. 1. Aufl. Wiesbaden: VS, Verlag für Sozialwissenschaften, 2009.

Magyar Nemzet. 'Dárdai magyar segítője nem ért mindenben egyet Gulácsi véleményével', 5 April 2021. https://magyarnemzet.hu/sport/2021/04/dardai-magyar-segitoje-nem-ert-mindenben-egyet-gulacsi-velemenyevel.

Magyar Nemzet. 'Gergely Gulyás: A nemzet még az országnál is fontosabb', 4 June 2020. https://magyarnemzet.hu/belfold/gulyas-gergely-a-nemzet-meg-az-orszagnal-is-fontosabb-8199818/.

Magyar Nemzet. 'Milyen is valójában a Soros-féle kolbász?', 2 October 2020. https://magyarnemzet.hu/belfold/milyen-is-valojaban-a-soros-fele-kolbasz-8751048/.

Magyari Péter. 'Az orrunk előtt rövidítik meg Magyarországot'. 444.hu, 9 April 2021. https://444.hu/2021/04/09/az-orrunk-elott-rovidi tik-meg-magyarorszagot.

Magyari Péter. 'Orbán a kommunista-ellenes röpiratokból német-ellenes kormányzati propagandát faragott'. 444.hu, 30 June 2021. https://444.hu/2021/06/30/orban-a-kommunista-ellenes-ropiratok bol-nemet-ellenes-kormanyzati-propagandat-faragott.

Makk, Ferenc. *A turulmadártól a kettőskeresztig: tanulmányok a magyarság régebbi történelméről*. Szeged: Szegedi Középkorász Műhely, 1998.

Makkai, Laszlo. 'Neo-Serfdom: Its Origin and Nature in East Central Europe'. *Slavic Review* 34, no. 2 (1975): 225–38.

Makszimov, Vlagyiszlav. 'Romanian Football Captain Complains to UEFA about Racist Comments'. Euractiv, 30 March 2021. www.euractiv.com/section/politics/short_news/romanian-football-captain-complains-to-uefa-about-racist-comments/.

Mark, James, Bogdan C. Iacob, Tobias Rupprecht, and Ljubica Spaskovska. *1989: A Global History of Eastern Europe*. New Approaches to European History. Cambridge: Cambridge University Press, 2019.

Marx, Karl, and Friedrich Engels. *Marx and Engels Collected Works: 1864–68*. Moscow: Progress Publishers, 1987.

Maslova, Irina. 'Irina Maslova, Saint Petersburg'. Amnesty International, 8 June 2018. www.amnesty.org/en/latest/campaigns/2018/06/irina-maslova-human-rights-defender-in-russia/.

Mathia, Jozef. 'Ako zas spraviť zdravotníctvo atraktívne pre lekárov a sestry II? (8.časť)'. LinkedIn, 16 April 2021. www.linkedin.com/pulse/ako-zas-spravi%C5%A5-zdravotn%C3%ADctvo-atrakt%C3%ADvne-pre-lek%C3%A1rov-sestry-mathia-1f.

Mathiesen, Karl, and Kalina Oroschakoff. 'Leaving No One behind in the Green Deal'. POLITICO, 24 November 2020. www.politico.eu/article/european-green-deal-policy-guide-farmers-coal-decarbonization/.

Matovič Igor. 'Igor Matovič trianoni beszéde – Először magyar fordításban a Körképen'. Körkép.sk, 3 June 2020. https://korkep.sk/cikkek/szemle/igor-matovic-trianoni-beszede-eloszor-magyar-forditasban-a-korkepen/.

Mbembe, Achille. *Necropolitics*. Theory in Forms. Durham, NC: Duke University Press, 2019.

Mbembe, Achille. *On the Postcolony*. Berkeley: University of California Press, 2001.

McAuliffe, Marie, Binod Khadria, and Céline Bauloz. 'World Migration Report 2020'. Geneva: International Organization for Migration, 2019. https://publications.iom.int/system/files/pdf/wmr_2020.pdf.

Media Education Centre. 'Aphorisms'. Accessed 28 September 2021. www.mediaeducationcentre.eu/eng/?page_id=442.

Meer, Nasar, ed. *Whiteness and Nationalism*. Abingdon, Oxon: Routledge, 2021.

Menand, Louis. 'Francis Fukuyama Postpones the End of History', 27 August 2018. www.newyorker.com/magazine/2018/09/03/francis-fukuyama-postpones-the-end-of-history.

Meuleman, Elisabeth, Stijn Bex, and Imade Annouri. Voorstel van resolutie over het opnemen van de kolonisatie en het dekolonisatieproces in de eindtermen van het Vlaamse basis- en secundair onderwijs, Pub. L. No. 349 (2019–2020) nr. 1 (2020). www.vlaamsparlement.be/parlementaire-documenten/parlementaire-initiatieven/1397176.

Mičúch, Peter. 'Obrovská smola ho pripravila o veľkú futbalovú kariéru'. MY Považská, 16 March 2021. https://mypovazska.sme.sk/c/22618239/obrovska-smola-ho-pripravila-o-velku-futbalovu-karieru.html.

Ministerstvo zahraničních věcí České republiky. 'Počet českých krajanů v zahraničí'. Accessed 24 September 2021. www.mzv.cz/jnp/cz/zahranicni_vztahy/vyrocni_zpravy_a_dokumenty/poskytnute_informace/pocet_ceskych_krajanu_v_zahranici.html.

Modood, Tariq. *Essays on Secularism and Multiculturalism*. London; New York: Rowman & Littlefield International Ltd, 2019.

Moeller van den Bruck, Arthur. 'Schicksal Ist Stärker Als Staatskunst'. *Deutsche Rundschau*, no. 169. Band. October–December (1916).

Moffitt, Benjamin. *Populism*. Key Concepts in Political Theory. Medford, MA: Polity Press, 2020.

Moïsi, Dominique. 'Racisme et violences policières: la France n'est pas l'Amérique'. *Institut Montaigne* (blog), 29 June 2020. www.institutmontaigne.org/blog/racisme-et-violences-policieres-la-france-nest-pas-lamerique.

Moláček, Jan. 'Česko si zvolilo šanci. Povinností politiků je nezahodit ji'. Deník N, 9 October 2021. https://denikn.cz/722978/cesko-si-zvolilo-sanci-povinnosti-politiku-je-nezahodit-ji/

Mondon, Aurelien, and Aaron Winter. 'Whiteness, Populism and the Racialisation of the Working Class in the United Kingdom and the United States'. *Identities* 26, no. 5 (3 September 2019): 510–28. https://doi.org/10.1080/1070289X.2018.1552440.

Mondon, Aurelien, and Aaron Winter. *Reactionary Democracy: How Racism and the Populist Far Right Became Mainstream*. Brooklyn, NY: Verso Books, 2020.

Mondon, Aurelien, and Aaron Winter. *Reactionary Democracy: How Racism and the Populist Far Right Became Mainstream*. Brooklyn, NY: Verso Books, 2020.

Montalbano, Giuseppe. 'Geopolitical Economy and Competing Capitalist Blocs in the EU Post-Crisis Financial Regulation: Two Cases from the Reform of the Banking Sector'. *World Review of Political Economy* 6, no. 4 (2015): 498–521. https://doi.org/10.13169/worlrevipoliecon.6.4.0498.

Morawski, Andrea, and Paolo Morawski. *Polonia mon amour: dalle Indie d'Europa alle Indie d'America*. Rome: Ediesse, 2006.

Moreh, Chris. 'The Asianization of National Fantasies in Hungary: A Critical Analysis of Political Discourse'. *International Journal of Cultural Studies* 19, no. 3 (May 2016): 341–53. https://doi.org/10.1177/1367877915573781.

Moroşanu, Laura, and Jon E. Fox. '"No Smoke without Fire": Strategies of Coping with Stigmatised Migrant Identities'. *Ethnicities* 13, no. 4 (2013): 438–56. https://doi.org/10.1177/1468796813483730.

Morvai, Krisztina. 'Krisztina Morvai (Jobbik, NI): Hungary Is Not a Colony'. Jobbik.com, 21 January 2014. http://jobbik.com/krisztina_morvai_jobbik_ni_hungary_is_not_a_colony.

Moskalewicz, Marcin, and Wojciech Przybylski. 'Making Sense of Central Europe: Political Concepts of the Region'. In *Understanding Central Europe*, edited by Marcin Moskalewicz and Wojciech Przybylski, 1–22. London; New York: Routledge, 2017.

Mozart, Wolfgang Amadeus. *Briefe*. Edited by Horst Wandrey. Neuausg. Diogenes-Taschenbuch 21610. Zürich: Diogenes-Verl, 1997.

Mudde, Cas, and Cristóbal Rovira Kaltwasser, eds. *Populism in Europe and the Americas: Threat or Corrective for Democracy?* Cambridge; New York: Cambridge University Press, 2012.

Müller, Jan-Werner. *What Is Populism?* Philadelphia: University of Pennsylvania Press, 2016.

Murphy, Francois. 'Austria's Kurz Steps Down Over Corruption Probe to Save Coalition'. Reuters, 10 October 2021. www.reuters.com/world/europe/austrias-kurz-says-stepping-down-chancellor-2021-10-09/

Mynář, Vratislav. 'Dopis disciplinární komisi UEFA'. Pražský hrad, 15 April 2021. www.hrad.cz/cs/pro-media/tiskove-zpravy/aktualni-tiskove-zpravy/dopis-disciplinarni-komisi-uefa-15891.

Nádoba, Jiří. '"Kolonie Bruselu"? Babiš usvědčuje ze střetu zájmů sám sebe'. Respekt, 24 April 2021. www.respekt.cz/komentare/kolonie-bruselu-babis-usvedcuje-ze-stretu-zajmu-sam-sebe.

Nagy, Gábor. 'Orbán: Közép-Európa működik, Nyugat-Európa kudarcot vallott'. 888.hu, 3 January 2018. https://888.hu/ketharmad/orban-kozep-europa-mukodik-nyugat-europa-kudarcot-vallott-4130062/.

Namier, Lewis Bernstein. *Germany and Eastern Europe*. London: Duckworth & Co, 1915.

Narkowicz, Kasia. 'Janion, Maria'. *Global Social Theory* (blog). Accessed 1 October 2021. https://globalsocialtheory.org/thinkers/janion-maria/.

Narkowicz, Kasia. 'White Enough, Not White Enough: Racism and Racialization among Poles in the UK'. *Journal of Ethnic and Migration Studies*, Forthcoming.

Naumann, Friedrich. *Central Europe*. London: P.S. King & Son, 1916.

Naumann, Friedrich. *Mitteleuropa*. Berlin: G. Reimer, 1916.

Népszava. 'Orbán Viktor tananyag lett! – Bekerült a történelemkönyvbe', 2 September 2016. https://nepszava.hu/1104821_orban-viktor-tananyag-lett-bekerult-a-tortenelemkonyvbe.

nextQuotidiano. 'Ma Salvini e Meloni che difendono Viktor Orbán sono gli stessi che accusano Conte "uomo solo al comando"?', 31 March 2020. www.nextquotidiano.it/salvini-e-meloni-che-difendono-viktor-orban-accusano-conte-uomo-solo-al-comando/.

Niček, Marie. 'Nespadám už do kategorie ,z Východu', nemusím tak ztvárňovat jen prostitutky, říká herečka Babišová'. Lidovky.cz, 29 October 2020. www.lidovky.cz/lide/nespadam-uz-do-kategorie-z-vychodu-nemusim-tak-ztvarnovat-jen-prostitutky-rika-herecka-babisova.A201028_180441_lide_rkj.

Novák Miklós. 'Visegrádi gimnasztika: csak semmi térdeplés!' Magyar Nemzet, 1 April 2021. https://magyarnemzet.hu/sport/visegradi-gimnasztika-csak-semmi-terdeples-9600839/.

Office for National Statistics. 'Median Full-Time Gross Weekly Earnings and Percentage Change from Previous Year, by Region,

UK, April 2018'. Accessed 10 September 2021. www.ons.gov.uk/ file?uri=/employmentandlabourmarket/peopleinwork/earnings andworkinghours/bulletins/annualsurveyofhoursandearnings/2018/ c794315d.xlsx.

Okamura, Tomio. '"Češi na členství v EU prodělali nejvíc a jsou poraženým národem", říká jasně světoznámý francouzský ekonom Thomas Piketty.' Facebook, 10 January 2021. www.facebook.com/ tomio.cz/posts/3632401420103980.

Okey, Robin. *Eastern Europe 1740–1985: Feudalism to Communism.* Vol. 47. University of Minnesota Press, 1986.

Orbán, Viktor. 'Orbán Viktor beszéde a XXVIII. Bálványosi Nyári Szabadegyetem és Diáktáborban'. Magyarország Kormánya, 22 July 2017. https://2015-2019.kormany.hu/hu/a-miniszterelnok/beszedek-publikaciok-interjuk/orban-viktor-beszede-a-xxviii-balvanyosi-nyari-szabadegyetem-es-diaktaborban.

Orbán, Viktor. 'Orbán Viktor beszéde a XXVIII. Bálványosi Nyári Szabadegyetem és Diáktáborban'. Magyarország Kormánya, 22 July 2017. https://2015-2019.kormany.hu/hu/a-miniszterelnok/beszedek-publikaciok-interjuk/orban-viktor-beszede-a-xxviii-balvanyosi-nyari-szabadegyetem-es-diaktaborban.

Orbán, Viktor. 'Orbán Viktor beszéde Nagy Imre és mártírtársai újratemetésén'. Magyar Nemzet, 16 June 2014. https://web.archive.org/web/20171207125017/https://mno.hu/belfold/orban_viktor_beszede_nagy_imre_es_martirtarsai_ujratemetesen-320290.

Orbán, Viktor. 'Orbán Viktor sajtónyilatkozata Mateusz Morawieckivel, Lengyelország miniszterelnökével és Matteo Salvinivel, az olasz kormánypárt elnökével történt tárgyalását követően'. Miniszterelnok.hu, 1 April 2021. www.miniszterelnok.hu/orban-viktor-sajtonyilatkozata-mateuszmorawieckivel-lengyelorszag-miniszterelnokevel-es-matteo-salvinivelaz-olasz-kormanypart-elnokevel-tortent-targyalasat-kovetoen/.

Orbán, Viktor. 'Orbán Viktor'. Facebook. Accessed 31 August 2021. www.facebook.com/orbanviktor.

Orbán, Viktor. 'Due Fratelli. Találkozó Giorgia Melonival'. Facebook, 28 August 2021. www.facebook.com/orbanviktor/posts/ 384108886420049?comment_id=577881210076046.

Orbán, Viktor. 'Közép-Európa lesz Európa jövője'. Miniszterelnok. hu, 17 November 2019. www.miniszterelnok.hu/kozep-europalesz-europa-jovoje/.

Orbán, Viktor. 'Full Text of Viktor Orbán's Speech at Băile Tuşnad (Tusnádfürdő) of 26 July 2014'. The Budapest Beacon, 29 July 2014. https://budapestbeacon.com/full-text-of-viktor-orbans-speech-atbaile-tusnad-tusnadfurdo-of-26-july-2014/.

Orbán, Viktor. 'Orban's Great Speech – a Must Read for Every European – 15 March 2016'. Rumeli Observer, 7 October 2016. www.esiweb.org/rumeliobserver/2016/10/07/orbans-great-speech-a-must-read-for-every-european-15-march-2016/.

Orbán, Viktor. 'Reply to Martin Schulz from Prime Minister Viktor Orbán'. Miniszterelnok.hu, 30 November 2020. https://miniszterelnok.hu/reply-to-martin-schulz-from-prime-minister-viktor-orban/.

Ortová, Jitka. *Julius Payer: Z Čech až k severnímu pólu*. Liberec: Severočeské nakladatelství, 1976.

Özyürek, Esra. 'Subcontracting Guilt: Muslim Minority and Holocaust Memory in Germany'. Lecture, Institute of Islamic Studies, Berlin, 5 February 2020.

Pachoński, Jan, and Reuel K. Wilson. *Poland's Caribbean Tragedy: A Study of Polish Legions in the Haitian War of Independence, 1802–1803*. Boulder, CO; New York: Columbia University Press, 1986.

Palacký, František. *Gedenkblätter. Auswahl von Denkschriften, Aufsätzen und Briefen aus den letzten fünfzig Jahren. Als Beitrag zur Zeitgeschichte*. Prague: FTempsky, 1874.

Palacký, František. 'Palacky's Famous Letter to the Frankfurt Parliament'. Age of the Sage. Accessed 21 September 2021. www.age-of-the-sage.org/history/1848/palacky_letter.html.

Palmer, R. R, and Joel Coulton. 'The Transformation of Eastern Europe, 1648–1740'. In *History of the Modern World*. New York: Alfred A. Knopf, 1965.

'Pandora Papers: Biggest Ever Leak of Offshore Data Exposes Financial Secrets of Rich and Powerful'. *The Guardian*, 3 October 2021. www.theguardian.com/news/2021/oct/03/pandora-papers-biggest-ever-leak-of-offshore-data-exposes-financial-secrets-of-rich-and-powerful

Parvulescu, Anca. 'European Racial Triangulation'. In *Postcolonial Transitions in Europe: Contexts, Practices and Politics*, edited by Sandra Ponzanesi and Gianmaria Colpani, 25–46. Frontiers of the Political. London; New York: Rowman & Littlefield International, 2016.

Pawłowska, Danuta, and Stanisław Dudzik. 'Wybory 2019. Rolnicy za PiS, kierownicy za KO. Wykształcenie i zawody wyborców'. *Gazeta Wyborcza*, 14 October 2019. https://wyborcza.pl/7,75398,25306309,rolnicy-za-pisem-kierownicy-za-ko-wyksztalcenie-i-zawody-wyborcow.html.

Pędziwiatr, Konrad. 'Imigranci w Polsce i wyzwania integracyjne'. *Infos zagadnienia społecznogospodarcze* 15, no. 1 (2015): 1–4.

Pędziwiatr, Konrad. 'The Catholic Church in Poland on Muslims and Islam'. *Patterns of Prejudice* 52, no. 5 (20 October 2018): 461–78. https://doi.org/10.1080/0031322X.2018.1495376.

Pędziwiatr, Konrad. 'Islamophobia in Poland. National Report 2016'. In *European Islamophobia Report 2016*, edited by Enes Bayrakli and Farid Hafez, 411–42. Ankara: SETA, 2017. www.islamophobiaeurope.com/wp-content/uploads/2017/03/EIR_2016.pdf.

Peschel, Andreas. *Friedrich Naumanns und Max Webers 'Mitteleuropa': eine Betrachtung ihrer Konzeptionen im Kontext mit den 'Ideen von 1914' und dem Alldeutschen Verband*. Dresden: TUD Press, 2005.

Pethő, András, and Szabó Szabó. 'Feltárul Simicska bukásának titkos története'. 444.hu, 13 January 2019. https://444.hu/2019/01/13/feltarul-simicska-bukasanak-titkos-tortenete.

Pető, Andrea. 'Feminist Stories from an Illiberal State: Revoking the License to Teach Gender Studies in Hungary at a University in Exile (CEU)'. In *Gender and Power in Eastern Europe*, edited by Katharina Bluhm, Gertrud Pickhan, Justyna Stypinska, and Agnieszka Wierzcholska, 35–44. Cham: Springer International Publishing, 2021.

Pew Research Center. 'Eastern and Western Europeans Differ on Importance of Religion, Views of Minorities, and Key Social Issues', 29 October 2018. www.pewforum.org/wp-content/uploads/sites/7/2018/10/Eastern-Western-Europe-FOR-WEB.pdf.

Pew Research Center. 'Eastern Europeans Are More Likely to Regard Their Culture as Superior to Others', 24 October 2018. www.pewforum.org/wp-content/uploads/sites/7/2018/10/PF.10.29.18_east.west_-00-03-.png.

Pieiller, Evelyne. 'Hungary Looks to the Past for Its Future'. Le Monde diplomatique, 1 November 2016. https://mondediplo.com/2016/11/10Hungary.

Piketty, Thomas. '2018, the Year of Europe'. *Le Monde* (blog), 16 January 2018. www.lemonde.fr/blog/piketty/2018/01/16/2018-the-year-of-europe/.

Piketty, Thomas. *Capital and Ideology*. Translated by Arthur Goldhammer. Cambridge, MA: Harvard University Press, 2020.

Piketty, Thomas. *Capital in the Twenty-First Century*. Translated by Arthur Goldhammer. Cambridge, MA: The Belknap Press of Harvard University Press, 2014.

Pithart, Petr. '"Tak co, Václave, rozhodni se konečně!" Havel chtěl v Česku volit jako v Americe, ale poddal se, vzpomíná Pithart'. Deník N, 17 November 2020, sec. Kontext N. https://denikn.cz/495018/pithart-proti-ceskemu-trumpovi-imunitu-nemame/.

Polskie Radio 24. 'Jan Tomaszewski o Klękaniu Przed Meczem: Piłkarze Reprezentują Polskę, Nas Ta Sprawa Nie Dotyczy'. PolskieRadio24.pl, 2021. https://polskieradio24.pl/art5925_2707921.

Popa, Bogdan. 'Ethnicity as a category of imperial racialization: What do race and empire studies offer to Romanian studies?' *Ethnicities* 21, no. 4 (2021):751-68.

Populism in Central and Eastern Europe. 'Populism in Central and Eastern Europe: FATIGUE and POPREBEL'. Accessed 10 September 2021. https://populism-europe.com.

Prague Morning. 'President Zeman Calls "Black Lives Matter" Slogan Racist', 1 July 2020. https://praguemorning.cz/president-zeman-calls-black-lives-matter-slogan-racist/.

Prague Morning. 'Czech Football Players Refused to Kneel for BLM Before Match with Wales', 2 April 2021. https://praguemorning.cz/czech-football-players-refused-to-kneel-for-blm-before-match-with-wales/.

Pravda.sk. 'Prieskum: Slováci odmietajú prijať utečencov, vidia v nich hrozbu', 17 June 2015. https://spravy.pravda.sk/domace/clanok/358731-slovensko-by-nemalo-prijat-utecencov-mysli-si-70-percent-respondentov/.

Přeučil, Pavel. 'Rasismus je svinstvo, ať už má podobu bílou, nebo černou. A ten černý současný 'rasismus naruby' může mít katastrofální důsledky'. Krajské listy, 14 April 2021. www.krajskelisty.cz/stredocesky-kraj/25521-rasismus-je-svinstvo-at-uz-ma-podobu-bilou-nebo-cernou-a-ten-cerny-soucasny-rasismus-naruby-muze-mit-katastrofalni-dusledky-streda-pavla-preucila.htm.

Procházka, Theodore. *The Second Republic: The Disintegration of Post-Munich Czechoslovakia, October 1938–March 1939*. East European Monographs, no. 90. Boulder, CO; New York: East European Monographs. Distributed by Columbia University Press, 1981.

Prokop, Daniel. 'Proč podle nesmíme zapomínat na pracoviště?' Twitter, 24 February 2021. https://twitter.com/dan_prokop/status/1364589470440431616?s=20.

Quora. 'What Are Eastern European Facial Features?' Accessed 16 September 2021. www.quora.com/What-are-Eastern-European-facial-features.

Radio Prague International. 'Zeman Describes Orban as "Genuine Leader" in Message of Congratulations', 9 April 2014. https://english.radio.cz/zeman-describes-orban-genuine-leader-message-congratulations-8299121.

Rádl, Emanuel. *Válka Čechů s Němci*. Prague: Čin, 1928.

Rapoport, Louis. *Stalin's War against the Jews: The Doctors' Plot and the Soviet Solution*. The Second Thoughts Series. New York: Free Press, 1990.

Renton, James, and Ben Gidley, eds. *Antisemitism and Islamophobia in Europe: A Shared Story?* London: Palgrave Macmillan, 2017.

Rényi, Pál Dániel. *Győzelmi kényszer: futball és hatalom Orbán világában.* Budapest: Magyar Jeti Zrt, 2021.

Reporters Without Borders. '2021 World Press Freedom Index', 2021. https://rsf.org/en/ranking.

Rieboldt, Mona. 'Entvolkt!' *ortner online* (blog), 30 June 2016. www.ortneronline.at/entvolkt/.

Roe, Joseph Wickham. 'Review of *Central Europe*, by Friedrich Naumann'. *Journal of Political Economy* 25, no. 2 (1917): 213–14. www.jstor.org/stable/1819728.

Ross, Alex. 'The Schorske Century'. *The New Yorker*, 28 September 2015. www.newyorker.com/culture/cultural-comment/the-schorske-century.

Rupnik, Jacques. 'Eastern Europe a Decade Later: The Postcommunist Divide'. *Journal of Democracy* 10, no. 1 (1 January 1999): 57–62. https://doi.org/10.1353/jod.1999.0016.

Rupnik, Jacques. 'The Crisis of Liberalism'. *Journal of Democracy* 29, no. 3 (2018): 24–38. https://doi.org/10.1353/jod.2018.0042.

Rzepnikowska, Alina. 'Racism and Xenophobia Experienced by Polish Migrants in the UK before and after Brexit Vote'. *Journal of Ethnic and Migration Studies* 45, no. 1 (2 January 2019): 61–77. https://doi.org/10.1080/1369183X.2018.1451308.

Said, Edward. *Orientalism.* New York: Vintage Books, 1978.

Salner, Peter. 'Ethnic Polarisation in an Ethnically Homogenous Town'. *Czech Sociological Review* 9, no. 2 (2001): 235–46. www.jstor.org/stable/41133186.

Sanfourche, Philippe, and Victor Goury-Laffont. 'PSG-OM: Neymar, Alvaro, Sakai … Que sait-on des incidents?' RTL, 2020. www.rtl.fr/sport/football/psg-om-neymar-alvaro-sakai-que-sait-on-des-incidents-lors-de-cette-rencontre-7800826829.

Santora, Marc. 'In Poland, Nationalism with a Progressive Touch Wins Voters'. *The New York Times*, 10 October 2019, sec. World. www.nytimes.com/2019/10/10/world/europe/poland-election-law-and-justice-party.html.

Santora, Marc, and Joanna Berendt. 'For Poland, Nobel Prize in Literature Is Cause for Conflict as Much as Congratulation'. *The New York Times*, 10 October 2019, sec. World. www.nytimes.com/2019/10/10/world/europe/for-poland-nobel-prize-in-literature-is-cause-for-conflict-as-much-as-congratulation.html.

Sargeson, Robin. 'More Footballers Stop Taking the Knee'. CBJSpotlight. Accessed 14 September 2021. https://cbjspotlight.co.uk/2021/03/16/more-footballers-stop-taking-the-knee/.

Sarkadi, Zsolt. '100 felvidéki magyart hívott trianoni megemlékezésre a szlovák miniszterelnök a pozsonyi várba'. 444.hu, 31 May 2020. https://444.hu/2020/05/31/100-felvideki-magyart-hivott-trianoni-megemlekezesre-a-szlovak-miniszterelnok-a-pozsonyi-varba.

Sarkadi, Zsolt. 'Magyarország megint megakadályozta, hogy az EU elítélje Kínát a hongkongi események miatt'. 444.hu, 6 May 2021. https://444.hu/2021/05/06/magyarorszag-megint-megakadalyozta-hogy-az-eu-elitelje-kinat-a-hongkongi-esemenyek-miatt.

Sarnyai, Gábor. 'Schmidt: Western Countries Want to "Civilize" Central Europe in a Colonial Fashion'. Hungary Today, 18 October 2018. https://hungarytoday.hu/schmidt-western-countries-want-to-civilize-central-europe-in-a-colonial-fashion/.

Sayyid, S. 'Islamophobia and the Europeanness of the Other Europe'. *Patterns of Prejudice* 52, no. 5 (20 October 2018): 420–35. https://doi.org/10.1080/0031322X.2018.1512481.

Scheffel, David Z., and Alexander Mušinka. '"Third-class" Slovak Roma and Inclusion: Bricoleurs vs Social Engineers'. *Anthropology Today* 35, no. 1 (2019): 17–21. https://doi.org/10.1111/1467-8322.12483.

Schenk, Dieter. *Auf Dem Rechten Auge Blind: Die Braunen Wurzeln Des BKA*. 1. Aufl. Köln: Kiepenheuer & Witsch, 2001.

Schneider, J. *Italy's 'Southern Question:' Orientalism in One Country*. Oxford; New York: Berg, 1998.

Schorske, Carl E. *Fin-de-Siècle Vienna: Politics and Culture*. London: Weidenfeld and Nicolson, 1979.

Schulze, Max-Stephan. *Engineering and Economic Growth: The Development of Austria-Hungary's Machine-Building Industry in the Late Nineteenth Century*. Forschungen Zur Wirtschafts-, Finanz- Und Sozialgeschichte, Bd. 3. Frankfurt am Main; New York: P. Lang, 1996.

Schutz, Peter. 'Kollárov sabatical je sabotážou na chod štátu (týždeň podľa Schutza)'. SME.sk, 25 March 2021. https://komentare.sme.sk/c/22625356/absolutny-lucifer-sabatical-s-kollarom-a-uzky-profil-ivermektin.html.

Schwaner, Wilhelm. 'Das Alte Und Das Neue Deutschland'. *Der Volkserzieher*, September 1914.

Scott, Corrie. 'How French Canadians Became White Folks, or Doing Things with Race in Quebec'. *Ethnic and Racial Studies* 39, no. 7 (27 May 2016): 1280–97. https://doi.org/10.1080/01419870.2015.1103880.

Senna, Danzy. 'White Progressives in Pursuit of Racial Virtue: What Two New Books Reveal About the Moral Limits of Anti-Racist Self-Help'. *The Atlantic*, September 2021, 90–93.

Shekhovtsov, Anton. 'Putin's Brain?' *New Eastern Europe*, no. 4 (13) (2014): 72–79.

Shekhovtsov, Anton. *Russia and the Western Far Right: Tango Noir*. Studies in Fascism and the Far Right. Abingdon, Oxon; New York: Routledge, 2017.

Shmidt, Victoria. 'Public Health as an Agent of Internal Colonialism in Interwar Czechoslovakia: Shaping the Discourse about the Nation's Children'. *Patterns of Prejudice* 52, no. 4 (2018): 355–87.

Shmidt, Victoria, and Bernadette Nadya Jaworsky. *Historicizing Roma in Central Europe: Between Critical Whiteness and Epistemic Injustice*. London: Routledge, 2020.

Shoshan, Nitzan. *The Management of Hate: Nation, Affect, and the Governance of Right-Wing Extremism in Germany*. Princeton, NJ: Princeton University Press, 2016.

Slačálek, Ondřej. 'The Postcolonial Hypothesis. Notes on the Czech "Central European" Identity'. *ALPPI Annual of Language & Politics and Politics of Identity* 10 (2016): 27–44.

Smith, Zadie. *Intimations: Six Essays*. Hamish Hamilton: Penguin Random House, 2020.

Snochowska-Gonzalez, Claudia. 'Post-Colonial Poland—On an Unavoidable Misuse'. *East European Politics and Societies* 26, no. 4 (1 November 2012): 708–23. https://doi.org/10.1177/0888325412448473.

Snyder, Timothy. *The Road to Unfreedom: Russia, Europe, America*. First paperback edition. New York: Tim Duggan Books, 2018.

Solzhenitsyn, Alexandr. 'A World Split Apart. Harvard Address'. American Rhetoric, 8 June 1978. www.americanrhetoric.com/speeches/alexandersolzhenitsynharvard.htm.

Sommaruga, Carlo. 'Sklaverei und Kolonialismus. Hat der Bundesrat nichts gelernt?'. Pub. L. No. 18.4067 (2018). www.parlament.ch/de/ratsbetrieb/suche-curia-vista/geschaeft?AffairId=20184067.

Sosnowski, Jerzy. 'W pustyni, w puszczy oraz na manowcach'. *Więź*, 8 June 2020. https://wiez.pl/2020/06/08/w-pustyni-w-puszczy-oraz-na-manowcach/.

Sowa, Jan. 'Forget Postcolonialism, There's a Class War Ahead'. *Nonsite.Org*, no. 12 (12 August 2014). https://nonsite.org/article/forget-postcolonialism-theres-a-class-war-ahead.

Spike, Justin. 'More than 600,000 Hungarians Could Be Living in Other EU Countries'. The Budapest Beacon, 1 September 2017. https://budapestbeacon.com/600000-hungarians-living-eu-countries/.

Sportnet. 'Slovan spoznal trest za transparent o bielych životoch', 17 July 2020. https://sportnet.sme.sk/spravy/slovan-bratislava-dostal-za-white-lives-matter-pokutu/.

Springer, Simon. 'Fuck Neoliberalism'. *ACME: An International Journal for Critical Geographies* 15, no. 2 (7 July 2016): 285–92. www.acme-journal.org/index.php/acme/article/view/1342.

Stanley, Ben. 'The Thin Ideology of Populism'. *Journal of Political Ideologies* 13, no. 1 (February 2008): 95–110. https://doi.org/10.1080/13569310701822289.

Stanley, Ben. 'Defenders of the Cross: Populist Politics and Religion in Post-Communist Poland'. *Saving the People*, 2016: 109–28.

Štatistický úrad Slovenskej republiky. 'Mzdy podľa ekonomickej činnosti zistené pracoviskovou metódou'. Accessed 10 September 2021. http://datacube.statistics.sk/#!/view/sk/VBD_SK_WIN/np3110rr/v_np3110rr_00_00_00_sk.

Štechrová, Věra, and Anna Urbanová. 'Od Kúdely to byla obrovská taktická chyba. V Británii jsou na rasismus hypercitliví, míní Hošek'. iROZHLAS, 19 March 2021. www.irozhlas.cz/sport/fotbal/fotbalovy-zapas-slavia-praha-glasgow-rangers-skotsko-nasili-hosek_2103191424_aur.

Steiner, Rudolf. *Mitteleuropa zwischen Ost und West. Zwölf Vorträge, gehalten in München zwischen dem 13. September und 1914 und dem 4. Mai 1918*. Dornach: Rudolf Steiner Verlag, 1982.

Stevens, Zachary. 'Arsenal Kick Slavia Prague and Racism out of Europa League'. Pain in the Arsenal, April 2021. https://paininthearsenal.com/2021/04/16/arsenal-kick-racism-slavia-prague/.

Stoker, Bram, and Maurice Hindle. *Dracula*. London: Penguin, 1993.

Stola, Dariusz. *Kampania antysyjonistyczna w Polsce 1967–1968*. Warszawa: Instytut Studiów Politycznych Polskiej Akademii Nauk, 2000.

'Střední Evropa a učitelstvo'. *Naše Doba* 23 (1 January 1916): 638. http://search.proquest.com/docview/1347989311?pq-origsite=summon.

Sundhaussen, Holm. *Der Einfluss der Herderschen Ideen auf die Nationsbildung bei den Völkern der Habsburger Monarchie*. Buchreihe der Südostdeutschen Historischen Kommission, Bd. 27. Munich: Oldenbourg, 1973.

Švec, Róbert. 'Švédsky predseda vlády sa pred samitom v Salzburgu vyjadril, že bude trvať na tom, aby všetky členské štáty EÚ prijali migrantov'. Facebook, 27 September 2018. www.facebook.com/robertsvecsho/posts/10156056708017462.

Švihlíková, Ilona. *Jak jsme se stali kolonií*. Prague: Rybka Publishers, 2015.

Sweet, James H. 'The Iberian Roots of American Racist Thought'. *The William and Mary Quarterly* 54, no. 1 (January 1997): 143. https://doi.org/10.2307/2953315.

Switzer, Terri. 'Nationalism and the Myth of Hungarian Origin: Attila and Árpád'. In *A Companion to Nineteenth-Century Art*, edited by Michelle Facos, 371–90. Hoboken, NJ: John Wiley & Sons, Inc., 2018.

Szałańska, Justyna. 'Uneasy Mission of NGOs in Protection and Reception of Asylum Seekers and Refugees in Poland. Reflections from Fieldwork'. RESPOND, 30 October 2019. https://respondmigration.com/blog-1/mission-ngos-protection-reception-asylum-seekers-refugees-poland.

Szelényi, Iván. 'Weber's Theory of Domination and Post-Communist Capitalisms'. *Theory and Society* 45, no. 1 (2016): 1–24.

Szikra, Dorottya. 'Interpreting Social Policy Change Under the "System of National Cooperation"'. In *Brave New Hungary: Mapping the 'System of National Cooperation'*, edited by János Mátyás Kovács and Balázs Trencsényi, 225–41. Lanham, MD: Lexington Books, 2020.

Tablet Magazine. 'The Worst Choice for "Greatest Slovak"', 6 November 2018. www.tabletmag.com/sections/news/articles/the-worst-choice-for-greatest-slovak.

Tacconi, Matteo. 'Kaczynski's Poland vs Europe. An Interview with Paolo Morawski'. *ResetDOC* (blog), 19 July 2017. www.resetdoc.org/story/kaczynskis-poland-vs-europe-interview-paolo-morawski/.

Tansel, Cemal Burak, ed. *States of Discipline: Authoritarian Neoliberalism and the Contested Reproduction of Capitalist Order*. Transforming Capitalism. London; New York: Rowman & Littlefield International, 2017.

Tarant, Zbyněk. *Czech Antisemitic Movements towards the Muslim World*. ISGAP. JBS, 2016. www.youtube.com/watch?v=E6xrOn1E_eM.

Taylor, Simon. 'Orbán Accuses EU of Colonialism'. POLITICO, 16 March 2012. www.politico.eu/article/orban-accuses-eu-of-colonialism/.

The New York Times. 'Free Vote Demanded for Subject Peoples', 26 October 1918.

The News. 'Slovakia's Ex-Police Chief Commits Suicide in Custody', 1 January 2021. www.thenews.com.pk/print/767563-slovakia-s-ex-police-chief-commits-suicide-in-custody.

The Slovak Spectator. 'A Canadian Professor Accused of Sexual Abuse Gets 7 Years in Slovak Prison', 19 June 2019. https://spectator.sme.sk/c/22148979/canadian-professor-david-scheffel-accused-of-sexual-abuse-gets-7-years-in-slovak-prison.html.

The Slovak Spectator. 'Slovakia Summoned Belgian Ambassador, Discussing the Slovak Citizen's Death in Belgium', 7 September 2020. https://spectator.sme.sk/c/22480687/jozef-chovanec-died-in-belgium-slovakia-responds-asking-for-proper-investigation.html.

Ther, Philipp. *Europe since 1989: A History*. Princeton, NJ: Princeton University Press, 2016.

Thompson, Ewa. 'A Jednak Kolonializm. Uwagi Epistemologiczne'. *Teksty*, no. 6 (2011): 289–302.

Tilles, Daniel. 'LGBT "Ideology Weakens the West and Terrorises People", Warns Polish Leader Kaczyński'. Notes From Poland, 2 April 2021. https://notesfrompoland.com/2021/04/02/lgbt-ideology-weakens-the-west-and-terrorises-people-warns-polish-leader-kaczynski/.

Todorova, Maria. 'The Balkans: From Discovery to Invention'. *Slavic Review* 53, no. 2 (1994): 453–82. https://doi.org/10.2307/2501301.

Todorova, Maria. *Imagining the Balkans*. Oxford; New York: Oxford University Press, 2009.

Toplišek, Alen. 'The Political Economy of Populist Rule in Post-Crisis Europe: Hungary and Poland'. *New Political Economy* 25, no. 3 (15 April 2020): 388–403. https://doi.org/10.1080/13563467.2019.1598960.

Trading Economics. 'Capital Flows'. Accessed 10 September 2021. https://tradingeconomics.com/country-list/capital-flows.

Transparency International. 'Corruption Perceptions Index 2020', 2020. www.transparency.org/en/cpi/2020.

Tuček, Milan. 'Vztah české veřejnosti k národnostním skupinám žijícím v ČR–březen 2017'. Centrum pro výzkum veřejného mínění, 2017. https://cvvm.soc.cas.cz/media/com_form2content/documents/c2/a4284/f9/ov170425.pdf.

Turda, Marius, ed. *The History of East-Central European Eugenics, 1900–1945: Sources and Commentaries*. London; New York: Bloomsbury Academic, 2015.

TVP Sport. 'Liga Narodów: rasizm i race. UEFA ukarała Polskę', 24 September 2018. https://sport.tvp.pl/39156896/liga-narodow-polska-ukarana-przez-uefa-rasizm-race.

U.S. Bureau of Labor Statistics. 'Quarterly Census of Employment and Wages'. Accessed 10 September 2021. https://data.bls.gov/cew/apps/table_maker/v4/table_maker.htm#type=2&st=28&year=2018&qtr=A&own=0&ind=10&supp=0.

Új, Péter. '444.Hu Blog', 17 February 2021.

UNAIDS. 'Key Populations Atlas'. Accessed 10 September 2021. https://kpatlas.unaids.org/dashboard.

United Nations Development Programme. 'Human Development Report 2020. The next Frontier. Human Development and the Anthropocene'. New York, 2020. http://hdr.undp.org/sites/default/files/hdr2020.pdf.

United Nations Development Programme. 'Human Development Index (HDI) | Human Development Reports'. Accessed 10 September 2021. http://hdr.undp.org/en/content/human-development-index-hdi.

Varga, Judit. 'No Power Grab in Hungary'. POLITICO, 27 March 2020. www.politico.eu/article/coronavirus-hungary-no-power-grab/.

Varoufakis, Yanis. 'Techno-Feudalism Is Taking Over'. Project Syndicate, 28 June 2021. www.project-syndicate.org/commentary/techno-feudalism-replacing-market-capitalism-by-yanis-varoufakis-2021-06.

Varoufakis, Yanis. *And the Weak Suffer What They Must? Europe's Crisis and America's Economic Future.* New York: Nation Books, 2016.

V-Dem Institute. 'Autocratization Turns Viral. Democracy Report 2021'. Gothenburg, Sweden, 2021.

Vermeiren, Jan. *The First World War and German National Identity: The Dual Alliance at War.* Cambridge: Cambridge University Press, 2016.

Virdee, Satnam. 'Racialized Capitalism: An Account of Its Contested Origins and Consolidation'. *The Sociological Review* 67, no. 1 (January 2019): 3–27. https://doi.org/10.1177/0038026118820293.

Visegrad Group. 'Visegrad Declarations'. (C) 2006–2010, International Visegrad Fund. Accessed 19 August 2021. www.visegradgroup.eu/documents/visegrad-declarations.

Wachtel, Eleanor. 'Zadie Smith's Latest Book, Intimations, Reflects Deeply on Isolation and Injustice'. Writers and Company. Accessed 16 September 2021. www.cbc.ca/radio/writersandcompany/zadie-smith-s-latest-book-intimations-reflects-deeply-on-isolation-and-injustice-1.5729946.

Walker, Mark. 'Slavia Chief Alleges Rangers Pushed for Czechs to Face Europa League Axe'. Daily Record, 2 May 2021. www.dailyrecord.co.uk/sport/football/football-news/slavia-prague-chief-claims-rangers-24022602.

Walker, Shaun. '"A Whole Generation Has Gone": Ukrainians Seek Better Life in Poland'. *The Guardian*, 18 April 2019. www.theguardian.com/world/2019/apr/18/whole-generation-has-gone-ukrainian-seek-better-life-poland-elect-president.

Walker, Shaun. 'Hungarian Leader Says Europe Is Now "Under Invasion" by Migrants'. *The Guardian*, 15 March 2018, sec.

World news. www.theguardian.com/world/2018/mar/15/hungarian-leader-says-europe-is-now-under-invasion-by-migrants.

Wallerstein, Immanuel Maurice. 'Semi-Peripheral Countries and the Contemporary World Crisis'. *Theory and Society; Amsterdam* 3, no. 4 (Winter 1976): 461–83.

Wallerstein, Immanuel Maurice. 'Semi-Peripheral Countries and the Contemporary World Crisis'. *Theory and Society; Amsterdam* 3, no. 4 (Winter 1976): 461–83. http://search.proquest.com/docview/1303209935?pq-origsite=summon.

Wallerstein, Immanuel Maurice. *Centrist Liberalism Triumphant, 1789/1914*. The Modern World-System 4. Berkeley: University of California Press, 2011.

Wallerstein, Immanuel Maurice. *Mercantilism and the Consolidation of the European World-Economy, 1600–1750*. Studies in Social Discontinuity 2. New York: Academic Press, 1980.

Wallerstein, Immanuel Maurice. *Capitalist Agriculture and the Origins of the European World-Economy in the Sixteenth Century*. Studies in Social Discontinuity 1. New York: Academic Press, 1974.

Wang, Zhaohui, and Zhiqiang Sun. 'From Globalization to Regionalization: The United States, China, and the Post-Covid-19 World Economic Order'. *Journal of Chinese Political Science* 26, no. 1 (March 2021): 69–87. https://doi.org/10.1007/s11366-020-09706-3.

Wasser, Bruno. *Himmlers Raumplanung Im Osten: Der Generalplan Ost in Polen, 1940–1944*. Band 15 Der Reihe Stadt, Planung, Geschichte. Basel; Boston, MA: Birkhäuser, 1993.

Wekker, Gloria. *White Innocence: Paradoxes of Colonialism and Race*. Durham, NC: Duke University Press, 2016.

Wilczek, Maria. '"Armored Marian" — the Man Who Has Poland's Law and Justice Party in His Sights'. POLITICO, 13 May 2021. www.politico.eu/article/marian-banas-poland-takes-on-law-and-justice-government/.

Wintour, Patrick. 'Growing Awareness of Colonial Past Fuels Radicalisation, Says Czech Minister'. *The Guardian*, 15 June 2017. www.theguardian.com/world/2017/jun/15/growing-awareness-of-colonial-past-fuels-radicalisation-says-czech-minister.

Wittfogel, Karl August. *Oriental Despotism: A Comparative Study of Total Power*. New Haven, CT: Yale University Press, 1957.

Wittgenstein, Ludwig. *Philosophical Investigations. Philosophische Untersuchungen*. Revised 4th edition. Chichester, UK; Malden, MA: Wiley-Blackwell, 2009.

Wolff, Larry. *Inventing Eastern Europe: The Map of Civilization on the Mind of the Enlightenment*. Stanford, CA: Stanford University Press, 2000.

World Bank. 'GDP per Capita, PPP (Current International $)'. Accessed 10 September 2021. https://data.worldbank.org/indicator/NY.GDP.PCAP.PP.CD.

Wroński, Paweł. 'Jak MSZ ratuje Europę przed diabłem gender'. Gazeta Wyborcza, 30 December 2020. https://wyborcza.pl/7,75398,26648124,jak-msz-ratuje-europe-przed-diablem-gender.html.

'Wybory parlamentarne: PILNE. Ostateczne wyniki wyborów: PiS – 43,59 proc., KO – 27,40 proc.' *Rzeczpospolita*, 14 October 2019. www.rp.pl/polityka/art9177301-wybory-parlamentarne-pilne-ostateczne-wyniki-wyborow-pis-43-59-proc-ko-27-40-proc.

Yavlinsky, Grigory. *The Putin System: An Opposing View*. New York: Columbia University Press, 2018.

Yendell, Alexander. 'Mythos "Jammer-Ossis"'. University of Leipzig Research Centre Global Dynamics, 14 December 2020. www.recentglobe.uni-leipzig.de/zentrum/detailansicht/artikel/blog-37-mythos-jammer-ossis-2020-12-14/.

Zakaria, Fareed. 'The Rise of Illiberal Democracy'. *Foreign Affairs* 76, no. 6 (1997): 22–43. https://doi.org/10.2307/20048274.

Zarycki, Tomasz. *Ideologies of Eastness in Central and Eastern Europe*. BASEES/Routledge Series on Russian and East European Studies 96. Abingdon, Oxon; New York: Routledge/Taylor & Francis Group, 2014.

Zia-Ebrahimi, Reza. *Antisémitisme et islamophobie: Une histoire croisée*. 1st edition. Amsterdam, 2021.

Zijl, Joop van. 'De Nikolaus Harnoncourt-Week: Mozart en Strauss door Harnoncourt'. *Geen dag zonder Bach*. concertzender, 6 May 2016. www.concertzender.nl/dossier-geen-dag-zonder-bach/.

Žižek, Slavoj. *Looking Awry: An Introduction to Jacques Lacan through Popular Culture*. Cambridge, MA: MIT Press, 1992.

Žižek, Slavoj. *The Puppet and the Dwarf: The Perverse Core of Christianity*. Cambridge, MA: The MIT Press, 2003.

Żuk, Piotr, Przemysław Pluciński, and Paweł Żuk. 'The Dialectic of Neoliberal Exploitation and Cultural-Sexual Exclusion: From Special Economic Zones to LGBT-Free Zones in Poland'. *Antipode* 53, no. 5 (September 2021): 1571–95. https://doi.org/10.1111/anti.12721.

Zúquete, José Pedro. *The Identitarians: The Movement against Globalism and Islam in Europe*. Notre Dame, IN: University of Notre Dame Press, 2018.

Index

1989 (fall of communist governments in Central Europe) 3, 16–20, 54, 68, 70, 72, 90–91, 95, 97, 109–110, 116, 129, 135, 143, 152, 161–167, 169, 173, 184, 186–187, 190–191, 193–195, 198–201, 204, 207

A

A Fish Called Wanda 68
abortion 149, 179
absolutism 40
acquis communautaire 111
Adamowicz, Paweł 178
Adriatic 82
AfD
  see Alternative for Germany
affective politics 4, 8
Afghanistan 178, 225
Africa 12, 35, 37, 44, 47, 65–66, 144, 174, 223–225
African–American 7, 33–34, 173, 243
  see also Blackness
Africans 38, 43, 50
Akroyd, Dan 68
Albania 60
Albanians 82
Aleichem, Sholem 222
Alexander II, of Russia, 50
Alexievich, Svetlana 129
Algeria 23, 217
Alhambra 39
Allen, Theodore 37, 49
Alternative for Germany (political party) 168
America (United States of)
  Americans 37, 53, 86
  see also United States of America
Anderson, Benedict 61, 236

Anglo-Saxons 53, 80
Anglo-Teutonic 43
Ankara 177
Antall, József 98, 110
Anti-Defamation League 171
anti-democratic 3, 206, 243
anti-Muslim 170, 172, 174, 176
anti-Semites 21, 166
anti-Semitism 1, 3, 20, 22–24, 31, 110, 161–162, 168, 172–173, 176, 178–181, 188, 246, 262, 268, 290
  see also blood libel
Applebaum, Anne 16, 111, 153
Arab 37, 174
Armenia 108
Arsenal (football team) 227, 231, 233–234, 239
art nouveau 89, 183
Aryans 36, 155
Ash, Timothy Garton 67, 74, 89, 90, 162
Asia 43–44, 47, 57, 81, 148, 152, 194
  Asian Americans 7, 41
Asians 37, 55, 125, 189
Aster, Ari 146
Atilla the Hun 155
Australia 12, 65, 142
Austria 9, 13, 22, 48, 50–52, 57, 59–60, 62, 65, 67, 76–78, 82, 83, 89–99, 107, 117, 158, 165, 192, 200, 223, 224
  Anschluss (annexation to Germany) 60
  Austro-Slavism 81
  see also Czechs, Slavs
  see also Austria-Hungary
Austria-Hungary 9, 59, 65, 76, 78, 82–83, 99, 222–224

312

INDEX

authoritarianism 3, 6, 16–17, 20, 26, 30–31, 51, 110, 113–114, 120–121, 123–24, 126, 131, 161, 187, 192, 195, 199–200, 203, 207, 211, 243–244, 246, 250
Azerbaijan 69
Aznavour, Charles 140

B

Babiš, Andrej 29, 117, 125, 214
Babišová, Martina 125
Bacon's Rebellion 38
Balcerowicz, Leszek 92, 95
Baldwin, Richard 211
Balkans 52, 54, 59–60, 97, 108, 127, 133
  Balkanism 52
Balogun, Leon 228
Baltic States 57, 82, 101, 111
  see also individual states
Banaś, Marian 121
Barcelona 128
baroque 87, 183
Barša, Pavel 7, 18, 197, 205
Bartók 87
Bata 225
Bavaria 52, 76
Belarus 6, 9, 82, 113, 118, 129, 218, 142, 177, 245–246
Belgium 33, 112–113, 118, 218
Benin 218
Berdimuhamedow, Gurbanguly 152
Berlin 44, 67, 73, 76, 95, 109, 166–168, 182, 190, 231–232
Berlin Wall 44, 95, 109, 190
  Fall of the (metaphor for the end of communist rule) *see* 1989
Berlusconi, Silvio 1
Besant, Annie 80
Bezos, Jeff 2, 212
Bhabha, Homi 186, 193
Biedroń, Robert 178
Bildungsbürgertum 63, 183
Bismarck, Otto von 77
Black Lives Matter 20, 227, 231, 233, 239, 240
Blackness 7, 13, 20, 33, 35, 38, 41–42, 159, 170, 192, 217–218, 227–231, 233–234, 236–237, 238, 240, 242, 244
  see also African-Americans
Blatter, Sepp 229
Blavatsky, Helena 80

blood libel 161
Boabdil, Muhammad II, ruler of Granada 39
Boatcă, Manuela 50, 70, 221
Bohemia 47–49, 51, 58, 59, 63, 65, 77–78, 97, 223
  Böhmer 58
  see also Bohemia and Moravia (Protectorate of), Czech Republic
Bohemia and Moravia, Protectorate of 65
Bolagun, Baloji 252, 272, 274, 278
Bolshevism 178
Bolsonaro, Jair 2, 8, 246
'Borat' 70
Böröcz, József 201, 219
Bosnia 52, 60, 151, 232
Bosnians 60
bourgeoisie 63–64, 68, 206, 212
brain drain 141–142
Bratislava 59, 68, 100, 102, 119, 128, 131, 138, 233, 249
  Pressburg (German name of Bratislava) 59
Brazil 8
Brexit 11, 14–15, 34
Britain
  see United Kingdom
Brodkin, Karen 37
Bruni, Carla 44
Brussels
  see European Union
Buchowski, Michał 97, 255, 262
Budapest 1–3, 29, 60, 63, 67, 77, 83, 89, 100, 128, 130–131, 138, 147–148, 151–152, 154, 164–165, 179, 213, 222, 249–250
Budweis
  see České Budějovice
Buffon, Georges-Louis Leclerc, Count of 41–42
Bulgaria 13, 97, 108, 112, 127, 130–131, 134, 136, 139, 142–144, 147, 150–152, 158, 166, 171–172, 179–181, 236
Byzantium 52, 85

C

café culture 88
Cala, Juan 236
Cameroon 224
Canada 8, 12, 166, 169, 171, 211, 250

313

Canadians 37, 53
capitalism 3, 5, 9, 12, 14, 16, 36, 40–41, 44, 45, 50, 54, 63, 69–72, 75, 83, 92–96, 103, 109–10, 123, 128, 139, 176, 187–188, 190, 193, 196, 202, 205–206, 213, 240, 242, 244, 247
  see also free market, market economy, national capitalists, neoliberalism
Čaputová, Zuzana 30
Carlson, Tucker 3, 147
Carnot, Lazare 192
Carpathian Basin 100–101
Casanova, Giacomo 49, 51, 57
Catholicism 24, 27, 38–39, 52, 76–77, 85, 162, 175, 178–179, 218, 243
Central Asia 155
Central Asians 125
Central Europe's Culture Wars 98
Central Europeans 4, 5, 6, 7, 9, 10, 11, 34, 35, 43, 45, 53, 72, 74, 81, 87, 88, 89, 93, 100, 101, 111, 116, 118, 129, 140, 141, 147, 148, 159, 160, 175, 182, 188, 189, 190, 19, 192, 197, 198, 200, 215, 216, 220, 236, 240, 242
České Budějovice 58–59
Ceylon (Sri Lanka) 225
Chamberlain, Houston 43, 79
China 26, 91, 136, 150, 205, 209–212, 244, 246
Chovanec, Jozef 33
Christianity 8, 23–24, 26, 31, 39, 51–52, 97, 153–154, 174, 195, 256
  and race 4, 25
Churchill, Winston 45–46, 66–67
civil liberties 112–113, 192
class 14, 182
  lower middle 14–15
  underclass 14
  upper middle 14
  upper working 14–15
Cleese, John 68
climate change 176, 240, 245, 247
Cohen, Sasha Baron 70
Cold War 5, 19, 45, 47, 50, 54, 59, 67–73, 75, 106, 109, 169, 183, 187, 202, 209, 220
Cologne 76

colonization 4, 5, 7, 11–13, 18, 38, 40, 45, 50, 54, 63, 65, 70–71, 147, 157–158, 186, 193–201, 210–212, 214–227, 231, 238, 242, 250
Columbus, Christopher 39
Commonwealth
  see White, Commonwealth
communism 1–3, 5, 6, 10, 11, 16, 18–22, 24, 29, 31–32, 35, 44, 46, 52, 55, 57, 66, 68–69, 71–73, 75, 83–86, 90, 91–98, 100, 108–111, 125, 135, 148–149, 152, 154, 165, 178, 185–188, 192, 197–200, 202–204, 212, 215, 225, 243, 252
  end of communist rule in Europe, *see* 1989
communists 1, 83, 91–95, 110, 152, 166, 184, 225, 243
Conan Doyle, Arthur 59
concentration camps 21, 161–164, 55
  Sobibor 162
Condee, Nancy 201
conspiracy theories 1, 28, 90, 119, 172
Constable, Henry S., 42–43
Corruption 19, 29, 30, 52, 106, 117–119, 121–123
COVID-19, 3, 30, 34, 100, 103, 150, 209, 240, 246
  Omicron variant 30
  see also Sputnik vaccine
Credit Suisse 210, 247
Crete 85
Croatia 9, 52, 65, 76, 112, 234
Croats 52, 65
Cronyism 31
Crystal Palace, Brighton 239
Cseh, Péter 102
Csoóri, Sándor 21
culture wars 18, 178
Cyprus 111–113
Czechia
  see Czech Republic
Czech Republic 2, 6, 9, 18, 23, 25, 28–30, 44, 47–49, 51, 58–59, 61–63, 76–77, 79, 81, 83–84, 88, 91, 95, 98, 108, 110, 113, 114–116, 118, 124–131, 133, 135, 138, 141, 142, 144, 150, 153, 166, 171–174, 180, 192, 203–204, 209, 215, 217–218, 222–223, 231, 234
  see also Czechs, Czechoslovakia, Moravia, Protectorate of Bohemia and Moravia

Czechoslovakia (former Republic of) 29, 30, 57, 59, 66–67, 69, 75, 82–84, 86, 88, 91–92, 97–99, 100–101, 110, 121, 153, 163, 165, 183, 192, 203, 224–225
  Velvet Divorce (dissolution of Czechoslovakia) 30, 110
Czechoslovakian Brothers 68
Czechs 9, 22–23, 28, 42, 53, 58, 59, 61, 63, 65, 81–82, 100, 110, 133, 141, 150, 163, 171, 182, 192, 215, 223, 227–229, 236
Czernowitz (Chernivtsi) 57

D

Danton, Georges Jacques 192
Danube 57, 250
Davidson, Neil 8
Deák, István 20
demagogy 151
Demjanjuk, John 162
democracy 8, 16, 17, 25, 26, 32, 44, 46, 66, 91, 98–100, 106, 109–114, 120, 157, 185, 191–192, 197, 240, 245, 246
  illiberal 100, 104, 150, 185, 187
  liberal 2, 4, 16, 17, 18, 19–20, 25, 44, 86, 97, 109, 112, 115–116, 168, 185, 187, 191, 196, 208
  majoritarian 6, 27
DEMOS (research project) 17
denazification 160, 168–169
Denmark 117, 124
depopulation 143–145
deregulation 19, 215, 252
Derganac, Franc 66
Déry, Tibor 84
Dessalines, Jean-Jacques 192
Diakhaby, Mouctar 236
Die Zeit 151
dissidents 20–21, 72, 75, 86, 88–90, 91, 93, 94, 96–98, 109–110, 184–185, 197–198, 202–203, 206, 262
Don Giovanni 58
Dracula 59–60
Drahoš, Jiří 218–219
Dresden 73
Dubček, Alexander 91–92
Duda, Andrzej 24, 149, 178
Dugin, Alexsandr 154–155
Duke, David 37, 59, 216
Dzenovska, Dace 157
Dzurinda, Mikuláš 28–29

E

Economist, The 112, 114, 118
Eastern Bloc 20, 34, 71, 165, 183, 215
Eastern Europeanism 5, 34–36, 39, 45, 47, 49, 54–55, 60, 64, 68, 70, 73, 105–106, 108–109, 113, 115, 123–124, 127–128, 136, 143, 158, 168, 171, 186, 192, 197, 201, 226, 229, 233–234, 236–237, 262
Eastern Orthodox 59, 85, 108, 191
Egyptians 37
Ekstraklasa 237
elites 14, 91, 94–95, 109, 129, 158, 175, 185, 187–188, 190, 194, 208, 216, 218–219, 242
  supranational 156
Engels, Friedrich 43, 81, 192
England 13, 47, 52, 53, 69, 80, 182, 183, 184, 222, 227, 231, 236
Enlightenment 19, 46, 47, 51, 54, 72, 191
Erdogan, Recep 2
Estonia 82
Eszterhazy (noble family) 77
ethnic cleansing 53, 66–67, 71
Etkind, Aleksandr 63, 167
eugenics 66
Eurasianism 155
Euro 138, 139, 234
European Commission 24, 28, 111, 118, 198, 220, 247
European League 230
European Union 2, 3, 5, 10–12, 16–19, 22, 24–25, 28–30, 34, 52, 72, 82, 98–99, 103–104, 111, 133, 156, 201, 211, 245–246
  'Brussels' (metonym for the European Union) 1, 28–29, 52, 99, 103, 111, 132–133, 148, 149–150, 152–154, 160, 175–177, 199, 200, 201, 208, 214, 244, 246–247
  see also European Commission
Euroscepticism 203
exekuce (debt repossession in the Czech Republic) 204

F

Fabry, Adam 18, 95, 117, 204
Facebook 3, 133
Farage, Nigel 216
far-right 110, 147, 175
fascism 6, 20, 60, 65, 104, 192

FATIGUE (research project) 17
Fekete, Liz 25–26, 153, 241
Felcsút 1
Ferdinand II of Aragon 39
Fico, Robert 30, 119, 214
Fiddler on the Roof 222
financial crisis of 2008, 18, 111, 175, 203–204, 246
Fin-de-siècle Vienna 89
Finland 6, 9, 82, 108, 113, 180
Finno-Ugric 62
Fidesz 1, 24, 25, 100, 103, 122, 151, 179, 213, 253
First World War 21, 65–66, 75, 78–81, 93, 224
free market 97, 199, 202, 215, 242
folk horror (film genre) 158–159
football 1, 82, 179, 187, 227–249, 277, 285, 290, 294, 303–304, 309
Fortuna Liga 237
Fragile States Index 141
France 3, 18, 23, 29, 35, 37, 44, 48, 49, 52–54, 65, 67, 75, 78, 83–84, 87, 113–114, 118, 124, 126–127, 136–137, 140, 142, 149, 175, 183, 192–193, 211, 214, 222, 234, 236, 244
  Vichy government 192
Francis Joseph I 224
Frankfurt 60, 73
Franz-Joseph Land 223
Franzos, Emil 57
Fratelli d'Italia (Italian political party) 3
Freedom House 114–115
Freud, Sigmund 84
From Russia With Love 69
Fudan University 151, 179
Fukuyama, Francis 109, 202

G

Gagyi, Agnes 206
Gajdoš, Marek 119
Galicia 57, 249
Gambia 157
gangsters 69–70, 106, 123–124, 125, 210
Guardian, The 242, 244, 275, 294, 300, 309–310
Gates, Bill 212
Gayà, José Luis 236
Gazeta Wyborcza 179
Gdańsk 178

gender 17, 25, 27, 41, 123, 149, 158, 178–179, 232, 242
  see also heteronormativity, homophobia, homosexuality, LGBTQ+, sexual orientation, transgender
'gender ideology'
  see gender
General Electric 92
General Motors 92
Generalplan Ost 65
Genghis Khan 56
geopolitics 11–12, 148, 197, 201
George Floyd 33, 227
Georgia 108, 234
Germans 19, 20, 42, 52–53, 55, 57, 59, 61–68, 71, 73, 75–76, 78, 80–81, 109, 151, 169, 170–172, 174, 176–177, 190, 200, 211, 226, 231–232
  see also Nazis
German–Slavic rivalry 55, 71
Germany 2, 9, 11, 19, 21–22, 29, 31, 36, 42–44, 47–55, 57–68, 71–84, 87, 89–90, 93, 96, 99, 104, 109, 143, 161–169, 182, 192, 203, 218, 223–224
  German Empire 78
  German far right 31
  German idealist philosophy 80
  'German question' 76
  German nationalists 62, 71, 76–77
  German occupation of Europe 60, 65, 162, 164
  Germanic racial pride 36
  see also denazification, German-Slavic rivalry, Gestapo, Nazis
Gestapo 169
Geva, Dorit 213
Gilman, Sander 41
Gini Index 136, 137
Girard, René 188, 191
Glasgow Rangers 227–229, 235–236, 240
Gleig, George Robert 47
Global Peace Index 123
Global South 4, 11, 182, 200, 220, 222, 225, 226, 242, 245, 246–247
globalism 1, 18, 96, 243–244, 246
globalization 3, 19, 109, 181, 185, 202, 210, 212, 214, 245, 247
Globo 235
Globsec 150

INDEX

Gogol 51
Golden Eye 69
Gonzalez, Álvaro 7, 235–236
Gorbachev, Mikhail 94, 153, 187
Gottfried, Jacquin von 47
governmentality 201
Granada 39
Grant, Charles 194–196
Greece 108, 115, 127, 130, 137, 170–171, 211, 216, 234
Greeks 82
Gross, Jan 23, 160–163, 166, 168, 170–171, 181
Gulácsi, Péter 231–232
Gulyás, Gergely 102
Gwiazda, Andrzej 92

H

Habermas, Jürgen 90, 193
Habsburgs 48, 57, 61, 76–79, 81, 83, 88–89, 93, 174, 175, 223, 224, 249
Habsburg Empire 57, 61, 76–77, 81, 93, 223, 249
HaCohen, Ran 41
Haiti 192
Halb-Asien 57
Halík, Tomáš 243
Hall, Stuart 40, 78, 196, 203
Halle 168
Hamburg 73, 76
Handlin, Oscar and Mary 38
harem 49
Haringey Borough FC 234
Harms, Victoria 93, 96
Harnoncourt, Nikolaus 89, 100
Harper, Kevin 229
hate speech 24
Hauskrecht, Gustav 169
Havel, Václav 77, 88, 91, 93, 98, 110, 184, 191, 202, 220
Hawker, Jonathan 60
Haydn, Joseph 77, 87
Hebrew 37, 70
Heng, Geraldine 38–39
Herder, Johann Gottfried 61–62
Hergé 60
Hertha BSC 231–232
Hesová, Zora 18
heteronormativity 149, 179
Hibernian F.C., 229
hillbillies 68, 159
Hispanics 37

Hitler, Adolf 33, 59, 65, 66, 89, 166–167, 192, 225
Hlinka Guard 163
Hobsbawm, Eric 49
Hohlmeier, Monika 29
Hollywood 68
Holmes, Stephen 16, 17, 90, 111, 143–144, 185–191, 193
Holocaust 21–23, 160–170, 173, 249, 250
Holt, Thomas, 7, 54
Holy Roman Empire 76
homophobia 25, 31, 101, 162, 178, 181, 231, 243
homosexuality 3, 24, 178–179
  see also same-sex marriage
Hong Kong 151, 210
Horizon 2020 (research grant programme) 17
Horthy, Miklós 164, 192
Hošek, Jiří 229
Hostel 123
How Jewish Folk Became White 37
How the Irish Became White 37
Hradec Králové 77
Hrutka, János 232
Human Genome Project 56
human rights 32, 98, 168
Human Development Index 126–127
Hungarians 9, 20–21, 22, 25, 53, 55, 59–63, 71, 80, 82, 89, 97, 99–102, 118, 141, 146, 150–151, 154, 164, 199, 204, 223–224, 233, 249
  see also Magyars
Hungary 1–3, 6, 8–9, 13, 21–26, 28–32, 35, 44, 51, 57, 60–61, 63, 65–66, 71, 76–78, 82–84, 86–88, 92–93, 95, 97–104, 108, 110, 114–115, 117–118, 122, 124–128, 136, 141, 144, 146–147, 149, 151, 153, 158, 163–166, 173–174, 177, 179, 181, 184–186, 192, 199, 202, 204–206, 213–216, 218, 222–225, 231, 233–234, 243, 249, 250
Eastern Opening 150
National Media and Info-Communications Authority 116
System of National Cooperation 121, 123, 135–137, 187, 209–210, 213
  see also Magyarization, Paks nuclear power plant, Trianon (Treaty of)
Husserl, Edmund 84

I

Iberians 42
Ibrox Stadium 227
identity
   cultural 86–87
   national 58, 98, 144
identitarians 86
Ignatiev, Noel 37–38, 42
illiberalism 1–6, 8–11, 14–20, 22, 25–32, 64, 72, 74–75, 86, 96, 98–100, 103–104, 106, 109–111, 115, 122, 124, 127, 131–132, 136, 143, 147–149, 153–155, 158–159, 166, 176, 178–179, 181, 183, 185–187, 193, 197, 199–200, 205–206, 208, 214–216, 218, 220, 234, 237, 240–247, 250, 252–253
illiberal democrats 1
   see also democracy, illiberal
Illyés, Gyula 102
Ilyin, Ivan 154–155
imitation 16, 185, 187–189, 191, 193–197
Imitation Imperative 16, 185–186
imperialism 54, 221–223
Imre, Aniko 7, 92, 146–147
Independence Hall 82
India 36, 80, 150–151, 195, 205
Indian National Congress 80
Indians, Northern 36
Indigeneity 7, 40, 65
Indo-European 36, 155
Industrial Revolution 50–51, 53–54, 70, 221–222
inferiority complex 53, 104
intelligentsia 183–184
Intermarium 82
International Organization for Migration 143
Iran 155, 170
Iranians 36
Iraq 170, 217
Ireland 38, 42–43, 50, 125, 142, 180, 233
Irish (people) 38, 274, 289
   and race 37–38, 40–44, 56
   in America 44
Iron Curtain 46, 66–67, 71, 73, 94, 181–182, 185, 200
Isabelle I of Castille 39
Islam 29, 97, 174
Islamophobia 3, 23–24, 29, 31, 170, 172–175, 177, 180–181, 238
Israel 22, 165–166
Istanbul 52
Italia-Irredenta (political party) 82
Italy 1, 30, 48, 60, 72, 76, 83, 113, 119, 121, 126–127, 130, 137, 148–149, 154, 165, 180, 192–193, 233, 234, 250
   see also Sicily

J

Jaguar (automobile assembly plant, Slovakia) 209
Jakeš, Miloš 153
'James Bond' 69
Janik, Allan 89
Janion, Maria 64
Japan 188, 210, 235, 246
Jędraszewski, Marek 24, 119, 149, 178
Jedwabne massacre 161, 166
Jerusalem 20, 23, 82
Jews 1, 20–23, 27, 37, 39, 41–44, 47, 57–59, 70, 82–84, 117, 120, 161–167, 169–173, 224, 249, 250, 255
jingoism 106, 108, 245
Jobbik (Hungarian political party) 30, 103
John III Sobieski 174
John the Baptist 62
Johnson, Lonnie 62
Joseph II of Austria 61
Judt, Tony 94
Juncker, Jean-Claude 198, 220, 247
justice system 28, 121, 124

K

Kaczyński, Jarosław 22, 24, 27–28, 30, 99, 149, 178, 246
Kaczyński, Jerzy 214
Kádár, János 95
Kaepernick, Colin 227
Kafka, Franz 84
Kafka, Hermann 84
Kamara, Glen 228–229, 235–236
Karosa 203
Kayaoglu, Kaya 173
Kazakh 70
Kielce massacre 161–164
KGB 69
Khodorovsky, Mikhail 209
Kiev 222
King, Electra 69

INDEX

King, Jeremy 39, 58, 78, 89
King, Martin Luther 243
Kis, Danilo 84
Klaus, Václav 30, 95, 203
Klebb, Rosa 69
klezmer 165
kneeling (gesture in support of racial justice) 227, 231, 233, 236, 239
Kočner, Marian 119
Kołakowski, Leszek 92, 95
Kolář, Ondřej 228
Kolíková, Mária 29
Komárno 31, 249
Konrád, György 88, 93, 94, 191
Kościuszko, Tadeusz 191
Kosovo 52
Kossuth, Lajos 2, 192
Kotleba, Milan 217
Kovács, Melinda 201
Kövér, László 101
Krajské Listy 217
Krakow 24, 77, 83, 149, 174, 178, 192
Krastev, Ivan 16–17, 90, 111, 143–144, 185–191, 193
Kremnička massacre 163, 169
Křetínský, Daniel 135–136
Ku Klux Klan 37
Kuciak, Ján 119
Kúdela, Ondřej 226, 228–230, 235–236
Kulka, Otto Dov 23
Kulturmensch 64, 86
Kulturvolk 64
Kundera, Milan 23, 83–88, 91, 93–94, 96, 183, 191, 198
Kurz, Sebastian 117
Kušnírová, Martina 119
Kwaśniewski, Aleksander 166

L

La Liga 236
labour activism 35
Lacan 168
Land, Franz-Joseph 40, 223
Lassalle, Ferdinand 43
Latin America 12, 61
Latvia 82, 143, 204
Latvians 157
Lázár, János 213
Le Monde 132, 136
Le Parisien 235
Le Pen, Marine 3, 149, 154

Leach, Archie 68
Lebanese 37
Lebanese-Americans 37
Lebanon 85
Lebensraum 65
Lefilliâtre, Jérôme 136
Lega (Italian political party) 154
Leipzig 73
Leuthard, Doris 218
Levitsky, Steven 17
Lewicki, Aleksandra 7, 18, 34
LGBTQ+, 24, 28, 149, 177–180, 246
liberalism 2–6, 8–9, 16–18, 19–22, 24–26, 28, 31, 44–45, 72, 75, 77, 79, 86, 91, 93, 97–99, 100, 104, 109–111, 123, 147–148, 150–151, 155, 157, 159, 175, 178, 181, 185, 187–188, 191–192, 197, 208, 243
see also democracy, liberal
Libya 66
Lisbon 128
Lisiewicz, Piotr 227
List, Friedrich 215
Liszt, Franz 2, 87
Lithuania 82, 143, 204
Lithuanians 82, 224
Loizou, Tom 235
London 13, 44, 170, 183, 234
Lopez-Gonzalez, Javier 211
Louis XIV 78
Lowe, Lisa 41
Lukashenko, Alexander 152, 177
Lusatians
  see Sorbians
Luther, Martin 29

M

Madrid 170
mafia 69, 119–120
Magnus, Hanz 93
Magyar Nemzet 122, 213, 231
Magyari, Péter 26, 179–180
Magyarization 102
Magyars 102–103, 151
Mahler, Gustav 84
Mali 23
Malta 111
Manchester 13, 34
Marček, Miroslav 120
Mark, James 7, 91, 95–96, 225
market economy 6, 18
Martin, Steve 68

Marx, Karl 43, 81, 192
Masaryk, Tomáš 81–82
Matovič, Igor 102–103
Mazowiecki, Tadeusz 2
Mbembe, Achille 65
McLuhan, Marshall 105, 109
Mečiar, Vladimír 30, 110, 121
mečiarizmus 110
Meer, Nasar 7, 44, 125
Meisl, Hugo 82–83
Meloni, Giorgia 3
Mennonites 37
Memorial to the Murdered Jews of Europe 166
Mercedes 190, 203
Merkel, Angela 2, 161
Mészáros, Lőrinc 1, 2, 212
Mexico 211–212
Michnik, Adam 88, 90
Mickiewicz, Adam 87
Middle Ages 63
Midsommar 146, 158
migrants 2, 4, 8, 11, 13, 18, 22–23, 25, 27–28, 30, 34–35, 43, 111, 124, 130, 140–142, 144, 145, 160–162, 169–170, 175–178, 199, 216–220, 222, 226, 232–233, 245–246
Milosz, Czeslaw 86, 191
Minneapolis 227
mission civilisatrice 195
Mississippi 131
Missouri 66
Mitropa Cup 82–83
Mitteleuropa 52, 68, 75, 77–84, 88–89, 93, 104
Moffit, Benjamin 17
Moldova 108, 127, 143, 170–171, 265
Mondon, Auriel 14–15
Mongols 55–56
Montalbano 210, 211
Montenegro 234
montovny 217
Moors 175, 244
Moravia 58, 65, 84, 223
 see also Bohemia and Moravia (Protectorate of), Czech Republic, Czechoslovakia
Morawiecki, Mateusz 22, 133, 154–155
Morawski, Paolo 148–149
Morvai, Krisztina 215

Moscow 121, 147–149, 165, 272
Moses 43
Moskalewicz, Marcin 74
Mozart, Wolfgang Amadeus 47–49, 51, 57–58, 61
Mrázik, Peter 209
Müller, Jan-Werner 17
multinational corporations 4, 12, 182, 202, 206, 208–209, 213–215, 224, 243, 246
Murzyn 218, 244
Muslims 2, 23, 27, 39, 47, 51, 86, 171, 173, 174–176, 217, 226
"Muslim ban" (declared by President Donald Trump), 170
Mussolini, Benito 66, 225
Mynář, Vratislav 230

N

Nagy, Imre 92, 152
Napoleon 75–76, 78, 191
National Association for the Advancement of White People 216
national capitalists 206–209, 213, 245
national conservativism 6
nationalism 17, 20, 21, 26, 31, 61–62, 64, 72, 81, 89, 98–101, 106, 109–110, 155, 162, 167, 203, 208, 213, 215, 246–247
NATO 10, 154, 202, 209–210
Naumann, Friedrich 79, 81
Nazis 21–22, 31, 33, 36, 37, 57, 60, 65, 71, 83, 110, 152, 155–156, 158, 160, 162–164, 166, 167–169, 217, 229
Ndrangheta 119
Němec, Vilém 224
Nemsila, Jozef 169
neo-fascism 3, 217
neo-feudalism 17
neoliberalism 3, 5, 6, 8, 16, 18, 19, 95–98, 109, 176, 181, 185, 198–200, 202, 204–206, 208, 213–215, 220, 243–244, 246, 252
neo-Marxism 24
Neo-traditionalism 17
Netanyahu, Benjamin 22
New Guinea 223
New York 44, 47, 68, 82, 130, 170, 222
Neymar 235
Nigeria 228

INDEX

Northwest Europeans 6
Norway 55, 108, 127
Nostitz-Rieneck, Count Franz Anton von 58
NSO (spying software) 115
Nuremberg Trials 169

O

Obama, Barrack 242
Observations on the State of Society among the Asiatic Subjects of Great Britain (1792) 194
occult 80
Ofori, Prince 233
Okamura, Tomio 133
OL'aNO (Slovak political party) 102
oligarchs 69, 70, 120
Oliyanka, Peter 228
Olympique of Marseilles 235
Open Society Foundation
  see Soros, George
Orbán, Victor 1–3, 8–10, 21–22, 24–30, 74–75, 79, 86, 96, 99–100, 102–104, 111, 114–118, 122, 133, 147, 149–156, 158, 177, 179, 184–185, 187, 199, 205–206, 212–214, 216, 232–233, 241–244, 246
Orient 47, 51
Orientalism 47, 49, 170, 183
Orthodox Church 85
Ossi 73, 176
Osteuropa (German term) 68, 80
Ottoman Empire 49, 51, 81, 97
Oxford, University of 1, 22, 157, 184
Özyürek, Esra 169

P

Pajetat, Valery 234
Paks nuclear power plant 151
Palacký, František 81
Palestine 41, 82
Panama Papers 117, 136
pandemic 121, 209, 147
pan-Slavism
  see Slavs
Paris 78, 128, 130, 170, 183, 222, 235
Paris Saint Germain FC 243
partial privilege 7, 11, 13–15, 173
Parvulescu, Anca 13
Passover 161
patriarchy 8, 25–27, 51, 123, 149, 153, 179

Paulista, Gabriel 236
Payer, Julius 223
Peace and Justice Party
  see PiS
Pędziwiatr, Konrad 7, 244
Pembroke College 184
Pence, Mike 3
people of colour 5–6, 11, 23, 35–36, 226, 238–239, 243–244
perestroika 94
periphery 2, 11–14, 51, 103, 121, 128, 131–132, 158, 211–212, 216, 242, 247
  see also semi-periphery, white periphery
Pétain, Philippe 166, 192
Pető, Andrea 25
Petőfi, Sándor 87
Petry, Zsolt 231
Pew Research Center 106–109, 170–172, 180–181
Philadelphia 82
Piketty, Thomas 132–133
Piłsudski, Józef 28
PiS (Polish political party) 15, 22, 24, 27, 103, 118, 121, 166, 178
Pithart, Petr 202–203
plantations 38, 40, 50, 221
plombier polonais 35
Poland 2, 6, 9, 13, 15–16, 21, 22–24, 27–28, 30, 34–35, 44, 51, 54, 57, 61, 63–66, 70–72, 75–76, 78, 82–84, 86–89, 92–93, 95, 97–98, 100–101, 103, 108, 110, 113–114, 115, 118, 121, 124, 127–129, 132, 139, 140, 142, 148–150, 155–156, 158, 162–166, 173–174, 177–179, 181, 192, 206, 214, 218, 221–225, 227, 231, 233–234, 237, 244, 249
  August Understandings 92
  parliamentary elections of 2019, 15
  presidential campaign of 2020, 24
Poles 9, 13, 22, 25, 35, 55, 59, 61, 63, 65, 71, 76, 97, 100, 118, 140–141, 148, 150, 161–164, 182, 223–224, 227, 233, 244, 247
Poldi 203
POLIS (research project) 174
'political correctness' 175, 238
Polonia Mon Amour: From the Indies of Europe to the Indies of America 148
Polska24.pl 231

POPREBEL (research project) 17
populism 6, 8, 17
Porsche 203
Portland, Oregon 31
Portugal 42, 108, 175, 181
postcoloniality 11, 18, 157, 194, 197, 200–202, 214, 219, 220–221, 224–225, 226, 250
Poznań 13, 59
Prague 42, 47, 49, 57–60, 63, 67, 77, 83–84, 86–87, 89, 91, 93, 100, 128, 183, 192, 197, 221–222, 224–225, 227, 234, 237–238, 249
Prague Spring 87, 91, 93
Premier League 239
Pressburg
  see Bratislava
Přeučil, Petr 217
Princeton University 168
privatization 45
Prokop, Daniel 209
'prostitutes'
  see sex workers
Provan, Davie 229
Prussia 50, 51, 61, 76–78
Przybylski, Wojciech 74
Pulaski, Casimir 191
purity of blood concept
  see Spain
Puskás Arena 1
Putin, Vladimir 2, 8, 24, 122, 149, 151, 154–155, 187, 209–210, 229, 245–246

Q

Quora 55–56

R

race 4–8, 11, 15, 18, 25–26, 36–43, 50, 53–54, 56, 65–66, 79, 104, 125, 146–147, 150, 154–155, 158, 196, 216, 224, 238, 242, 245, 247
racialization 13, 34, 36, 40, 159, 175
racism 3–7, 11, 20, 26, 31, 34–36, 39–40, 54, 66, 73, 104, 125, 147, 157–159, 162, 173, 181, 197, 216, 226, 229–231, 233–240, 243–244
  see also blackness, Eastern Europeanism, people of colour, whiteness
Rada Języka Polskiego 244
Rádl, Emanuel 61
Ranger, Terrence 49

Rassemblement National (French Political party) 3, 175
Reagan, Ronald 3, 95
refugees 158, 160–161, 166, 170, 174, 177, 183, 198–199, 217, 220
Renaissance 83, 154, 244
Renault 203
Rényi, Pál Dániel 241
Reporters Without Borders 115–116
restorative nostalgia 153
Roma (people) 4, 14, 20, 25–27, 30, 35, 98, 104, 125, 163, 173–174, 213–214, 226, 233, 237, 243, 245
Romania 9, 51, 57, 71, 76, 82–83, 99–100, 102, 108, 143, 156, 205, 234, 254
Romanians 22, 35, 55, 60, 71, 80, 97, 143, 233
Romanova, Tatiana 69
Rome 85
Roofe, Kemar 228
Roosevelt, Franklin Delano 45, 67
Roth, Joseph 84
Rumanians 82
Rupnik, Jacques 18
Russia 8, 10–11, 16, 19, 24–28, 45, 47, 49, 50–54, 56–57, 59–64, 68–70, 75, 78, 80–82, 84–86, 88, 92–93, 97, 103, 105, 108, 111, 114, 116–117, 120–122, 124–125, 136, 147–155, 170, 179, 181–182, 187, 191, 209–210, 212, 221–222
  see also Sputnik vaccine, St. Petersburg
Russia Today 136
Russians 19, 28, 53, 57, 68, 97, 121, 182, 187, 224
Rzepnikowska-Phillips, Alina 34–35

S

Said, Edward 47, 86, 170
Sakai, Hiroki 235
Salvini, Matteo 3, 149, 154
same-sex marriage 178, 180–181, 231
Sanfourche, Phillipe 235
Šanov 223
Sarkozy, Nicolas 35, 44
Saturday Night Live 68
Sayyid, Salman 7
Scandinavia 146, 211
Schengen Zone 22
Schlögel, Karl 93
Schmidt, Mária 216

Schönberg 87
Schorske, Carl 89
Schreckbild 123
Schwaner, Wilhelm 79
Schwarzenbergs
　Felix of Schwarzenberg 77
　Schwarzenberg, Karel 77
Scotland 8, 229
Second World War 53, 57–59, 66, 67, 71, 85, 163, 255
Sejm 191
Sellers, Peter 68
semi-periphery 11, 12, 14, 211, 221, 240, 242, 247
　see also periphery
Semites 36, 37
Senna, Danzy 243
Serbia 22, 52, 76, 143, 234, 236
serfs 49–51, 64, 70, 72, 221
sexual assault 23
sexual orientation 24, 158, 179
sex workers 106, 123–125
Shekhovtsov, Anton 147, 155
Sherlock Holmes 59
Shoshan, Nitzan 7, 168
Shprygin, Alexander 229
Sicily 51
Siemens 203
Silesia 78, 91
Sima, Abdallah 228
Simicska, Lajos 122, 213
Singapore 150
Škoda 202–203
Slačálek, Ondřej 7, 18, 219
slave labour 39–40
Slavia Prague 235–237, 239, 241–245, 247–248, 274, 285, 289–290, 306, 309
Slavic Studies 47, 272
Slavs 43, 47–48, 52–53, 55–66, 68, 71, 76, 79–81, 88–89, 100, 149–150, 192, 222
　anti-Slavism 47, 55, 68, 72
　pan-Slavism 149–150
　see also Austro-Slavism, German–Slavic rivalry
Slovakia 2, 6, 9, 21, 23, 26, 28–31, 33, 44, 51, 59, 61, 63, 65, 76, 81, 92, 102–103, 108, 110, 113, 115, 118, 119–121, 123–124, 127–128, 132, 141–142, 150, 163–164, 169–171, 173–174, 192, 202, 209, 214–215, 217–218, 221, 224–225, 234, 249

　see also Hlinka Guard
Slovaks 9, 22, 28, 30, 59, 63, 65, 100, 102, 110, 118, 141–142, 150, 174, 217, 223
Slovania (television series) 150
Slovenia 9, 52, 76, 111
Słupsk 178
Smith, Zadie 36
Smolensk 27, 28
Snochowska-Gonzalez, Claudia 220–221
Snyder, Timothy 16
soccer
　see football
social welfare 8, 103–104, 214
socialism 43, 67, 71, 75, 80, 83, 91–94, 96, 103–104, 109, 176, 191, 252
　with a human face 92, 93, 94, 104
Solzhenitsyn, Aleksandr 184
Sorbians 60–61, 76
Soros, George 21, 104, 117, 151, 184, 213
Sosnowski, Jerzy 218
South Asians 37
South Korea 210
Southern European 7, 55, 130
Soviet Union 20, 28, 34, 44–45, 56, 57, 66–67, 69–71, 83, 85–88, 91, 94, 95–97, 109, 127, 129, 153, 165, 169, 187, 192, 200–221, 223, 225
　see also KGB
Sowa, Jan 214
Spain 39–40, 42, 126–127, 130, 137, 175, 200, 234, 236
　conquistadores 40
　marranos 39
　moriscos 39
　New Christians 39
　purity of blood concept 39
　reconquista 39
　see also Madrid
SPECTRE 69
Spivak, Gayatri Chakravorty 200
Sputnik vaccine 103, 150
St Petersburg 57, 58
St. Stephen 151
Stalin, Joseph 45, 56, 67, 85, 101, 165
Stanciu, Nicolae 228
Stanford University 109
Stanley, Ben 103
statism 104

Steiner, Rudolf 79–81, 93, 155
stereotypes 100, 106, 123, 128, 137
Stoker, Bram 59–60
essentialism, strategic 38–39
Strauss, Johann 89
subaltern empires 219
Supreme Audit Office (Poland) 121
Švec, Róbert 217
Švihlíková, Ilona 215
swastika 36
Sweden 114, 146, 173
Switzerland 6, 108, 218
Syria 41
Syrians 37
Szabó, Tomáš 120
Szelényi, Iván 206
Szikra, Dorottva 104
Szydło, Beata 178

T

Tarant, Zdeněk 7, 172
Tatars 55
Tatra 203
Teutonic 53
 see also Anglo-Teutonic
Thatcher, Margaret 3, 8, 95, 203
The Invention of the White
 Race 37, 49
The Light That Failed 16, 111, 186
The Modern World System 12
The Party 68
The Sorrow and the Pity 166
The Texas Chainsaw Massacre 158
'The Tragedy of Central Europe' 84
The Twilight of Democracy 16, 111
The Witcher 147
theosophy 80
Ther, Philipp 16, 106, 202
Third Way 93–94, 96, 104
'Tintin' 60
Tiso, Jozef 21, 192
Tobago 157
Tokarczuk, Olga 224
Tolstoy 51
Tomaszewski, Jan 231
totalitarianism 23, 75, 90, 92
Toulmin, Steven 89
tourism 123, 125, 165
Transcarpathian 225
transgender 25
transitologists 110
Transparency International 120
Transylvania 60, 175, 225

Trevelyan, Alec 69
Trianon, Treaty of 99–102
TripAdvisor 126
Trošková, Mária 119
Trump, Donald 1–4, 8, 14–16, 29,
 31–32, 90, 111–112, 149, 153,
 156, 158, 170, 231, 239, 242, 246
Tucker and Dale vs Evil 159
tunelování 207
Turkey 6, 9, 26, 52, 78, 102, 113,
 150–151, 177
Turks 175
Tusk, Donald 178
Tvrdík, Jaroslav 237
Tyre 85

U

UEFA (Union of European Football
 Associations) 228, 230–231,
 234, 239
Ugro-Ruthones 82
Új, Péter 116
Ukrainians 57, 82, 97, 142, 182–183,
 224, 259
Ukraine 4, 9, 13, 57, 71, 76, 82,
 113–114, 124, 136, 142–143, 148,
 151, 164, 275, 234, 245, 248–249
'Un occident kidnappé ou la tragédie
 de l'Europe Centrale' 84
United Kingdom 8, 11, 18, 34, 38,
 40, 44, 46, 49–50, 52, 54, 67, 69,
 80, 82, 108, 129, 136, 173,
 194–196, 209, 216, 233, 234
United Kingdom Independence
 Party 216
 see also Brexit
United Nations 126
United States of America 2, 3, 7, 8,
 12, 14, 16, 20–22, 31–34, 37–39,
 49–50, 58, 61, 67–68, 74, 75, 79,
 81–82, 93–94, 106, 111–115, 125,
 147–149, 153, 155, 158, 173, 181,
 192, 210–211, 242, 250
 presidential election of 2016,
  14, 111
University of Debrecen 151
University of Gothenburg 114
urbanization 64, 71
USMCA 211

V

Vadalà, Antonio 119
Valencia FC 236

van der Bruck, Arthur Moeller 79
Varoufakis, Yanis 211
Vergangenheitsbewältigung 167, 169
Vermeersch, Wouter 218
Vienna 48, 49, 57, 63, 67, 77, 83, 84, 89, 174, 222
Virdee, Satnam 40
Visegrád Alliance 2, 6, 29, 75, 96–100, 102, 110–111, 113, 127, 129, 132–133, 136, 150, 176, 178, 198, 209, 220, 223, 231
Vlaams Belang (Belgian political party) 218
Voltaire 49
von der Leyen, Ursula 24

W

Wales 132, 231, 239
Wałęsa, Lech 92, 98, 110
Wallachians 63
Wallenberg, Raoul 164
Wallerstein, Immanuel 11–14, 211
Warsaw 2, 13, 29, 67, 86, 100, 132, 137, 139–140, 151, 222, 237
Washington 1, 201
Weber, Max 79
welfare regulations 103
welfare state 5, 176, 214
Wenden
  see Sorbians
White House 3, 156
white
  Commonwealth 12
  innocence 147
  privilege 5, 6–7, 11, 27, 43–44, 173, 197, 223, 226, 242
whiteness 4–7, 11–15, 18, 26–27, 31, 33–38, 41–45, 52–53, 56, 59, 64–65, 70, 78, 89, 98, 104, 146–147, 151, 158, 219
Więź 218
Wild Nineties 207

Wilhelm I 78
Winter, Aaron 14–15
Wittgenstein, Karl 203
Wittgenstein, Ludwig 6, 8, 89, 203
Wolff, Larry 47–51, 54, 57–58, 67
World Cup (football) 229, 233, 239
World Happiness Report 127
World Values Survey 173
World War I
  see First World War

X

xenophobia 98, 239
Xiao-Ping, Deng 212

Y

Yalta Conference 45, 67, 70–71, 73
Yavlinsky, Grigory 120–121, 210
Yeltsin, Boris 120, 187
Yeovil 234–235
Yiddish 221–222
YouTube 228, 244
Yugoslavia 82, 99, 108

Z

Zaha, Wilfried 239
Zakaria, Fareed 8
Zaorálek, Lubomír 217
Zarycki, Tomasz 155, 219
Zeman, Miloš 2, 23, 29, 153, 218–219, 230–231, 239
Zemmour, Eric 3
'Zero Degree of Decolonialization' 220
Zeus 85
Zeyer, Julius 84
Zhukovksy, Valentin Dimitrovich 69
Ziblatt, Daniel 17
Zionism 82, 165
Žižek, Slavoj 52, 54, 167
Zsuzsová, Alena 120